OSF/1 User's Guide

Revision 1.2

Open Software Foundation

P T R Prentice Hall, Englewood Cliffs, New Jersey 07632

Cover design
 and cover illustration: **BETH FAGAN**

This book was formatted with troff

Published by PTR Prentice Hall
A Simon & Schuster Company
Englewood Cliffs, New Jersey 07632

The information contained within this document is subject to change without notice.

OSF MAKES NO WARRANTY OF ANY KIND WITH REGARD TO THIS MATERIAL, INCLUDING, BUT NOT LIMITED TO, THE IMPLIED WARRANTIES OF MERCHANTABILITY AND FITNESS FOR A PARTICULAR PURPOSE.

OSF shall not be liable for errors contained herein or for any direct or indirect, incidental, special or consequential damages in connection with the furnishing, performance, or use of this material.

Copyright © 1990, 1991, 1992, 1993 Open Software Foundation, Inc.

This documentation and the software to which it relates are derived in part from materials supplied by the following:

- © Copyright 1987, 1988, 1989 Carnegie-Mellon University
- © Copyright 1985, 1988, 1989, 1990 Encore Computer Corporation
- © Copyright 1985, 1987, 1988, 1989, 1990, 1991, 1992, 1993 International Business Machines Corporation
- © Copyright 1988, 1989, 1990 Mentat Inc.
- © Copyright 1987, 1988, 1989, 1990, 1991, 1992, 1993 SecureWare, Inc.
- THIS SOFTWARE AND DOCUMENTATION ARE BASED IN PART ON THE FOURTH BERKELEY SOFTWARE DISTRIBUTION UNDER LICENSE FROM THE REGENTS OF THE UNIVERSITY OF CALIFORNIA. WE ACKNOWLEDGE THE FOLLOWING INDIVIDUALS AND INSTITUTIONS FOR THEIR ROLE IN ITS DEVELOPMENT: KENNETH C.R.C ARNOLD, GREGORY S. COUCH, CONRAD C. HUANG, ED JAMES, SYMMETRIC COMPUTER SYSTEMS, ROBERT ELZ © COPYRIGHT 1980, 1981, 1982, 1983, 1985, 1986, 1987, REGENTS OF THE UNIVERSITY OF CALIFORNIA.

All rights reserved.
Printed in the U.S.A.

Printed in the United States of America

10 9 8 7 6 5 4 3 2 1

ISBN 0-13-014291-3

Prentice-Hall International (UK) Limited, *London*
Prentice-Hall of Australia Pty. Limited, *Sydney*
Prentice-Hall Canada Inc., *Toronto*
Prentice-Hall Hispanoamericana, S.A., *Mexico*
Prentice-Hall of India Private Limited, *New Delhi*
Prentice-Hall of Japan, Inc., *Tokyo*
Simon & Schuster Asia Pte. Ltd., *Singapore*
Editora Prentice-Hall do Brasil, Ltda., *Rio de Janeiro*

THIS DOCUMENT AND THE SOFTWARE DESCRIBED HEREIN ARE FURNISHED UNDER A LICENSE, AND MAY BE USED AND COPIED ONLY IN ACCORDANCE WITH THE TERMS OF SUCH LICENSE AND WITH THE INCLUSION OF THE ABOVE COPYRIGHT NOTICE.

TITLE TO AND OWNERSHIP OF THE DOCUMENT AND SOFTWARE REMAIN WITH OSF OR ITS LICENSORS.

FOR U.S. GOVERNMENT CUSTOMERS REGARDING THIS DOCUMENTATION AND THE ASSOCIATED SOFTWARE

These notices shall be marked on any reproduction of this data, in whole or in part.

NOTICE: Notwithstanding any other lease or license that may pertain to, or accompany the delivery of, this computer software, the rights of the Government regarding its use, reproduction and disclosure are as set forth in Section 52.227-19 of the FARS Computer Software-Restricted Rights clause.

RESTRICTED RIGHTS NOTICE: Use, duplication, or disclosure by the Government is subject to the restrictions as set forth in subparagraph (c)(1)(ii) of the Rights in Technical Data and Computer Software clause at DFARS 52.227-7013.

RESTRICTED RIGHTS LEGEND: Use, duplication or disclosure by the Government is subject to restrictions as set forth in paragraph (b) (3)(B) of the rights in Technical Data and Computer Software clause in DAR 7-104.9(a). This computer software is submitted with "restricted rights." Use, duplication or disclosure is subject to the restrictions as set forth in NASA FAR SUP 18-52.227-79 (April 1985) "Commercial Computer Software-Restricted Rights (April 1985)." If the contract contains the Clause at 18-52.227-74 "Rights in Data General" then the "Alternate III" clause applies.

US Government Users Restricted Rights - Use, duplication or disclosure restricted by GSA ADP Schedule Contract.

Unpublished - All rights reserved under the Copyright Laws of the United States.

This notice shall be marked on any reproduction of this data, in whole or in part.

Open Software Foundation, OSF, the OSF logo, OSF/1, OSF/Motif, and Motif are trademarks of the Open Software Foundation, Inc.

AT&T is a registered trademark of American Telephone & Telegraph Company in the U.S. and other countries.

Ethernet is a registered trademark of Xerox Corporation.

UNIX is a registered trademark of UNIX System Laboratories, Inc. in the U.S. and other countries.

Contents

Preface xv
    Audience xvi
    Applicability xvi
    Purpose xvi
    Document Usage xvii
    Related Documents xix
    Reference Section Numbers xx
    Typographic and Keying Conventions xxi
    Problem Reporting xxii

Part 1. General User Tasks

Chapter 1. Getting Started on OSF/1 1–1
    Logging In 1–2
    Logging Out 1–5
    Using Commands 1–5
    Stopping Command Execution 1–7
    Setting Your Password 1–7
        Password Guidelines 1–8
        Password Procedure 1–9
    Getting Help 1–11
        Displaying and Printing Online Reference Pages
        (man) 1–11
        Finding Out About Commands (apropos) 1–13
Chapter 2. Overview of Files and Directories 2–1
    Overview of Text Editors 2–2

Contents

Creating Sample Files With the vi Text Editor	2–2
Understanding Files, Directories, and Pathnames	2–6
Files and Filenames	2–7
Directories and Subdirectories	2–8
Displaying the Name of Your Current Directory (pwd)	2–8
The Tree-Structure File System and Pathnames	2–9
Specifying Files With Pattern Matching	2–13
Chapter 3. Managing Files	**3–1**
Listing Files (ls)	3–2
Listing Contents of the Current Directory	3–3
Listing Contents of Other Directories	3–3
Flags Used With the ls Command	3–4
Displaying Files	3–7
Displaying Files Without Formatting (pg, more, cat)	3–7
Displaying Files With Formatting (pr)	3–9
Printing Files (lpr, lpq, lprm)	3–12
Linking Files (ln)	3–16
Hard Links and Soft Links	3–16
Links and File Systems	3–17
Using Links	3–18
How Links Work—Understanding Filenames and i-Numbers	3–19
Removing Links	3–20
Copying Files (cp)	3–22
Copying Files in the Current Directory	3–23
Copying Files into Other Directories	3–24
Renaming or Moving Files (mv)	3–26
Renaming Files	3–26
Moving Files into a Different Directory	3–27
Comparing Files (diff)	3–29
Sorting File Contents (sort)	3–31
Removing Files (rm)	3–32
Removing a Single File	3–33
Removing Multiple Files—Matching Patterns	3–34
Determining File Type (file)	3–35
Chapter 4. Managing Directories	**4–1**
Creating a Directory (mkdir)	4–2
Changing Directories (cd)	4–4

Contents

Changing Your Current Directory	4–4
Using Relative Pathname Notation	4–5
Accessing Directories Through Symbolic Links	4–8
Displaying Directories (ls -F)	4–9
Copying Directories (cp)	4–10
Renaming Directories (mv)	4–11
Removing Directories (rmdir)	4–12
Removing Empty Directories	4–13
Removing Multiple Directories	4–14
Removing Your Current Directory	4–15
Removing Files and Directories at the Same Time (rm -r)	4–15
Chapter 5. Controlling Access to Your Files and Directories	5–1
Understanding Password and Group Security Files	5–2
The /etc/passwd File	5–3
The /etc/group File	5–4
Protecting File and Directories	5–5
Displaying File and Directory Permissions (ls)	5–7
Setting File and Directory Permissions (chmod)	5–9
Specifying Permissions with Letters and Operation Symbols	5–10
Specifying Permissions With Octal Numbers	5–14
Setting the User Mask	5–16
Changing Your Identity to Access Files (su, whoami)	5–20
Superuser Concepts	5–21
Changing Owners and Groups	5–23
Additional Security Considerations	5–24
Using Enhancements to the Security System	5–25
Chapter 6. Using Processes	6–1
Understanding Programs and Processes	6–2
Understanding Standard Input, Output, and Error	6–2
Redirecting Input and Output	6–3
Redirecting Standard Error to a File	6–5
Redirecting Both Standard Error and Standard Output	6–7
Running Several Processes Simultaneously	6–8
Running Foreground Processes	6–8
Running Background Processes	6–9

OSF/1 User's Guide   iii

Contents

Monitoring and Terminating Processes	6–11
Checking Process Status	6–11
Canceling a Foreground Process (Ctrl-c)	6–14
Canceling a Background Process (kill)	6–15
Suspending and Resuming Processes (C Shell Only)	6–16
Displaying Information About Users and Their Processes	6–18
Chapter 7. OSF/1 Shell Overview	**7–1**
Purpose of OSF/1 Shells	7–2
Summary of Bourne, C, and Korn Shell Features	7–3
More Information on C and Korn Shell Features	7–4
The Restricted Bourne Shell	7–5
Changing Your Shell	7–5
Determining What Shell You Are Running	7–6
Temporarily Changing Your Shell	7–7
Permanently Changing Your Shell	7–8
Command Entry Aids	7–8
Using Multiple Commands and Command Lists	7–8
Using Pipes and Filters	7–11
Grouping Commands	7–13
Quoting	7–14
The Shell Environment	7–17
The login Program	7–17
Environment Variables	7–18
Shell Variables	7–21
Login Scripts and Your Environment	7–22
Using Variables	7–24
Setting Variables	7–25
Referencing Variables (Parameter Substitution)	7–27
Displaying the Values of Variables	7–28
Clearing the Values of Variables	7–29
How the Shell Finds Commands	7–30
Using Logout Scripts	7–32
Logout Scripts and the Shell	7–32
A Sample .logout File	7–33
Using Shell Procedures	7–34
Writing and Running Shell Procedures	7–34
Specifying a Run Shell	7–36
Chapter 8. OSF/1 Shell Features	**8–1**
Comparison of C, Bourne, and Korn Shell Features	8–2
C Shell Features	8–3

Sample .cshrc and .login Scripts 8–3
Metacharacters 8–7
Command History 8–9
Filename Completion 8–11
Aliases 8–12
Built-In Variables 8–14
Built-In Commands 8–15

Bourne Shell Features 8–17
Sample .profile Login Script 8–17
Metacharacters 8–20
Built-In Variables 8–21
Built-In Commands 8–23

Korn Shell Features 8–24
Sample .profile and .kshrc Login Scripts 8–25
Metacharacters 8–29
Command History 8–31
Editing Command Lines 8–33
Filename Completion 8–36
Aliases 8–36
Built-In Variables 8–39
Built-In Commands 8–41

Chapter 9. Useful Productivity Tools 9–1

Searching Files for Text Patterns (grep) 9–1

Finding Files (find) 9–5

Part 2. Communications Tasks

Chapter 10. Using Simple Communications Facilities 10–1

Sending Messages (write) 10–2
Having a Conversation 10–3
Retaining a Local Connection 10–5
Sending a Long Message 10–6
System Errors 10–7

Conducting an Online Talk Session (talk) 10–7

Controlling Messages and Online Talk Sessions (mesg) 10–9
Using the mesg Command 10–9
Changing the mesg Start-Up Procedure 10–11

Chapter 11. Using the UUCP Networking Utilities 11–1

Introduction to the UUCP Networking Utilities 11–2

Identifying Compatible Systems (uuname) 11–2

Contents

  Pathnames Used With UUCP Commands 11–3
  Communicating With a Remote System 11–5
    Connecting to a Remote Computer With the cu
    Command 11–6
    Connecting to a Remote Computer With the tip
    Command 11–18
    Connecting a Remote Terminal to Your System Using a Modem
    (ct) 11–29
  Running Remote Commands (uux) 11–34
    The uux Examples 11–37
    Additional Information About the uux Command 11–38
  Sending and Receiving Files (uucp) 11–40
    The uucp Command and System Security 11–43
    The uucp Examples (Bourne and Korn Shells) 11–44
    The uucp Examples (C Shell) 11–45
  Another Method for Transferring and Handling Files (uuto,
    uupick) 11–46
    Sending Files to a Specific ID (uuto) 11–47
    Locating Files for a Specific ID (uupick) 11–49
  Displaying the Status of UUCP Jobs 11–52
    Getting Status Information About UUCP Jobs
    (uustat) 11–52
    Additional Information About the uustat Command 11–56

Chapter 12. Using TCP/IP Commands 12–1

  Requesting Information About Users (finger) 12–2
  Requesting Information About Remote Systems (ruptime) . . . 12–3
  Transferring Files with ftp 12–4
    Using ftp Subcommands 12–6
  Transferring Files With tftp 12–14
    Interactive tftp 12–14
    Command-Line tftp 12–18
  Copying Files (rcp) 12–19
  Logging Into Remote Systems 12–21
    Logging In With rlogin 12–21
    Logging In With telnet 12–23
  Executing Commands Remotely (rsh) 12–26
  Displaying Who Is on Remote Systems (rwho) 12–27

Part 3. System Administration Tasks for the User

Contents

Chapter 13. Adding and Removing Users and Groups	13–1
Adding Users	13–2
Adding a New User Interactively	13–3
Adding a New User Manually	13–4
Adding a User Account to the /etc/passwd File	13–4
Adding a User Account to the /etc/group File	13–7
Creating the Login ($HOME) Directory	13–8
Providing the Default Shell Scripts	13–9
Creating a Mail File	13–11
Assigning an Initial Password	13–12
Removing a User	13–12
Removing the User's Files and Directories	13–13
Removing the User's Account from the /etc/group File	13–13
Removing the User's Account from the /etc/passwd File	13–14
Adding and Removing Groups	13–14
Adding a New Group to the /etc/group File	13–15
Removing a Group	13–17
Chapter 14. Shutting Down and Rebooting Your System	14–1
Shutdown and Reboot Concepts	14–2
Shutdown and Automatic Reboot Procedure	14–4
Chapter 15. Backing Up the System	15–1
Why Backups are Essential	15–2
Sample Backup Procedures	15–3
Appendix A. A Beginner's Guide to Using vi	A–1
Getting Started	A–3
Opening a File	A–3
Moving Within the File	A–4
Entering New Text	A–6
Editing Text	A–8
Finishing Your Edit Session	A–10
Using Advanced Techniques	A–10
Searching for Strings	A–11
Moving Text	A–11
Copying Text	A–12
Other vi Features	A–13
Using the Underlying ex Commands	A–13

Contents

Making Substitutions	A-14
Writing a Whole File or Parts of a File	A-16
Deleting a Block of Text	A-17
Moving and Copying Blocks of Text	A-17
Customizing Your Environment	A-17
Saving Your Customizations	A-19
Appendix B. Creating and Editing Files With ed	**B-1**
Understanding Text Files and the Edit Buffer	B-2
Creating and Saving Text Files	B-2
Starting the ed Program	B-3
Entering Text—The a (Append) Subcommand	B-3
Displaying Text—The p (Print) Subcommand	B-4
Saving Text—The w (Write) Subcommand	B-5
Leaving the ed Program—The q (Quit) Subcommand	B-7
Loading Files into the Edit Buffer	B-8
Using the ed (Edit) Command	B-8
Using the e (Edit) Subcommand	B-9
Using the r (Read) Subcommand	B-10
Displaying and Changing the Current Line	B-11
Finding Your Position in the Buffer	B-12
Changing Your Position in the Buffer	B-13
Locating Text	B-15
Searching Forward Through the Buffer	B-15
Searching Backward Through the Buffer	B-16
Changing the Direction of a Search	B-16
Making Substitutions—The s (Substitute) Subcommand	B-17
Substituting on the Current Line	B-18
Substituting on a Specific Line	B-18
Substituting on Multiple Lines	B-19
Changing Every Occurrence of a String	B-19
Removing Characters	B-20
Substituting at Line Beginnings and Ends	B-21
Using a Context Search	B-21
Deleting Lines—The d (Delete) Subcommand	B-22
Deleting the Current Line	B-23
Deleting a Specific Line	B-24
Deleting Multiple Lines	B-24
Moving Text—The m (Move) Subcommand	B-25
Changing Lines of Text—The c (Change) Subcommand	B-26
Changing a Single Line	B-27
Changing Multiple Lines	B-28

Contents

Inserting Text—The i (Insert) Subcommand	B–28
Using Line Numbers	B–29
Using a Context Search	B–30
Copying Lines—The t (Transfer) Subcommand	B–31
Using System Commands from ed	B–32
Ending the ed Program	B–33

Appendix C. Using Internationalization Features   C–1

Understanding Locale	C–2
How Locale Affects Processing and Display of Data	C–4
Collation	C–4
Date and Time Conventions	C–6
Numeric and Monetary Formatting	C–7
Program Messages	C–7
Yes/No Prompts	C–8
Determining Whether a Locale Has Been Set	C–8
Setting Locale	C–9
Locale Functions	C–11
Limitations of Locale Variables	C–13
Your Terminal Setup and Locale	C–14
Background on OSF/1 Terminal Devices	C–15
Determining the Active Code Set	C–18
Changing the Active Code Set	C–19
Checking the Terminal Device Stream	C–19
Changing the Terminal Device Stream Configuration	C–21

Appendix D. Sending and Receiving Mail   D–1

Understanding the Mail System	D–2
Parts of the Mail System	D–2
Addressing Mail	D–8
Addressing for Users on Your Local System	D–9
Addressing for Users on Your Network	D–9
Addressing for Users on a Different Network	D–11
Addressing for Users Connected with a UUCP Link	D–14
Creating Aliases and Distribution Lists	D–16
Sending Mail	D–18
Composing and Sending a Message	D–19
Sending a File	D–19
Receiving Mail	D–20
Forwarding Your Mail	D–22
Looking at Your Personal Mailbox	D–24
Looking at a Mail Folder	D–25
Processing Messages in a Mailbox	D–26

Contents

        Using Mailbox Commands D–27
        Looking at a Mailbox D–30
        Leaving the Mailbox D–30
        Getting Help D–31
        Finding the Name of the Current Mailbox D–31
        Changing Mailboxes D–32
        Reading a Message from a Mailbox D–32
        Displaying the Contents of a Mailbox D–34
        Deleting and Recalling Messages D–35
        Saving Messages in a File or Folder D–36
        Editing a Message D–38
        Creating a Message D–39
        Listing Defined Aliases D–41
    Using the Mail Editor D–42
        Starting the Mail Editor D–42
        Sending a Message D–42
        Quitting Without Sending the Message D–43
        Getting Help D–43
        Using the Escape Character D–43
        Displaying a Message D–44
        Changing a Message D–44
        Reformatting a Message D–46
        Checking for Misspelling D–46
        Changing the Header D–47
        Including Information from Another File D–51
        Including Another Message D–52
        Resending Undelivered Messages D–53
    Changing Mail to Meet Your Needs D–53
        Commands for Customizing Mail D–54
        Checking Mail Characteristics D–56
        Prompting for a Subject: Field D–57
        Prompting for a Cc: Field D–58
        Changing How Mail Displays a Message D–59
        Creating and Using Folders D–63
        Keeping a Record of Messages Sent D–65
        Selecting a Different Editor D–66
        Defining How to Exit the Mail Editor D–67
        Defining How Mail Stores Messages D–67

Glossary GL-1
Index Index-1

List of Figures

Figure 1–1. Shell Interaction with the User and the Operating System . . . 1–6
Figure 2–1. A Typical OSF/1 File System 2–10
Figure 2–2. Relative and Full Pathnames 2–12
Figure 3–1. Removing Links and Files 3–21
Figure 4–1. Relationship Between a New Directory and the Current Directory 4–3
Figure 4–2. Copying a Directory Tree 4–11
Figure 5–1. File and Directory Permission Fields 5–8
Figure 7–1. Flow Through a Pipeline 7–11
Figure C–1. Terminal Device Stream in OSF/1 . . . . C–16
Figure D–1. Parts of the Mail System D–3
Figure D–2. General Domain Naming Structure with Example Connections D–13
Figure D–3. Example of UUCP Connection on a Network D–16

List of Tables

Table 2–1. Summary of Pattern-Matching Characters	2–15
Table 2–2. Summary of Internationalized Pattern-Matching Characters	2–16
Table 3–1. The ls Command Options	3–5
Table 3–2. The ls -l Command Information	3–6
Table 3–3. The pr Command Flags	3–10
Table 3–4. The lpr Command Flags	3–14
Table 5–1. Differences Between File and Directory Permissions	5–6
Table 5–2. Permission Combinations	5–15
Table 5–3. How Octal Numbers Relate to Permission Fields	5–15
Table 5–4. The umask Permission Combinations	5–17
Table 6–1. Shell Notation for Reading Input and Redirecting Output	6–3
Table 7–1. Shell Filenames and Default Prompts	7–7
Table 7–2. Multiple Command Operators	7–9
Table 7–3. Command Grouping Symbols	7–13
Table 7–4. Shell Quoting Conventions	7–15
Table 7–5. Selected Shell Environment Variables	7–18
Table 7–6. System and Local Login Scripts	7–23
Table 7–7. Description of Example Shell Script	7–35
Table 8–1. C, Bourne, and Korn Shell Features	8–2
Table 8–2. Description of an Example .cshrc Script	8–4
Table 8–3. Description of an Example .login Script	8–6
Table 8–4. C Shell Metacharacters	8–7
Table 8–5. Reexecuting C Shell History Buffer Commands	8–11

Table 8–6. Built-In C Shell Variables	8–14
Table 8–7. Built-In C Shell Commands	8–15
Table 8–8. Description of an Example Bourne Shell .profile Script	8–18
Table 8–9. Bourne Shell Metacharacters	8–20
Table 8–10. Built-In Bourne Shell Variables	8–22
Table 8–11. Built-In Bourne Shell Commands	8–23
Table 8–12. Description of an Example Korn Shell .profile Script	8–26
Table 8–13. Description of an Example .kshrc Script	8–28
Table 8–14. Korn Shell Metacharacters	8–29
Table 8–15. Reexecuting Korn Shell History Buffer Commands	8–32
Table 8–16. Built-In Korn Shell Variables	8–39
Table 8–17. Built-In Korn Shell Commands	8–41
Table 9–1. The grep Command Flags	9–3
Table 10–1. Login Script Information	10–11
Table 11–1. The cu Command Flags and Entries	11–8
Table 11–2. The cu Local Commands	11–13
Table 11–3. The tip Command Flags and Entries	11–20
Table 11–4. The tip Local Commands	11–24
Table 11–5. The ct Command Flags and Entries	11–31
Table 11–6. The uux Command Flags and Entries	11–35
Table 11–7. The uucp Command Flags and Entries	11–41
Table 11–8. The uuto Command Flags and Entries	11–47
Table 11–9. The uupick Command Options	11–50
Table 11–10. The uustat Command Flags	11–54
Table 12–1. The ftp Subcommands	12–7
Table 12–2. The tftp Subcommands	12–16
Table 12–3. The telnet Subcommands	12–25
Table 13–1. Shells and Their Login Scripts	13–10
Table A–1. Selected vi Environment Variables	A–18
Table C–1. OSF/1 Locale Names	C–9
Table C–2. Environment Variables That Influence Locale Functions	C–12

Contents

Table D–1. Mailbox Information D–21

Preface

The *OSF/1 User's Guide* introduces users to the basic features of the OSF/1™ operating system.

This preface covers the following topics:

- Audience
- Applicability
- Purpose
- Document Usage
- Related Documents
- Typographic and Keying Conventions
- Problem Reporting

Preface

Audience

This guide is written for those who have little or no familiarity with computers, and no extensive knowledge of UNIX compatible systems or any other operating systems. As a result, the guide explains important concepts, provides tutorials, and is organized according to task.

Applicability

This is Revision 1.2 of this guide, which applies to Release 1.2 of OSF/1.

Purpose

This guide introduces you to the features of OSF/1. After reading the guide, you should be able to do the following:

- Gain access to your system and issue commands
- Understand file and directory concepts
- Manage files and directories
- Control access to your files and directories
- Manage processes
- Understand and manage your shell environment
- Use the **grep** and **find** productivity tools
- Use electronic mail and other facilities for communications between your system and other systems
- Perform basic system administrator tasks
- Use the **mail** program as well as the **ed** and **vi** text editors
- Use internationalization features

Document Usage

This guide is organized into three parts:

Part 1. General User Tasks

- Chapter 1 shows you how to log into and out of your system, enter commands, set your password, and obtain online help.

- Chapter 2 gives an overview of the OSF/1 file system, consisting of the files and directories that are used to store text, programs, and other data. This chapter also introduces you to the **vi** text editor, a program that allows you to create and modify files.

- Chapter 3 shows you how to manage files. You will learn how to list, display, copy, move, link, and remove them.

- Chapter 4 explains how to manage directories. You will learn how to create, change, display, copy, rename, and remove them.

- Chapter 5 shows you how to control access to your files and directories by setting appropriate permissions. It also describes standard password and group security issues as well as provides an overview of optional security enhancements.

  Note that the OSF/1 operating system provides one of the following security levels:

  — Standard level: a version equivalent to most UNIX implementations.

  — C2 level: a version that provides National Center for Computer Security (NCSC) C2 level security features.

  — B1 level: a version that provides NCSC B1 security level features.

  If your system provides C2 level or B1 level security enhancements, see your system administrator and the *OSF/1 Security Features User's Guide* for details.

- Chapter 6 describes how OSF/1 creates and keeps track of processes. It tells you how to redirect process input, output, and error information, run processes simultaneously, display process information, and cancel processes.

- Chapter 7 introduces you to features common to the three shells available with OSF/1: the Bourne, C, and Korn shells. You learn how to

Preface

change your shell, use command entry aids, understand some features of your shell environment (login scripts, environment and shell variables), set and clear variables, write logout scripts, and write and run basic shell procedures. The Korn Shell (**ksh**) is available only to AT&T Tool Chest Licensees.

- Chapter 8 provides detailed reference information about the C, Bourne, and Korn shells, comparing their features. It details the commands and environment variables of each program and shows you how to set up your login script.

- Chapter 9 describes the **grep** and **find** commands that allow you to examine the contents of files and to determine their location in the system.

Part 2. Communications Tasks

- Chapter 10 shows you how to use simple communications programs that permit you to send mail to and hold 2-way conversations with other users.

- Chapter 11 describes the UUCP Networking Utilities, which allow you to connect to remote systems, transfer files between remote systems, and run programs on remote systems.

- Chapter 12 describes how to use the Transmission Control Protocol/Internet Protocol (TCP/IP), which allows you to connect to, transfer files between, and run programs on remote systems.

Part 3. System Administration Tasks for the User

- Chapter 13 shows you how to add and remove individual user accounts and user groups.

- Chapter 14 describes the system shutdown and reboot procedures, which you may occasionally perform to correct operational problems.

- Chapter 15 provides basic conceptual information about backups, where you save copies of files and directories on a storage medium. It also provides you with simple backup and restore procedures.

The following appendixes provide reference information for this guide:

- Appendix A teaches you how to use the basic features of the **vi** text editor.

- Appendix B teaches you how to use the **ed** text editor. Detailed information about **ed** is provided because all systems have this editor

Preface

and because it can be used in critical system management situations when no other editor can be used.

- Appendix C describes the internationalization features of OSF/1 that allow users to process data and interact with the system in a manner appropriate to their native language, customs, and geographic region.
- Appendix D instructs you in the use of the **mail** program.

Related Documents

The following OSF/1 documents are currently available from Prentice-Hall:

- *OSF/1 Command Reference*
- *OSF/1 Programmer's Reference*
- *OSF/1 System and Network Administrator's Reference*
- *Application Environment Specification — Operating System Programming Interfaces Volume*

In addition, versions of the following documents may be available from your system vendor:

- *OSF/1 System Programmer's Reference Volume 1*
- *OSF/1 System Administrator's Guide*
- *OSF/1 Network and Communications Administrator's Guide*
- *OSF/1 Applications Programmer's Guide*
- *OSF/1 System Extension Guide*
- *OSF/1 Network Applications Programmer's Guide*
- *OSF/1 Security Features User's Guide*
- *OSF/1 Security Features Programmer's Guide*
- *OSF/1 Security Features Administrator's Guide*
- *OSF/1 Security Detailed Design Specification*

Preface

- *Design of the OSF/1 Operating System*
- *OSF/1 POSIX Conformance Document*

Reference Section Numbers

In descriptive text, all references appear without their reference section numbers. Reference section numbers correspond with OSF documentation as follows:

Section Number	Content	Manual
(1)	User commands	*OSF/1 Command Reference*
(2)	System calls	*OSF/1 Programmer's Reference* *OSF/1 System Programmer's Reference Volume 1*
(3)	Library calls	*OSF/1 Programmer's Reference*
(4)	File formats and data structures	*OSF/1 Programmer's Reference* *OSF/1 System and Network Administrator's Reference* *OSF/1 System Programmer's Reference Volume 1* *OSF/1 Command Reference*
(5)	Miscellaneous functions	*OSF/1 Programmer's Reference*
(7)	Special files	*OSF/1 Programmer's Reference*
(8)	Administrator commands	*OSF/1 System and Network Administrator's Reference*

Typographic and Keying Conventions

This document uses the following typographic conventions:

Bold	**Bold** words or characters represent system elements that you must use literally, such as commands, flags, and pathnames.
Italic	*Italic* words or characters represent variable values that you must supply.
`Constant width`	Examples and information that the system displays appear in typeface.
[ ]	Brackets enclose optional items in format and syntax descriptions.
{ }	Braces enclose a list from which you must choose an item in format and syntax descriptions.
|	A vertical bar separates items in a list of choices.
< >	Angle brackets enclose the name of a key on the keyboard.
...	Horizontal ellipsis points indicate that you can repeat the preceding item one or more times. Vertical ellipsis points indicate that you can repeat the preceding item one or more times.

This document uses the following keying conventions:

<Ctrl-*x*> or ^*x*	The notation **<Ctrl-*x*>** or ^ followed by the name of a key indicates a control character sequence. For example, **<Ctrl-c>** means that you hold down the control key while pressing **<c>**.
<Delete>	The notation **<Delete>** refers to the key on your terminal or workstation that is labeled with the word Delete or with a left arrow.
<Return>	The notation **<Return>** refers to the key on your terminal or workstation that is labeled with the word Return or Enter, or with a left arrow.

Preface

Entering commands   When instructed to *enter* a command, type the command name and then press < **Return**>. For example, the instruction ''Enter the **ls** command'' means that you type the **ls** command and then press **<Return>** (enter = type command + press **<Return>**).

Problem Reporting

If you have any problems with the software or documentation, please contact your software vendor's customer service department.

Part 1
General User Tasks

Chapter 1
Getting Started on OSF/1

This chapter introduces you to the basic tasks for using the OSF/1 operating system. Before you read this chapter, familiarize yourself with your system's hardware components.

If you are new to computing, you will find this chapter to be especially useful. If you are familiar with the UNIX operating system or other operating systems, you may wish to skim this chapter.

After completing this chapter, you will be able to do the following:

- Log into and log out of the system
- Execute commands
- Stop command execution
- Change your password
- Know how to access online help

Next, you must learn how to create and modify files with a text editing program. See Chapter 2 for an overview of text editors, and Appendixes A and B for information on the **vi** and **ed** text editors, respectively. Once you learn how to use a text editor, you should have the basic skills necessary to start using the operating system.

Logging In

To use the OSF/1 operating system, your system must be running and you must be logged in. Logging in identifies you as a valid system user and creates a work environment that belongs to you alone.

Before you can log in, you must obtain your username and password from the system administrator. A username (typically, your surname or given name) identifies you as an authorized user. A password (a word or group of characters that is easy for you to remember, but hard for others to guess) verifies your identity.

You may wish to think of your username and password as electronic keys that give you access to the system. When you enter them during the login process, you identify yourself as an authorized user.

Your password is an important part of system security because it prevents unauthorized use of your data. For more information on passwords, see "Password Guidelines" later in this chapter.

The first step in the login process is to display the login prompt. When your system is running and your workstation is on, the following login prompt appears on your screen:

```
login:
```

On some systems, you may have to press **<Return>** a few times to display the login prompt.

Your system's login prompt screen may be somewhat different. For example, in addition to the login prompt, the screen may display the system name and the version number of the operating system.

To log in, perform the following steps:

1. Enter your username at the login prompt. If you make a mistake, use **<Delete>** to correct it.

    For example, if your username is **larry**, enter:

    ```
    login: larry
    ```

Getting Started on OSF/1

The password prompt appears:

```
login: larry
Password:
```

2. Enter your password. For security reasons, the password does not display on the screen as you type it.

    If you think you made a mistake while typing your password, press **<Return>**. If your password is incorrect, the system tells you so and asks you to enter your username and password again.

    After you enter your username and password correctly, the system displays the shell prompt, usually a dollar sign ($) or a percent sign (%). Your system's shell prompt may be different.

    Note: In this guide, the shell prompt display is a dollar sign ($).

The shell prompt display tells you that your login is successful and that the system is ready to go to work for you. The shell prompt is your signal that the shell is running. The shell is a program that interprets all commands you enter, runs the programs you have asked for, and sends the results to your screen. For more information about commands and the shell prompt, see "Using Commands" later in this chapter and Chapter 7.

When you first log in, you are automatically placed in your login directory. See Chapter 2 for information about your login directory.

If your system does not display the shell prompt, you are not logged in. You may, for example, have entered your username or your password incorrectly. Try to log in again. If you still cannot log in, see your system administrator.

Note: Your system may not require you to have a password, or you may have been assigned a password that is common to all new users. To ensure security in these cases, it is usually a good idea to set your own password. For information on how to create or change a password, see "Setting Your Password."

Many systems display a welcome message and announcements whenever users log in.

General User Tasks

For example, the following is a typical login screen (your screen may vary):

```
Welcome to the OSF/1 Operating System
Fri Dec 7 09:48:25 EDT 19nn
You have mail.
$ _$
```

The preceding announcements contain the following pieces of information:

- A greeting
- The date and time of your last login.

    Note this information whenever you log in, and tell your system administrator if you have not logged in at the time specified. A wrong date and time might indicate that someone has been breaking into your system.

- Whether you have mail messages waiting to be read.

    Briefly, **mail** is a program that allows you to both send and receive electronic mail. The system displays the message You have mail when there are mail messages for you that are waiting to be read. If you have no mail messages, this line does not appear.

    For more information about mail, see Appendix D.

Note: Your system may contain enhanced security features in addition to those provided with all OSF/1 systems. These enhancements may result in a system that is certified at either the B1 or C2 security levels specified by the National Center for Computer Security (NCSC). As a result, you may be required to enter more than just a username and password during the login process. If so, see your system administrator for details.

OSF/1 User's Guide

Logging Out

When you are ready to end your work session, log out of the system. Logging out leaves the operating system running for other users and also ensures that no one else can use your work environment.

To log out, perform the following steps:

1. Make sure that the shell prompt is displayed.
2. Press **<Ctrl-d>**. If **<Ctrl-d>** does not work, enter **exit** or **logout**.

   The system displays the login prompt. On some systems, a message may also be displayed.

At this point, you or another user may log in.

Using Commands

Operating system commands are programs that perform tasks on the OSF/1 system. The OSF/1 operating system has a large set of commands that are described in the remaining chapters of this guide and in the related reference pages.

A shell reads every command you enter and directs the OSF/1 operating system to do what is requested. Therefore the shell is a command interpreter. Think of entering a command as an interactive process in which you enter a command, the shell interprets that command, and then gives an appropriate response—that is, the system either runs the program or displays an error message.

The shell acts as a command interpreter in the following way:

- The shell displays a shell prompt and waits for you to enter a command.
- When you enter a command, the shell analyzes it and locates the requested program.
- The shell asks the system to run the program, or it returns an error message.
- When the program completes execution, control returns to the shell, which again displays the prompt.

General User Tasks

Figure 1-1 shows the relationship between the user, the shell, and the operating system. The shell interacts with both the user (to interpret commands) and with the OSF/1 operating system (to request command execution).

Figure 1-1. Shell Interaction with the User and the Operating System

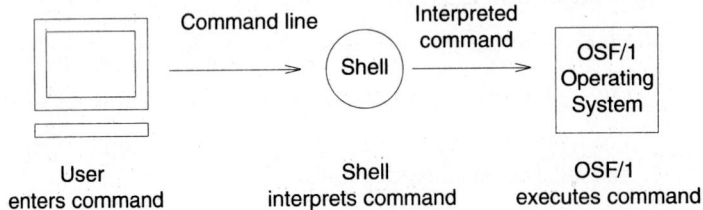

The OSF/1 operating system supports three different shells: the Korn, C, and Bourne shells. Your system administrator determines which shell you get when you log in for the first time. For more information on OSF/1 shells, see Chapter 7.

When you use the OSF/1 operating system, you typically enter commands following the shell prompt on the command line. For example, to display today's date and time, enter:

$ **date**

If you make a mistake while typing a command, use **<Delete>** to erase the incorrect characters and then retype them.

An argument is a string of characters that follows a command name. An argument specifies the data the command uses to complete its action. For example, the **man** command gives you information about OSF/1 commands. If you wish to display complete information about the **date** command, you would enter:

$ **man date**

Last, OSF/1 commands can have options that modify the way a command works. These options are called flags and immediately follow the command name. Most commands have several flags. If you use flags with a command, arguments follow the flags on the command line.

Getting Started on OSF/1

For example, suppose that you wish to use the **-f** flag with the **man** command. This flag displays a one-line description of a specified OSF/1 command. To display a one-line description of the **date** command, you would enter:

$ **man -f date**

While a command is running, the system does not display the shell prompt because the control passes to the program you are running. When the command completes its action, the system displays the shell prompt again, indicating that you can enter another command.

In addition to using the commands provided with the system, you can also create your own personalized commands. Refer to "Writing and Running Shell Procedures" in Chapter 7 for information about creating these special commands.

Stopping Command Execution

If you enter a command and then decide that you do not want it to complete execution, press **<Ctrl-c>**. The command stops executing, and the system displays the shell prompt. You can now enter another command.

Setting Your Password

Your username is public information and generally does not change. Your password, on the other hand, is private. In most instances, when your system account is established, the system administrator assigns you a password that is common to new users. After getting familiar with the system, you should select your own password to protect your account from unauthorized access. In addition, you should change your password periodically to protect your data from unauthorized access.

To set your password, use the **passwd** command. If your account does not have a password, you can use the **passwd** command to set one. For information on the **passwd** command, see "Password Procedure" later in this chapter.

OSF/1 User's Guide   1–7

Password Guidelines

You may find the following guidelines useful in selecting a password.

Here is a list of things you *should not do*:

- Do not choose a word found in a dictionary.
- Do not use personal information as your password, or as a substring of it, such as your username, names (yours, your family's, your company's), initials, or the make or model of your car.
- Do not use the default password you received with your account.
- Do not use old passwords or the same prefix or suffix you used in previous passwords. This rule also applies to any passwords you may have used in previous jobs.
- Do not choose a password that is easy to guess (includes all of the above options) even if you reverse its spelling. Choose a password that is hard to guess, not hard to remember.
- Do not choose passwords shorter than six characters in length. Your password can be up to eight characters long. (Strictly speaking, password length is measured in bytes, rather than characters, but we can regard these terms as the same, for now.)
- Do not write your password on paper or place it into a file.

Here is a list of things you *should do*:

- If possible, use a mixture of uppercase and lowercase letters in your password. You also should include any combination of numbers, punctuation marks, underscores (_), or spaces. Put them in the middle of your password, or at the end.
- Change your password frequently, especially if you think it might have been compromised.

On most systems, you can change your password as frequently, or as rarely, as you like. However, to protect system security, your system administrator may set limits on how often you may change your password, on the length of time your password remains valid, or on the nature of changes you can make.

Getting Started on OSF/1

Some typical password restrictions could be the following:

- Character restrictions
  - Minimum number of alphabetic characters
  - Minimum number of "other" characters, such as punctuation or numbers
  - Minimum number of characters in a new password that must be different from the old password
  - Maximum number of consecutive duplicate characters allowed in a password
- Time restrictions
  - Maximum number of weeks before your password expires
  - Number of weeks before you can change a password

See your system administrator for more information about password restrictions.

Password Procedure

To set or change your password, perform the following steps:

1. Enter the **passwd** command:

   $ **passwd**

   The system displays the following message (identifying you as the user) and prompts you for your old password:

   ```
   Changing password for username
   Old password:
   ```

   If you do not have an old password, the system does not display this prompt. Go to step 3.

2. Enter your old password. For security reasons, the system does not display your password as you type it.

General User Tasks

After the system verifies your old password, it is ready to accept your new password and displays the following prompt:

```
New password:
```

3. Enter your new password following the prompt. Remember that your new password entry does not appear on the screen.

    Finally, to verify the new password (since you cannot see it as you type), the system prompts you to enter the new password again:

    ```
    Re-enter new password:
    ```

4. Enter your new password once again. As before, the new password entry does not appear on the screen.

    Your password should be no more than eight bytes. For security reasons, it should be easy for you to remember, but difficult for anyone else to guess.

    When the shell prompt returns to the screen, your new password is in effect.

If you change your password and the new password is not proper, you receive a message stating the specific problem and the restrictions in effect for the system.

Note: Try to remember your password because you cannot log into the system without it. If you do forget your password, see your system administrator.

Getting Help

Most OSF/1 operating system commands needed for your work are described in this guide. In addition, you can quickly access online command documentation by using one of the following commands:

- The **man** command displays online reference pages.
- The **apropos** command displays a one-line summary of each command pertaining to a specified subject.

The following subsections describe these features.

Displaying and Printing Online Reference Pages (man)

Online reference pages contain complete information about OSF/1 commands. To view a reference page, use the **man** command. For example, to view the reference page for the **date** command, enter the following (your screen may vary):

$ man date

```
date(1)              Open Software Foundation              date(1)


NAME
     date - Displays or sets the date

SYNOPSIS
   With Superuser Authority:
     date [-nu] [MMddhhmm.ssyy | alternate_date_format]
     [+field_descriptor ...]

   Without Superuser Authority:
     date [-u] [+field_descriptor ...]

     The date command writes the current date and time to
     standard output.
```

General User Tasks

```
FLAGS
     -n   Does not set the time globally on all machines in a
          local area network that have their clocks synchronized
          (superuser only).

     -u   Performs operations as if the TZ environment variable was
          set to the string GMT0.  Otherwise, date uses the timezone
          indicated by the TZ environment variable or the system
          default if that variable is not set.

DESCRIPTION

     The date command writes the current date and time to
     standard output if called with no flags or with a flag list
     that begins with a + (plus sign).  Only a user operating with
     superuser authority can change the date and time.  The
     LC_TIME variable, if it is defined, controls the ordering of
     the day and month numbers in the date specifications.  The
     default order is MMddhhmm.ssyy where:

     o    MM is the month number (01=January)

     o    dd is the number of the day in the month
--More--(30%)
```

The symbol `--More--(30%)` at the bottom of the page indicates that 30% of the reference page is currently displayed. Press the space bar to display more, or type **q** to quit and return to the shell prompt.

To print the reference page for the **date** command, enter:

$ man date | lpr
$ _

The reference page is now queued for printing. See Chapter 3 for more information about the **lpr** command.

Getting Started on OSF/1

To display a brief, one-line description of an OSF/1 command, use the **man -f** command. For example, to display a brief description of the **who** command, enter:

$ **man -f who**
```
who (1)     - Identifies users currently logged in
$ _
```

For complete information on the **man** command and its options, you can display the reference page by entering the following:

$ **man man**

Finding Out About Commands (apropos)

Because the OSF/1 operating system provides many powerful commands, you may forget a command name now and then. At those times, the **apropos** command and the **man -k** command are useful tools.

The **apropos** and **man -k** commands do exactly the same thing. They allow you to describe a command, and then they list commands that answer that description.

For example, assume that you cannot remember the name of the command that sets passwords. To display the names and descriptions of all commands that have something to do with passwords, enter one of the following:

$ **apropos password**
or
$ **man -k password**

A portion of what the system displays is the following:

```
passwd (1)     - Changes password file information
passwd (4)     - Password files
```

You can now use the **passwd** command to set your password.

Chapter 2
Overview of Files and Directories

This chapter introduces you to files, file systems, and text editors. A file is a collection of data stored together in the computer. Typical files contain memos, reports, correspondence, programs, or other data. A file system is the useful arrangement of files into directories.

A text editor is a program that allows you to create new files and modify existing ones.

After completing this chapter, you will be able to do the following:

- Create files with the **vi** text editor. These files will be useful for working through the examples later in this guide.

- Understand OSF/1 file system components and concepts.

This knowledge can help you design a file system that is appropriate for the type of information you use and the way you work.

Overview of Text Editors

An editor is a program that allows you to create and change files containing text, programs, or other data. An editor does not provide the formatting and printing features of a word processor.

With a text editor, you can do the following:

- Create, read, and write files
- Display and search data
- Add, replace, and remove data
- Move and copy data
- Run OSF/1 commands

Your editing takes place in an edit buffer that you can save or discard.

The following text editing programs are available on the OSF/1 operating system: **vi** and **ed**. Each editor has its own methods of displaying text as well as its own set of subcommands and rules.

For information on **vi**, see the following section and Appendix A. For information on **ed**, see Appendix B. Your system may contain additional editors, so see your system administrator for details.

Creating Sample Files With the vi Text Editor

This section shows you how to create three files with the **vi** text editor. Teaching you how to use the **vi** editor is not the purpose of this section. Instead, the goal is to have you create, with a minimal set of commands, files that can be used for working through the examples later in this guide. For more information on **vi**, see Appendix A and the **vi** reference page.

Note: If you are familiar with a different editing program, you can use that program to create the three example files described next. If you have already created three files with an editing program, you can use those files by substituting their names for the filenames used in the examples.

Overview of Files and Directories

When trying the following procedures, you should enter the text that is printed in **boldface** characters. System prompts and output are shown in a different typeface, `like this`.

To create three sample files, perform the following steps:

1. Start the **vi** program by typing the command **vi** and the name of a new file, and then pressing **<Return>**:

    $ **vi file1**

    This is a new file, so the system responds by putting your cursor at the top of a screen that looks like the following:

    ~
    ~
    ~
    ~
    ~
    ~
    `"file1" [New file]`

    Note the blank lines on your screen that begin with a ~ (tilde). These tildes indicate the lines that contain no text. Because you have not entered any text, all lines begin with a tilde.

2. Specify that you want to add text to the new file by typing the letter **i** (insert text). The system does not display the **i** that you type.

3. Enter the following text. If you make mistakes and wish to correct them before moving to the next line, use **<Delete>** to erase backward over the current line of text.

    You start the vi program by entering
    the command vi, optionally followed by the name
    of a new or existing file.
    ~
    ~
    ~
    ~
    ~
    `"file1" [New file]`

OSF/1 User's Guide   2–3

General User Tasks

That is all you need to enter for the text of **file1**.

4. Indicate that you have finished your current work by pressing **<Esc>** and then typing a : (colon). The colon is displayed as a prompt at the bottom of the screen as follows:

```
You start the vi program by entering
the command vi, optionally followed by the name
of a new or existing file.
~
~
~
~
~
:
```

Then enter the letter **w**. Entering the letter **w** indicates to the system that you want to *write*, or save a copy of the new file.

Your screen will look like the following:

```
You start the vi program by entering
the command vi, optionally followed by the name
of a new or existing file.
~
~
~
~
~
~
"file1" [New file] 3 lines, 112 characters
```

Note that the system displays the name of the new file as well as the number of lines and characters it contains.

You are still in **vi**, so you can create two more sample files. The process is the same as the one you used to create **file1**, but the text you enter will be different.

2–4   OSF/1 User's Guide

Overview of Files and Directories

5. To create the second file, **file2**, type a : (colon). The colon is displayed as a prompt at the bottom the screen. Then enter the **vi file2** command.

   The system responds with a screen that looks like the following:

   ```
   ~
   ~
   ~
   ~
   ~
   ~
   ~
   "file2" No such file or directory
   ```

   The message `"file2" No such file or directory` indicates that **file2** is a new file.

   Indicate that you want to add text to the new file by typing the letter **i**. Then enter the following text:

   **If you have created a new file, you will find
   that it is easy to add text.**

   Then, press **<Esc>**, type a : (colon), and enter the letter **w** to save the file.

   Your screen will look like the following:

   ```
   If you have created a new file, you will find
   that it is easy to add text.
   ~
   ~
   ~
   ~
   ~
   ~
   "file2" [New file] 2 lines, 75 characters
   ```

6. To create the third file, follow the instructions in step 5. However, name the file **file3**, and enter the following text:

   **You will find that vi is a useful
   editor that has many features.**

   Then, press **<Esc>**, type a : (colon), and enter the **wq** command.

   The **wq** command writes the file, exits the editor, and returns you to the shell prompt.

Understanding Files, Directories, and Pathnames

A file is a collection of data stored in a computer. A file stored in a computer is like a document stored in a filing cabinet because you can retrieve it, open it, process it, close it, and store it as a unit. Every computer file has a filename that both users and the system use to refer to the file.

A file system is the arrangement of files into a useful pattern. Any time you organize information, you create something like a computer file system. For example, the structure of a manual file system (file cabinets, file drawers, file folders, and documents) resembles the structure of a computer file system. (The software that manages the file storage is also known as the file system, but that usage of the term does not occur in this chapter.)

Once you have organized your file system (manual or computer), you can find a particular piece of information quickly because you understand the structure of the system. To understand the OSF/1 file system, you should first become familiar with the following three concepts:

- Files and filenames
- Directories and subdirectories
- Tree structures and pathnames

Files and Filenames

A file can contain the text of a document, a computer program, records for a general ledger, the numerical or statistical output of a computer program, or other data.

A filename can contain any character except the **/** (slash) but, to prevent difficulties, construct your filenames without the characters that have a special meanings to your shell. For example, the following characters have special meaning to the shell: **** (back slash), **&** (ampersand), **< >** (angle brackets), **?** (question mark), **$** (dollar sign), **[ ]** (brackets), ***** (asterisk), or **|** (vertical bar or pipe symbol). You may use a **.** (period or dot) in the middle of a filename, but never at the beginning of the filename, unless you wish the file to be "hidden" when doing a simple listing of files. For information about characters with special meanings to your shell, refer to Chapter 8. For information about listing hidden files, see Chapter 3.

Note: Unlike some operating systems, the OSF/1 operating system distinguishes between uppercase and lowercase letters in filenames (that is, it is case sensitive). For example, the following three filenames specify three distinct files: **filea**, **Filea**, and **FILEA**.

It is a good idea to use filenames that reflect the actual contents of your files. For example, a filename such as **memo.advt** could indicate that the file contains a memo dealing with advertising. On the other hand, a filename such as **a**, **b**, or **c** tells you little or nothing about the contents of that file.

It is also a good idea to use a consistent pattern to name related files. For example, suppose you have a report that is divided into chapters, with each chapter contained in a separate file. You might name these files in the following way:

    chap1
    chap2
    chap3
    and so on ...

The maximum length of a filename depends upon the file system used on your computer. For example, your file system may allow a maximum filename length of 255 bytes (the default), or it may allow a maximum filename length of only 14 bytes. Because knowing the maximum filename length is important for helping you name files meaningfully, see your system administrator for details.

Directories and Subdirectories

You can organize your files into groups and subgroups that resemble the cabinets, drawers, and folders in a manual file system. These groups are called directories, and the subgroups are called subdirectories. A well-organized system of directories and subdirectories lets you retrieve and manipulate the data in your files quickly.

Directories differ from files in two significant ways:

- Directories are organizational tools; files are storage places for data.
- Directories contain the names of files, other directories, or both.

When you first log in, the system automatically places you in your login directory. This directory was created for you when your computer account was established. However, a file system in which all files are arranged under your login directory is not necessarily the most efficient method of organizing your data.

As you work with the system, you may want to set up additional directories and subdirectories so you can organize your files into useful groups. For example, assume that you work for the Sales department and are responsible for four lines of automobiles. You may wish to create a subdirectory under your login directory for each automobile line. Each subdirectory can contain all memos, reports, and sales figures applicable for the automobile model.

Once your files are arranged into a directory structure that you find useful, you can move easily between directories as you work first with File A, located in Directory X, and then with File B, located in Directory Y. See Chapter 4 for information on creating directories and moving between them.

Displaying the Name of Your Current Directory (pwd)

The directory in which you are working at any given time is your current or working directory. Whenever you are uncertain what directory you are working in, or where that directory exists in the file system, enter the **pwd** (print working directory) command as follows:

$ **pwd**

Overview of Files and Directories

The system displays the name of your current directory in a form such as the following:

/usr/msg

indicating that you are currently working in a directory named **msg** that is located under the **usr** directory. The **/usr/msg** notation is called the pathname of your working directory. See the following section for information about pathnames.

The Tree-Structure File System and Pathnames

The files and directories in the OSF/1 file system are arranged hierarchically in a structure that resembles an upside-down tree with the roots at the top and the branches at the bottom. This arrangement is called a tree structure. You can find more detailed information about OSF directory structure in the **hier** reference page.

Figure 2-1 shows a typical OSF/1 file system arranged in a tree structure. The names of directories are printed in bold, and the names of files are printed in italics.

General User Tasks

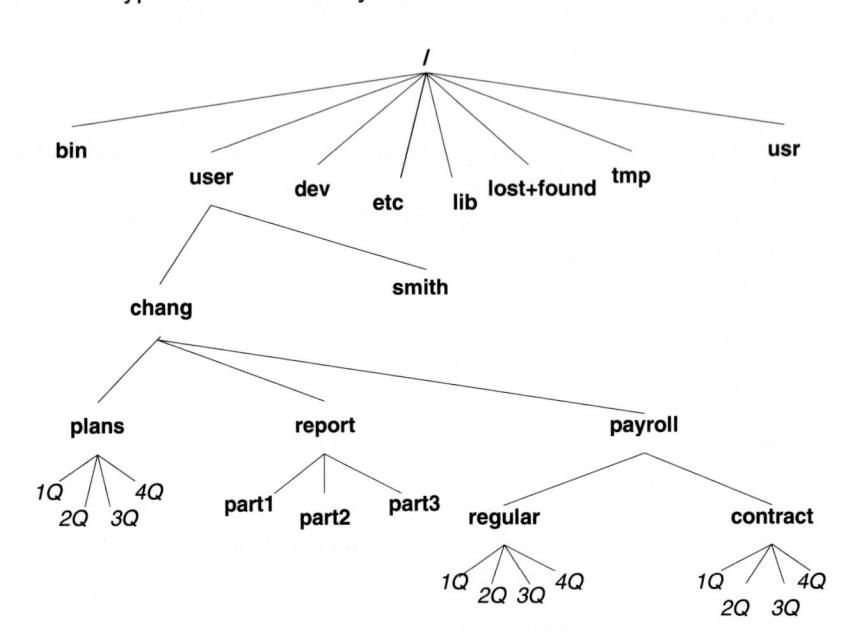

Figure 2–1. A Typical OSF/1 File System

```
                                    /
       ┌───────┬───────┬────┬────┬────┬─────────┬─────┬──────┐
      bin    user    dev  etc  lib  lost+found  tmp   usr
             ┌──────┴──────┐
           chang         smith
      ┌──────┼──────────────────┐
    plans  report            payroll
   ┌─┬─┬─┐  ┌─┼─┐         ┌──────┴──────┐
   1Q 2Q   part1 part2   regular      contract
   3Q 4Q         part3   ┌─┬─┬─┐      ┌─┬─┬─┐
                         1Q 2Q        1Q 2Q
                         3Q 4Q        3Q 4Q
```

At the top of the file system shown in Figure 2-1 (that is, at the root of the inverted tree structure) is a directory called the root directory. The symbol that represents this first major division of the file system is a **/** (slash).

At the next level down from the root of the file system are eight directories, each with its own system of subdirectories and files. Figure 2-1, however, shows only the subdirectories under the directory named **user**. These are the login directories for the users of this system.

The third level down the tree structure contains the login directories for two of the system's users, **smith** and **chang**. It is in these directories that **smith** and **chang** begin their work after logging in.

The fourth level of the figure shows three directories under the **chang** login directory: **plans, report,** and **payroll**.

The fifth level of the tree structure contains both files and subdirectories. The **plans** directory contains four files, one for each quarter. The **report** directory contains three files that make up the three parts of a report. Also on the fifth level are two subdirectories, **regular** and **contract**, which further organize the information in the **payroll** directory.

Overview of Files and Directories

A higher level directory is frequently called a parent directory. For example, in Figure 2-1, the directories **plans**, **report**, and **payroll** all have **chang** as their parent directory.

A pathname specifies the location of a directory or a file within the file system. For example, when you want to change from working on File A in Directory X to File B in Directory Y, you enter the pathname to File B. The OSF/1 operating system then uses this pathname to search through the file system until it locates File B.

A pathname consists of a sequence of directory names separated by slashes (/) that ends with a directory name or a filename. The first element in a pathname specifies where the system is to begin searching, and the final element specifies the target of the search. The following pathname is based on Figure 2-1:

/user/chang/report/part3

The first / represents the root directory and indicates the starting place for the search. The remainder of the pathname indicates that the search is to go to the **user** directory, then to directory **chang**, next to directory **report**, and finally to the file **part3**.

Whether you are changing your current directory, sending data to a file, or copying or moving a file from one place in your file system to another, you use pathnames to indicate the objects you wish to manipulate.

A pathname that starts with a / (the symbol representing the root directory) is called a full pathname or an absolute pathname. You can also think of a full pathname as the complete name of a file or a directory. Regardless of where you are working in the file system, you can always find a file or a directory by specifying its full pathname.

The OSF/1 file system also lets you use relative pathnames. Relative pathnames do not begin with the / that represents the root directory because they are *relative* to the current directory.

You can specify a relative pathname in one of four ways:

- As the name of a file in the current directory.

- As a pathname that begins with the name of a directory one level below your current directory.

General User Tasks

- As a pathname that begins with **..** (dot dot, the relative pathname for the parent directory).

- As a pathname that begins with **.** (dot, which refers to the current directory). This relative pathname notation is useful when you wish to run your own version of an operating system command in the current directory (for example **./ls**).

Every directory contains at least two entries: **..** (dot dot), and **.** (dot, which refers to the current directory).

In Figure 2-2, for example, if your current directory is **chang**, the relative pathname for the file **1Q** in directory **contract** is **payroll/contract/1Q**. By comparing this relative pathname with the full pathname for the same file, **/user/chang/payroll/contract/1Q**, you can see that using relative pathnames means less typing and more convenience.

Figure 2-2. Relative and Full Pathnames

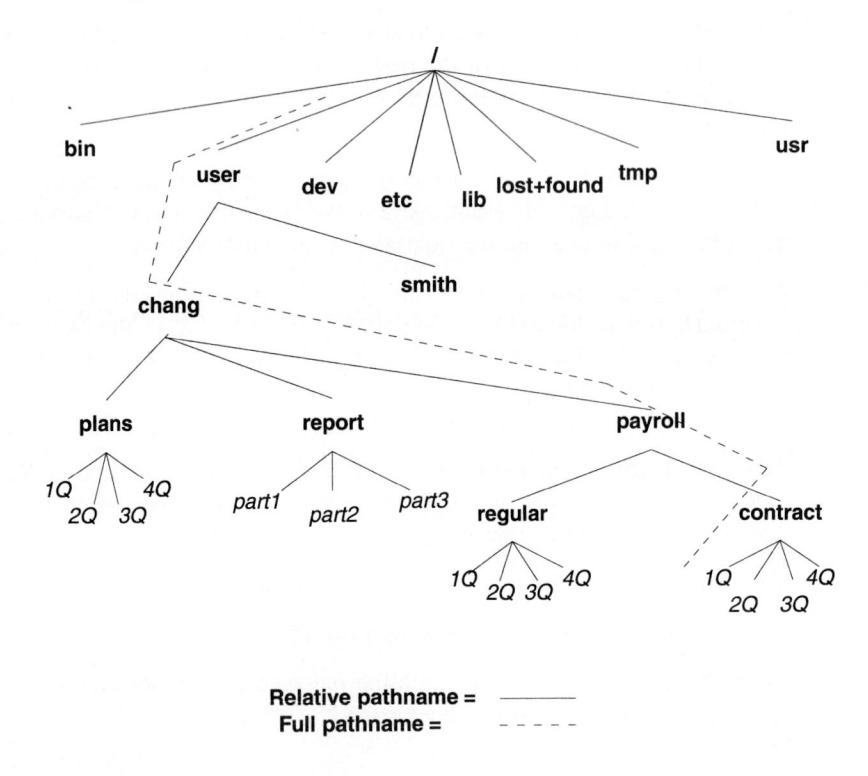

```
                              /
      ┌─────┬────┬────┬────┬──────────┬─────┬─────┐
     bin  user  dev  etc  lib    lost+found tmp  usr
           │
           │         smith
         chang
       ┌───┼──────────────┐
     plans  report       payroll
     ╱│╲    ╱│╲          ╱    ╲
    1Q 4Q  part1 part3  regular contract
    2Q 3Q   part2        ╱│╲    ╱│╲
                        1Q 4Q  1Q 4Q
                        2Q 3Q  2Q 3Q
```

Relative pathname = ─────────
Full pathname =   - - - - -

In the C shell and the Korn shell, you may also use a ~ (tilde) at the beginning of relative pathnames. The tilde character specifies a user's login (home) directory. For example, to specify your own login directory, use the tilde alone. To specify the login directory of user **chang**, specify ~**chang**.

For more information on using relative pathnames, see "Using Relative Pathname Notation" in Chapter 4.

Note: If there are other users on your system, you may or may not be able to get to their files and directories, depending upon the permissions set for them. For more information about file and directory permissions, see Chapter 5. In addition, your system may contain enhanced security features that may affect access to files and directories. If so, see your system administrator for details.

Specifying Files With Pattern Matching

Commands often take filenames as arguments. To use several different filenames as arguments to a command, you can type out the full name of each file, as the next example shows:

$ **ls first.t second.t third.t fourth.t fifth.t**

However, if the filenames have a common pattern (in this example, the **.t** suffix), the shell can match that pattern, generate a list of those names, and automatically pass them to the command as arguments.

The ***** (asterisk) matches any string of characters. In the following example, **ls** finds the name of every text file in this directory that includes the suffix **.t**:

$ **ls *.t**

The ***.t** matches any filename that begins with a character string and ends with **.t**. The shell passes every filename that matches this pattern as an argument for **ls**.

Thus, you do not have to type (or even remember) the full name of each file in order to use it as an argument. Both commands (**ls** with all filenames typed out, and **ls *.t**) do the same thing—they pass all files with the **.t** suffix in the directory as arguments to **ls**.

There is one exception to the general rules for pattern matching. When the first character of a filename is a period, you must match the period explicitly. For example, **ls *** displays the names of all files in the current directory that do not begin with a period. The command **ls -a** prints all filenames that begin with a period.

This restriction prevents the shell from automatically matching the relative directory names. These are **.** (called "dot," standing for the current directory) and **..** (called "dot dot," standing for the parent directory). For more information on relative directory names, see Chapter 4.

If a pattern does not match any filenames, the shell displays a message informing that no match has been found.

In addition to the ***** (asterisk), OSF/1 shells provide other ways to match character patterns. Table 2-1 summarizes pattern-matching characters and provides examples.

Table 2–1. Summary of Pattern-Matching Characters

Character	Action
*	Matches any string, including the null string. For example, **th*** matches **th**, **theodore**, and **theresa**.
?	Matches any single character. For example, **304?b** matches **304Tb**, **3045b**, **304Bb**, or any other string that begins with **304**, ends with **b**, and has one character in between.
[...]	Matches any one of the enclosed characters. For example, **[A G X]*** matches all filenames in the current directory that begin with **A**, **G**, or **X**.
[.-.]	Matches any character that falls within the specified range, as defined by the current locale. For more information on locale, see Appendix C. For example, **[T-W]*** matches all filenames in the current directory that begin with **T**, **U**, **V**, or **W**.
[!...]	Matches any single character except one of those enclosed. For example, **[!abyz]*** matches all filenames in the current directory that begin with any character except **a**, **b**, **y**, or **z**. This pattern matching is available only in the Bourne and Korn shells.

Because OSF/1 is an internationalized operating system, it also provides additional pattern-matching features. Table 2-2 summarizes internationalized pattern-matching characters and provides examples.

Table 2–2. Summary of Internationalized Pattern-Matching Characters

Character	Action
[[:*class*:]]	A character class name enclosed in bracket-colon delimiters matches any of the set of characters in the named class.
	The supported classes are **alpha, upper, lower, digit, alnum, xdigit, space, print, punct, graph, cntrl**. For example, the **alpha** character class name specifies that you wish to match any alphabetic character (uppercase and lowercase) as defined by the current locale. If you are running an American-based locale, **alpha** would match any character in the alphabet (A-Z, a-z).
[[=*char*=]*]	A character enclosed in bracket-equal delimiters matches any equivalence class character.
	An equivalence class is a set of collating elements that all sort to the same primary location. It is generally designed to deal with primary-secondary sorting; that is, for languages such as French that define groups of characters as sorting to the same primary location, and then having a tie-breaking, secondary sort. For example, if your current locale is France, **[[=a=]*]** would match any filename starting with the following characters: a, á, à, or â.

For more information on internationalized pattern-matching characters, see the **grep** reference page. For more information on OSF/1 internationalization features, see Appendix C, "Using Internationalization Features."

Chapter 3
Managing Files

This chapter shows you how to manage files on your system. After completing this chapter, you will be able to do the following:

- List files
- Display and print files
- Link files
- Copy, rename, and move files
- Compare and sort files
- Remove files from the system
- Determine file type

A good way to learn about managing files is to try the examples in this chapter. Do each example in order so that the information on your screen is consistent with the information in this guide.

Before you can work through the examples, you must be logged in, and your login directory must contain the following three files created in Chapter 2: **file1**, **file2**, and **file3**. To produce a listing of the files in your login directory, enter the **ls** command, which is explained in the following section. If you are using files with different names, make the appropriate substitutions as you work through the examples.

General User Tasks

In the following examples, when you are asked to return to your login directory, enter the **cd** (change directory) command as follows:

$ **cd**
$ _

Note that, in the preceding example, the $ indicates the shell prompt, and the _ (underscore) represents the cursor. Your shell prompt and cursor may vary.

In addition, before working on the examples in this chapter, create a subdirectory called **project** in your login directory. To do so, enter the following **mkdir** (make directory) command from your login directory:

$ **mkdir project**
$ _

For more information on the **cd** and **mkdir** commands, see Chapter 4.

Listing Files (ls)

You can display a listing of the contents of one or more directories with the **ls** (list directory) command. This command produces a list of the files and subdirectories (if any) in your current directory. You can also display other types of information, such as the contents of directories other than your current directory.

The general format of the **ls** command follows:

ls

The **ls** command has a number of options, called flags that enable you to display different types of information about the contents of a directory. Refer to "Flags Used With the **ls** Command" for information about these flags.

3–2   OSF/1 User's Guide

Listing Contents of the Current Directory

To list the contents of your current directory, enter:

ls

Used without flags in this format, the **ls** command simply lists the names of the files and directories in your current directory:

```
$ ls
file1      file2      file3      project
$ _
```

You may also list portions of your current directory's contents by using the command format:

ls *filename*

The *filename* entry can be the name of the file or a list of filenames separated by spaces. You may also use pattern-matching characters to specify files. See Chapter 2 for information on pattern matching.

For example, to list the files whose names begin with the characters **file**, you would enter the following command:

```
$ ls file*
file1   file2   file3
$ _
```

Listing Contents of Other Directories

To display a listing of the contents of a directory other than your current directory, use the following command:

ls *dirname*

The *dirname* entry is the pathname of the directory whose contents you want to display.

General User Tasks

In the following example, the current directory is your login directory, and you wish to display the **/users** directory. (Your system may contain another directory with a name similar to the **/users** directory.) Note that the name of the **/users** directory is preceded by a slash (/), which indicates that the system should begin searching in the root directory.

```
$ ls /users
amy     beth     chang    george   jerry    larry
mark    monique  ron
$ _
```

The **ls** command ordinarily lists directory and filenames in collated order as determined by the current locale.

Flags Used With the ls Command

In its simplest form, the **ls** command displays only the names of files and directories contained in the specified directory. However, **ls** has several flags that provide additional information about the listed items or change the way in which the system displays the listing.

When you want to include flags with the **ls** command, use the following format:

ls *-flagname(s)*

The *-flagname(s)* entry specifies one or more flags (options) that you are using with the command. For example, the **-l** flag produces a long listing of the directory contents. Note also that all **ls** flags are preceded by the - (dash) character.

If you want to use multiple flags with the command, enter the flag names together in one string:

$ **ls -ltr**

Table 3-1 lists some of the most useful **ls** command flags.

Table 3–1. The ls Command Options

Flag	Action
-l	Lists in **long** format. An **-l** listing provides the type, permissions, number of links, owner, group, size, and time of last modification for each file or directory listed.
-t	Sorts the files and directories by the **time** they were last modified (latest first), rather than collated by name.
-r	Reverses the order of the sort to get **reverse collated** order (**ls -r**), or **reverse time** order (**ls -tr**).
-a	Lists **all** entries including hidden files. Without this flag, the **ls** command does not list the names of entries that begin with a . (dot), such as **.profile**, **.login**, and relative pathnames.

The following example shows a long (-l) listing of a current directory. (The name `larry` shows the owner of the files. Your username will replace `larry` on your screen.)

```
$ ls -l
total 4
-rw-r--r--   1 larry    system      101 Jun  5 10:03 file1
-rw-r--r--   1 larry    system       75 Jun  5 10:03 file2
-rw-r--r--   1 larry    system       65 Jun  5 10:06 file3
drwxr-xr-x   2 larry    system       32 Jun  5 10:07 project
$ _
```

Table 3-2 explains the information displayed on your screen after you enter the **ls -l** command.

Table 3-2. The ls -l Command Information

Field	Information
`total 4`	Number of 512-byte blocks taken up by files in this directory.
`drwxr-xr-x`	File type and permissions set for each file or directory. The first character in this field indicates file type: - (dash) for ordinary files **b** for block-special files **c** for character-special files **d** for directories **l** for symbolic links **p** for pipe-special files (first in, first out) **s** for local sockets The remaining characters indicate what **r**ead, **w**rite, and **ex**ecute permissions are set for the owner, group, and others. In addition, other permission information may also be displayed. For more information on permissions, see Chapter 5.
`1`	Number of links to each file. For an explanation of *file links*, see "Linking Files (**ln**)."
`larry`	Username of the file's owner.
`system`	Group to which the file belongs.
`101`	Number of bytes in the file.
`Jun 5 10:03`	Date and time the file was created or last modified in the format defined by your current locale.
`file1`	Name of the file or directory.

There are other **ls** command flags that you may find useful as you gain experience with the OSF/1 operating system. For detailed information about the **ls** command flags, see the **ls** reference page.

Displaying Files

You can view any text file stored on your system with a text editor. However, if you wish to just look at a file without making any changes, you may view it (with or without screen formatting) using a variety of OSF/1 commands. The following subsections describe these commands.

Displaying Files Without Formatting (pg, more, cat)

The following commands display a file just as it is, without adding any special characteristics that govern the appearance of the contents:

- **pg**
- **cat**
- **more**

For information on displaying files with formatting, see the following subsection. To display a file without formatting, the general format is the following:

command filename

The *command* entry is one of the following command names: **pg**, **more**, or **cat**. The *filename* entry can be the name of one file or a series of filenames separated by spaces. You may also use pattern-matching characters to specify your files. See Chapter 2 for information on using pattern-matching characters.

The **pg** command allows you to view one or more files. In the following example, the **pg** command displays the contents of **file1** in your login directory:

```
$ pg file1
You start the vi program by entering
the command vi, optionally followed by the name
of a new or existing file.
$ _
```

Now, view the contents of both **file1** and **file2**. Note that the command displays both files without a break between them.

$ **pg file1 file2**
```
You start the vi program by entering
the command vi, optionally followed by the name
of a new or existing file.
If you have created a new file, you will find
that it is easy to add text.
$ _
```

The **pg** command always displays multiple files in the order in which you listed them on the command line. When you display files that contain more lines than will fit on the screen, the **pg** command pauses as it displays each screen. To see the next screen of information, press **<Return>**.

The **more** command is very much like the **pg** command in the way that it handles long files. If the file contains more lines than are on your screen, **more** pauses and displays a message telling you what percentage of the file you have viewed thus far. At this point, you can do one of the following:

- Press the space bar to display the remainder of the file a page at a time.
- Press **<Return>** to display a line at a time.
- Type **q** to quit viewing the file.

The **cat** command also displays text. However, it is less useful for viewing long files because it does not paginate files. When viewing a file that is larger than one screen, the contents will display too quickly to be read. When this happens, press **<Ctrl-s>** to halt the display. You can then read the text. When you wish to display the rest of the file, press **<Ctrl-q>**. Because **cat** is not very easy to use for viewing long files, you may prefer using the **pg** or **more** command in these cases.

The **pg**, **more**, and **cat** commands all have additional options that you may find useful. For more information, refer to the reference pages for these commands.

Displaying Files With Formatting (pr)

Formatting is the process of controlling the way the contents of your files appear when you display or print them. The **pr** command formats a file in a simple but useful style.

To display a file with formatting, the general format is the following:

pr *filename*

The *filename* entry can be simply the name of the file, the relative pathname of the file, the full pathname of the file, or a list of filenames separated by spaces. The format you use depends on where the file is located in relation to your current directory. You may also use pattern-matching characters to specify files. See Chapter 2 for information on pattern matching.

Used without any options, the **pr** command does the following:

- Divides the contents of the file into pages
- Puts the date, time, page number, and filename in a heading at the top of each page
- Leaves five blank lines at the end of the page

When you use the **pr** command to display a file, its contents may scroll off your screen too quickly for you to read them. When this happens, you can view the formatted file by using the **pr** command along with the **more** command. The **more** command instructs the system to pause at the end of each screenful of text. See the immediately preceding section for information on the **more** command.

For example, suppose that you wish to display a long file, **report**, so that it pauses when the screen is full. To do so, enter the following command:

$ **pr report|more**
$ _

When the system pauses at the first screenful of text, press **<Return>** to display the next screen. The previous command uses the | (pipe) symbol to take the output from the **pr** command and use it as input to the **more** command. For more information on pipes, see ''Using Pipes and Filters'' in Chapter 7.

General User Tasks

Sometimes you may prefer to display a file in a more sophisticated format. You can use a number of flags in the command format to specify additional formatting features. Table 3-3 explains several of these flags.

Table 3-3. The pr Command Flags

Flag	Action
+*page*	Begins formatting on page number *page*. Otherwise, formatting begins on page 1. For example, the **pr +2 file1** command starts formatting **file1** on page 2.
-*column*	Formats page into *column number* columns. Otherwise, **pr** formats pages with one column. For example, the **pr -2 file1** command formats **file1** into two columns.
-m	Formats all specified files at the same time, side-by-side, one per column. For example, the **pr -m file1 file2** command displays the contents of **file1** in the left column, and that of **file2** in the right column.
-d	Formats double-spaced output. Otherwise, output is single-spaced. For example, the **pr -d file1** command displays **file1** in double-spaced format.
-f	Uses a formfeed character to advance to a new page. (Otherwise, **pr** issues a sequence of linefeed characters.) Pauses before beginning the first page if the standard output is a tty.
-F	Uses a formfeed character to advance to a new page. (Otherwise, **pr** issues a sequence of linefeed characters.) Does not pause before beginning the first page if the standard output is a tty.
-w*num*	Sets line width to *num* bytes. Otherwise, line width is 72 bytes.

Managing Files

Flag	Action
	For example, the **pr -w40 file1** command sets the line length of **file1** to 40 bytes.
-onum	Offsets (indents) each line by num byte positions. Otherwise, offset is 0 (zero) byte positions.
	For example, the **pr -o5 file1** command indents each line of **file1** five spaces.
-lnum	Sets page length to num lines. Otherwise, page length is 66 lines.
	For example, the **pr -l30 file1** command sets the page length of **file1** to 130 lines.
-h	Uses the next string of characters, rather than the filename, in the header (title) that is displayed at the top of every page. If the string includes blanks or special characters, it must be enclosed in ' ' (single quotes).
	For example, the **pr -h 'My Novel' file1** command specifies "My Novel" as the title.
-t	Prevents **pr** from formatting headings and the blank lines at the end of each page.
	For example, the **pr -t file1** command specifies that **file1** be formatted without headings and blank lines at the end of each page.
-schar	Separates columns with the character char rather than with blank spaces. You must enclose special characters in single quotes.
	For example, the **pr -s'*' file1** command specifies that asterisks separate columns.

You can use more than one flag at a time with the **pr** command. In the following example, you instruct **pr** to format **file1** with these characteristics:

- In two columns (**-2**)
- With double spacing (**d**)
- With the title **My Novel** rather than the name of the file

    $ pr -2dh 'My Novel' file1

General User Tasks

```
$ _
```

For detailed information about **pr** and its flags, refer to the **pr** reference page. The **pr** command can also be used to format files for printing. See the following section for more information.

Printing Files (lpr, lpq, lprm)

Use the **lpr** command to send one or more files to the system printer. The **lpr** command actually places files in a print queue, which is a list of files waiting to be printed. Once the **lpr** command places your files in the queue, you can continue to do other work on your system while you wait for the files to print.

The general format of the **lpr** command is

lpr *filename*

The *filename* entry can be simply the name of the file, the relative pathname of the file, the full pathname of the file, or a list of filenames separated by spaces. The format you use depends on where the file is located in relation to your current directory. You may also use pattern-matching characters to specify files. See Chapter 2 for information on pattern matching.

If your system has more than one printer, use the following format to specify where you want the file to print:

lpr -P*printername filename*

The **-P** flag indicates that you wish to specify a printer. The *printername* entry is the name of a printer. Printers often have names such as **lp0, lp1,** and **lpn**. Ask your system administrator for the printer names. If your system has more than one printer, one of them is the default printer. When you do not enter a specific *printername*, your print request goes to the default printer.

Managing Files

The following example shows how to use the **lpr** command to print one or more files on a printer named **lp0**:

$ **lpr -Plp0 file1**
$ **lpr -Plp0 file2 file3**
$ _

The first **lpr** command sends **file1** to the **lp0** printer and then displays the $ prompt. The second **lpr** command sends **file2** and **file3** to the same print queue, and then displays the shell prompt before the files finish printing.

You may wish to use the **lpr** command together with the **pr** command so that your file will be formatted. The **pr** command is described in the immediately preceding subsection. For example, suppose that you wish to format a long file, **report**, and then print it. To do so, enter the following command:

$ **pr report | lpr**
$ _

This command uses the | (pipe) symbol to take the output from the **pr** command and use it as input to the **lpr** command. For more information on pipes, see ''Using Pipes and Filters'' in Chapter 7.

Several **lpr** command flags enable you to control the way in which your file prints. Following is the general format for using a flag with this command:

lpr *flag filename*

Table 3-4 explains some of the most useful **lpr** command flags.

OSF/1 User's Guide

General User Tasks

Table 3–4. The lpr Command Flags

Flag	Action
-#*num*	Prints *num* copies of the file. Otherwise, **lpr** prints one copy. For example, the **lpr -#2 file1** command prints two copies of **file1**.
-w*num*	Sets line width to *num* bytes. Otherwise, line width is 72 bytes. For example, the **lpr -w40 file1** command prints **file1** with lines that are 40 bytes long.
-i*num*	Offsets (indents) each line by *num* space positions. Otherwise, offset is eight spaces. For example, the **lpr -i5 file1** command prints **file1** with lines that are indented five spaces.
-p	Formats the file using **pr** as a filter.
-T	Uses the next string of characters, rather than the filename, in the header used by **pr**. The **-p** option must be used along with this flag. If the string includes blanks or special characters, it must be enclosed in ' ' (single quotes). For example, the **lpr -p -T 'My Novel' file1** command specifies "My Novel" as the title.
-m	Sends mail when the file completes printing. For example, the command **lpr -m file1** specifies that you wish mail to be sent to you once **file1** prints.

Once you have entered the **lpr** command, your print request is entered into the print queue.

If you wish to see the position of the request in the print queue, use the **lpq** command. To look at the print queue, enter:

$ **lpq**

If your request has already been printed, or if there are no requests in the print queue, the system responds with the following message:

```
no entries
```

Managing Files

If there are entries in the print queue, the system lists them and indicates which request is currently being printed. Following is a typical listing of print queue entries (your listing will vary):

```
Rank    Owner     Job   Files              Total Size
active  marilyn   489   report             8470 bytes
1st     sue       135   letter             5444 bytes
2nd     juan      360   (standard input)   969 bytes
3rd     larry     490   travel             1492 bytes
```

As shown, the system displays the following for each print queue entry:

- Its priority
- Its owner
- Its job number
- Name of the file
- Size of the file in bytes

For example, Marilyn's report (job number 489) is currently being printed, and the requests of Sue, Juan, and Larry are pending.

When you print files, the position of the request in the queue as well as its size may help you estimate when your request may be finished. Generally, the higher the priority number in the queue and the larger the print request, the more time it will take. If your system has more than one printer, use the following format to specify which print queue you wish to see:

lpq -P*printername filename*

The **-P** flag indicates that you wish to specify a print queue. The *printername* entry is the name of a particular printer. Use the **lpstat -s** command to learn the names of all the printers.

If you decide not to print your request, you can delete it from the print queue by using the **lprm** command. The general format of the **lprm** command is the following:

lprm *jobnumber*

OSF/1 User's Guide   3–15

General User Tasks

The *jobnumber* entry specifies the job number that the system has assigned to your print request. (You can see the job number by entering the **lpq** command.)

For example, if Larry wishes to cancel his print request, he can enter:

$ **lprm 490**
$ _

The **travel** file will be removed from the print queue.

Linking Files (ln)

A link is a connection between a filename and the file itself. Usually, a file has one link—a connection to its original filename. However, you can use the **ln** (link) command to connect a file to more than one filename at the same time.

Links are convenient whenever you need to work with the same data in more than one place. For example, suppose you have a file containing assembly-line production statistics. You use the data in this file in two different documents, such as a monthly report prepared for management, and in a monthly synopsis prepared for the line workers.

You can link the statistics file to two different filenames, for example, **mgmt.stat** and **line.stat**, and place these filenames in two different directories. In this way, you save storage space because you have only one copy of the file. More importantly, you do not have to update multiple files. Because **mgmt.stat** and **line.stat** are linked, editing one automatically updates the other, and both filenames always refer to the same data.

Hard Links and Soft Links

There are two kinds of links available for your use:

- Hard links
- Soft (symbolic) links

Managing Files

Hard links allow you to link only files in the same file system. When you create a hard link, you are providing another name for the same file. All the hard link names for a file, including the original name, are on equal footing. It is incorrect to think of one file name as the "real name," and another as "only a link."

Soft links or symbolic links allow you to link both files and directories. In addition, you may link both files and directories across different file systems. A symbolic link is actually a distinct file that contains a pointer to another file or directory. This pointer is simply the pathname to the destination file or directory. Only the original filename is the real name of the file or directory. Unlike a hard link, a soft link is actually "only a link."

With both hard and soft links, changes made to a file through one name appear in the file as seen through another name.

A major difference between hard and soft links occurs when removing them. A file with hard-linked names persists until all its names have been removed. A file with soft-linked names vanishes when its original name has been removed; any remaining soft links then point to a nonexistent file. See "Removing Links" later in this chapter.

Links and File Systems

The term "file system" as used in this discussion of links differs from its earlier usage in this guide. Previously, a file system was defined as a useful arrangement of files into a directory structure. Here, the same term acquires a more precise meaning: the files and directories contained within a single disk partition. A disk partition is a physical disk, or a portion of one, that has been prepared to contain file directories.

You can use the **df** command to discover the name of the disk partition that holds any particular directory on your OSF/1 system. Here is an example in which **df** shows that the directories **/u1/info** and **/etc** are in different file systems, but that **/etc** and **/tmp** are in the same file system:

```
$ df /u1/info
Filesystem 512-blks    used   avail capacity  Mounted on
/dev/rz2c     196990 163124   14166     92%   /u1
$ df /etc
Filesystem 512-blks    used   avail capacity  Mounted on
```

General User Tasks

```
/dev/rz3a      30686    19252   8364    70%       /
$ df /tmp
Filesystem 512-blks    used  avail capacity Mounted on
/dev/rz3a      30686    19252   8364    70%       /
$ _
```

Using Links

To link files in the same file system, use the following command format:

ln /*dirname1*/*filename1* /*dirname2*/*filename2*

The /*dirname1*/*filename1* entry is the pathname of an existing file. The /*dirname2*/*filename2* entry is the pathname of a new filename to be linked to the existing /*dirname1*/*filename1*. The *dirname1* and *dirname2* arguments are optional if you are linking files in the same directory.

If you wish to link files and directories across file systems, you can create symbolic links. To create a symbolic link, add an **-s** flag to the **ln** command sequence and specify the full pathnames of both files. The **ln** command for symbolic links takes the following form:

ln -s /*dirname1*/*filename1* /*dirname2*/*filename2*

The /*dirname1*/*filename1* entry is the pathname of an existing file. The /*dirname2*/*filename2* entry is a pathname of a new filename in a different file system.

In the following example, the **ln** command links the new filename **checkfile** to the existing file named **file3**:

```
$ ln file3 checkfile
$ _
```

Now use the **more** command to verify that **file3** and **checkfile** are two names for the same file:

$ **more file3**

3–18   OSF/1 User's Guide

Managing Files

The system displays the following:

```
You will find that vi is a useful
editor that has many features.
$ _
```

Now display the text of **checkfile**:

$ **more checkfile**
```
You will find that vi is a useful
editor that has many features.
$ _
```

Notice that both **file3** and **checkfile** contain the same information. Any change that you make to the file under one name will show up when you access the file by its other name. Updating **file3**, for example, will also update **checkfile**.

If your two files were located in directories that are in two different file systems, you need to create a symbolic link to link them. For example, to link a file called **newfile** that is in the **/reports** directory to the file called **mtgfile** in the **/summary** directory, you can create a symbolic link by using the following:

$ **ln -s /reports/newfile /summary/mtgfile**
$ _

The information in both files is still updated in the same manner as previously explained.

How Links Work—Understanding Filenames and i-Numbers

Each file has a unique identification number called an i-number. The i-number refers to the file itself—data stored at a particular location—rather than to the filename. The i-number distinguishes the file from other files within the same file system.

A directory entry is simply a link between an i-number that represents a physical file and a filename. It is this relationship between files and filenames that enables you to link multiple filenames to the same physical

General User Tasks

file; that is, to the same i-number. To display the i-numbers of files in your current directory, use the **ls** command with the **-i** (print i-number) flag in the following form:

ls -i

Now, examine the identification numbers of the files in your login directory. The number preceding each filename in the listing is the i-number for that file.

```
$ ls -i
1079 checkfile   1077 file1   1078 file2   1079 file3
$ _
```

The i-numbers in your listing will probably differ from those shown in this example. However, the important thing to note is the identical i-numbers for **file3** and **checkfile**, the two files linked in the previous example. In this case, the i-number is 1079.

Because an i-number represents a file within a particular filesystem, hard links cannot exist between separate file systems. However, the situation is entirely different with symbolic links, where the link becomes a new file with its own, new i-number. The symbolic link is not another filename on the original file's i-number, but instead is a separate file with its own i-number. Because the symbolic link refers to the original file *by name*, rather than by i-number, symbolic links work correctly between separate file systems.

Removing Links

The **rm** (remove file) command does not always remove a file. For example, suppose that a file is linked to more than one filename; that is, several names refer to the same i-number. In this case, the **rm** command removes the link between the i-number and that filename, but leaves the physical file intact. The **rm** command actually removes a physical file only after it has removed the last link between that file and a filename, as shown in Figure 3-1. When a symbolic link is removed, the filename specifying the pointer to the destination file or directory is removed.

Managing Files

For detailed information about the **rm** command, refer to "Removing Files" later in this chapter.

Figure 3–1. Removing Links and Files

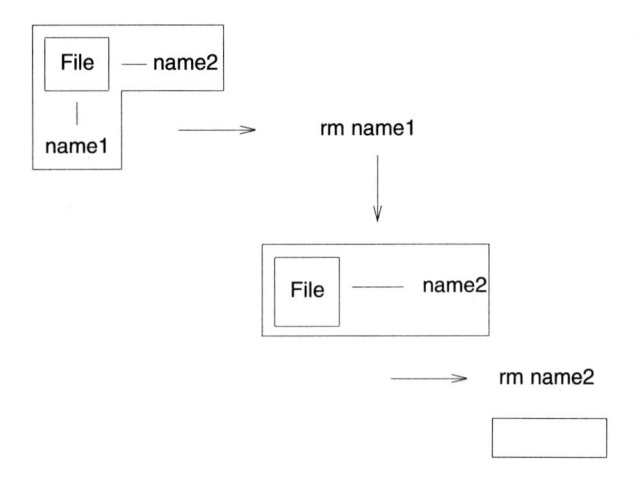

To display both the i-numbers and the number of filenames linked to a particular i-number, use the **ls** command with the **-i** (print i-number) and the **-l** (long listing) flags, in the following format:

ls -il

Now examine the links in your login directory. Remember that the i-numbers displayed on your screen will differ from those shown in the example and that your username and your group's name will replace the `larry` and `system` entries.

```
$ ls -il
total 3
 1079 -rw-r--r--  2 larry system   65 Jun 5 10:06 checkfile
 1077 -rw-r--r--  1 larry system  101 Jun 5 10:03 file1
 1078 -rw-r--r--  1 larry system   75 Jun 5 10:03 file2
 1079 -rw-r--r--  2 larry system   65 Jun 5 10:06 file3
 1080 drwxr-xr-x  2 larry system   32 Jun 5 10:07 project
$ _
```

Again, the first number in each entry shows the i-number for that filename. The second element in each line shows the file permissions, described in detail in Chapter 5.

The third field for each entry, the number to the left of the username, represents the number of links to that i-number. Notice that **file3** and **checkfile** have the same i-number, 1079, and that both show two links. Each time the **rm** command removes a filename, it reduces the number of links to that i-number by one.

In the following example, use the **rm** command to remove the filename **checkfile**:

```
$ rm checkfile
$ _
```

Now, list the contents of the directory with the **ls -il** command. Notice that the **rm** command has reduced the number of links to i-number 1079, which is the same i-number that **file3** is linked to, by one.

```
$ ls -il
total
 1077 -rw-r--r--  1 larry system   101 Jun 5 10:03 file1
 1078 -rw-r--r--  1 larry system    75 Jun 5 10:03 file2
 1079 -rw-r--r--  1 larry system    65 Jun 5 10:06 file3
 1080 drwxr-xr-x  2 larry system    32 Jun 5 10:07 project
$ _
```

Copying Files (cp)

The **cp** (copy) command copies files either within your current directory or from one directory into another directory.

The **cp** command is especially useful in making backup copies of important files. Because the backup and the original are two distinct files, you can make changes to the original while still maintaining an unchanged copy in the backup file. This is helpful in case something happens to the original version. Also, if you decide you do not want to save your most recent changes to the original file, you can begin again with the backup file.

Note: Compare the **cp** command, which actually copies files, with the **ln** command, which creates multiple names for the same file. The section "Linking Files (**ln**)" explains the **ln** command in some detail. Refer also to the **cp** and **ln** reference pages.

To copy a file, the general format of the **cp** command is the following:

cp *source destination*

The *source* entry is the name of the file to be copied. The *destination* entry is the name of the file to which you want to copy *source*. The *source* and *destination* entries can be filenames in your current directory or pathnames to different directories.

To copy files to a different directory, the general format of the **cp** command is the following:

cp *source destination*

In this case, *source* is a series of one or more filenames, and *destination* is a pathname that ends with the name of the target directory. In the *source* entry you can also use pattern-matching characters, as described in Chapter 2.

Copying Files in the Current Directory

The **cp** command creates the destination file if it does not already exist. However, if a file with the same name as the destination file does exist, **cp** copies the source file over the existing destination file.

Caution: If the destination file exists, your shell may allow the **cp** command to erase the contents of that file before it copies the source file. As a result, be certain that you do not need the contents of the destination file, or that you have a backup copy of the file, before you use it as the destination file for the **cp** command. If you use the C shell, see Table 8-6 for the **noclobber** variable that can be set to prevent the erasure of the destination file.

General User Tasks

In the following example, the destination file does not exist, so the **cp** command creates it. First, list the contents of your login directory:

```
$ ls
file1    file2    file3    project
$ _
```

Now, copy the source file, **file2**, into the new destination file, **file2x**:

```
$ cp file2 file2x
$ _
```

List the contents of the directory to verify that the copying process was successful:

```
$ ls
file1    file2    file2x    file3    project
$ _
```

Copying Files into Other Directories

You need a subdirectory to work through the following example, so create one called **reports** with the **mkdir** command:

```
$ mkdir reports
$ _
```

To copy the file **file2** into the directory **reports**, enter:

```
$ cp file2 reports
$ _
```

Now, list the contents of **reports** to verify that it contains a copy of **file2**:

```
$ ls reports
file2
$ _
```

You can also use the **cp** command to copy multiple files from one directory into another directory. The general format of the command is the following:

cp *filename1 filename2 dirname*

In the following example, enter the **cp** command to copy both **file2** and **file3** into the **reports** directory, and then list the contents of that directory:

$ **cp file2 file3 reports**
$ **ls reports**
```
file2   file3
$ _
```

Note that, in the above example, you do not have to specify **file2** and **file3** as part of the *dirname* entry. This is because the files being copied are retaining their original filenames.

You may also use pattern-matching characters to copy files. For example, to copy **file2** and **file3** into **reports**, enter:

$ **cp file* reports**
```
$ _
```

To change the name of a file when you copy it into another directory, enter the name of the source file (the original file), the directory name, a / (slash), and then the new filename. In the following example, copy **file3** into the **reports** directory under the new name **notes**. Then list the contents of the **reports** directory:

$ **cp file3 reports/notes**
$ **ls reports**
```
file2   file3   notes
$ _
```

OSF/1 User's Guide   3–25

Renaming or Moving Files (mv)

You can use the **mv** (move) command to perform the following actions:

- Move one or more files from one directory into another directory
- Rename files

Following is the general format of the **mv** command:

mv *oldfilename newfilename*

The *oldfilename* entry is the name of the file you wish to move or rename. The *newfilename* entry is the new name you wish to assign to the original file. Both entries can be names of files in the current directory, or pathnames to files in a different directory. You may also use pattern-matching characters.

The **mv** command links a new name to an existing i-number and breaks the link between the old name and that i-number. It is useful to compare the **mv** command with the **ln** and **cp** commands, which are explained in "Linking Files (**ln**)" and "Copying Files (**cp**)." Refer also to the reference pages for these commands.

Renaming Files

You can use the **mv** command to rename files.

In the following example, first list the i-number of each file in your current directory with the **ls -i** command. Then, enter the **mv** command to change the name of file **file2x** to **newfile**. The i-numbers displayed on your screen will differ from the numbers in the example.

```
$ ls -i
1077 file1     1088 file2x    1080 project
1078 file2     1079 file3     1085 reports
$ mv file2x newfile
$ _
```

Again, list the contents of the directory:

```
$ ls -i
1077 file1     1079 file3     1080 project
1078 file2     1088 newfile   1085 reports
$ _
```

Note two things in this example:

- The **mv** command changes the name of file **file2x** to **newfile**.
- The i-number for the original file (**file2x**) and **newfile** is the same—1088.

The **mv** command removes the connection between i-number 1088 and filename **file2x**, replacing it with a connection between i-number 1088 and filename **newfile**. However, the command does not change the file itself.

Moving Files into a Different Directory

You can also use the **mv** command to move one or more files from your current directory into a different directory.

Note: Type the target directory name carefully because the **mv** command does not distinguish between filenames and directory names. If you enter an invalid directory name, the **mv** command simply takes that name as a new filename. The result is that the file is renamed rather than moved.

In the following example, the **ls** command lists the contents of your login directory. Then, the **mv** command moves **file2** from your current directory into the **reports** directory. The **ls** command then verifies that the file has been removed:

```
$ ls
file1    file2    file3    newfile   project   reports
$ mv file2 reports
$ ls
file1    file3    newfile   project   reports
$ _
```

General User Tasks

Finally, list the contents of the **reports** directory to verify that the command has moved the file:

```
$ ls reports
file2    file3    notes
$ _
```

You may also use pattern-matching characters to move files. For example, to move **file1** and **file3** into **reports**, you could enter the following command:

```
$ mv file* reports
$ _
```

Now list the contents of your login directory to verify that **file1** and **file3** have been moved:

```
$ ls
newfile    project    reports
$ _
```

Now, copy **file1**, **file2**, and **file3** back into your login directory. The . (dot) in the following command line specifies the current directory, which, in this case, is your login directory:

```
$ cp reports/file* .
$ _
```

Now, verify that the files are back in your login directory:

```
$ ls
file1    file2    file3    newfile    project    reports
$ _
```

Last, verify that **file1**, **file2**, and **file3** are still in the **reports** directory:

```
$ ls reports
file1    file2    file3    newfile    project    reports
$ _
```

Comparing Files (diff)

You can compare the contents of text files with the **diff** command. This command compares the files and displays the differences between them. Use the **diff** command when you wish to pinpoint the differences in the contents of two files that are expected to be somewhat different.

The general format of the **diff** command is the following:

diff *file1 file2*

The **diff** command scans each line in both files looking for differences. When it finds a line (or lines) that differ, it reports the following:

- Line numbers of any changes
- Whether the difference is an addition, a deletion, or a change to the line

If the change is caused by an addition, **diff** displays the following form:

`l[,l] a r[,r]`

where `l` is a line number in *file1* and `r` is a line number in *file2*. The `a` indicates an addition. If the difference were a deletion, **diff** would specify `d`, and if it were a change to a line, **diff** would specify `c`. The actual differing lines then follow. In the leftmost column, a left angle bracket (<) indicates lines from *file1*, and a right angle bracket (>) indicates lines from *file2*.

General User Tasks

For example, suppose that you wish to quickly compare the following meeting rosters in the files **jan15mtg** and **jan22mtg**:

jan15mtg	jan22mtg
alice	alice
colleen	brent
daniel	carol
david	colleen
emily	daniel
frank	david
grace	emily
helmut	frank
howard	grace
jack	helmut
jane	jack
juan	jane
lawrence	juan
rusty	lawrence
soshanna	rusty
sue	soshanna
tom	sue
	tom

Instead of tediously comparing the list by sight, you can use the **diff** command to compare **jan15mtg** with **jan22mtg** as follows:

```
$ diff jan15mtg jan22mtg
2a3,4
> brent
> carol
10d11
< howard
$ _
```

3-30   OSF/1 User's Guide

Here we find that Brent and Carol attended the meeting on January 22, and Howard did not. We know this because the line number and text output indicate that **brent** and **carol** are additions to file **jan22mtg** and that **howard** is a deletion.

In cases where there are no differences between files, the system will merely return your prompt. For more information, see the **diff** reference page.

Sorting File Contents (sort)

You can sort the contents of text files with the **sort** command. You can use this command to sort a single file or multiple files.

Following is the general format of the **sort** command:

sort *filename*

The *filename* entry can be simply the name of the file, the relative pathname of the file, the full pathname of the file, or a list of filenames separated by spaces. You may also use pattern-matching characters to specify files. See Chapter 2 for information on pattern matching.

A good example of what the **sort** command can do for you is to sort a list of names and put them in collated order as defined by your current locale. For example, assume that you have lists of names that are contained in three files: **list1**, **list2**, and **list3**.

list1	list2	list3
Zenith, Andre	Rocca, Carol	Hambro, Abe
Dikson, Barry	Shepard, Louis	Anastio, William
D'Ambrose, Jeanette	Hillary, Mimi	Saluccio, William
Julio, Annette	Chung, Jean	Hsaio, Peter

To sort the names in all three files, enter:

$ **sort list***
```
Anastio, William
Chung, Jean
```

General User Tasks

```
D'Ambrose, Jeanette
Dickson, Barry
Hambro, Abe
Hillary, Mimi
Hsaio, Peter
Julio, Annette
Rocca, Carol
Saluccio, Julius
Shepard, Louis
Zenith, Andrew
$ _
```

You can also capture the sorted list by redirecting the screen output to a file that you name by entering the following:

$ sort list* >newlist
$ _

For more information on redirecting output, see Chapter 6. For a detailed description of the **sort** command and its many options, see the **sort** reference page.

Removing Files (rm)

When you no longer need a file, you can remove it with the **rm** (remove file) command. You use this command to remove a single file or multiple files.

Following is the general format of the **rm** command:

rm *filename*

The *filename* entry can be simply the name of the file, the relative pathname of the file, the full pathname of the file, or a list of filenames. The format you use depends on where the file is located in relation to your current directory.

Removing a Single File

In the following example, you remove the file called **file1** from your login directory. First, return to your login directory with the **cd** (change directory) command. Next, enter the **pwd** (print working directory) command to verify that your login directory is your current directory, and then list its contents. Remember that the system substitutes the name of your login directory for the notation */u/uname* in the example.

```
$ cd
$ pwd
/u/uname
$ ls
file1     file2     file3     newfile   project   reports
$ _
```

Enter the **rm** command to remove **newfile**, and then list the contents of the directory to verify that the system has removed the file.

```
$ rm newfile
$ ls
file1     file2     file3     project   reports
$ _
```

You must have permission to access a directory before you can remove files from it. For information about directory permissions, see Chapter 5.

Note: In addition to removing one or more files, **rm** also removes the links between files and filenames. The **rm** command actually removes the file itself only when it removes the last link to that file. For information about using the **rm** command to remove links, see ''Removing Links'' earlier in this chapter.

General User Tasks

Removing Multiple Files—Matching Patterns

You can remove more than one file at a time with the **rm** command by using pattern-matching characters. See ''Specifying Files With Pattern Matching'' in Chapter 2 for a description of pattern-matching characters.

For example, suppose your current directory contains the following files: **receivable.jun**, **payable.jun**, **payroll.jun**, and **expenses.jun**. You can remove all four of these files with the **rm *.jun** command.

Caution: Be certain that you understand how the * (asterisk) pattern-matching character works before you use it. For example, the **rm *** command removes *every file* in your current directory. Be especially careful with * at the beginning or end of a filename. If you mistakenly type **rm * name** instead of **rm *name**, you will remove all your files, rather than just those ending with *name*. You may prefer to use the **-i** flag with the **rm** command, which prompts you for verification before deleting a file or files. See the end of this section for details.

You can also use the pattern-matching character **?** (question mark) with the **rm** command to remove files whose names are the same, except for a single character. For example, if your current directory contains the files **record1**, **record2**, **record3**, and **record4**, you can remove all four files with the **rm record?** command.

When using pattern-matching characters, you may find the **-i** (interactive) flag of the **rm** command particularly useful. The **rm -i** command allows you to selectively delete files. For each file selected by the command, you are prompted, allowing you to delete the file or to retain the file.

For example, suppose that your directory contains the files **record1**, **record2**, **record3**, and **record4**, **record5**, and **record6**. Create those files now in your login directory by using the **touch** command as follows:

```
$ touch record1 record2 record3 record4 record5 record6
$ _
```

The **touch** command is useful when you wish to create empty files, as you are doing now. For complete information on the **touch** command, see the **touch** reference page.

Managing Files

For example, if you wish to remove four of the six files that begin with the characters **record**, enter:

$ rm -i record?
rm: remove record1? **n**
rm: remove record2? **y**
rm: remove record3? **y**
rm: remove record4? **y**
rm: remove record5? **y**
rm: remove record6? **n**
$ _

Note that, in the preceding example, you have deleted all files except for **record1** and **record6**.

Note: In addition to removing one or more files, the **rm** command also provides an option, the **-r** flag, that removes files and directories at the same time. See Chapter 4 for more information.

Determining File Type (file)

Use the **file** command when you wish to see what kind of data a file contains without having to display its contents. The **file** command displays whether the file is one of the following:

- A text file
- A directory
- Input for one of the text formatting packages **troff**, **nroff**, or **eqn** input text
- Source code for the C or FORTRAN programming languages
- An executable file

The **file** command is especially useful when you suspect that a file contains a compiled program. This is because displaying the contents of a compiled program can produce disconcerting results on your screen.

OSF/1 User's Guide   3–35

Following is the general format of the **file** command:

file *filename*

The *filename* entry can be simply the name of the file, the relative pathname of the file, the full pathname of the file, or a list of filenames. The format you use depends on where the file is located in relation to your current directory. You may also use pattern-matching characters to specify files. See Chapter 2 for information on pattern matching.

For example, to determine the file type of entries in your login directory, enter the following (and remember that your login directory will appear instead of /u/uname):

```
$ cd
$ pwd
/u/uname
$ file *
file1:    ascii text
file2:    ascii text
file3:    ascii text
project:  directory
record1:  empty
record6:  empty
reports:  directory
$ _
```

Note that the **file** command has identified **file1**, **file2**, and **file3** as ASCII text files, **project** and **reports** as directories, and **record1** and **record6** as empty files.

For more information on the **file** command, see the **file** reference page.

Chapter 4
Managing Directories

This chapter shows you how to manage directories on your system. After completing this chapter, you will be able to do the following:

- Create directories
- Change directories
- Display, copy, and rename directories
- Remove directories

A good way to learn about managing directories is to try the examples in this chapter. You should do each example in order so that the information on your screen is consistent with the information in this guide.

Before you can work through the examples, you must be logged in, and your login directory should be in the state that you left it after doing the examples in Chapter 3. As a result, your login directory should contain the following:

- The files **file1**, **file2**, **file3**, **record1**, and **record6**
- The **reports** subdirectory that contains the files **file1**, **file2**, **file3**, and **notes**
- The empty **project** subdirectory

General User Tasks

If you are using files with different names, make the appropriate substitutions as you work through the examples. To produce a listing of the files in your current directory, enter the **ls** command, which is explained in Chapter 3.

Note: Your system may contain enhanced security features that may affect how you manage directories. If so, see your system administrator for details.

Creating a Directory (mkdir)

Directories allow you to organize individual files into useful groups. For example, you could put all the sections of a report in a directory named **reports**, or the data and programs you use in cost estimating in a directory named **estimate**. A directory can contain files, other directories, or both.

Your login directory was created for you when your computer account was established. However, you will probably need additional directories to organize the files you create and edit while working with the system. You create new directories with the **mkdir** (make directory) command.

The form of the **mkdir** command is the following:

mkdir *dirname*

The *dirname* entry is the name you wish to assign to the new directory. The system creates *dirname* as a subdirectory of your working directory. This means that the new directory is located at the next level below your current directory.

In the following example, return to your login directory by entering the **cd** command, and create a directory named **project2**:

```
$ cd
$ mkdir project2
$ _
```

Managing Directories

Now, create a subdirectory in the **reports** directory by entering a relative pathname:

```
$ mkdir reports/status
$ _
```

Note the new file system tree structure in Figure 4-1. The **project**, **project2**, and **reports** directories are located one level below your login directory, and **status** is located one level below the **reports** directory.

Figure 4–1. Relationship Between a New Directory and the Current Directory

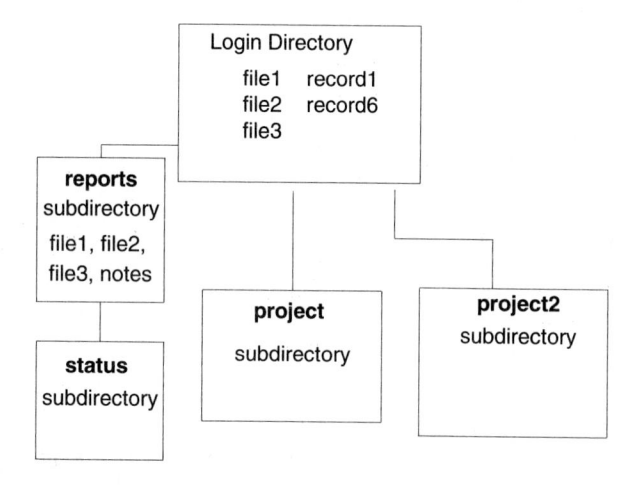

```
                    ┌─────────────────────┐
                    │   Login Directory   │
                    │    file1  record1   │
                    │    file2  record6   │
                    │    file3            │
                    └─────────────────────┘
                   /           |           \
    ┌──────────────┐    ┌──────────────┐    ┌──────────────┐
    │   reports    │    │   project    │    │   project2   │
    │ subdirectory │    │ subdirectory │    │ subdirectory │
    │ file1, file2,│    └──────────────┘    └──────────────┘
    │ file3, notes │
    ├──────────────┤
    │    status    │
    │ subdirectory │
    └──────────────┘
```

Like filenames, the maximum length of a directory name depends upon the file system used on your computer. For example, your file system may allow a maximum directory name length of 255 bytes (the default), or it may allow a maximum directory name length of only 14 bytes. Because knowing the maximum directory name length is important for helping you name directories meaningfully, see your system administrator for details.

Note that the system does not have a symbol or notation that automatically distinguishes between a filename and a directory name, so you may find it useful to establish your own naming conventions to designate files and directories. However, you may use the **ls -F** command to distinguish between filenames and directory names when the contents of your current directory are displayed. For more information on this command, see "Displaying Directories (**ls -F**)" later in this chapter.

General User Tasks

Changing Directories (cd)

The **cd** (change directory) command changes your current (working) directory. You can move to any directory in the file system from any other directory in the file system by executing **cd** with the proper pathname.

Note: You must have permission to access a directory before you can use the **cd** command to make that directory your current directory. For information about directory permissions, see Chapter 5.

The general format of the **cd** command is the following:

cd *pathname*

The *pathname* entry can either be the full pathname or the relative pathname of the directory that you want to set as your current directory.

If you enter the **cd** command without a pathname, the system returns you to your login directory.

To check the name of your current directory, enter the **pwd** (print working directory) command. See Chapter 2 for information on the **pwd** command.

Changing Your Current Directory

In the following example, which shows you how to change directories, you first enter the **pwd** command to display the name (which is also the pathname) of your working directory. You then use the **cd** command to change your current directory.

First return to your login directory, if necessary, by entering the **cd** command without a pathname. Next, enter the **pwd** command to verify that your login directory is your current directory. Remember that the system substitutes the name of your login directory for the notation */u/uname* in the example.

4–4   OSF/1 User's Guide

Managing Directories

```
$ cd
$ pwd
/u/uname
$ _
```

Now enter the **cd** command with the relative pathname **project2** to change to the **project2** directory:

```
$ cd project2
$ _
```

Enter **pwd** again to verify that **project2** is the current directory. Then, enter **cd** to return to your login directory:

```
$ pwd
/u/uname/project2
$ cd
$ _
```

To change your current directory to the **status** directory, a different branch of the file system tree structure, enter the **cd** command with a full pathname:

```
$ cd reports/status
$ pwd
/u/uname/reports/status
$ _
```

Using Relative Pathname Notation

You can use the following relative pathname notation to change directories quickly:

- Dot notation (. and ..)
- Tilde notation (~)

This subsection describes both of the above notations.

OSF/1 User's Guide   4-5

General User Tasks

Every directory contains at least two entries represented by . (dot) and .. (dot dot). These entries refer to directories relative to the current directory:

. (dot)　　　　　This entry refers to the current directory.

.. (dot dot)　　　This entry refers to the parent directory of your working directory. The parent directory is the directory immediately above the current directory in the file system tree structure.

To display the . and .. entries as well as any files beginning with a period, use the **-a** flag with the **ls** command.

In the following example, change to the **reports** directory by changing first to your login directory:

```
$ cd
$ cd reports
$ _
```

Then, the first **ls** command displays the directory contents as well as the **status** subdirectory you created earlier:

```
$ ls
file1    file2    file3    notes    status
$ _
```

Now, execute the **ls -a** command to list all directory entries as well as those relative directory names that begin with a . (dot):

```
$ ls -a
./   ../   file1   file2   file3   notes   status
$ _
```

You can use the relative directory name .. (dot dot) to refer to files and directories located above the current directory in the file system tree structure. That is, if you wish to move up the directory tree one level, you can use the relative directory name for the parent directory rather than using the full pathname.

In the following example, the **cd ..** command changes the current directory from **reports** to your login directory, which is the parent directory of **reports**. Remember that the /u/*uname* entry represents your login directory.

4–6　　　　　　　　　　　　　　　　　　　　　　　　　　　　　OSF/1 User's Guide

```
$ pwd
/u/uname/reports
$ cd ..
$ pwd
/u/uname
$ _
```

To move up the directory structure more than one level, you can use a series of relative directory names, as shown in the following example. The response to the following **pwd** command, the **/** (slash) entry, represents the root directory.

```
$ cd ../..
$ pwd
/
$ _
```

In the C shell and the Korn shell, you may use a ~ (tilde) to specify a user's login directory. For example, to specify your own login directory, use the tilde alone as follows:

```
$ cd ~
$ _
```

The above tilde notation does not save you keystrokes because in all OSF/1 shells you may get the same results by merely entering **cd** from any place in the file system.

However, if you wish to access a directory below your login directory, tilde notation can save you keystrokes. For example, to access the **reports** directory from anywhere in the file system, enter the following:

```
$ cd ~/reports
$ _
```

Tilde notation is also very useful when you wish to access a file or directory either in or below another user's login directory. You may not know the precise location of that user's login directory, but assuming you have the appropriate permissions, you could get there with a minimum of keystrokes.

General User Tasks

For example, from any place in the file system, you could specify the login directory of a hypothetical user **jones** by entering the following:

```
$ cd ~jones
$ _
```

In addition, if user **jones** tells you that you can find a file in the **status** directory immediately below the login directory, you can access the directory by entering the following:

```
$ cd ~jones/status
$ _
```

Accessing Directories Through Symbolic Links

When directories are connected through a symbolic link, the parent directory you access with the **cd** command differs depending upon whether you are specifying the actual directory name or the relative directory name. In particular, using the full pathname to find the parent of a symbolically linked directory results in accessing the actual parent directory.

For example, suppose **user2** is working on a file in the **/u/user2/project** directory, which is the symbolic link to **/u/user1/project**. In order to change to the actual parent directory (**/u/user2**), **user2** types the following:

```
$ cd /u/user2
$ pwd
/u/user2
$ _
```

On the other hand, if **user2** specified the relative directory name (**..**), the parent directory of the *symbolic link* would be accessed. For example, suppose **user2** is working on the same file in the **/u/user2/project** directory,

4–8 OSF/1 User's Guide

which is the symbolic link to **/u/user1/project**. In order to access the parent directory of the symbolic link, **user2** enters the following:

```
$ cd ..
$ pwd
/u/user1
$ _
```

Instead of being in the **/u/user2** directory, **user2** is now in the directory called **/u/user1**.

For background information on symbolic (or soft) links, see Chapter 3.

Displaying Directories (ls -F)

A directory can contain subdirectories as well as files. To display subdirectories, use the **ls -F** command. This command displays the contents of the current directory and marks each directory with a **/** (slash) character so that it can be readily distinguished from a file.

The general format of the **ls -F** command is the following:

ls -F

In the following example, return to your login directory and enter the **ls -F** command to display the directory contents. Note that the **project**, **project2**, and **reports** directories are marked with a slash.

```
$ cd
$ ls -F
file1     file3       project2/   record6
file2     project/    record1     reports/
$ _
```

Note that some C and Korn Shell users define an alias for the **ls** command so that, whenever they enter **ls**, the **ls -F** command is executed. For more information on defining aliases, see Chapter 8.

Copying Directories (cp)

You can use the **cp** command with the **-r** flag to copy directories and directory trees to another part of the file system. The **cp -r** command has the following format:

cp -r *source destination*

The *source* entry is the name of the directory to be copied. The *destination* entry is the name of the directory location to which you want to copy *source*.

Figure 4-2 shows how the **cp -r** command in the following example copies the directory tree **reports** into the directory **project**. It is assumed that the command is entered from the login directory.

$ **cp -r reports project**
$ _

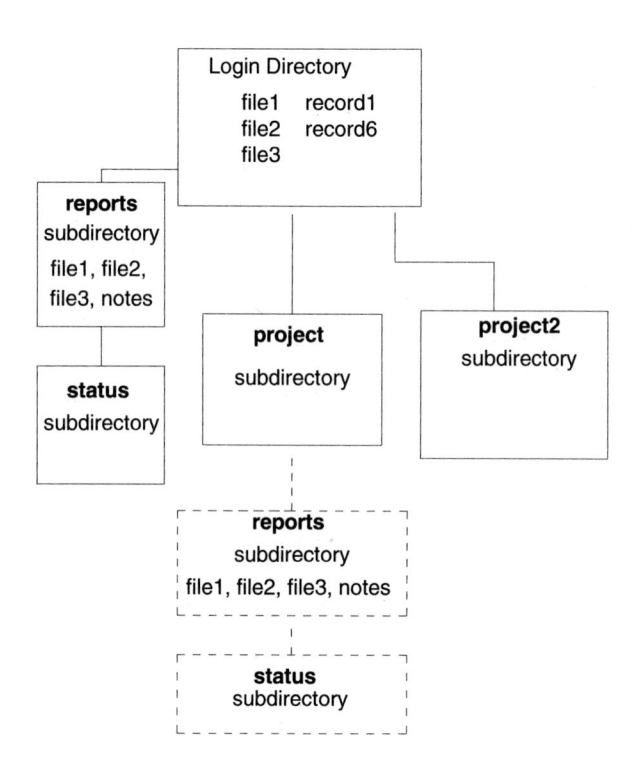

Figure 4–2. Copying a Directory Tree

```
                    Login Directory
                      file1   record1
                      file2   record6
                      file3

    reports
    subdirectory
    file1, file2,
    file3, notes
                         project              project2
                         subdirectory         subdirectory
        status
        subdirectory


                         reports
                         subdirectory
                         file1, file2, file3, notes


                         status
                         subdirectory
```

Note that the **reports** directory files **file1**, **file2**, **file3**, and **notes**, as well as the subdirectory **status**, have been copied to **project**.

Renaming Directories (mv)

You can use the **mv** command to rename a directory *only* when that directory is contained in the same disk partition.

Following is the general format of the **mv** command:

mv *olddirectoryname newdirectoryname*

The *olddirectoryname* entry is the name of the directory you wish to move

OSF/1 User's Guide   4–11

or rename. The *newdirectoryname* entry is the new name you wish to assign to the original directory.

In the following example, first change to the **reports** directory. Then, enter the **ls -i -d** command to list the i-number for the **status** directory:

$ **cd reports**
$ **ls -i -d status**
1091 status
$ _

Now, enter the **mv** command to change the name of **status** to **newstatus**. Then, list the i-number for the **newstatus** directory:

$ **mv status newstatus**
$ **ls -i -d newstatus**
1091 newstatus
$ _

Notice that the second **ls -i -d** command does not list the original directory name **status**. However, it does list the new directory **newstatus**, and it displays the same i-number (1091 in this example) for the new directory as for the original **status** directory.

Removing Directories (rmdir)

When you no longer need a particular directory, you can remove it from the file system with the **rmdir** (remove directory) command. This command removes only empty directories; that is, those that contain no files or subdirectories. For information about removing files from directories, see "Removing Files and Directories Simultaneously (**rm -r**)" and Chapter 3.

Following is the general format of the **rmdir** command:

rmdir *dirname*

The *dirname* entry is the name, or pathname, of the directory you wish to remove.

Before working through the examples in the following sections, create three subdirectories in the directory **project2**.

First, use the command **cd project2** to set **project2** as your current directory. Next, use the **mkdir** command to create the directories **schedule**, **tasks**, and **costs**. Then, list the contents of the **project2** directory:

$ **cd project2**
$ **mkdir costs schedule tasks**
$ **ls**
costs   schedule   tasks
$ _

Finally, use the **cd** command to return to your login directory:

$ **cd**
$ **pwd**
/u/uname
$ _

Removing Empty Directories

The **rmdir** command removes only empty directories. If you try to remove a directory that contains any files or subdirectories, the **rmdir** command gives you an error message, as the following example shows:

$ **rmdir project2**
rmdir: project2 not empty
$ _

Note: You cannot remove a directory while you are positioned in it. In order to remove a directory, you must be elsewhere in the directory tree. See ''Removing Your Current Directory'' later in this chapter for more information.

General User Tasks

Before you can remove the directory **project2**, you must first remove the contents of that directory. In the following example, the **cd** command makes **project2** your current directory, and then the **ls** command lists the contents of **project2**:

```
$ cd project2
$ ls
costs   schedule   tasks
```

Now remove the directory **schedule** from the current directory, and then list the remaining contents of the **project2** directory:

```
$ rmdir schedule
$ ls
costs   tasks
$ _
```

The **project2** directory still contains two subdirectories: **costs** and **tasks**. You can remove them by using pattern-matching characters, as described in the next section. Once these subdirectories are removed, you can delete the **project2** directory, as described in ''Removing Your Current Directory.''

Removing Multiple Directories

You can remove more than one directory at a time with the **rmdir** command by using pattern-matching characters. See ''Specifying Files With Pattern Matching'' in Chapter 2 for detailed information about pattern-matching characters.

For example, suppose that you are in the **project2** directory and wish to remove two subdirectories: **costs** and **tasks**. To do so, enter the **rmdir *s?s** command. Then, enter the **ls** command to verify that the **project2** directory contains no entries:

```
$ rmdir *.s?s
$ ls
$ _
```

Managing Directories

Caution: Entering the **rmdir** command with the * (asterisk) character alone (**rmdir** *) removes *all* empty directories from your current directory. As a result, use the * pattern-matching character with care.

Removing Your Current Directory

You cannot remove your current directory while you are still working in it. You can remove it only after you move into another directory. You generally enter the **cd ..** (dot dot) command to move into the parent directory of your current directory, and then enter **rmdir** with the pathname of the target directory.

The directory **project2** is empty. To remove **project2**, first move to your login directory, which is the parent directory of **project2**. Then, use the **rmdir** *dirname* command to remove **project2**, and enter **ls** to confirm the removal:

```
$ cd
$ rmdir project2
$ ls
file1    file2    file3    project/    record1    record6    reports/
$ _
```

Your login directory no longer contains the **project2** directory.

Removing Files and Directories at the Same Time (rm -r)

As you now know, the **rmdir** command removes only directories, not files. You can, however, remove files and directories at the same time by using the **rm** command with the **-r** (recursive) flag.

The **rm -r** command first deletes the files from a directory and then deletes the directory itself. It deletes the directory you specify as well as any subdirectories (and the files they contain) below it on the directory tree. As a result, this command should be used with caution.

General User Tasks

Following is the format for the **rm -r** command:

rm -r *pathname*

The *pathname* entry can either be the full pathname or the relative pathname of the directory that you wish to remove. You may also use pattern-matching characters to specify files.

Caution: Be certain that you understand how the **-r** flag works before you use it. For example, entering the **rm -r *** command from your login directory *deletes all files and directories to which you have access*. If you have superuser authority and are in the root directory, this command will *delete all system files*. See Chapter 5 for more information on superuser authority.

When using the **rm -r** command to remove files or directories, it is a good idea to include the **-i** flag in the command line, in the following form:

rm -ri *pathname*

When you enter the command in this form, the system prompts you for verification before actually removing the specified item(s). In this way, by answering **y** (yes) or **n** (no) in response to the prompt, you control the actual removal of a file or directory.

Chapter 5
Controlling Access to Your Files and Directories

This chapter shows you how to control access to your system as well as your files and directories. After reading this chapter, you will be able to do the following:

- Understand password, group, and system security issues
- Understand file and directory permissions
- Display and set file and directory permissions
- Change owners and groups
- Change your identity to access files
- Understand superuser concepts
- Learn where to find information about enhancements to security that may be installed on your system

A good way to learn about the preceding topics is to try the examples in this chapter. You should do each example in order so that the information on your screen is consistent with the information in this guide.

Before you can work through the examples, you must be logged in, and your login directory should be in the state that you left it after doing the examples in Chapter 4.

As a result, your login directory should contain the following:

- The files **file1**, **file2**, **file3**, **record1**, and **record6**
- The **reports** subdirectory that contains the files **file1**, **file2**, **file3**, and **notes**, and the subdirectory **newstatus**
- The **project** subdirectory that contains the files **file1**, **file2**, **file3**, and **notes**, as well as the **status** subdirectory

If you are using files with different names, make the appropriate substitutions as you work through the examples.

Understanding Password and Group Security Files

Before a user can log in successfully, he or she must be made known to the system by the creation of a user account. Adding a user account is a routine, but critical, activity that is usually performed by the system administrator.

When a user account is created, the new user is added to the following two files:

- **/etc/passwd**

    This file contains individual user information for all users of the system.

- **/etc/group**

    This file contains group information for all groups on the system.

These files define who can use the system and each user's access rights. In addition, all other system security controls depend upon password and group security. The following subsections describe the **/etc/passwd** and **/etc/group** files.

The /etc/passwd File

The **/etc/passwd** file contains records that define login accounts and attributes for all system users. This file can be altered only by a user with superuser privileges. See "Superuser Concepts" later in this chapter for more information.

Each record in the **/etc/passwd** file defines a login account for an individual user. The fields are separated by colons, and the last field ends with a newline character. The following text shows the format of an **/etc/passwd** file entry and describes the meaning of each field:

username:*password*:*UID*:*GID*:*user_info*:*login_directory*:*login_shell*

username	Your login name.
password	Your password stored in encrypted form. Encryption prevents unauthorized users or programs from discovering your actual password. If no password has been specified for a user, this field will be blank.
UID	(User ID) A unique number identifying you to the system.
GID	(Group ID) A number identifying your default group. You can belong to one or more groups.
user_info	This field can contain the following: • Your full name. • Maximum file size. This is a number limiting the maximum size of any file you create or extend. • Site-specific information. This is an attribute serving various purposes for each installation. It normally records biographical information.
login_directory	Your current directory after logging into the system. It is usually a directory you own and use to store private files.
login_shell	The program run by the **login** program after you successfully log into the system. It is normally a shell program used to interpret commands. For more information on shells, see Chapter 7.

General User Tasks

A sample entry in the **/etc/passwd** file would look like this:

```
lee:NebPsa9qxMkbD:201:20:Lee Voy,sales,x1234:/users/lee:/usr/bin/bsh
```

In this example, the user account **lee** has user ID 201 and group ID 20. Lee's full name is Lee Voy, and his department and telephone are listed. The login directory is **/users/lee** and the Bourne shell (**/usr/bin/bsh**) is defined as the command interpreter. The password field contains Lee's password in encrypted form (NebPsa9qxMkbD).

The /etc/group File

The **/etc/group** file defines login accounts for all groups using the system. This file can be altered only by a user with superuser privileges. See "Superuser Concepts" later in this chapter for more information.

Each record in the group database defines the login account of one group. Groups provide a convenient way to share files among users with a common interest or who are working on the same project.

Each entry in the **/etc/group** file is a single line that contains four fields. The fields are separated by colons, and the last field ends with a newline character. The following text shows the format of each entry and describes the meaning of each field:

groupname:*password*:*GID*:*user1*[,*user2*,...,*userN*]

groupname	A unique character string that identifies the group to the system.
password	This field is left empty. Entries in this field are ignored.
GID	(Group ID) A unique number that identifies the group to the system.
usernames	A list of users who belong to the group.

Controlling Access to Your Files and Directories

Protecting File and Directories

The OSF/1 operating system has a number of commands that enable you to control access to your files and directories. You can protect a file or directory by setting or changing its permissions, which are simply codes that determine the way in which anyone working on your system can use the stored data.

Setting or changing permissions is also referred to as setting or changing the protections on your files or directories. You generally protect your data for one or both of the following reasons:

- Your files and directories contain sensitive information that should not be available to everyone who uses your system.

- Not everyone who has access to your files and directories should have the permission to alter them.

Caution: Your system may allow two or more users to make changes to the same file at the same time without informing them. If this is so, the system saves the changes made by the last user to close the file; changes made by the other users are lost (some text editors warn users of this situation). It is, therefore, a good idea to set file permissions to allow only authorized users to modify files. The specified users should then communicate about when and how they are using the files.

Each file and each directory has nine permissions associated with it. Files and directories have the following three *types of permissions*:

- **r** (read)
- **w** (write)
- **x** (execute)

OSF/1 User's Guide

General User Tasks

These three permissions occur for each of the following three *classes of users*:

- **u** (user/owner)
- **g** (group)
- **o** (all others; also known as "world")

The **r** permission allows users to view or print the file. The **w** permission allows users to write to (modify) the file. The **x** permission allows users to execute (run) the file or to search directories.

The **user/owner** of a file or directory is generally the person who created it. If you are the owner of a file, you can change the file permissions with the **chmod** command, which is described next in "Setting File and Directory Permissions (**chmod**)."

The **group** specifies the group to which the file belongs. If you are the owner of a file, you can change the *group ID* of the file with the **chgrp** command, which is described later in "Changing Owners and Groups."

Note: If you do not own a file, you cannot change its permissions or group ID unless you have superuser authority. See "Superuser Concepts" later in this chapter for more information.

The meanings of the three types of permissions differ slightly between ordinary files and directories, as shown in Table 5-1.

Table 5–1. Differences Between File and Directory Permissions

Permission	For a File	For a Directory
r (read)	Contents can be viewed or printed.	Contents can be read, but not searched. Normally **r** and **x** are used together.
w (write)	Contents can be changed or deleted.	Entries can be added or removed.
x (execute)	File can be used as a program.	Directory can be searched.

Displaying File and Directory Permissions (ls)

To display the current file permissions, enter the **ls** command with the **-l** flag. To display the permissions for a single file or selected files, enter the following format:

ls -l *filename*

The *filename* entry can be the name of the file or a list of filenames separated by spaces. You may also use pattern-matching characters to specify files. See "Using Pattern-Matching Characters" later in this chapter for more information.

To display the permissions for all of the files in your current directory, enter the **ls -l** command, as shown in the following example:

```
$ ls -l
total 7
-rw-r--r--  1 larry   system   101 Jun 5 10:03 file1
-rw-r--r--  1 larry   system   171 Jun 5 10:03 file2
-rw-r--r--  1 larry   system   130 Jun 5 10:06 file3
drwxr-xr-x  2 larry   system    32 Jun 5 10:07 project
-rw-r--r--  1 larry   system     0 Jun 5 11:03 record1
-rw-r--r--  1 larry   system     0 Jun 5 11:03 record6
drwxr-xr-x  2 larry   system    32 Jun 5 10:31 reports
$ _
```

The first string of each entry in the directory shows the permissions for that file or directory. For example, the fourth entry, drwxr-xr-x, shows the following:

- That this is a directory (the d notation)

- That the owner can view it, write in it, and search it (the rwx sequence)

- That the group can view it and search it, but not write in it (the first r-x sequence)

- That all others can view it and search it, but not write in it (the second r-x sequence)

The third field shows the file's owner, (in this case, larry), and the fourth field shows the group to which the file belongs, in this case system).

General User Tasks

To list the permissions for a single directory, use the **ls -ld** command:

```
$ ls -ld reports
drwxr-xr-x   2 larry    system      32 Jun  5 10:31 reports
$ _
```

Taken together, all the permissions for a file or directory are called its permission code. As Figure 5-1 shows, a permission code consists of four parts:

- A single character shows the file type. The - (dash) indicates an ordinary file, **d** a directory, and **l** a symbolic link. Any other character indicates an I/O device.

- A 3-character permission field shows user (owner) permissions, which may be any combination of read, write, and execute.

- Another 3-character permission field shows group permissions.

- Another 3-character permission field shows permissions for all others.

Figure 5-1. File and Directory Permission Fields

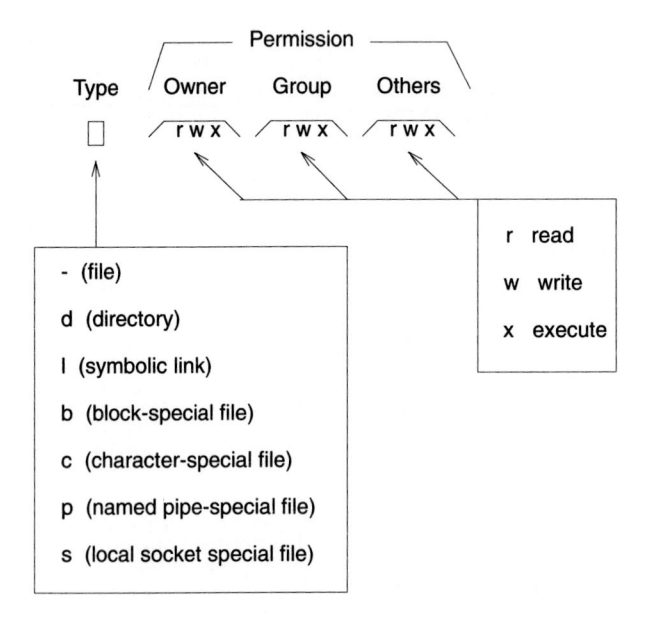

```
                        Permission
              ┌─────────────────────────┐
      Type   / Owner    Group    Others \
       □    / r w x  / r w x  / r w x \
                ↑         ↑        ↑
                │         │        │
       ┌────────────────────────────┐   ┌──────────────┐
       │  - (file)                  │   │ r   read     │
       │  d (directory)             │   │ w   write    │
       │  l (symbolic link)         │   │ x   execute  │
       │  b (block-special file)    │   └──────────────┘
       │  c (character-special file)│
       │  p (named pipe-special file)│
       │  s (local socket special file)│
       └────────────────────────────┘
```

When you create a file or directory, the system automatically supplies a predetermined permission code. A typical file permission code is

-rw-r--r--

This file permission code specifies that the owner has read and write permissions while the group and all others have read permission. The - (dashes) in some positions following the file-type notation indicate that the specified class of user does not have permission for that operation.

A typical directory permission code is

drwxr-xr-x

This directory permission code specifies that owner has read, write, and execute permissions, while the group and all others have read and execute permissions.

The default permission codes that your system provides relieve you from the task of specifying them explicitly every time you create a file or directory. If you wish to create your own default permission codes, you must change your user mask with the **umask** command. For an explanation of **umask**, see the description of the command in "Setting the User Mask" later in this chapter.

Setting File and Directory Permissions (chmod)

Your ability to change permissions gives you a great deal of control over the way your data can be used. Use the **chmod** (change mode) command to set or change the permissions for your files and directories.

For example, you obviously permit yourself to read, modify, and execute a file. You generally permit members of your group to read a file. Depending upon the nature of your work and the composition of your group, you often allow them to modify or execute it. You generally prohibit all other system users from having any access to a file.

General User Tasks

Note: You must be the owner of the file or directory (or have superuser authority) before you can change its permissions. This means that your username must be in the third field in an **ls -l** listing of that file.

It is important to realize that whatever restrictions you impose on file/directory access, the superuser can always override them. For example, suppose that you used the **chmod** command to specify that only you can have access to the file **report20**. The superuser can still access this file. For more information on this topic, see "Superuser Concepts" later in this chapter.

There are two ways to specify the permissions set by the **chmod** command:

- You can specify permissions with letters and operation symbols.
- You can specify permissions with octal numbers.

It is more difficult to learn to specify permissions with octal numbers than it is to specify them with letters. However, once you are familiar with the octal number system, you may find using it more efficient than setting permissions with letters and operation symbols.

The following subsections describe how to specify permissions with letters and operation symbols, as well as with octal numbers.

Specifying Permissions with Letters and Operation Symbols

You can use letters and operation symbols to change file and directory permissions. Following is the format of the **chmod** command when using letters and operation symbols:

chmod *userclass-operation-permission filename*

The *userclass-operation-permission* entry actually represents three codes that specify the user class, group, operation, and permission code that you wish to activate. The *filename* entry is the name of the file or files whose permissions you want to change. You may also use pattern-matching characters to specify files. See "Using Pattern-Matching Characters" later in this chapter for more information.

Controlling Access to Your Files and Directories

User classes, operations, and permissions are defined as follows:

- Use one or more of these letters to represent the *userclass*:

    u   User (owner)
    g   Group
    o   All others (besides owner and group)
    a   All (user, group, and all others)

- Use one of these symbols to represent the *operation*:

    +   Add permission
    -   Remove permission
    =   Assign permission regardless of previous setting

- Use one or more of these letters to represent the type of *permission*:

    r   Read
    s   Set user or group ID
    w   Write
    x   Execute

Changing File Permissions

This subsection shows you how to change the access permissions for a file. In the following example, first enter the **ls -l** command to display the permissions for the file **file1**:

```
$ ls -l file1
-rw-r--r--   1 larry      system       101 Jun  5 10:03 file1
$ _
```

Note that the owner (larry) has read/write permissions while the group and others have only read permissions.

Now, enter the **chmod** command with the flags **go+w**. This command expands the permissions for both the group (**g**) and for others (**o**) by giving them write access (**+w**) to **file1** in addition to the read access they already enjoy:

```
$ chmod go+w file1
$ _
```

OSF/1 User's Guide   5-11

Next, list the new permissions for the file:

```
$ ls -l file1
-rw-rw-rw-  1 larry     system      101 Jun  5 10:03 file1
$ _
```

Note that you have given your group and all other system users write permission to **file1**.

Changing Directory Permissions

The procedure for changing directory permissions is the same as that for changing file permissions. However, to list the information about a directory, you use the **ls -ld** command, as shown in the following example:

```
$ ls -ld project
drwxr-xr-x  2 larry   system   32 Jun 5 10:07 project
$ _
```

Now change the permissions with the **chmod g+w** command so that the group (**g**) has write permission (**+w**) for the directory **project**:

```
$ chmod g+w project
$ ls -ld project
drwxrwxr-x  2 larry   system   32 Jun 5 10:07 project
$ _
```

Using Pattern-Matching Characters

If you want to make the same change to the permissions of all entries in a directory, you can use the pattern-matching character * (asterisk) with the **chmod** command. For information on pattern-matching characters, see Chapter 2.

Controlling Access to Your Files and Directories

In the following example, the command **chmod g+x *** gives execute (**x**) permission to the group (**g**) for all files (*****) in the current directory:

$ **chmod g+x ***
$ _

Now enter the **ls -l** command to show that the group now has execute (**x**) permission for all files in the current directory:

```
$ ls -l
total 7
-rw-rwxrw-  1 larry  system  101 Jun 5 10:03 file1
-rw-r-xr--  1 larry  system  171 Jun 5 10:03 file2
-rw-r-xr--  1 larry  system  130 Jun 5 10:06 file3
drwxrwxr-x  2 larry  system   32 Jun 5 10:07 project
-rw-r-xr--  1 larry  system    0 Jun 5 11:03 record1
-rw-r-xr--  1 larry  system    0 Jun 5 11:03 record6
drwxr-xr-x  2 larry  system   32 Jun 5 10:31 reports
$ _
```

Setting Absolute Permissions

An absolute permission assignment (=) resets all permissions for a file or files, regardless of how the permissions were set previously. In the following example, the **ls -l** command lists the permissions for the **file3** file. Then the command **chmod a=rwx** gives all three permissions (**rwx**) to all users (**a**):

```
$ ls -l file3
-rw-r-x-r--  1 larry  system  130 Jun 5 10:06 file3
$ chmod a=rwx file3
$ ls -l file3
-rwxrwxrwx  1 larry  system  130 Jun 5 10:06 file3
$ _
```

OSF/1 User's Guide   5–13

General User Tasks

You can also use an absolute assignment to remove permissions. In the following example, the command **chmod a=rw newfile** removes the execute permission (**x**) for all groups (**a**) from the file **file3**:

```
$ chmod a=rw file3
$ ls -l file3
-rw-rw-rw-   1 larry  system   130 Jun 5 10:06 file3
$ _
```

Specifying Permissions With Octal Numbers

You can also use octal numbers to change file and directory permissions. To use octal number permission codes with the **chmod** command, enter the command in the following form:

chmod *octalnumber filename*

The *octalnumber* entry is a 3-digit octal number that specifies the permissions for owner, group, and others. The *filename* entry is the name of the file whose permissions you want to change. It can be the name of the file or a list of filenames separated by spaces. You may also use pattern-matching characters to specify files. See "Using Pattern-Matching Characters" earlier in this chapter for more information.

An octal number corresponds to each type of permission:

4 = **read**
2 = **write**
1 = **execute**

To specify a group of permissions (a permissions field), add together the appropriate octal numbers (**r**, **w**, and **x** denote read, write, and execute, respectively):

3 = -**wx** (2 + 1)
6 = **rw**- (4 + 2)
7 = **rwx** (4 + 2 + 1)
0 = --- (no permissions)

Table 5-2 lists the eight possible permission combinations for easy reference.

5–14   OSF/1 User's Guide

Table 5–2. Permission Combinations

Octal Number	Permissions	Description
0	None	No permissions granted
1	--x	Execute
2	-w-	Write
3	-wx	Write/execute
4	r--	Read
5	r-x	Read/execute
6	rw-	Read/write
7	rwx	Read/write/execute

The entire permission code for a file or directory is specified with a 3-digit octal number, one digit each for owner, group, and others. Table 5-3 shows some typical permission codes and how they relate to the permission fields.

Table 5–3. How Octal Numbers Relate to Permission Fields

Octal Number	Owner Field	Group Field	Others Field	Complete Code
777	rwx	rwx	rwx	rwxrwxrwx
755	rwx	r-x	r-x	rwxr-xr-x
700	rwx	---	---	rwx------
666	rw-	rw-	rw-	rw-rw-rw-

Enter the following example to change the permission of **file3** using octal numbers:

```
$ ls -l file3
-rw-rw-rw-  1 larry   system   130 Jun 5 10:06 file3
$ chmod 754 file3
$ ls -l file3
-rwxr-xr--  1 larry   system   130 Jun 5 10:06 file3
$ _
```

Setting the User Mask

Every time you create a file or a directory, the program you are running automatically establishes default permission codes for it. This relieves you from the task of specifying permission codes explicitly every time you create a file or directory.

If you wish to further restrict whatever permissions are established by a program when it creates a file or directory, you must specify a user mask with the **umask** command. The user mask is a numeric value that determines the maximum access permissions when a file or directory is created. As a result, when you create a file or directory, its permissions are set to what the creating program specifies, *minus* what the **umask** value forbids.

The **umask** command has the following format:

umask *octalnumber*

The *octalnumber* entry is a 3-digit octal number that specifies the default maximum permissions for owner, group, and others.

Setting the user mask is very similar to setting the permission bits discussed earlier in "Specifying Permissions With Octal Numbers." The permission code for a file or directory is specified with a 3-digit octal number. Each digit represents a type of permission. The position of each digit (first, second, or third) represents 3 bits that correspond to the following:

- The first is for the **owner** of the file (you).
- The second is for the **group** of the file.
- The third is for the default class **others**.

However, when you set the user mask, you are actually specifying which permissions are *not* to be granted regardless of the permissions requested by the file-creating program.

Table 5-4 lists the eight possible **umask** permission combinations for easy reference. Note that the **umask** permission values are the inverse of those specified for regular permission codes. Also note that these permission values are applied to those set by the creating program.

Table 5–4. The umask Permission Combinations

Octal Number	Maximum Allowed Permissions	Description
0	rwx	read/write/execute
1	rw-	read/write
2	r-x	read/execute
3	r--	read
4	-wx	write/execute
5	-w-	write
6	--x	execute
7	none	no permissions granted

For example, if you specify a user mask of 027:

- The owner is allowed all permissions requested by the program creating the file.
- The group is not allowed write permission.
- The others are not allowed any permissions.

A good user mask value to set for your own files and directories depends upon how freely information resources are shared on your system. The following guidelines may be useful:

- In a very open computing environment, you might specify 000 as a user mask value, which allows no restrictions on file/directory access. As a result, when a program creates a file and specifies permission codes for it, the user mask imposes no restrictions on what the creating program has specified.

- In a more secure computing environment, you might specify 066 as a user mask value, which allows you total access but prevents all others from being able to read or write to your files. As a result, when a file is created, its permissions are set to what the creating program specifies, minus the user mask restrictions that prevent read/write access for everyone but you.

- In a very secure computing environment, you might specify 077 as a user mask value, which means that only you have access to your files.

General User Tasks

As a result, when a file is created, its permissions are set to what the creating program specifies, minus the user mask restrictions that prevent anyone else from reading, writing, or executing your files.

To show you how **umask** would work, assume that you have entered the following command:

$ **umask 037**
$ _

This command establishes the following conditions:

- You (the owner) are allowed all permissions.
- Members of your group are not allowed write and execute permissions.
- The others are not allowed any permissions.

Also, assume that you have just created a file. By default, your editor always assigns the following default permissions: owners are allowed all permissions, and all others only read and execute permissions. However, since you have previously set a user mask of 037, it further restricts the file permissions. As a result, the owner still has all permissions, but the group cannot execute the file, and all others have no permissions.

You can activate the **umask** command in two ways:

- Include it in your login script. This is the most common and efficient way to specify your user mask because the specified value is set automatically for you whenever you log in. For a discussion of login scripts, see Chapter 7. For examples of **umask** commands in login scripts, see Chapter 8.
- Enter it at the shell prompt during a login session. The user mask value you set is in effect *for that login session only*.

For a more detailed example of how your user mask works in restricting permissions for files you create with a text editor, you may perform the following procedure:

1. Enter the following command to find out what the current value of your user mask is:

    $ **umask**

Controlling Access to Your Files and Directories

If the user mask value is 000, there are no restrictions on the permissions established by file-creating programs. Go to step 3.

If the user mask value is set, jot it down. Then, go to step 2.

2. Set the user mask value to 000 so that that there will be no restrictions on the permissions established by file-creating programs. Before resetting the user mask, make sure you have written down the current value should you need to reset it.

   Enter the following:

   $ **umask 000**
   $ _

3. Create a file, save it, and then exit your editor.

4. Display the permissions of the file by using the **ls -l** command. We will assume for the sake of the example that read/write permissions are granted for all users:

   $ **ls -l**
   -rw-rw-rw-   1 *user*   15 Oct 27 14:42 afile
   $_

5. Reset the user mask to **022** by entering the following:

   $ **umask 022**
   $_

   A user mask of 022 establishes the following maximum permission restrictions: owners are allowed all permissions, and all others only read and execute permissions.

6. Create another file, save it, and then exit your editor.

7. Display the permissions of the file by using the **ls -l** command.

   $ **ls -l**
   -rw-r--r--   1 *user*   15 Oct 27 14:42 afile2
   $_

   Note that the write permissions for the group and all others have been removed in accordance with the user mask value of 022.

OSF/1 User's Guide

8. Reset the user mask to its original value or to another value (optional).

Note: It is important to know that, whatever restrictions you impose on file/directory access with your user mask, a user with superuser privileges can override them. For more information on this topic, see "Superuser Concepts" later in this chapter.

On occasion, the results you obtain when specifying a user mask may vary from what you intended. If so, see your system administrator.

The OSF/1 operating system provides a default user mask value of 022, which allows the owner all permissions, but prevents members of your group or any other users from writing to your files. However, your system's user mask default may vary.

Changing Your Identity to Access Files (su, whoami)

The **su** command allows you to alter your identity during a login session. A reason for altering your identity is to be able to access files that you do not own. To protect system security, you should not assume another identity without the owner's or the system administrator's permission.

The **su** command allows you to log into another user's account only if you know that user's password. The **su** command authenticates you and then resets both the process's user ID and *effective* user ID to the value of the newly specified user ID. The effective user ID is the user ID currently in effect for the process, although it may not be the user ID of the person logged in.

The format of the **su** command is the following:

su *username*

The *username* entry is the username of the person whose identity you wish to assume.

If after altering your identity, you wish to confirm what identify you have assumed, use the **whoami** command. This command displays the username of the identity you have assumed. After completing your work under a new

Controlling Access to Your Files and Directories

identity, you should return to your own login identity. To do so, press **<Ctrl-d>** or enter the **exit** command.

The following example shows how Juan assumes Lucy's identity with the **su** command, confirms it with the **whoami** command, removes a file, and then returns to his own login identity with the **exit** command:

```
$ su lucy
Password: ...
$ whoami
lucy
$ rm file9
$ exit
$ whoami
juan
$ _
```

For more information, see the **su** and **whoami** reference pages.

Superuser Concepts

Every system has a superuser who has permissions that supersede those of ordinary users. This superuser is often referred to as root. The root user has absolute power over the running of the system. This user has access to all files and all devices and can make any changes to the system. The root user is said to have superuser privileges.

The following is a list of sample tasks ordinarily performed by root users:

- Edit files not normally changeable by ordinary users (for example, **/etc/passwd**).
- Be able to change ownership and permissions of all files.
- Execute restricted commands like **mount** or **reboot**.
- Kill any process running on your system.
- Add and remove users.

- Boot and shut down the system.
- Back up the system.

Many of the preceding tasks are typically performed by system administrators, who require superuser privileges. Basically, the system administrator's job is to manage the system by performing the preceding tasks, installing new software, analyzing system performance, and reporting hardware failures.

Depending upon your computing environment, you may or may not be the system administrator for your system or have root privileges. Your site configuration as well as your job responsibilities will determine your privileges.

For example, if you work from a terminal that accesses a centralized system, you will probably not be the system administrator or have root privileges. In this situation, the system administrator, who is in charge of maintaining, configuring, and upgrading the system, will be the person who has root privileges.

On the other hand, if you perform your tasks from a workstation that is either independent or networked to other workstations or systems, you may indeed have root privileges for your own workstation, but you may not be the system administrator of your site. In this situation, you would maintain *your own workstation only*. However, the system administrator would still maintain shared machines and networks.

To become a root user, use the **su** command. You must also know the password for the root user. The format of the **su** command is the following:

su root

The following example shows how Juan becomes a root user to perform an administrative task:

```
$ su root
Password: ...
# _
```

Controlling Access to Your Files and Directories

The new prompt, a # (number sign), indicates that Juan has become a root user and that a shell has been created for his use. The root user shell (often the C shell) is defined in the **/etc/passwd** file. Juan may now perform the administrative task. See Chapter 13 for some examples of administrative tasks that require root user privileges.

Caution: Because the root user had absolute power over the system, the password should be carefully protected. Otherwise, unauthorized use of the system may result in corruption or destruction of data.

After completing your work as the root user, you should return to your own login identity. To do so, press **<Ctrl-d>** or enter the **exit** command. You are then returned to the system prompt.

Changing Owners and Groups

In addition to setting permissions, you can control how a file or directory is used by changing its owner or group. Use the **chown** command to change the owner and the **chgrp** command to change the group.

Note: In order to use the **chown** command, you must have superuser privileges. For more information on this topic, see "Superuser Concepts" earlier in this chapter.

Enter the **chown** command in the following form:

chown *owner filename*

The *owner* entry is the username of the new owner of the file. The *filename* entry is a list of one or more files whose ownership you want to change. You may also use pattern-matching characters to specify files. See "Using Pattern-Matching Characters" earlier in this chapter for more information.

Enter the **chgrp** command in the following form:

chgrp *group file*

The *group* entry is the group ID or group name of the new group. Note that, to change the group ownership of a file, you must be a member of the

OSF/1 User's Guide 5–23

General User Tasks

group to which you are changing the file. The *file* entry is a list of one or more files whose ownership you want to change.

For more information, see the **chown** and **chgrp** reference pages.

Additional Security Considerations

The security guidelines enforced at your site protect your files from unauthorized access. See your system administrator for complete information about security guidelines and follow them scrupulously.

In addition, it is wise to avoid running untrusted software (software that is from an unknown source or that has not been validated for system security). When you run a program, that program has all of your access rights, and nothing prevents the program from being used to illicitly access, observe, or alter sensitive files.

You should be aware of three types of programs that compromise security:

- Trojan horse

    A trojan horse is a program that performs, or appears to perform, its defined task properly; however, it also performs hidden functions that may be malevolent. A trojan horse program emulates the program that you intended to run, but may perform an unwanted action. It might vandalize your files by altering or deleting them, or compromise the files by making illegal copies of them.

    A typical trojan horse is the **login** trojan horse, which mimics the system's login prompt on the display and waits for you to enter a username and password. The program mails or copies this information to the user responsible for the trojan horse. As the trojan horse exits, it displays `Login incorrect`. The real **login** program then runs. Most users assume they typed the password incorrectly, and are unaware that they were deceived.

- Computer worm

    A computer worm is a program that moves around a computer network, making copies of itself. For example, a **login** computer worm can log into a system, copy itself into the system, start running, log into another system, and then continue this process indefinitely.

- Computer virus

    A computer virus program is really a type of trojan horse. Normally, a trojan horse waits passively for the right user to run it (usually a privileged user). Viruses spread themselves by inserting themselves in other executable files, thus increasing the threat and extent of compromise of privacy or integrity.

Be careful of programs that were not installed by the person who administers your system. Programs that are obtained from bulletin boards and other unknown origins are particularly suspect. Even if the program includes source code, it is not always possible to examine the program carefully enough to determine if it is trustworthy.

Using Enhancements to the Security System

Your system may contain OSF/1 enhanced security features that may affect access to the overall system, files, and directories. These enhancements result in a system that can be certified at either the B1 or C2 security classes defined by the U.S. Department of Defense. OSF/1 enhanced security features expand system security in the following areas:

- Accountability-Identification and Authentication

    The system keeps track of all logins and maintains an extensive profile of each user. As a result, an unauthorized penetration (or attempted penetration) into an account is extremely difficult.

- Accountability-Audit

    The system maintains an audit trail that records every relevant security event. Each file open, file creation, login, and print job is recorded.

- Discretionary Access Control (DAC)

    In addition to the traditional UNIX file protection (owner, group, and permission bits), users can associate an Access Control List (ACL) with each file. This list contains entries that specify exact permissions for users and groups.

General User Tasks

- Mandatory Access Control (MAC)

    The system enforces its own access rules (mandatory rules) based upon sensitivity labels. Sensitivity labels define the level of trust. The system maintains sensitivity labels on all users, processes, files, and directories. The system checks that the user (or the process on the system doing the work for the user) is cleared to access information.

- Data Interchange

    The system ensures that classified data maintains its classification even if it leaves the system.

- Privilege Mechanism

    The privilege mechanism extends traditional root user security by implementing the concept of least privilege. Least privilege refers to the security doctrine that states that a program should have only enough power to do the specific task it is assigned, and only for the duration of that task. Therefore, if a program performs a highly sensitive operation, it must be privileged only during that operation, and not longer.

    OSF/1 enhanced security features do not completely replace the need for a superuser; instead they do redefine the way the operating system checks for privilege. All privilege checks in the operating system check for possession of a privilege rather than for a superuser. System commands either were converted to enable an appropriate privilege on every privileged operation, or require that a privileged user run them.

    See your system administrator for details.

Chapter 6
Using Processes

This chapter explains OSF/1 operating system processes. After completing this chapter, you will be able to do the following:

- Understand programs and processes
- Redirect process input, output, and errors
- Run processes in the foreground and background
- Check the status of processes
- Cancel processes
- Display information about users and their processes

A good way to learn about the preceding topics is to try the examples in this chapter. You should do each example in order so that the information on your screen is consistent with the information in this guide.

Understanding Programs and Processes

A program is a set of instructions that a computer can interpret and run. You may think of most programs as belonging to one of two categories:

- Application programs such text editors, accounting packages, or electronic spreadsheets
- Programs that are components of the OSF/1 operating system such as commands, the shell (or shells), and your login procedure

While a program is running, it is called a process. The OSF/1 operating system assigns every process a unique number known as a process identifier.

The OSF/1 operating system can run a number of different processes at the same time. When more than one process is running, a scheduler built into the operating system gives each process its fair share of the computer's time, based on established priorities.

Understanding Standard Input, Output, and Error

When a process begins executing, the OSF/1 operating system opens three files for the process: **stdin** (standard input), **stdout** (standard output), and **stderr** (standard error). Programs use these files as follows:

- Standard input is the place from which the program expects to read its input. By default, processes read **stdin** from the keyboard.
- Standard ouput is the place to which the program writes its output. By default, processes write **stdout** to the screen.
- Standard error is the place to which the program writes its error messages. By default, processes write **stderr** to the screen.

In most cases, the default standard input, output, and error mechanisms will serve you well. However, there are times when it is useful to redirect the standard input, output, and error. The following subsections describe these procedures.

Using Processes

Redirecting Input and Output

A command usually reads its input from the keyboard (standard input) and writes its output to the display (standard output). Often, though, you may want a command to read its input from a file, write its output to a file, or both. You can select input and output files for a command with the shell notation shown in Table 6-1. This notation can be used in all OSF/1 shells.

Table 6–1. Shell Notation for Reading Input and Redirecting Output

Notation	Action	Example
<	Reads standard input from a file.	wc <file3
>	Writes standard output to a file.	ls >file3
>>	Adds standard output to the end of a file.	ls >>file3

The following subsections explain how to read input from a file and how to write output to a file.

Reading Input from a File—The < Symbol

All OSF/1 shells allow you to redirect the standard input of a process so that input is read from a file instead of from the keyboard. You can use input redirection with any command that accepts input from **stdin** (your keyboard). You cannot use input redirection with commands, such as **who**, that do not accept input.

To redirect input, use the < (less-than symbol), as the following example shows:

```
$ wc <file3
      3      27     129
$ _
```

OSF/1 User's Guide   6–3

The **wc** (word count) command counts the number of lines, words, and bytes in the named file. So **file3** contains 3 lines, 27 words, and 129 bytes. If you do not supply an argument, the **wc** command reads its input from the keyboard. In this example, however, input for **wc** comes from the file named **file3**.

Note that, in the preceding example, you could have entered the following, and displayed the same output:

```
$ wc file
      3      27     129
$ _
```

This is because most OSF/1 commands allow the input file to be specified without the < symbol. However, there are a few commands like **mail** that require the use of the < symbol for special functions. For example, note the following command:

mail juan <report

This command mails to the user **juan** the file **report**. For more information about mail, see Appendix D.

Redirecting Output—The > and >> Symbols

All OSF/1 shells allow you redirect the standard output of a process from the screen (the default) to a file. As a result, you can store the text generated by a command into a new or existing file. To send output to a file, use either the > (greater-than symbol) or the >> symbol.

The > symbol causes the shell to do the following:

- Replace the contents of the file with the output of the command, if the file exists
- Create the file, if the file does not exist

The >> symbol adds (appends) the output of the command to the end of a file that exists. If you use the >> symbol to write output to a file that does not exist, the shell creates it.

In the next example, the output of **ls** goes to the file named **file**:

$ **ls >file**
$ _

If the file already exists, the shell replaces its contents with the output of **ls**. If **file** does not exist, the shell creates it.

In the following example, the shell adds the output of **ls** to the end of the file named **file**:

$ **ls >>file**
$ _

If **file** does not exist, the shell creates it.

In addition to their standard output, processes often produce error or status messages known as diagnostic output. For information about redirecting diagnostic output, see the following section.

Redirecting Standard Error to a File

When a command executes successfully, it displays the results on the standard output. When a command executes unsuccessfully, it displays error messages on the default standard error file, the screen. However, the shell allows you to redirect the standard error of a process from the screen to a file.

Redirection symbols and syntax vary among OSF/1 shells. The following subsections describe standard error redirection for the Bourne, Korn, and C shells.

Bourne and Korn Shell Error Redirection

The general format for Bourne and Korn shell standard error redirection is the following:

command **2>** *errorfile*

General User Tasks

The *command* entry is an OSF/1 command. The *errorfile* entry is the name of the file to which the process writes the standard error. The **2>** is a file descriptor digit combined with the output redirection symbol. The file descriptor digit tells the shell what standard file to access so that its contents may be redirected. The file descriptor digit **2** indicates that the standard error file is being redirected.

In fact, for the Bourne and Korn shells, a file descriptor digit is associated with each of the files a command ordinarily uses:

- File descriptor 0 (same as <) specifies standard input (the keyboard).
- File descriptor 1 (same as >) specifies standard output (the screen).
- File descriptor 2 specifies standard error (screen).

In the following example, an error is redirected to the file **error** when the **ls** command attempts to display the nonexistent file, **reportx**. The contents of file **error** are then displayed:

```
$ ls reportx 2> error
$ cat error
reportx not found
$ _
```

Although only standard error is redirected to a file in the preceding example, typically you would redirect both standard error and standard output. See the next section, "Redirecting Both Standard Error and Standard Output," for more information.

For many commands, the difference between standard output and standard error is difficult to see. For instance, if you use the **ls** command to display a nonexistent file, an error message displays on the screen. If you redirect the error message to a file as in the previous example, the output is identical.

C Shell Error Redirection

The general format for C shell standard error redirection is the following:

(*command* > *outfile*) >&*errorfile*

Using Processes

The *command* entry is an OSF/1 command. The *outfile* entry is the name of the file to which the process writes the standard output. The **>&** symbol redirects the standard error to a file. The *errorfile* entry is the name of the file to which the process writes the standard error. Note that, in this command format, the parentheses are mandatory.

Redirecting Both Standard Error and Standard Output

In the preceding section, you learned how to redirect standard output and standard error separately. Usually, however, you would redirect both standard output and standard error at the same time. Standard output and standard error can be written to different files or to the same file.

For the Bourne and Korn shells, the general format for redirecting both standard output and standard error to different files is the following:

command **>** *outfile* **2>***errorfile*

The *command* entry is an OSF/1 command. The *outfile* entry is the file to which the process writes the standard output. The **2>** symbol redirects the error output. The *errorfile* entry is the file where the process writes the standard error.

For the C shell, the general format for redirecting both standard output and standard error to different files is the following:

(*command* **>** *outfile*) **>&***errorfile*

The *command* entry is an OSF/1 command. The *outfile* entry is the file to which the process writes the standard output. The **>&** symbol redirects the error output. The *errorfile* entry is the file where the process writes the standard error. Note that, in this command format, the parentheses are mandatory. See ''C Shell Error Redirection'' earlier in this chapter for more information.

For the Bourne and Korn shells, the general format for redirecting both standard output and standard error to the same file is the following:

command **1>** *outfile* **2>&1**

The *command* entry is an OSF/1 command. The **1>** symbol redirects the standard output. The *outfile* entry is the file to which the process writes the standard output. The **2>&1** symbol tells the shell to write the standard error (file descriptor **2**) in the file associated with the standard output (**>&1**), *outfile*.

For the C shell, the general format for redirecting both standard output and standard error to the same file is the following:

command **>&** *outfile*

The *command* entry is an OSF/1 command. The *outfile* entry is the file to which the process writes the standard output. The **>&** symbol tells the shell to write the standard output and standard error to the same file specified by *outfile*.

Running Several Processes Simultaneously

The OSF/1 operating system can run a number of different processes at the same time. This capability makes it a multitasking operating system, which means that the processes of several users can run at the same time.

These different processes can be from one or multiple users. As a result, you do not have to enter commands one at a time at the shell prompt. Instead, you can run both foreground and background processes simultaneously. The following subsections describe both foreground and background processes.

Running Foreground Processes

Normally, when you enter a command on the command line, you wait for the results to display on your screen. Commands entered singly at the shell prompt are called "foreground processes."

Most commands take a short time to execute—perhaps a second or two. However, some commands require longer execution times. If a long-duration command runs as a foreground process, you cannot execute others commands until the current one finishes. As a result, you may wish to run a long-duration command as a background process.

Using Processes

Running Background Processes

Generally, background processes are most useful with commands that take a long time to run. Instead of tying up your workstation by having a long-duration command run as a foreground process, you can execute a command as a background process. You can then continue with other work in the foreground.

To run a background process, you end the command with **&** (an ampersand). Once a process is running in the background, you can perform additional tasks by entering other commands at your workstation.

After you create a background process, the following takes place:

- The Process Identification Number (PID) is displayed. The OSF/1 operating system creates and assigns PIDs so that all processes currently running on the system can be tracked. (In the Korn or the C shell, job numbers are assigned as well.)

- The prompt returns so that you can enter another command.

- In the C shell, a message is displayed when the background process is complete.

When you create a background process, note its PID number. The PID number helps you to monitor or terminate the process. See "Monitoring and Terminating Processes" later in this chapter for more information.

Because background processes increase the total amount of work the system is doing, they may also slow down the rest of the system. This may or may not be a problem, depending upon how much the system slows and the nature of the other work you or others do while background processes run.

Most processes direct their output to standard output, even when they run in the background. Unless redirected, standard output goes to your workstation. Because the output from a background process may interfere with your other work on the system, it is usually good practice to redirect the output of a background process to a file or to a printer. Then you can look at the output whenever you are ready. For more information about redirecting output, see the examples later in this chapter as well as "Redirecting Input and Output" earlier in this chapter.

General User Tasks

The examples in the rest of this chapter use a command that takes more than a few seconds to run:

find / -type f -print

This command displays the pathnames for all files on your system. You do not need to study the **find** command in order to complete this chapter—it is used here simply to demonstrate how to work with processes. However, if you want to learn more about the **find** command, see Chapter 9 and the **find** reference page. In the following example, the **find** command runs in the background (**&**) and redirects its output to a file named **dir.paths** (with the **>** operator):

```
$ find / -type f -print >dir.paths &
24
$ _
```

When the background process starts, the system assigns it a PID number, displays it (24 in this example), and then prompts you for another command. (Your process number probably will be different from the one shown in this and following examples.)

If you use the Korn or C shell, job numbers are assigned as well. In the C shell, the preceding example looks like this:

```
% find / -type f -print >dir.paths &
[1] 24
% _
```

Note that the job number [1] is displayed to the left of the PID number.

You can then check the status of the process with the **ps** (process status) or the **jobs** command (Korn and C shells). You can also terminate a process with the **kill** command. See the following section for more information on the these commands.

In the C shell, when the background process is completed, a message is displayed as in the following:

```
[1]  24   Done     find / -type f -print >dir.paths
```

The completion message displays the job number and the PID, the status Done, and the command that was executed.

Monitoring and Terminating Processes

Use the **ps** (process status) command to find out which processes are running and to display information about those processes. In the Korn and C shells, you also can use the **jobs** command to monitor background processes.

If you need to stop a process before it is finished, use the **kill** command.

The following subsections describe how to monitor and terminate processes.

Checking Process Status

The **ps** command allows you to monitor the status of all active processes, both foreground and background. In the Korn and C shell, you also can use the **jobs** command to monitor background processes only. The following subsections describe the **ps** and the **jobs** command.

The ps Command

The **ps** command has the following form:

ps

In the following example, the **ps** command displays the status of all processes associated with your workstation under the following headings:

```
$ ps

PID     TT      STAT    TIME    COMMAND
29670   p4      I       0:00    -sh (csh)
  515   p5      S       0:00    -sh (csh)
28476   p5      R       0:00    ps
  790   p6      I       0:00    -sh (csh)
$ _
```

General User Tasks

You interpret the display under these entry headings as follows:

PID   Process identification. The system assigns a process identification number (PID number) to each process when that process starts. There is no relationship between a process and a particular PID number; that is, if you start the same process several times, it will have a different PID number each time.

TT   Controlling tty device name. On a system with more than one workstation, this field tells you which workstation started the process. On a system with only one workstation, this field can contain the designation `console` or the designation for one or more virtual terminals.

STAT   Symbolic process status. The system display the state of the process, with a sequence of up to four alphanumeric characters. For more information, see the reference page for the **ps** command.

TIME   Time devoted to this process by the computer is displayed in minutes and seconds as of when you enter **ps**.

COMMAND   The name of the command (or program) that started the process.

You can also check the status of a particular process by using the **-p** flag and the PID number with the **ps** command. The general format for checking the status of a particular process is the following:

ps -p*PIDnumber*

The **ps** command also displays the status of background processes. If there are any background processes running, they will be displayed along with the foreground processes. The following example shows how to start a **find** background process and then check its status:

```
$ find / -type f -print >dir.paths &
25
$ ps -p25
PID    TTY        TIME    COMMAND
 25    console    0:40    find
$ _
```

6–12   OSF/1 User's Guide

Using Processes

You can check background process status as often as you like while the process runs. In the following example, the **ps** command displays the status of the preceding **find** process five times:

```
$ ps -p25
PID     TTY      TIME    COMMAND
25      console  0:18    find
$ ps -p25
PID     TTY      TIME    COMMAND
25      console  0:29    find
$ ps -p25
PID     TTY      TIME    COMMAND
25      console  0:49    find
$ ps -p25
PID     TTY      TIME    COMMAND
25      console  0:58    find
$ ps -p25
PID     TTY      TIME    COMMAND
25      console  1:02    find
$ ps -p25
PID     TTY      TIME COMMAND
$ _
```

Notice that the sixth **ps** command returns no status information because the **find** process ended before the last **ps** command was entered.

Generally, the simple **ps** command described here tells you all you need to know about processes. However, you can control the type of information that the **ps** command displays by using more of its flags. One of the most useful **ps** flags is **-e**, which causes **ps** to return information about *all* processes, not just those associated with your workstation. For an explanation of all **ps** command flags, see the **ps** reference page.

The jobs Command

The Korn shell and the C shell display both a job number and a PID number when a background process is created. The **jobs** command reports the status of all background processes only, based upon the job number.

OSF/1 User's Guide 6-13

General User Tasks

The **jobs** command has the following form:

jobs

Adding the **-l** flag displays both the job number and the PID.

The following example shows how to start a **find** process and then check its status in the C shell with the **jobs -l** command:

```
% find / -type f -print >dir.paths &
[2] 26
% jobs -l
[2] +26 Running    find / -type f -print >dir.paths &
%
```

The status message displays both the job number (`[2]`) and the PID number (`26`), the status (`Running`), and the command executed.

Canceling a Foreground Process (Ctrl-c)

To cancel a foreground process (stop an executing command), press **<Ctrl-c>**. The command stops executing, and the system displays the shell prompt. Note that canceling a foreground process is the same as stopping command execution (described in Chapter 1).

Most simple OSF/1 operating system commands are not good examples for demonstrating how to cancel a process because they run so quickly that they finish before you have time to cancel them. However, the following **find** command runs long enough for you to cancel it (after the process runs for a few seconds, you can cancel it by pressing **<Ctrl/c>**):

```
$ find / -type f -print
/usr/sbin/acct/acctcms
/usr/sbin/acct/acctcon1
/usr/sbin/acct/acctcon2
/usr/sbin/acct/acctdisk
/usr/sbin/acct/acctmerg
/usr/sbin/acct/accton
/usr/sbin/acct/acctprc1
/usr/sbin/acct/acctprc2
/usr/sbin/acct/acctwtmp
```

Using Processes

```
/usr/sbin/acct/chargefee
/usr/sbin/acct/ckpacct
/usr/sbin/acct/dodisk
```
<Ctrl-c>
$ _

The system returns the shell prompt to the screen. Now you can enter another command.

Canceling a Background Process (kill)

If you decide, after starting a background process, that you do not want the process to finish, you can cancel the process with the **kill** command. Before you can cancel a background process, however, you must know its PID number.

If you have forgotten the PID number of that process, you can use the **ps** command to list the PID numbers of all processes. Or, if you are a C or Korn Shell user, it is more efficient to use the **jobs** command to list background processes only.

The general format for terminating a particular process is the following:

kill *PIDnumber*

Note: If you wish to end all the processes you have started since login, use the **kill 0** command. You do not have to know the PID numbers to use **kill 0**. Because this command deletes all of your processes, use this command with care.

The following example shows how to start another **find** process, check its status, and then terminate it:

```
$ find / -type f -print >dir.paths &
38
$ ps
PID     TT      STAT    TIME    COMMAND
520     p4      I       0:11    sh
738     p5      I       0:10    find
1216    p6      S       0:01    qdaemon
839     p7      R       0:03    ps
```

OSF/1 User's Guide   6-15

General User Tasks

```
$ kill 738
$ ps
38 Terminated
PID     TT      STAT    TIME    COMMAND
520     p4      I       0:11    sh
1216    p6      S       0:01    qdaemon
839     p7      R       0:03    ps
$ _
```

The command **kill 738** stops the background **find** process, and the second **ps** command returns no status information about PID number 738. The system does not display the termination message until you enter your next command. Note that, in this example, **kill 738** and **kill 0** have the same effect because only one process was started from this workstation.

In the C shell, the **kill** command has the following format:

kill %jobnumber

The following example uses the C shell to start another **find** process, to check its status with the **jobs** command, and then to terminate it:

```
% find / -type f -print >dir.paths &
[3] 40
% jobs -l
[3] +40 Running    find / -type f -print >dir.paths &
% kill %3
% jobs -l
[3]  +Terminated    find / -type f -print > dir.paths
% _
```

Suspending and Resuming Processes (C Shell Only)

Stopping a process and resuming it can be helpful when you have a long-duration process absorbing system resources, and you need to do something quickly. Rather than waiting for process completion, you can stop the process temporarily (suspend it), perform your more critical task, and then resume the process. Suspending a process is available for C shell users only.

Using Processes

To suspend a process, press **<Ctrl-z>.** A message will display the job number, the status Suspended, and the command executed.

Once you are ready to resume the process, enter:

% *n*

To resume the process in the background, instead, enter:

% *n* **&**

The *n* entry is the number of the stopped job.

The following example starts a **find** process, suspends it, checks its status, resumes it, and then terminates it:

```
% find / -type f -print >dir.paths &
[4] 41
% jobs -l
[4] +41 Running    find / -type f -print >dir.paths &
% <Ctrl-z>
Suspended
% jobs -l
[4] +Stopped    find / -type f -print > dir.paths
% %4 &
[4] find / -type f -print >dir.paths &
% kill %4
[4] +Terminated    find / -type f -print > dir.paths
% _
```

Once a process is suspended, you may also resume it by entering the **fg** command. Or, if a currently running process is taking too long to run and is tying up your keyboard, you can use the **bg** command to place the process in the background and enter other commands.

The following example starts a **find** process, suspends it, puts the process in the background, copies a file, and then resumes the process in the foreground:

```
% find / -type f -print >dir.paths
Ctrl-z
Suspended
% bg
```

OSF/1 User's Guide   6–17

General User Tasks

```
[5]     find / -type f -print > dir.paths &
% cp salary1 salary2
% fg
find / -type f -print > dir.paths
% _
```

Displaying Information About Users and Their Processes

The OSF/1 operating system provides the following commands that can tell you who is using the system and what they are doing:

- **who**

    This command displays currently logged-in users.

- **w**

    This command displays currently logged-in users and what they are currently running on their workstations.

- **ps -au**

    This command displays currently logged-in users and information about processes they are running.

The **who** command allows you to determine who is logged into the system. It may be especially useful, for example, when you wish to send a message and want to know whether the person is currently available.

In the following example, all currently logged-in users are displayed:

```
$ who
juan    tty01   Jan 15   08:33
chang   tty05   Jan 15   08:45
larry   tty07   Jan 15   08:55
tony    tty09   Jan 15   07:53
lucy    pts/2   Jan 15   11:24    (boston)
$ _
```

Note that the **who** command lists the username of each user on the system, the workstation being used, and when the person logged in. In addition, if a

6–18   OSF/1 User's Guide

user is logged in from a remote system, the name of the system is listed (in this case, boston). For example, lucy logged in remotely from the system boston on Jan 15 at 11:24.

The **who -u** command gives all the information of the **who** command and also displays the PID of each user, and the number of hours and minutes since there was activity at a workstation. Activity for less than a minute is indicated by a dot (.).

In the following example, all currently logged-in users are displayed:

```
$ who -u
juan    tty01   Jan 15   08:33   01:02   50
chang   tty05   Jan 15   08:45      .    52
larry   tty07   Jan 15   08:55      .    58
tony    tty09   Jan 15   07:53   01:20   60
lucy    pts/5   Jan 15   11:24      .    65   (boston)
$ _
```

Note that, in the preceding example, juan and tony have been inactive for over an hour, while chang, larry, and lucy have been inactive for less than a minute.

Now that you know how to find out who is active on your system, you may wish to find out what command each person is currently executing. The **w** command displays what command is currently running at each user's workstation.

In the following example, all users (the User column) and their current commands (the what column) are displayed:

```
$ w
11:02am up 23 days, 2:40, 5 users, load average: 0.32, 0.20, 0.00
User    tty     login@   idle   JCPU   PCPU   what
juan    tty01   8:33am    12      54     14   -csh
chang   tty05   8:45am          6:20     26   mail
larry   tty07   8:55           1:58      8   -csh
tony    tty09   7:53     3:10    22      4   mail
lucy    tty02   11:24    1:40    18      4   -csh
$ _
```

OSF/1 User's Guide   6-19

General User Tasks

In addition, the **w** command also displays the following information:

- The `tty` column

  This column displays the user's workstation.

- The `login@` column

  This column displays the user's login time.

- The `idle` column

  This column displays the amount of time since the user entered a command.

- The `JCPU` column

  This column displays the total CPU time used during the current login session.

- The `PCPU` column

  This column displays the CPU time used by the command that is currently executing.

On certain occasions, you may wish to have a detailed listing of current processes (both foreground and background) and the users who are running them. To get such a listing, use the **ps -au** command. In the following example, five users and their active processes are displayed:

```
$ ps -au
USER     PID %CPU %MEM   SZ  RSS TT  STAT  TIME   COMMAND
juan   26300 16.5  0.8  441  327 p3  R     0:02   ps -au
chang  25821  7.0  0.2  149   64 p4  R     0:12   mail -n
larry  25121  6.1  0.2  107   83 p22 R    26:25   tip modem
tony   11240  4.5  0.6  741  225 p19 R     1:57   emacs
lucy   26287  0.5  0.1   61   28 p1  S     0:00   more
$ _
```

The most important fields for the general user are the USER, PID, TIME, and COMMAND fields. For information on the remaining fields, see the **ps** reference page.

Chapter 7
OSF/1 Shell Overview

This chapter introduces you to the OSF/1 shells. After completing this chapter, you will be able to do the following:

- Understand the purpose and general features of the Bourne, C, and Korn shells
- Change your shell
- Use command entry aids common to all shells
- Understand your shell environment as well as the role of login scripts, environment variables, and shell variables
- Set and clear environment and shell variables
- Understand how the shell finds commands on your system
- Write logout scripts
- Write and run shell procedures

This chapter covers features common to all OSF/1 shells, with some descriptions of shell differences. For detailed information on specific Bourne, C, and Korn shell features, see Chapter 8.

Purpose of OSF/1 Shells

The user interfaces to the OSF/1 operating system are called "shells." The shells are programs that interpret the commands you enter, run the programs you have asked for, and send the results to your screen.

The OSF/1 operating system provides the following shells:

- The Bourne shell
- The C shell
- The Korn shell

Note: The Korn Shell (**ksh**) is available only to AT&T Tool Chest Licensees.

You may access any shell, depending upon the security restrictions in effect on your system as well as upon the licensing restrictions of the Korn shell. In any case, all shells perform the same basic function; that is, they allow you to perform work on your system by executing commands.

The **sh** command invokes the shell **/usr/bin/sh**, which is a link to either the Korn shell or the Bourne shell, depending on the configuration of the system.

In addition to interpreting commands, the shell can also be used as a programming language. This is because you can create a shell procedure that contains commands and execute the procedure like a program. Shell procedures provide an easy means of carrying out tedious commands, large or complicated sequences of commands, and routine or repetitive tasks.

See "Using Shell Procedures" later in this chapter for more information on shell programming.

Summary of Bourne, C, and Korn Shell Features

The OSF/1 operating system provides the following shells that have both command execution and programming capabilities:

- The Bourne shell (**bsh**)

  This is a simple shell that is easily used in programming. It is usually represented by a $ (dollar sign) prompt. This shell does not provide either the interactive features or the complex programming constructs (arrays and integer arithmetic) of the C shell or the Korn shell.

  The Bourne shell also provides a restricted shell (**Rsh**). For more information, see "The Restricted Bourne Shell" later in this chapter.

- The C shell (**csh**)

  This shell is designed for easy interactive use. It is usually represented by a % (percent sign) system prompt. The C shell provides some features for entering commands interactively:

  — A command history buffer

  — Command aliases

  — Filename completion

  For more information on these features, see the following subsection.

- The Korn shell (**ksh**)

  This shell combines the ease of use of the C shell and the ease of programming of the Bourne shell. The system prompt is usually a $ (dollar sign) prompt. The Korn shell provides these features:

  — The interactive features of the C shell

  — The simple programming syntax of the Bourne shell

  — Inline command editing

  — The fastest execution time

  — Upward compatibility with the Bourne shell (that is, most Bourne shell programs will run under the Korn shell)

  For more information on these features, see the following subsection.

General User Tasks

More Information on C and Korn Shell Features

Both the C and the Korn shells offer the following interactive features:

- Command history

    The command history buffer stores the commands you enter and allows you to display them at any time. As a result, you can select a previous command, or parts of previous commands, and then reexecute them. This feature may save you time because it allows you to reuse long commands instead of retyping them.

- Command aliases

    The command aliases feature allows you to abbreviate long command lines or rename commands. You do this by creating aliases for long command lines that you frequently use. For example, assume that you often need to move to the directory **/usr/chang/reports/status**. You could create an alias **status** that could move you to that directory whenever you enter **status** on the command line. In addition, aliases allow you to make up more descriptive names for OSF/1 commands. For example, you could define an alias named **rename** for the **mv** command.

- Filename completion

    The filename completion feature saves typing by allowing you to enter a portion of the filename which the shell will complete for you. In addition, you may ask the shell to display a list of filenames that match the partial name you entered. You may then choose among the displayed filenames.

The Korn shell provides an inline editing feature that allows you to retrieve a previously entered command and edit it. To use this feature, you must know how to use a text editor such as **vi** or **emacs**.

For more information on all of these shell features, see Chapter 8.

OSF/1 User's Guide

The Restricted Bourne Shell

The OSF/1 operating system enhances system security by providing specified users a limited set of functions with a restricted version of the Bourne shell (**Rsh**). When these specified users log into the system, they are given access to the restricted Bourne shell only. Your system administrator determines who has access to the restricted Bourne shell.

A restricted shell is useful for installations that require a more controlled shell environment. As a result, the system administrator can create user environments that have a limited set of privileges and capabilities. For example, all users who are guests to your system might be allowed access under the username **guest**. When logging into your system, user **guest** would be assigned a restricted shell.

The actions of **Rsh** are identical to those of **bsh**, except that the following actions are not allowed:

- Changing directories. (The **cd** command is deactivated.)
- Specifying pathnames or command names containing **/** (slash).
- Setting the value of the **PATH** or the **SHELL** variables. For more information on these variables, see "Environment Variables" later in this chapter.
- Redirecting output (with > and >>).

For more detailed information on **Rsh**, see the **bsh** reference page. For information on how system administrators create restricted shells, see your system administrator.

Changing Your Shell

Whenever you log in, you are automatically placed in a shell specified by your system administrator. However, depending upon the security features

General User Tasks

in effect on your system, you can enter commands that will allow you to do the following:

- Determine which shell you are running
- Temporarily change your shell
- Permanently change your shell

The following subsections describe these operations.

Determining What Shell You Are Running

To determine what shell you are currently running, enter the following at your system prompt:

echo $SHELL

The filename of the shell you are running will display.

In the following example, assume that you are running the Bourne shell (**bsh**):

```
$ echo $SHELL
/usr/bin/bsh
$ _
```

Table 7-1 lists the filename that displays for each shell as well as the default system prompt (your system prompt may vary).

Table 7–1. Shell Filenames and Default Prompts

Shell	Shell Filename	Default Prompt
Bourne	**bsh**	$
Restricted Bourne	**Rsh**	$
C	**csh**	%
Korn	**ksh**	$

Temporarily Changing Your Shell

You may experiment with using other shells if the security features on your system allow it. To temporarily change your shell, enter the following command:

shellname

where *shellname* is the filename of the shell. See Table 7-1 for valid shell filenames to enter on the command line. Once the shell is invoked, the correct shell prompt is displayed.

Once you are done using the new shell, you can return to your default shell by entering **exit** or by pressing **<Ctrl-d>**.

For example, assume that the Korn shell is your default shell. To change to the C shell and then back to the Korn shell, perform the following steps:

```
$ /usr/bin/csh
% exit
$ _
```

Note: If you are using the restricted Bourne shell, you cannot change to another shell.

Permanently Changing Your Shell

You may permanently change your default shell if the security features on your system allow it. To change your default shell, use the **chsh** command. For example, assuming that your current shell is the C shell, to change your default shell, enter:

```
% chsh
Changing login shell for user.
Old shell: /usr/bin/csh
New shell:
```

Enter the name of the new shell. See Table 7-1 for valid shell names to enter on the command line.

Note: After entering the **chsh** command, you must log out and log in again for the change to take effect.

Command Entry Aids

These features of all OSF/1 shells help you do your work easily and efficiently. The following subsections describe these features:

- The ability to enter multiple commands and command lists
- Pipes and filters
- The ability to group commands
- Quoting

Using Multiple Commands and Command Lists

The shell usually takes the first word on a command line as the name of a command, and then takes any other words as arguments to that command. That is, the shell usually considers each command line as a single command. However, you can use the operators in Table 7-2 to execute multiple commands on a single command line.

OSF/1 Shell Overview

Table 7–2. Multiple Command Operators

Operator	Action	Example
; (semicolon)	Causes commands to run in sequence.	*cmd1* ; *cmd2*
&&	Runs the next command if the current command succeeds.	*cmd1*&& *cmd2*
||	Runs the next command if the current command fails.	*cmd1* || *cmd2*
|	Creates a pipeline.	**ls | wc**

The following subsections describe running commands in sequence (;), running commands conditionally (\|\|), and using pipelines (\|).

Running Commands in Sequence with a Semicolon (;)

You can type more than one command on a line if you separate commands with the operator ; (semicolon). In the following example, the shell runs **ls** and waits for it to finish. When **ls** is finished, the shell runs **who**, and so on through the last command:

```
$ ls ; who ; date ; pwd
change   file3   newfile
amy      console/1      Jun 4 14:41
Tue Jun 4  14:42:51  CDT  1991
/u/amy
$ _
```

Note that, if any one command fails, the others still execute successfully.

To make the command line easier to read, you can separate commands from the ; (semicolon) with blanks or tabs. The shell ignores blanks and tabs used in this way.

General User Tasks

Running Commands Conditionally—The || and && Operators

When you connect commands with the **&&** or **||** operators, the shell runs the first command and then runs the remaining commands only under the following conditions:

&& The shell runs the next command only if the current command completes. (A command indicates successful completion when it returns a value of 0 (zero).

|| The shell runs the next command only if the current command does not complete.

In the following example, the shell runs the next command if the current command has executed successfully:

$ *cmd1* **&&** *cmd2* **&&** *cmd3* **&&** *cmd4* **&&** *cmd5*

If *cmd1* succeeds, the shell runs *cmd2*. If *cmd2* succeeds, the shell runs *cmd3*, and on through the series until a command fails or the last command ends. (If any command fails, the shell stops executing the command line).

In the following example, the shell runs the next command only if the current command has failed:

$ *cmd1* || *cmd2*
$ _

If *cmd1* fails, the shell runs *cmd2*. If *cmd1* succeeds, the shell stops executing the command line.

For example, suppose that the command **mysort** is a sorting program that creates a temporary file (**mysort.tmp**) during its sorting process. When **mysort** finishes successfully, it cleans up after itself, deleting the temporary file. If, on the other hand, **mysort** fails, it may neglect to clean up. To ensure deletion of **mysort.tmp**, use the following command line:

$ **mysort || rm mysort.tmp**
$ _

The second command, which deletes the temporary file, executes only if the first fails.

7–10   OSF/1 User's Guide

Using Pipes and Filters

A pipe is a one-way connection between two related commands. One command writes its output to the pipe, and the other process reads its input from the pipe. When two or more commands are connected by the | (pipe) operator, they form a pipeline. Figure 7-1 represents the flow of input and output through a pipeline. The output of the first command (*cmd1*) is the input for the second command (*cmd2*); the output of the second command is the input for the third command (*cmd3*).

Figure 7–1. Flow Through a Pipeline

cmd1 ⟶ cmd2 (filter) ⟶ cmd3 (filter) ⟶

A filter is a command that reads its standard input, transforms that input, and then writes the transformed input to standard output. Filters are typically used as intermediate commands in pipelines; that is, they are connected by a | (pipe) operator. For example,

ls -R | pg

causes the **ls** command to list recursively the contents of all directories from the current directory to the bottom of the hierarchy, and then to display the results. The **pg** command is the filter because it transforms the output from the **ls -R** command and displays it one screenful at a time.

Certain commands that are not filters have a flag that causes them to act like filters. For example, the **diff** (compare files) command ordinarily compares two files and writes their differences to standard output. The usual format for **diff** follows:

diff *file1 file2*

However, if you use the - (dash) flag in place of one of the filenames, **diff** reads standard input and compares it to the named file.

In the following pipeline, **ls** writes the contents of the current directory to standard output. The **diff** command compares the output of **ls** with the

General User Tasks

contents of a file named **dirfile**, and writes the differences to standard output one page at a time (with the **pg** command):

$ **ls | diff - dirfile | pg**

In the following example, another kind of filter program (**grep**) is used:

```
$ ls -l | grep r-x | wc -l
      12
$ _
```

In this example, the following takes place:

- The **ls -l** command lists in long format the contents of the current directory.

- The output of **ls -l** becomes the standard input to **grep r-x**, a filter that searches for the files in its standard input for patterns with permissions of **r-x**, and writes all lines that contain the pattern to its standard output.

- The standard output of **grep r-x** becomes the standard input to **wc -l**, which displays the number of files matching the **grep** criteria in the standard input.

To get the same results without using a pipeline, you would have to do the following:

1. Direct the output of **ls -l /user** to a file. For example:

   ```
   $ ls -l >file1
   $ _
   ```

2. Use **file1** as input for **grep r-x** and redirect the output of **grep** to another file. For example:

   ```
   $ grep r-x file1 >file2
   $ _
   ```

3. Use the output file of **grep** as input for **wc -l**. For example:

   ```
   $ wc -l file2
         12
   ```

OSF/1 Shell Overview

As the preceding cumbersome procedure demonstrates, using a pipeline is a much easier way to perform the same operations.

Each command in a pipeline runs as a separate process. Pipelines operate in one direction only (left to right), and all processes in a pipeline can run at the same time. A process pauses when it has no input to read or when the pipe to the next process is full.

Grouping Commands

The shell provides two ways to group commands, as shown in Table 7-3.

Table 7–3. Command Grouping Symbols

Command Grouping Symbol	Action
( ) (parentheses)	The shell creates a subshell to run the grouped commands as a separate process.
{ } (braces)	The shell runs the grouped commands as a unit. Braces can only be used in the Korn shell.

The following subsections describe the command grouping symbols of Table 7-3 in greater detail.

Using Parentheses ( )

In the following command grouping, the shell runs the commands enclosed in ( ) (parentheses) as a separate process:

$ **(cd reports;ls);ls**

The shell creates a *subshell* (a separate shell program) that moves to directory **reports** and lists the files in that directory. After the subshell

OSF/1 User's Guide   7–13

General User Tasks

process is complete, the shell lists the files in the current directory (**ls**).

If this command were written without the ( ), the original shell would move to directory **reports**, list the files in that directory, and then list the files in that directory again. There would be no subshell and no separate process for the **cd reports;ls** command.

The shell recognizes the ( ) wherever they occur in the command line. To use parentheses literally (that is, without their command-grouping action), quote them by placing a \ (backslash) immediately before either the ((open parenthesis) or the) (close parenthesis), for example, \(. For more information on quoting in the shell, see "Quoting" later in this chapter.

Using Braces { }

Using { } (braces) is valid only in the Korn shell.

When commands are grouped in { }, the shell executes them without creating a subshell. In the following example, the shell runs **date**, writing its output to the file **today.grp**, and then runs **who**, writing its output to **today.grp**:

```
$ { date; who }>today.grp
$ _
```

If the commands were not grouped together with braces, the shell would write the output of **date** to the display and the output of **who** to the file.

The shell recognizes { } in pipelines and command lists, but only if the { (left brace) is the first character on a command line.

Quoting

Reserved characters are characters such as < > |& ? and * that have a special meaning to the shell. See Chapter 8 for lists of reserved characters for each OSF/1 shell. To use a reserved character literally (that is, without its special meaning), quote it with one of the three shell quoting conventions, as shown in Table 7-4.

OSF/1 Shell Overview

Table 7–4. Shell Quoting Conventions

Quoting Convention	Action
\	(Backslash) Quotes a single character.
' '	(Single quotes) Quotes a string of characters (except the single quotation marks themselves).
" "	(Double quotes) Quotes a string of characters (except $, ', and \).

The following subsections describe the quoting conventions of Table 7-4 in greater detail.

Using the Backslash (\)

To quote a single character, place a \ (backslash) immediately before that character, as in the following:

$ **echo \?**
?
$ _

This command displays a single **?** (question mark) character.

Using Single Quotes (' ')

When you enclose a string of characters in single quotes, the shell takes every character in the string (except the ' itself) literally.

OSF/1 User's Guide   7–15

General User Tasks

Single quotes are useful when you do not wish the shell to interpret

- Reserved characters such as **$** (dollar sign), **`** (grave accent), and **** (backslash) so that they keep their special meanings
- Variable names

The following example shows how single quotes are used when you wish to display a variable name without having it be interpreted by the shell:

$ echo 'The value of $USER is' $USER
```
The value of $USER is amy
$ _
```

The **echo** command displays the variable name **$USER** when it appears within single quotes, but interprets the value of **$USER** when it appears outside the single quotes.

For information on variable assignments, see "Setting Variables" later in this chapter.

Using Double Quotes (" ")

Double quotes provide a special form of quoting. Within double quotes, the reserved characters **$** (dollar sign), **`** (grave accent), and **** (backslash) keep their special meanings. The shell takes literally all other characters within the double quotes. Double quotes are most frequently used in variable assignments.

The following example shows how double quotes are used when you wish to display brackets (normally reserved characters) in a message containing the value of the shell variable:

echo "<<Current shell is $SHELL>>"
```
<<Current shell is /usr/bin/csh>>
$ _
```

For information on variable assignments, see "Setting Variables."

The Shell Environment

Whenever you log in, your default shell defines and maintains a unique working environment for you. Your environment defines such characteristics as your user identity, where you are working on the system, and what commands you are running.

Your working environment is defined by both environment variables and shell variables. Your default login shell uses environment variables and passes them to all processes and subshells that you create. Shell variables are valid only for your current shell and are not passed to subshells.

The following subsections discuss the shell environment, how it is configured, and how you can tailor it.

The login Program

Whenever you log in, the program **login** is run. This program actually begins your login session using data stored in the **/etc/passwd** file, which contains one line of information about each system user. The **/etc/password** file contains your username, your password (in encrypted form), your home directory, and your default shell. For more information, see "The **/etc/passwd** File" in Chapter 5.

The **login** program runs after you enter your username at the `login:` prompt. It performs the following functions:

- Displays the `Password:` prompt (if you have a password)
- Verifies the username and password you entered against what is contained in the **/etc/passwd** file
- Assigns default values to the shell environment
- Starts running the shell process
- Runs system login scripts and your personal login scripts. See "Login Scripts and Your Environment" later in this chapter for more information.

General User Tasks

Environment Variables

Your shell environment defines and maintains a unique working environment for you. Most of the characteristics of your working environment are defined by environment variables.

Environment variables consist of a name and a value. For example, the environment variable for your login directory is named **HOME**, and its value is defined automatically when you log in.

Some environment variables are set by the **login** program, and some can be defined in the login script that is appropriate for your shell. For example, if you use the C shell, environment variables will typically be set in the **.cshrc** login script. For more information on login scripts, see ''Login Scripts and Your Environment'' later in this chapter.

Table 7-5 lists selected environment variables that can be used by all OSF/1 shells. Most of the values of these variables are set during the login process, and are then passed to each process that you create during your session.

Table 7–5. Selected Shell Environment Variables

Environment Variable	Description
HOME	Specifies the name of your login directory, the directory that becomes the current directory upon completion of a login. The **cd** command uses the value of **HOME** as its default value. The **login** program sets this variable, and it cannot be changed by the individual user.
LOGNAME	Specifies your login name; for example, **chang**.
MAIL	Specifies the pathname of the file used by the mail system to detect the arrival of new mail. The **login** program sets this variable based upon your username.

7–18   OSF/1 User's Guide

OSF/1 Shell Overview

Environment Variable	Description
PATH	Specifies the directories and the directory order that your system uses to search for, find, and execute commands. This variable is set by your login scripts.
SHELL	Specifies your default shell. This variable is set by **login** using the shell specified in your entry in the **/etc/passwd** file.
TERM	Specifies the type of terminal you are using. This variable is usually set by your login script.
TZ	Specifies the current time zone and difference from Greenwich mean time. This variable is set by the system login script.
LANG	Specifies the locale of your system, which is comprised of three parts: language, territory, and character code set. The default value is the C locale, which implies English for language, U.S. for territory, and ASCII for code set. However, your system may specify another locale; for example, French Canadian. **LANG** can be set in a login script. This variable is one aspect of the internationalization features of the system. For more information on this variable and internationalization features, see Appendix C.
LC_COLLATE	Specifies the collating sequence to use when sorting names and when character ranges occur in patterns. The default value is the ASCII collating sequence. **LC_COLLATE** can be set in a login script. This variable is one aspect of the internationalization features of the system. For more information on this variable and internationalization features, see Appendix C.

OSF/1 User's Guide   7–19

Environment Variable	Description
LC_CTYPE	Specifies the character classification rules for the current locale that are used in the **ctype** functions. The default value is the classification for ASCII characters. **LC_TYPE** can be set in a login script. This variable is one aspect of the internationalization features of the system. For more information on this variable and internationalization features, see Appendix C.
LC_MESSAGES	Specifies the language in which system messages will appear. In addition, this variable specifies the strings that indicate "yes" and "no" in yes/no prompts. The default value is American English, but your system may specify another language. This variable is one aspect of the internationalization features of the system. For more information on this variable and internationalization features, see Appendix C.
LC_MONETARY	Specifies the monetary format for your system. The default value is the American format for monetary figures. **LC_MONETARY** can be set in a login script. This variable is one aspect of the internationalization features of the system. For more information on this variable and internationalization features, see Appendix C.
LC_NUMERIC	Specifies the numeric format for your system. The default value is the American format for numeric quantities. **LC_NUMERIC** can be set in a login script. This variable is one aspect of the internationalization features of the system. For more information on this variable and internationalization features, see Appendix C.
LC_TIME	Specifies the date and time format for your system. The default value is the American format for dates and times. **LC_TIME** can be

OSF/1 Shell Overview

Environment Variable	Description
	set in a login script. This variable is one aspect of the internationalization features of the system. For more information on this variable and internationalization features, see Appendix C.
LC_ALL	Specifies the behavior for all aspects of the locale. If set, this variable overrides all other locale-specific environment variables. Use this variable with care only. This variable is one aspect of the internationalization features of the system. For more information on this variable and internationalization features, see Appendix C.

Many of these environment variables can be set during the login process by the appropriate login script (see "Login Scripts and Your Environment" later in this chapter). However, you may reset them as well as set those for which no default values have been provided. See "Setting Variables" later in this chapter for more information.

You may also create your own environment variables. For example, some systems have more than one mail program available to users. Assume that **mail**, **mh**, and **elm** are available on your system and that each has its own pathname. As a result, you could define a variable for the pathname of each mail program.

For more information about environment variables specific to each OSF/1 shell, see Chapter 8. For a complete list of OSF/1 shell environment variables, see the **bsh**, **csh**, and **ksh** reference pages.

Shell Variables

Shell variables are valid only for your current shell and are not passed to subshells. Consequently, they can be used only in the shell in which they are defined. In other words, they may be thought of as "local variables."

For example, the C and Korn shells allow you to store commands in a command history buffer so that you can display and reexecute them at any time. As a result, you can set the **history** variable (C shell) and the **HISTSIZE** variable (Korn shell) to store any number of commands you wish.

You may also create your own shell variables. For example, some mail programs use the **pager** variable to define the program that displays mail. Suppose that your mail program is **mhrmail**. You could define the **pager** variable to use the **more** program to display your mail.

For all information on how to set shell variables, see ''Setting Variables'' later in this chapter.

Login Scripts and Your Environment

A login script is a file that contains commands that set up your user environment. There are two kinds of login scripts:

- System login scripts for all users of a particular shell.

  These scripts create a default environment for all users and are maintained by your system administrator. The Bourne and Korn shells use a system login script called **/etc/profile**. The C shell uses a script called **/etc/csh.login**. See Table 7-6 for the pathnames of system login scripts. When you log in, the commands in the system login script are executed first.

- Local login scripts in your default login directory.

  These scripts allow you to tailor your environment, and you maintain the appropriate file. For example, you could change the default search path or shell prompt.

  The Bourne shell uses a file called **.profile**, which sets both environment and shell variables. The Korn shell uses two login scripts: **.profile**, which sets environment variables, and **.kshrc**, which sets shell variables. The C shell also uses two login scripts: **.login**, which sets environment variables, and **.cshrc**, which sets shell variables. The commands in the local login script are executed after the system login script.

  Creating your own login script is not mandatory because the system login script for your shell is sufficient for most operations. In some

OSF/1 Shell Overview

installations, your system administrator may have created a local login script that you can modify by using any editor. See Table 7-6 for the pathnames of local login scripts.

When you are new to the system, you may wish to use the default environment established for you. However, as you become more familiar with the system, you may wish to create or modify your own login script.

Table 7-6 lists the system login and local login scripts for each OSF/1 shell. All scripts run whenever you log into your system. In addition, the login scripts that end in **rc** run whenever the current shell creates a subshell. For example, when you enter **csh** at any shell prompt, the **.cshrc** file executes and a C shell subshell is created.

Table 7-6. System and Local Login Scripts

Shell	Pathname	System Login Script	Local Login Script
Bourne	/usr/bin/bsh	/etc/profile	.profile
Korn	/usr/bin/ksh	/etc/profile	.profile .ksh
C	/usr/bin/csh	/etc/csh.login	.cshrc .login

To verify whether you have any local login scripts in your home directory, use the **ls -a** command. This command displays all files that begin with a . (dot) as well as all other entries.

The following customization features are commonly set in login scripts:

- Terminal characteristics
- Search path and other environment variables
- Shell variables
- Maximum permissions for new files with **umask** (see Chapter 5)
- Allowing or stopping messages to your workstation
- The trap command (Bourne and Korn shells only)
- Command aliases, history variables (C and Korn shells only)
- Displaying system status information and other messages

General User Tasks

- Checking for mail
- Checking for news

It is a good idea to check the contents of your system login script so that you can avoid duplication in your local login script. For example, if your system login script checks for news, there is no need to do the same in your local login script.

See Chapter 8 for specific examples of Bourne, Korn, and C login scripts.

Using Variables

All OSF/1 shells use environment and shell variables to define user environment characteristics. As part of the set-up process, your system administrator has provided default environment and shell variable values in the appropriate login scripts.

For most users, the default environment and shell variable values are sufficient. As you become more familiar with the system, however, you may wish to modify some values. For example, you may wish to reset the variable that defines your shell prompt so that it is more personalized. Or you may wish to set a shell variable that specifies a very long directory pathname so that you can save time keying commands that use the directory (see examples in "Setting Variables" in the next section). Or you may find setting variables useful when writing shell procedures. In short, you will find that you can use variables creatively to enhance your work environment.

Note that some environment variables can be reset and some are read-only and cannot be reset. That is, these variables can be used, but not modified. For more information on this topic, see the appropriate shell reference page (**bsh**, **csh**, or **ksh**).

To reset environment variables as well as define your own shell variables, do one of the following:

- Edit the appropriate login script if you want these values set for you whenever you log in. For more information, see "Login Scripts and Your Environment" earlier in this chapter.

- Set them on the command line if you want these values set only for the current login session.

At any time, you may reference the value of any variable as well as display its value. You may also clear the value of any variable. The following subsections describe how to set, reference, display, and clear variable values.

Setting Variables

This section describes how to set variables in the Bourne, Korn, and C shells.

Bourne and Korn Shell Variables

In the Bourne and Korn shells, you set variables with an assignment statement. The general format for setting variables is the following:

name=value

The *name* entry specifies the variable name. The *value* entry specifies the value assigned to the variable. Be sure you do not type spaces on the command line.

For example, you can create a variable called **place** by assigning it a value of **U. S. A.** with the following statement:

```
$ place='U. S. A.'
$ _
```

From then on, you can use the variable **place** just as you would use its value.

For a more useful example, assume that you are using the Bourne shell and that you temporarily wish to personalize your shell prompt. The default Bourne shell prompt is a $ set by the **PS1** environment variable. As a result, to set it to What Shall I Do Next? >, enter:

```
$ PS1='What Shall I Do Next? >'
What Shall I Do Next? > _
```

If you wish to make the shell prompt available to subshells, enter:

What Shall I Do Next? > **export PS1**
What Shall I Do Next? > _

This What Shall I Do Next? > prompt will be in effect throughout your session. If you wish to make the new prompt more permanent, enter the same assignment statement and the **export** command in your **.profile** file. When you export a shell variable, it becomes in effect an environment variable.

For another example, assume that to save keying time, you wish to define a variable for a long pathname that you often use. To define the variable **reports** for the directory **/usr/sales/shoes/women/retail/reports**, enter the following:

What Shall I Do Next? > **reports=/usr/sales/shoes/women/retail/reports**
What Shall I Do Next? > _

To reference the variable, type a **$** before the variable name; for example, **$reports**. For more information on referencing variables, see ''Referencing Variables (Parameter Substitution)'' later in this chapter.

You can now use the variable **reports** in any commands you enter during this session. If you wish to make this variable permanent, enter the same assignment statement in your **.profile** file.

C Shell Variables

In the C shell, you set environment variables with the **setenv** command. The general format of the **setenv** command is the following:

setenv *name value*

The *name* entry specifies the variable name. The *value* entry specifies the value assigned to the variable. For a good example of setting the **PATH** environment variable, see ''How the Shell Finds Commands'' later in this chapter.

You set shell variables with the **set** command. The general format of the **set** command is the following:

set *name=value*

The *name* entry specifies the variable name. The *value* entry specifies the value assigned to the variable. For example, assume that you wish to change your prompt. The default C shell is %. As a result, to set it to Ready? >, enter the following on the command line:

% set prompt = 'Ready? >'
Ready? >

The Ready? > prompt will be in effect throughout your session. If you wish to make the new prompt permanent, enter the same command in your **.cshrc** file.

Setting Variables in All Shells

To set or reset environment or shell variables in any OSF/1 shell, do one of the following:

- Edit the appropriate login script if you wish these values set for you whenever you log in. For more information, see "Login Scripts and Your Environment" earlier in this chapter.

- Set them on the command line if you wish these values set only for the current login session.

Referencing Variables (Parameter Substitution)

To reference the value of a variable in a command line, type a **$** before the variable name. The **$** causes the shell you are using to substitute the value of the variable for the variable name. This is known as parameter substitution.

For example, assume that you have previously defined the variable **sales** for the long pathname **/user/reports/Q1/march/sales**, and that you wish to use this variable with the **cd** command. To do so, enter the **cd** command with the **sales** variable:

$ cd $sales
$ _

Then, enter the **pwd** command to verify that the directory has been changed:

```
$ pwd
/user/reports/Q1/march/sales
$ _
```

In this example, the shell substitutes the actual pathname of the directory **/user/reports/Q1/march/sales** for the variable name **sales**.

Displaying the Values of Variables

You can display the value of any variable currently set in your shell. Variable values can be displayed either singly or as a group.

To display the value of a single variable, use the **echo** command in the following general format:

echo $*variable*

The *variable* entry specifies the variable for which you wish the value displayed.

For example, assume that you use the Korn shell and wish to display the value of the **SHELL** environment variable. To do so, enter:

```
$ echo $SHELL
/usr/bin/ksh
$ _
```

For the Bourne and Korn shells, to display the value of all currently set variables, use the **set** command without any options. For example, the following example lists the currently set values in the Bourne shell (your output may vary):

```
$ set
EDITOR=emacs
```

OSF/1 Shell Overview

```
HOME=/users/chang
LOGNAME=chang
MAIL=/usr/mail/chang
PATH=:/usr/bin:/usr/bin/X11
PS1=$
SHELL=/usr/bin/bsh
TERM=xterm
$ _
```

For the C shell, to display the value of all currently set shell variables, use the **set** command without any options. To display the value of all currently set environment variables, use the **setenv** command or the **printenv** command without any options.

Clearing the Values of Variables

You may remove the value of any current variable. Please note, however, that the following variables cannot be cleared:

- **PATH**
- **PS1** (Bourne and Korn shell)
- **PS2** (Bourne and Korn shell)
- **MAILCHECK** (Bourne and Korn shell)
- **IFS** (Bourne and Korn shell)

For more information on these variables, see the appropriate shell reference page (**bsh**, **csh**, or **ksh**).

In the Bourne and Korn shells, you clear both environment and shell variables with the **unset** command. The general format for the **unset** command is the following:

unset *name*

The *name* entry specifies the variable name.

OSF/1 User's Guide   7–29

In the C shell, you clear environment variables with the **unsetenv** command. The general format of the **unsetenv** command is the following:

unsetenv *name*

The *name* entry specifies the variable name.

You clear shell variables with the **unset** command. The general format of the **unset** command is the following:

unset *name*

The *name* entry specifies the variable name.

For an example, assume that you use the Korn shell and have created a variable called **place** and have assigned it a value of **U. S. A.** To clear the variable, enter the following:

```
$ unset place
$ _
```

For more detailed information about setting and referencing variables, see the appropriate shell reference page (**bsh**, **csh**, or **ksh**).

How the Shell Finds Commands

Every time you enter a command, your shell searches through a list of directories to find the command. This list of directories is specified by the **PATH** environment variable. At many installations, system administrators specify default **PATH** directories for new users. However, more experienced users may need to change these **PATH** directories.

The **PATH** variable contains a list of directories to search, separated by **:** (colons). The order in which the directories are listed is the search order that the shell uses to search for the commands that you enter.

To determine the value of **PATH**, use the **echo** command. For example, assume that you are using the C shell and have entered the following:

% echo $PATH
/usr/bin:/usr/bin/X11
%

This output from the **echo** command (your output may vary) tells you that the search order of the preceding example is the following:

- The **/usr/bin** directory is searched first.
- The **/usr/bin/X11** directory is searched second.

Typically, **PATH** is set as an environment variable in the appropriate login script. In the Bourne and Korn shells, the **PATH** variable is normally set in the **.profile** script. In the C shell, it is normally set in the **.login** script.

If you wish to change the search path, you can assign a new value to the **PATH** variable. For example, assume that you use the Bourne shell and that have you have decided to use your own versions of some OSF/1 commands. As a result, you wish to add **$HOME/usr/bin/** to the search path. To do so, enter the following on the command line if you wish the new **PATH** variable value to be in effect for the current login session:

$ **PATH=$HOME/usr/bin:/usr/bin:/usr/bin/X11**

If you wish this new **PATH** variable value to be in effect for all future sessions, modify the **PATH** variable in your **.profile** script. When you next log in, the changes you have made in your **.profile** script will take effect.

Using Logout Scripts

You can create a logout script that automatically runs every time you end your session. Just like login scripts, the **.logout** file must reside in your home directory. You can use logout scripts for the following purposes:

- To clear your screen
- To display a logout message
- To run long background processes after you log out
- To run a file cleanup routine

To create a logout script, do the following:

1. Create a file called **.logout** in your home directory with a text editor.
2. In the file, place the commands you want to use. See "A Sample **.logout** File" later in this chapter for ideas.
3. Save the text and exit the editor.
4. Enter the following command to ensure that the **.logout** file has the appropriate executable permissions:

    $ **chmod +x .logout**
    $ _

Note that using a **.logout** file is not mandatory. Rather, it is a convenience that may enhance your work environment.

Logout Scripts and the Shell

If you are using the C shell, the **.logout** script executes automatically when you log out.

If you are using the Bourne or the Korn shell and wish to use a logout script, you must ensure that a special trap is set in your **.profile** script. A trap is a command sequence that looks for a specified signal from a terminal, and then runs a specified command or set of commands. If the following line is not set in your **.profile** script, you must add it with a text editor:

trap $HOME/.logout 0

This statement tells your system to run the **.logout** script whenever it receives a 0 (zero) signal, which occurs when you log out.

A Sample .logout File

The following example **.logout** file does the following:

- Clears the screen
- Displays a logout message that provides the name of your system, your username, and the logout time
- Displays a parting message
- Runs a file cleanup routine in the background after you log out

Note that lines beginning with **#** (the number sign) are comment lines that describe the commands below them.

```
# Clear the screen
clear

# Display the name of your system, your username,
# and the time and date that you logged out
echo 'hostname' :  'whoami' logged out on 'date'

# Runs the find command in the background. This command
# searches your login directory hierarchy for all
# temporary files that have not been accessed in
# 7 days, and then deletes them.
find ~ -name '*.tmp' -atime +7 -exec rm {} \; &

# A parting message
echo "Good Day. Come Back Soon"
```

General User Tasks

Using Shell Procedures

In addition to running commands from the command line, the shell can read and run commands contained in a file. Such a file is called a shell procedure or shell script.

Shell procedures are easy to develop, and using them can help you work more efficiently. For example, you may find shell procedures useful because you can place frequently used commands in one file, and then execute them by entering only the name of the procedure. As a result, they are useful for doing repetitious tasks that would normally require entering a number of commands on the command line.

Furthermore, because shell procedures are text files that do not have to be compiled, they are easy to create and to maintain.

Note that each shell has its own native programming language. The following are some programming language features that apply to all shells:

- Storing values in variables
- Testing for predefined conditions
- Executing commands repeatedly
- Passing arguments to a program

For more information on specific programming features of your shell, see Chapter 8.

Writing and Running Shell Procedures

To write and run a shell procedure, do the following:

1. Create a file of the commands you need to accomplish a task. Create this file as you would any text file; that is, with **vi** or another editing program. The file can contain any system command or shell command (described on the **bsh**, **csh**, or **ksh** reference pages).

2. Use the **chmod +x** command to give the file **x** (execute) status. For example, the command **chmod g+x reserve** gives execute status to the file named **reserve** for any user in your group (**g**). See Chapter 5 for information on using the **chmod** command.

3. Run the procedure by simply entering its name. Enter the pathname if the procedure file is not in your current directory.

The following is a simple shell procedure named **lss** that sorts **ls -l** command output by file size.

```
# ! /usr/bin/csh
# lss: list, sorting by size
ls -l | sort -n +4
```

Table 7-7 describes each line in **lss**.

Table 7-7. Description of Example Shell Script

Shell Command	Description
#! /usr/bin/csh	Specifies the shell under which the procedure should run. See "Specifying a Run Shell" for more information.
#lss: list, sorting by size	Comment line describing the purpose of the procedure.
**ls -l	sort -n +4**	The commands of the shell procedure itself. This procedure lists the files in a directory (**ls -l**). Output from the **ls -l** command is then piped to the **sort** command (**| sort -n +4**). This command skips over the first four columns of the **ls -l** output, sorts the fifth column (the file size column) numerically, and writes the lines to the standard output.

General User Tasks

To run the **lss** procedure, simply enter **lss**. Sample system output looks similar to the following:

```
$ lss
-rw-rw-rw-  1 larry  system   65 Mar 13 14:46 file3
-rw-rw-rw-  1 larry  system   75 Mar 13 14:45 file2
-rw-rw-rw-  1 larry  system  101 Mar 13 14:44 file1
$ _
```

Note: When you run a shell procedure, your current shell creates or spawns a subshell. A subshell is a new shell your current shell creates to run a program. Thus, any command the shell procedure executes (for example, **cd**) leaves the invoking shell unaffected.

Specifying a Run Shell

At times, you may wish to specify the shell under which a shell procedure should run. This is because of possible syntactic differences between the shells but is especially true of differences between the C shell and the other shells.

By default, the OSF/1 operating system assumes that any shell procedure you run should be executed in the same shell as your login shell. For example, if your login shell is the Korn shell, by default your shell procedures will run in that same shell.

The ability to override the default is very useful for shell procedures that many users run because it ensures that the procedure executes in the correct shell, regardless of the user's login shell. To change this default run shell, include the following command as the first line of the shell procedure:

#! *shell_path*

The *shell_path* entry specifies the full pathname of the shell under which you want the procedure to run.

For example, if you wish a shell procedure to run under the C shell, the first line of the procedure should be the following:

#! /usr/bin/csh

Chapter 8
OSF/1 Shell Features

This chapter functions as a reference source for C, Bourne, and Korn shell features. Unlike other chapters of this guide that present conceptual and/or tutorial information, the purpose of this chapter is to provide very brief reference information about each shell. To get the most out this chapter, you should already be familiar with the introductory shell overview information in Chapter 7.

After completing this chapter, you should be able to do the following:

- Understand the main differences between OSF/1 shells
- Understand specific features of each OSF/1 shell
- Understand the specifics of login scripts for each shell

Comparison of C, Bourne, and Korn Shell Features

Table 8-1 compares C, Bourne, and Korn shell selected features. For detailed information on shell features, see the appropriate shell reference page (**bsh**, **csh**, or **ksh**).

Table 8-1. C, Bourne, and Korn Shell Features

Feature	Description	C	Bourne	Korn
Shell programming	A programming language that includes features such as loops, condition statements, and variables.	Yes	Yes	Yes
Signal trapping	Mechanisms for trapping interruptions and other signals sent by the OSF/1 operating system.	Yes	Yes	Yes
Restricted shells	A security feature that provides a controlled shell environment with limited features.	No	Yes	No
Command aliases	A feature that allows you to abbreviate long command lines or to rename commands.	Yes	No	Yes
Command history	A feature that stores commands and allows you to edit and reuse them.	Yes	No	Yes
Filename completion	A feature that allows you to enter a portion of a filename. The system automatically completes it or suggests a list of possible choices.	Yes	No	Yes

Feature	Description	C	Bourne	Korn
Command-line editing	A feature that allows you to edit a current or previously entered command line.	No	No	Yes
Array	The ability to group data and call it by a name.	Yes	No	Yes
Integer arithmetic	The ability to perform arithmetic functions within the shell.	Yes	No	Yes
Job control	Facilities for monitoring and accessing background processes.	Yes	No	Yes

C Shell Features

This section describes the following C shell features:

- Sample **.cshrc** and **.login** scripts
- Metacharacters
- Command history and aliases
- Built-in variables and commands

Sample .cshrc and .login Scripts

The **.cshrc** login script sets up your C shell environment by defining variables and operating parameters for the local shell process. The **.login** script defines variables and operating parameters that you want executed at the beginning of your session, and that you wish to be valid for all shell processes during the current login session.

When you log in, the OSF/1 operating system executes the **.cshrc** file in your home directory first, and the **.login** file second. The **.login** script is

General User Tasks

executed only when you log in. However, the **.cshrc** file is executed each time you create a subshell.

In the following **.cshrc** script, shell variables, command aliases, and command history variables are set. Table 8-2 explains every part of the script.

```
# Set shell variables
set noclobber
set ignoreeof
set notify
set autologout 600

# Set command aliases
alias h 'history \!* | more'
alias l 'ls -l'
alias c clear

# Set history variables
set history=40
set savehist=40

# Set prompt
setenv PROMPT = "[\!] % "
```

Table 8-2. Description of an Example .cshrc Script

Command	Description
Shell Variables	
set noclobber	Stops files from being overwritten. If set, places restrictions on output redirection > to ensure that files are not accidentally destroyed, and that >> redirections refer to existing files.
set ignoreeof	Specifies that you cannot use <Ctrl-d> to end your login session. Instead, you must use either the

OSF/1 User's Guide

OSF/1 Shell Features

Command	Description
	exit or the logout commands.
set notify	Informs you when background processes have completed.
set autologout 600	Logs you out automatically if you are idle for 600 seconds (10 minutes).
Command Aliases	
alias h 'history \!* | more'	Defines the **h** command that pipes the contents of the command history buffer through the **more** command. The \!* string specifies that all the history buffer should be piped.
alias l 'ls -l'	Defines a short name, **l**, for the **ls -l** command that lists directory files in the long format.
alias c clear	Defines a short name, **c**, for the **clear** command that clears your screen.
History Variables	
history=40	Instructs the shell to store the last 40 commands in the history buffer.
savehist=40	Instructs the shell to store the last 40 commands and use them as the starting history for the next login session.
Prompt Variable	
setenv PROMPT = "[\!] % "	Changes your prompt so that it tells you the command number of the current command.

In the following **.login** script, the permissions for file creation are set, the **PATH** environment variable is set, and the editor and printer are specified. Table 8-3 explains every part of the script.

OSF/1 User's Guide 8–5

General User Tasks

```
# Set file creation permissions
umask 027

# Set environment variables
setenv PATH=/usr/bin:/usr/local/bin:
setenv CDPATH .:...:$HOME
setenv EDITOR emacs
setenv MAILHOST boston
setenv PRINTER sales
```

Table 8–3. Description of an Example .login Script

Command	Description
File Permissions	
umask 027	Specifies the maximum permissions for all new files created. This command provides all permissions for the owner, read and execute permissions for members of the same group, and no permissions for all others.
Environment Variables	
setenv PATH /usr/bin:/usr/local/bin:	Specifies the search path. In this case, **/usr/bin** is searched first, and **/usr/local/bin** is searched second.
setenv CDPATH .:...:$HOME	**CDPATH** is a variable that sets the search path for the **cd** command. This variable assignment specifies that the **cd** command should search for the named directory in the current directory (**.**) first, in the parent directory (**..**) second, and the home directory (**$HOME**) third.

OSF/1 User's Guide

OSF/1 Shell Features

Command	Description
setenv EDITOR emacs	Specifies the **emacs** editor as the default editor when running a program that allows you to edit a file. For example, various mail programs allow you to use an editor to compose and edit messages.
setenv MAILHOST boston	Specifies **boston** as your mail handling system.
setenv PRINTER sales	Specifies the printer **sales** as your default printer.

Metacharacters

Table 8-4 describes C shell metacharacters (characters that have special meaning to the shell).

Table 8–4. C Shell Metacharacters

Metacharacter	Description
Syntactic	
;	Separates commands that should be executed sequentially.
|	Separates commands that are part of a pipeline.
&&	Runs the next command if the current command succeeds.
||	Runs the next command if the current command fails.
( )	Groups commands to run as a separate process in a subshell.

Metacharacter	Description
&	Runs commands in the background.
Filename	
/	Separates the parts of a file's pathname.
?	Matches any single character except a leading dot (.).
*	Matches any sequence of characters except a leading dot (.).
[ ]	Matches any of the enclosed characters.
~	Specifies a home directory when used at the beginning of filenames.
Quotation	
\	Specifies that the following character should be interpreted literally; that is, without its special meaning to the shell.
'...'	Specifies that any of the enclosed characters (except for the ') should be interpreted literally; that is, without their special meaning to the shell.
"..."	Provides a special form of quoting. Specifies that the $ (dollar), ` (grave accent), and \ (backslash) characters keep their special meaning, while all other enclosed characters are interpreted literally; that is, without their special meaning to the shell. Double quotes are useful in making variable assignments.
Input/Output	
<	Redirects input.
>	Redirects output to a specified file.
<<	Redirects input and specifies that the shell should read input up to a specified line.

OSF/1 Shell Features

Metacharacter	Description
>>	Redirects output and specifies that the shell should add output to the end of a file.
>&	Redirects both diagnostic and standard output and appends them to a file.
>>&	Redirects both diagnostic and standard output to the end of an existing file.
>!	Redirects ouput and specifies that, if the **noclobber** variable is set (prevents overwriting of files), it should be ignored so that the file can be overwritten.
E Expansion/Substitution	
$	Specifies variable substitution.
!	Specifies history substitution.
:	Precedes substitution modifiers.
^	Used in special kinds of history substitution.
`	Specifies command substitution.

Command History

The command history buffer stores the commands you enter and allows you to display them at any time. As a result, you can select a previous command, or parts of previous commands, and then reexecute them. This feature may save you time because it allows you to reuse long commands instead of reentering them.

You may wish to enter the following three commands in your **.cshrc** file:

- **set history=**n

    Creates a history buffer that stores the command lines you enter. The n entry specifies the number of command lines you wish to store in the history buffer.

OSF/1 User's Guide   8–9

- **set savehist=**_n_

    Saves the command lines you entered during the current login session and makes them available for the next login session. The _n_ entry specifies the number of command lines you wish to store in the history buffer when you log out.

- **set prompt=[\!] %**

    Causes your C shell prompt to display the number of each command line.

To see the contents of the history buffer, use the **history** command. The displayed output will be similar to the following (your output will vary):

```
[18] % history
   3 set history=15
   4 pwd
   5 cd /usr/sales
   6 ls -l
   7 cp report report5
   8 mv /usr/accounts/new .
   9 cd /usr/accounts/new
  10 mkdir june
  11 cd june
  12 mv /usr/accounts/new/june .
  13 ls -l
  14 cd /usr/sales/Q1
  15 vi earnings
  16 cd /usr/chang
  17 vi status
  18 history
[19] % _
```

To reexecute any command in the command history buffer, use the commands listed in Table 8-5. Note that each command starts with an ! (exclamation point), which tells the C shell that you are using commands in the history buffer.

Table 8–5. Reexecuting C Shell History Buffer Commands

Command	Description
!!	Reexecutes the previous command.
!*n*	Reexecutes the command specified by *n*. For example, using the history buffer shown in the previous display, **!5** reexecutes command number 5, **cd /usr/sales**.
!-*n*	Reexecutes a previous command relative to the current command. For example, using the history buffer shown in the previous display, **!-2** invokes command number **17**, **vi status**.
!*string*	Reexecutes the most recent command that has first characters matching those specified by *string*. For example, using the history buffer shown in the previous display, **!cp** invokes command number **7**, **cp report report5**.
!?*string*	Reexecutes the most recent command line that has any characters matching those specified by *string*. For example, using the history buffer shown in the previous display, **!?Q1** invokes command number **14**, **cd /usr/sales/Q1**.

The command history buffer also allows you to reuse previous command arguments as well as modify previous command lines. For information on these features, see the **csh** reference page.

Filename Completion

The C shell allows you to enter a portion of a filename or pathname at the shell prompt, and the shell will automatically match and complete the name. This feature saves you time when you are trying to display long, unique filenames. For example, assume that you have the file **meetings_sales_status** in your current directory. To display a long listing of the file, enter:

% **ls -l meetings<Esc>**

General User Tasks

The system displays the following on the same command line:

% **ls -l meetings_sales_status**

You can now execute the command by pressing **<Return>**.

For more detailed information on filename completion, see the **csh** reference page.

Aliases

The command aliases feature allows you to abbreviate long command lines or rename commands. You do this by creating aliases for long command lines that you frequently use.
For example, assume that you often need to move to the directory **/usr/chang/reports/status**. You can create an alias **status**, which will move you to that directory whenever you enter it on the command line. In addition, aliases allow you to make up more descriptive names for commands. For example, you could define an alias named **rename** for the **mv** command.

To create aliases, use the **alias** command. The general format of the **alias** command is the following:

alias *aliasname command*

The *aliasname* entry specifies the name you wish to use. The *command* entry specifies either the original command or a series of commands. If the *command* has more than one part (has spaces), enclose the whole expression in single quotes.

For example, to create the alias **status** that moves you to the directory **/usr/chang/reports/status**, enter the following:

% **alias status 'cd /usr/chang/reports/status'**
%

The usual way to define aliases is to make them a permanent part of your environment by including them in your **.cshrc** file. As a result, you can use the aliases whenever you log in or start a new shell. See ''Sample **.cshrc** and

.login Scripts'' earlier in this chapter for an example.

To display all alias definitions, enter:

% **alias**

To display the definition of a particular alias, enter:

alias *aliasname*

The *aliasname* entry specifies the particular alias for which you are requesting a definition.

To remove an alias for the current login session, use the **unalias** command. The general format of the **unalias** command is the following:

unalias *aliasname*

The *aliasname* entry specifies the alias you wish to remove.

To remove an alias for the current and all future login sessions, do the following:

1. Enter the following command:

   unalias *aliasname*

   The *aliasname* entry specifies the alias you wish to remove.

2. Edit the **.cshrc** file and remove the alias definition. Then, save the file.

3. Enter the following command to reexecute the **.cshrc** file:

   % **source .cshrc**
   % _

For complete information on using aliases with the C shell, see the **csh** reference page.

Built-In Variables

The C shell provides variables that can be assigned values. These variables can be very useful for storing values that can be later used in commands. In addition, you can directly affect shell behavior by setting those variables to which the shell itself refers.

Table 8-6 describes selected C shell built-in variables that are of the most interest to general users. For a complete list of C shell built-in variables, see the **csh** reference page.

Table 8–6. Built-In C Shell Variables

Variable	Description
argv	Contains a value or values that can be used by the shell or shell scripts.
autologout	Logs you off the system automatically if you are idle for a specified time. This variable is usually set in the **.cshrc** file. If you wish to disable **autologout**, specify the following: **set autologout = 0**.
cwd	Contains the pathname to your current directory. The value of this variable changes every time you use the **cd** command.
home	Contains the pathname of your home directory. The default value for this variable is specified in the **/etc/passwd** file.
ignoreeof	Specifies whether **<Ctrl-d>** can be used to log out from the system. If set, you must use either **logout** or **exit** to log out. If unset, you may use **<Ctrl-d>** to log out. This variable is usually set in the **.cshrc** file.
cdpath	Specifies alternative directories to be searched by the system when locating subdirectories with the **cd**, **chdir**, or **pushd** commands. This variable is usually set in the **.login** file.
noclobber	Specifies whether a file can be overwritten. If set, places restrictions on output redirection **>** to ensure that files are not accidentally destroyed, and that **>>** redirections refer to

Variable	Description
	existing files. If set, a file cannot be overwritten. This variable is usually set in the **.cshrc** file.
notify	Specifies whether you wish to be notified when a background process has completed. If set, you are notified; if unset, you are not notified. This variable is usually set in the **.cshrc** file.
path	Specifies the search path that the shell uses to find commands. This variable is usually set in the **.login** file.
prompt	Can be used to customize your C shell prompt. This variable is usually set in the **.cshrc** file.
shell	Specifies the shell to create when a program creates a subshell. This variable is usually set in the **.login** file.
status	Specifies whether the most recently executed command completed without error (a value of zero is returned) or with an error (a nonzero value is returned).

Built-In Commands

Table 8-7 describes selected C shell commands that are of the most interest to general users. For a complete list of C shell built-in commands, see the **csh** reference page.

Table 8–7. Built-In C Shell Commands

Command	Description
alias	Assigns and displays alias definitions. For more information and the command format, see the "Aliases" section earlier in this chapter.
bg	Puts a suspended process in the background. For more information and the command format, see Chapter 6.

General User Tasks

Command	Description
echo	Writes arguments to the shell's standard output. For more information and the command format, see the **csh** reference page.
fg	Puts a currently running background process in the foreground. For more information and the command format, see Chapter 6.
history	Displays the contents of the command history buffer. For more information and the command format, see the "Command History" section earlier in this chapter.
jobs	Displays the job number and the PID number of current background processes. For more information and the command format, see Chapter 6.
logout	Terminates the login session.
rehash	Tells the shell to recompute the hash table of command locations. Use this command if you add a command to a directory in the shell's search path and want the shell to be able to find it. If you do not use **rehash**, the command cannot be executed because it was not in the directory when the hash table was originally created.
repeat	Repeats a command a specified number of times. For more information and the command format, see the **csh** reference page.
set	Assigns and displays shell variable values. For more information and the command format, see "Setting Variables" in Chapter 7.
setenv	Assigns environment variable values. For more information and the command format, see "Setting Variables" in Chapter 7.
source	Executes commands in a file. This can be used to update the current shell environment. For more information and the command format, see the "Aliases" section earlier in this chapter and the **csh** reference page.

8–16 OSF/1 User's Guide

OSF/1 Shell Features

Command	Description
time	Displays the execution time of a specified command. For more information, see the **csh** reference page.
unalias	Removes alias definitions. For more information and the command format, see the "Aliases" section earlier in this chapter.
unset	Removes values that have been assigned to variables. For more information and the command format, see "Setting Variables" in Chapter 7.
unsetenv	Removes values that have been assigned to environment variables. For more information and the command format, see "Setting Variables" in Chapter 7.

Bourne Shell Features

This section describes the following Bourne shell features:

- A sample **.profile** login script
- Metacharacters
- Built-in variables and commands

Sample .profile Login Script

If your login shell is the Bourne shell, the OSF/1 operating system executes the **.profile** login script to set up your environment. The **.profile** login script variables that are exported are passed to any subshells and subprocesses that are created. Variables that are not exported are used only by the login shell.

In the following **.profile** login script, shell variables are set and exported, a trap is set for the logout script, and the system is instructed to display information. Table 8-8 explains every part of the script.

```
# Set PATH
PATH=/usr/bin:/usr/local/bin:
```

General User Tasks

```
# Export search path
export PATH

# Set shell variables
PS1='$LOGNAME $ '
CDPATH=.:...:$HOME

# Set up for logout script
trap "echo logout; $HOME/.logout" 0

# Display status information
date
echo "Currently logged in users:" ; users
```

Table 8–8. Description of an Example Bourne Shell .profile Script

Command	Description
Set Search Path	
PATH=/usr/bin:/usr/local/bin:	Specifies the search path. In this case, **/usr/bin** is searched first and **/usr/local/bin** searched second.
Export Search Path	
export PATH	Specifies that the search path is to be passed to all commands that you execute.
Set Shell Variables	
PS1='$LOGNAME $ '	**PS1** is the variable that specifies the Bourne shell prompt, and its default value is **$**. However, this variable assignment specifies that your prompt should be changed to the following: *username* **$**. For example, if your username were **amy**, your prompt would be the following: amy $.

8–18   OSF/1 User's Guide

Command	Description
CDPATH=.:..:$HOME	**CDPATH** is a variable that sets the search path for the **cd** command. This variable assignment specifies that the **cd** command should search for the named directory in the current directory (**.**) first, in the parent directory (**..**) second, and the home directory (**$HOME**) third.
Set Up Logout Script	
trap "echo logout; $HOME/.logout" 0	Specifies that your shell should display `logout` and execute your **.logout** script when the **trap** command captures the exit signal (0). For more information on the **trap** command, see "Logout Scripts and the Shell" in Chapter 7.
Display Status Information	
date	Displays the date and time.
echo "Currently logged in users:" ; users	Specifies that the shell display the users who are currently logged in.

Metacharacters

Table 8-9 describes Bourne shell metacharacters (characters that have special meaning to the shell).

Table 8-9. Bourne Shell Metacharacters

Metacharacter	Description
Syntactic	
|	Separates commands that are part of a pipeline.
&&	Runs the next command if current command succeeds.
||	Runs the next command if the current command fails.
;	Separates commands that should be executed sequentially.
;;	Separates elements of a case construct.
&	Runs commands in the background.
( )	Groups commands to run as a separate process in a subshell.
Filename	
/	Separates the parts of a file's pathname.
?	Matches any single character except a leading dot (.).
*	Matches any sequence of characters except a leading dot (.).
[ ]	Matches any of the enclosed characters.
Quotation	
\	Specifies that the following character should be interpreted literally; that is, without its special meaning to the shell.
'...'	Specifies that any of the enclosed characters (except for the &') should be interpreted literally; that is, without their special meaning to the shell.

Metacharacter	Description
"..."	Provides a special form of quoting. Specifies that the $ (dollar sign), ` (grave accent), and \ (backslash) characters keep their special meaning, while all other enclosed characters are interpreted literally; that is, without their special meaning to the shell. Double quotes are useful in making variable assignments.
Input/Output	
<	Redirects input.
>	Redirects output to a specified file.
<<	Redirects input and specifies that the shell should read input up to a specified line.
>>	Redirects output and specifies that the shell should add output to the end of a file.
2>	Redirects diagnostic output to a specified file.
Substitution	
${...}	Specifies variable substitution.
`...`	Specifies command output substitution.

Built-In Variables

The Bourne shell provides variables that can be assigned values. The shell sets some of these variables, and you can set or reset all of them.

Table 8-10 describes selected Bourne shell built-in variables that are of most interest to general users. For complete information on all Bourne Shell built-in variables, see the **bsh** reference page.

Table 8–10. Built-In Bourne Shell Variables

Variable	Description
HOME	Specifies the name of your login directory, the directory that becomes the current directory upon completion of a login. The **cd** command uses the value of **HOME** as its default value. **HOME** is set by the **login** command.
PATH	Specifies the directories through which your system should search to find and execute commands. The shell searches these directories in the order specified here. Usually, **PATH** is set in the **.profile** file.
CDPATH	Specifies the directories that the **cd** command will search to find the specified argument to **cd**. If **cd**'s argument is null, or if it begins with a **/** (slash), **.** (dot), or **..** (dot dot), then **CDPATH** is ignored. Usually, **CDPATH** is set in your **.profile** file.
MAIL	The pathname of the file where your mail is deposited. You must set **MAIL**, and this is usually done in your **.profile** file.
MAILCHECK	Specifies in seconds how often the shell checks for mail (600 seconds is the default). If the value of this variable is set to 0, the shell checks for mail before displaying each prompt. **MAILCHECK** is usually set in your **.profile** file.
SHELL	Specifies your default shell. This variable should be set and exported by your **.profile** file.
PS1	Specifies the default Bourne shell prompt, and its default value is **$**. **PS1** is usually set in your **.profile** file. If **PS1** is not set, the shell uses the standard primary prompt string.

Variable	Description
PS2	Specifies the secondary prompt string; that is, the string that the shell displays when it requires more input after you enter a command line. The standard secondary prompt string is > (a > symbol followed by a space). **PS2** is usually set in your **.profile** file. If **PS2** is not set, the shell uses the standard secondary prompt string.

Built-In Commands

Table 8-11 describes selected Bourne shell commands that are of the most interest to general users. For a complete list of Bourne shell built-in commands, see the **bsh** reference page.

Table 8–11. Built-In Bourne Shell Commands

Command	Description
cd	Allows you to change directories. If no directory is specified, the value of the **HOME** shell variable is used. The **CDPATH** shell variable defines the search path for this command. For more information and the command format, see "Changing Directories (**cd**)" in Chapter 4 and the **bsh** reference page.
echo	Writes arguments to the standard output. For more information and the command format, see "Sample **.profile** Login Script" earlier in this chapter and the **bsh** reference page.
export	Marks the specified variable for automatic export to the environments of subsequently executed commands. For more information and the command format, see "Sample **.profile** Login Script" earlier in this chapter and the **bsh** reference page.

General User Tasks

Command	Description
pwd	Displays the current directory. For more information and the command format, see "Displaying the Name of Your Current Directory (**pwd**)" in Chapter 2.
set	Assigns and displays variable values. For more information and the command format, see "Setting Variables" in Chapter 7.
times	Displays the accumulated user and system times for processes run from the shell.
trap	Runs a specified command when the shell receives a specified signal. For more information and the command format, see "Logout Scripts and the Shell" in Chapter 7.
umask	Specifies the maximum permissions for all new files created. For more information and the command format, see "Setting the User Mask" in Chapter 5 and "Sample **.cshrc** and **.login** Scripts" earlier in this chapter.
unset	Removes values that have been assigned to variables. For more information and the command format, see "Setting Variables" in Chapter 7.

Korn Shell Features

This section describes the following Korn shell features:

- Sample **.profile** and **.kshrc** login scripts
- Metacharacters
- Command history
- Editing command lines
- Filename completion
- Aliases
- Built-in variables and commands

Sample .profile and .kshrc Login Scripts

If your login shell is the Korn shell, the OSF/1 operating system processes the **.profile** login script in your home directory. The **.profile** login script defines environment variables. These variables are used by your login shell as well as any subshells and subprocesses that are created. The **.profile** login script is executed only when you log in.

The **.kshrc** login script sets up your Korn shell environment by defining variables and operating parameters for the local shell process. It is executed each time you create a subshell.

In the following **.profile** login script, global environment variables are set and exported, and shell variables are set. Table 8-12 explains every part of the script.

```
# Set environment variables
PATH=/usr/bin:/usr/local/bin:
ENV=$HOME/.kshrc
EDITOR=vi
FCEDIT=vi
PS1="'hostname' [!] $ "

# Export global variables
export PATH ENV EDITOR FCEDIT PS1

# Set mail variables
MAIL=/usr/spool/mail/$LOGNAME
MAILCHECK=300
```

General User Tasks

Table 8–12. Description of an Example Korn Shell .profile Script

Command	Description
Set Environment Variables	
PATH=/usr/bin:/usr/local/bin:	Specifies the search path. In this case, **/usr/bin** is searched first and **/usr/local/bin** searched second.
ENV=$HOME/.kshrc	Specifies **$HOME/.kshrc** as the login script.
EDITOR=vi	Specifies **vi** as the default editor for command-line editing at the shell prompt and for filename completion.
FCEDIT=vi	Specifies **vi** as the default editor for the **fc** command. For information on the **fc** command, see "Editing Command Lines" later in this chapter.
PS1="'hostname' [!] $ "	**PS1** is the variable that specifies the Korn shell prompt, and its default value is **$**. However, this variable assignment specifies that your prompt should be changed to the following: the output of the **hostname** command, followed by the command number of the current command, followed by the **$** (dollar sign). For example, if the name of your system is **boston**, and the current command is numbered **30**, your prompt would be the following: `boston[30] $ `.
Export Global Variables	
export PATH ENV EDITOR FCEDIT PS1	Specifies that the values of the **PATH**, **ENV**, **EDITOR**, **FCEDIT**, and **PS1** variables should be exported to all subshells.

8–26   OSF/1 User's Guide

OSF/1 Shell Features

Command	Description
Set Mail Variables	
MAIL=/usr/spool/mail/$LOGNAME	Specifies the pathname of the file used by the mail system to detect the arrival of new mail. In this case, the mail system would look in your username subdirectory under the **/usr/spool/mail** directory.
MAILCHECK=300	Specifies that the shell should check for mail every 300 seconds (5 minutes).

In the following **.kshrc** login script, shell variables, command aliases, and command history variables are set, as well as the permissions for file creation. Table 8-13 explains every part of the script.

```
# Set shell variables
set -o monitor
set -o trackall

# Set command aliases
alias rm='rm -i '
alias rename='mv '
alias h 'history \!* | more'
alias l 'ls -l'
alias c clear

# Set history variables
HISTSIZE=40

# Set file creation permissions
umask 027
```

General User Tasks

Table 8–13. Description of an Example .kshrc Script

Command	Description
Shell Variables	
set -o monitor	Specifies that the shell should monitor all background processes and display a completion message when the process finishes.
set -o trackall	Specifies that the shell should track all commands that you execute. Once a command is tracked, the shell stores the location of the command and finds the command more quickly the next time you enter it.
Command Aliases	
alias rm='rm -i '	Specifies the use of the **-i** option (which prompts you for file deletion) with the **rm** command.
alias rename='mv '	Specifies **rename** as a new name for the **mv** command.
alias h 'history \!* | more'	Defines a command that pipes the contents of the command history buffer through the **more** command. The **\!*** string specifies that all of the history buffer should be piped.
alias l 'ls -l'	Defines a short name for the **ls -l** command that lists directory files in the long format.
alias c clear	Defines a short name for the **clear** command that clears your screen.
History Variables	
HISTSIZE=40	Instructs the shell to store the last 40 commands in the history buffer.

8–28　　　　　　　　　　　　　　　　　　　　　　　　　　　OSF/1 User's Guide

Command	Description
Set File Creation Permissions	
umask 027	Specifies the maximum permissions for all new files created. This command provides all permissions for the owner, read and execute permissions for members of the same group, and no permissions for all others.

Metacharacters

Table 8-14 describes Korn shell metacharacters (characters that have special meaning to the shell).

Note: Before creating a **.kshrc** file in your home directory, make sure that the **ENV=$HOME/.kshrc** environment variable is set and exported in your **.profile**. Once this is done, the **.kshrc** login script will execute each time you log in and each time you create a subshell.

Table 8-14. Korn Shell Metacharacters

Metacharacter	Description
Syntactic	
|	Separates commands that are part of a pipeline.
&&	Runs the next command if the current command succeeds.
||	Runs the next command if the current command fails.
;	Separates commands that should be executed sequentially.

General User Tasks

Metacharacter	Description
;;	Separates elements of a case construct.
&	Runs commands in the background.
( )	Groups commands to run as a separate process in a subshell.
{ }	Groups commands without creating a subshell.
Filename	
/	Separates the parts of a file's pathname.
?	Matches any single character except a leading dot (.).
*	Matches any sequence of characters except a leading dot (.).
[ ]	Matches any of the enclosed characters.
~	Specifies a home directory when used at the beginning of filenames.
Quotation	
\	Specifies that the following character should be interpreted literally; that is, without its special meaning to the shell.
'...'	Specifies that any of the enclosed characters (except for the ') should be interpreted literally; that is, without their special meaning to the shell.
"..."	Provides a special form of quoting. Specifies that the $ (dollar sign), ` (grave accent), and \ (backslash) characters keep their special meaning, while all other enclosed characters are interpreted literally; that is, without their special meaning to the shell. Double quotes are useful in making variable assignments.

8–30   OSF/1 User's Guide

Metacharacter	Description
Input/Output	
<	Redirects input.
>	Redirects output to a specified file.
<<	Redirects input and specifies that the shell should read input up to a specified line.
>>	Redirects output and specifies that the shell should add output to the end of a file.
>&	Redirects both diagnostic and standard output and appends them to a file.
Expansion/Substitution	
${...}	Specifies variable substitution.
%	Specifies job number substitution.
'...'	Specifies command output substitution.

Command History

The command history buffer stores the commands you enter and allows you to display them at any time. As a result, you can select a previous command, or parts of previous commands, and then reexecute them. This feature may save you time because it allows you to reuse long commands instead of reentering them.

To see the contents of the history buffer, use the **history** command. The displayed output will be similar to the following (your output will vary):

```
[18] $ history
    3  ls -l
    4  pwd
    5  cd /usr/sales
    6  ls -l
    7  cp report report5
    8  mv /usr/accounts/new .
    9  cd /usr/accounts/new
```

General User Tasks

```
10 mkdir june
11 cd june
12 mv /usr/accounts/new/june .
13 ls -l
14 cd /usr/sales/Q1
15 vi earnings
16 cd /usr/chang
17 vi status
[19] $
```

To reexecute any command in the command history buffer, use the commands listed in Table 8-15. Note that each command starts with the letter **r**.

Table 8-15. Reexecuting Korn Shell History Buffer Commands

Command	Description
r	Reexecutes the previous command.
r *n*	Reexecutes the command specified by *n*. For example, using the history buffer shown in the previous display, **r 5** reexecutes command number 5, **cd /usr/sales**.
r -*n*	Reexecutes a previous command relative to the current command. For example, using the history buffer shown in the previous display, **r-2** invokes command number **16**, **cd /usr/chang**.
r *string*	Reexecutes the most recent command that has first characters matching those specified by *string*. For example, using the history buffer shown in the previous display, **r cp** invokes command number **7**, **cp report report5**.

For more information on reexecuting history buffer commands, see the **ksh** reference page.

If you want to increase or decrease the number of commands stored in your history buffer, set the **HISTSIZE** variable in your **.profile** file. This variable has the following format:

HISTSIZE=*n*

The *n* entry specifies the number of command lines you wish to store in the history buffer. For example, to store 15 commands in the history buffer, use the following command:

HISTSIZE=15

The Korn shell also allows you to edit current command lines as well as reuse those already entered in the command history buffer. To use this feature, you must know how to use a text editor such as **vi** or **emacs**. For information on these features, see the following section.

Editing Command Lines

The Korn shell allows you to list and/or edit the command lines in your command history buffer. As a result, you may modify any element of a previous command line and then reexecute the command line.

The command-line editing functions for the Korn shell are extensive. This section covers only the most basic functions. For more detailed information, see the **ksh** reference page.

To display the command history buffer and/or to edit its contents, use the built-in command **fc** (fix command). The **fc** command has the following two formats:

- **fc** [**-e** *editor*] [**-nlr**] [*first*] [*last*]

    This command format allows you to display and/or edit any number of command lines in your buffer.

    — The **-e** *editor* entry specifies the editor (usually **vi** or **emacs**) you wish to use in editing the command line. If you do not specify **-e**, the **fc** command displays the lines but does not allow you to edit them.

    — The **-n** flag specifies that you wish to list the command lines in the buffer *without* numbers. The **-l** flag specifies that you wish to list the command lines in the buffer *with* numbers. If you do not specify a line number or a range of line numbers, the last 16 lines you entered will be listed.

    — The **-r** flag specifies that you wish to list the command in the buffer in reverse order.

General User Tasks

— The *first* and *last* entries specify a range of command lines in the buffer. You may specify them either with numbers or with strings.

If you want to specify a default editor for the **-e** flag, define the **FCEDIT** variable in your **.profile** script. For example, if you want to make **emacs** your default editor, enter the following variable definition:

FCEDIT=emacs

- **fc -e -** [*old=new*] [*string*]

    This command allows you to immediately replace an *old* string with a *new* string within any previous command line.

    — The **-e -** entry specifies that you wish make a replacement.

    — The *old=new* specifies that you wish to replace the *old* string with the *new* string.

    — The *string* entry specifies that the Korn shell should make the edit to the most recent command line in the buffer containing the *string*.

The following section contains some examples of **fc** use.

Note that the Korn shell also allows you to edit individual command lines at the shell prompt by using a command set similar to the **vi** or the **emacs** editors. For more information on this feature, see the **ksh** reference page.

Examples of Command-Line Editing

This section contains examples that show you how to use the **fc** command to edit command lines.

Example 1: Displaying Command Lines in the Command History Buffer

To display command lines 15 to 18, enter:

```
$ fc -l 15 18
15  ls -la
16  pwd
17  cd /u/ben/reports
18  more sales
$ _
```

8-34   OSF/1 User's Guide

You may also list the same command lines by specifying command strings instead of line numbers, as in the following example:

```
$ fc -l ls more
15 ls -la
16 pwd
17 cd /u/ben/reports
18 more sales
$ _
```

Example 2: Editing and Executing Command Lines

To display and edit command lines 15 to 18 with the **vi** editor, enter:

```
$  fc -e vi 15 18
ls -la
pwd
cd /u/ben/reports
more sales
~
~
~
~
"/tmp/sh10268.3"  4 lines  40 characters
```

After making your edits, write and exit the file with the **:wq!** command. The command lines in the file are then reexecuted.

Example 3: Replacing and Reexecuting Command Lines

Assume that you have just entered the **echo hello** command, and now wish to replace **hello** with **goodbye**. To do the replacement and reexecute the command line, enter:

```
$ echo hello
hello
$ fc -e - hello=goodbye echo
echo goodbye
goodbye
```

For more detailed information on the **fc** command and command-line editing, see the **ksh** reference page.

General User Tasks

Filename Completion

The Korn shell allows you to enter a portion of a filename or pathname at the shell prompt. The shell will then automatically match and complete the name. If there is more than one filename or pathname that matches the criterion, the shell will provide you with a list of possible matches.

To activate the filename completion mechanism, define the **EDITOR** variable in your **.profile** file. For example, if you wish to use the **vi** editor, enter the following variable definition in your **.profile** file:

EDITOR=vi

To demonstrate how filename completion works, assume that your editor is **vi** and that you have the following three files in your current directory: **salesreport1**, **salesreport2**, **salesreport3**. To display a long listing and to activate filename completion, enter:

```
$ ls -l salesreport<Esc>=
1)  salesreportfeb
2)  salesreportjan
3)  salesreportmar
$ ls -l salesreport
```

The system redisplays your command, and your cursor is now at the end of **salesreport**. Assume that you wish to choose **salesreportjan**. Type **a** (the **vi** append command) followed by **jan**. Then press **<Return>**. The listing for **salesreportjan** will be displayed.

For more detailed information on filename completion, see the **ksh** reference page.

Aliases

The command aliases feature allows you to abbreviate long command lines or rename commands. You do this by creating **aliases** for long command lines that you frequently use.

For example, assume that you often need to move to the directory **/usr/chang/reports/status**. You can create an alias **status**, which will move

8–36 OSF/1 User's Guide

you to that directory whenever you enter it on the command line.

In addition, aliases allow you to make up more descriptive names for commands. For example, you could define an alias named **rename** for the **mv** command.

To create aliases, use the **alias** command. The general format of the **alias** command is the following:

alias *aliasname=command*

The *aliasname* entry specifies the name you wish to use. The *command* entry specifies either the original command or a series of commands. If the *command* has more than one part (has spaces), enclose the whole expression in single quotes.

For example, to create the alias **status** that moves you to the directory **/usr/chang/reports/status**, enter:

$ **alias status='cd /usr/chang/reports/status'**
$ _

The usual way to define aliases is to place them in your **.kshrc** file so that you can use them whenever you log in or start a new shell. See ''Sample **.profile** and **.kshrc** Login Scripts'' earlier in this chapter for an example.

To display all alias definitions, enter:

$ **alias**

To display the definition of a particular alias, enter:

alias *aliasname*

The *aliasname* entry specifies the particular alias for which you are requesting a definition.

The Korn shell allows you to export the aliases you create. Variables that are exported are passed to any subshells that are created so that, when you execute a shell procedure or new shell, the alias remains defined. (Variables that are not exported are used only by the login shell.)

General User Tasks

To export an alias, use the following form of the **alias** command:

alias -x *aliasname=command*

The **-x** flag specifies that you wish to export the alias. The *aliasname* entry specifies the name you wish to use. The *command* entry specifies either the original command or a series of commands. If the *command* has more than one part, enclose the whole expression in single quotes.

For example, to export an alias definition for the **rm** command, enter:

```
$ alias -x rm='rm -i'
$ _
```

You can enter the preceding command in one of two ways:

- By editing the **.kshrc** or **.profile** file if you want an alias exported whenever you log in

- By exporting an alias on the command line if you want the alias exported only for the current login session

To remove an alias for the current login session, use the **unalias** command. The general format of the **unalias** command is the following:

unalias *aliasname*

The *aliasname* entry specifies the alias you wish to remove.

To remove an alias for the current and all future login sessions, do the following:

1. Enter the following command:

   unalias *aliasname*

   The *aliasname* entry specifies the alias you wish to remove.

2. Edit the **.kshrc** file (or the file on your system that contains alias definitions) and remove the alias definition. Then, save the file.

3. Enter the following command to reexecute the **.kshrc** file:

   ```
   $ . .kshrc
   $ _
   ```

OSF/1 Shell Features

The Korn shell provides additional aliasing features that may be of interest to you. For complete information on using aliases with the Korn shell, see the **ksh** reference page.

Built-In Variables

The Korn shell provides variables that can be assigned values. The shell sets some of these variables, and you can set or reset all of them.

Table 8-16 describes selected Korn shell built-in variables that are of the most interest to general users. For complete information on all Korn shell built-in variables, see the **ksh** reference page.

Table 8–16. Built-In Korn Shell Variables

Variable	Description
HOME	Specifies the name of your login directory. The **cd** command uses the value of **HOME** as its default value. In Korn shell procedures, you can use **HOME** to avoid having to use full pathnames—something that is especially helpful if the pathname of your login directory changes. **HOME** is set by the **login** command.
PATH	Specifies the directories through which your system should search to find and execute commands. The shell searches these directories in the order specified here. Usually, **PATH** is set in the **.profile** file.
CDPATH	Specifies the directories that the **cd** command will search to find the specified argument to **cd**. If **cd**'s argument is null, or if it begins with a **/** (slash), **.** (dot), or **..** (dot dot), then **CDPATH** is ignored. Usually, **CDPATH** is set in your **.profile** file.
MAIL	The pathname of the file where your mail is deposited. **MAIL** is usually set in your **.profile** file.

General User Tasks

Variable	Description
MAILCHECK	Specifies in seconds how often the shell checks for mail (600 seconds is the default). If the value of this variable is set to 0, the shell checks for mail before displaying each prompt. **MAILCHECK** is usually set in your **.profile** file.
SHELL	Specifies your default shell. This variable should be set and exported by your **.profile** file.
PS1	Specifies the default Korn shell prompt, and its default value is **$**. **PS1** is usually set in your **.profile** file. If **PS1** is not set, the shell uses the standard primary prompt string.
PS2	Specifies the secondary prompt string; that is, the string that the shell displays when it requires more input after entering a command line. The standard secondary prompt string is **>** (a > symbol followed by a space). **PS2** is usually set in your **.profile** file. If **PS2** is not set, the shell uses the standard secondary prompt string.
HISTFILE	Specifies the pathname of the file that will be used to store the command history. This variable is usually set in your **.profile** file.
EDITOR	Specifies the default editor for command-line editing at the shell prompt and for filename completion. This variable is usually set in your **.profile** file.
FCEDIT	Specifies the default editor for the **fc** command. This variable is usually set in your **.profile** file.
HISTSIZE	Specifies the number of previously entered commands that are accessible by this shell. The default is 128. This variable is usually set in your **.kshrc** file.

Built-In Commands

Table 8-17 describes selected Korn shell commands that are of the most interest to general users. For a complete list of Korn shell built-in commands, see the **ksh** reference page.

Table 8–17. Built-In Korn Shell Commands

Command	Description
alias	Assigns and displays alias definitions. For more information and the command format, see "Aliases" earlier in this chapter.
cd	Allows you to change directories. If no directory is specified, the value of the **HOME** shell variable is used. The **CDPATH** shell variable defines the search path for this command. For more information and the command format, see "Changing Directories (**cd**)" in Chapter 4 and the **ksh** reference page.
echo	Writes arguments to the standard output. For more information and the command format, see the **ksh** reference page.
export	Marks the specified variable for automatic export to the environments of subsequently executed commands. For more information and the command format, see "Sample **.profile** and **.kshrc** Login Scripts" earlier in this chapter and the **ksh** reference page.
fc	Allows you to display, edit, and reexecute the contents of the command history buffer. For more information and the command format, see "Editing Command Lines" earlier in this section.
history	Displays the contents of the command history buffer. For more information and the command format, see "Command History" earlier in this section.
jobs	Displays the job number and the PID number of current background processes.

General User Tasks

Command	Description
pwd	Displays the current directory. For more information and the command format, see "Displaying the Name of Your Current Directory (**pwd**)" in Chapter 2.
set	Assigns and displays variable values. For more information and the command format, see "Setting Variables" in Chapter 7.
times	Displays the accumulated user and system times for processes run from the shell.
trap	Runs a specified command when the shell receives a specified signal. For more information and the command format, see "Logout Scripts and the Shell" in Chapter 7.
umask	Specifies the maximum permissions for all new files created. For more information and the command format, see "Setting the User Mask" in Chapter 5 and "Sample **.profile** and **.kshrc** Login Scripts" earlier in this chapter.
unalias	Removes alias definitions. For more information and the command format, see "Aliases" earlier in this section.
unset	Removes values that have been assigned to variables. For more information and the command format, see "Setting Variables" in Chapter 7.

Chapter 9
Useful Productivity Tools

This chapter describes two productivity tools that may enhance your work. After completing this chapter, you will be able to do the following:

- Use the **grep** command to search files
- Use the **find** command to locate files

Both the **grep** and the **find** commands provide extensive functions. As a result, this chapter does not provide detailed discussions of these commands. Instead, it provides a few simple examples that are likely to assist general users.

Searching Files for Text Patterns (grep)

The **grep** command allows you to search files for text patterns. You may use the command to search for the following kinds of text patterns:

- Specific text patterns, such "John Smith"

General User Tasks

- All kinds of regular expressions such as the following samples:
  - all lines ending in "1989"
  - all words beginning with "reports"
  - all names of employees whose last names are "Smith"

The **grep** command is very useful when you are trying to locate information that you know is in a file somewhere on your system.

The general format of the **grep** command is the following:

grep [*flag*] *expression file*

The *flag* entry specifies an option that modifies the operation of the command. Table 9-1 describes selected flags. The *expression* entry specifies the text for which you are looking. You may use pattern-matching characters (described in Chapter 2) to specify the *expression*. If the text is more than one word, enclose it in " " (double quotes). The *file* entry can be the name of the file, the relative pathname of the file, the full pathname of the file, or a list of files separated by spaces. You may also use pattern-matching characters to specify files.

As an example of using the **grep** command, suppose that you maintain the following employee telephone list files for your company:

- **empsales** (sales)
- **empmarket** (marketing)
- **empaccount** (accounting)
- **emphr** (human resources)
- **empad** (advertising)

To find the phone number of Mario Garcia, enter the following command:

```
$ grep "Mario Garcia" emp*
empad: Mario Garcia   X3871
$ _
```

As a result of the preceding command, you have learned that `Mario Garcia` is in the Advertising Department (`empad`), and that he can be reached at extension 3871.

Useful Productivity Tools

You may also use a number of flags in the **grep** command format to specify additional features. Table 9-1 explains several of these flags.

Table 9–1. The grep Command Flags

Flag	Action
-c	Displays the filename and the number of matching lines.
-i	Ignores the case of letters in searching for the specified test. That is, uppercase and lowercase characters in the input are considered to be identical (see Example 1 later in this section).
-l	Displays only the filenames that contain the specified text.
-n	Displays the filenames and line numbers of matching lines.
-v	Displays all lines *except* those that match the specified pattern. Useful for filtering unwanted lines out of a file if you redirect the output to another file (see Example 3 later in this section).

Because **grep** functions are so extensive, we can only provide a few examples of its usage. However, the following examples will give you some idea of how to use the **grep** command.

Example 1: Using the -i Option

Suppose that you want to search for all files that contain any information about a client of your company, a Mr. DeSantis. You realize that you have seen Mr. DeSantis's name spelled two ways: as "DeSantis" and "Desantis." Because the **grep** command is by default case-sensitive, you enter the following command so that the system can find any spelling of the name:

```
$ grep -i "Desantis" *
file1: DeSantis Enterprises
file2: Mr. DeSantis
file3: In response to your letter, Mr. Desantis
file4: Thank for your talk, Mr. Desantis
$ _
```

Example 2: Extracting Lines and Saving Them in Another File

Suppose that you maintain a file that lists everyone in your company by department. You have been asked to produce a list of everyone in your company who works in the Accounting Department. Instead of visually scanning the personnel file and then creating another file, you can enter the following command sequence to sort and display employees in the Accounting Department:

```
$ grep "Accounting" employees | sort >acctlist
$ more acctlist
Alicia Herstring         Accounting
Bob Beenie               Accounting
Sophire Smith            Accounting
$ lpr acctlist
$ _
```

Example 3: Deleting Lines and Saving the Output in Another File

Suppose that you maintain a file that lists everyone in your company by medical insurance carrier. You have been asked to produce a list of everyone not insured by Acme Insurance. Instead of visually scanning the medical file and then creating another file, you can enter the following command sequence to sort and print employees:

```
$ grep -v "Acme Insurance" medlist | sort >medlist2
$ more medlist2
Alice Herstring          Great Insurance
Bernard Smith            ABC Insurance
Bob Beenie               ABC Insurance
Connie Brown             Best Insurance
Cranston Applewood       Best Insurance
Randy Sparks             Great Insurance
$ lpr medlist
$ _
```

Example 4:

Suppose that you maintain a file that lists everyone in your company by hire date. You have been asked to produce a list of everyone who was hired at your firm between January 1983 and December 1989. Instead of visually

Useful Productivity Tools

scanning the employee file and then creating another file, you can enter the following command sequence to sort and print employees:

$ **grep "198[3-9]" employees | sort >emp80s**
$ **more emp80s**
```
Alice Herstring         September 1984
Bernard Smith           March 1988
Bob Beenie              July 1987
Connie Brown            February 1983
Cranston Applewood      August 1989
Randy Sparks            October 1986
```
$ **lpr emp80s**
$ _

Note the use of the bracketed range **[3-9]** in the first command line. This expression matches any *single* character that meets the qualifications expressed by the range.

The **grep** command has many more features. For complete information on the **grep** command and its options, see the **grep** reference page.

Finding Files (find)

The **find** command allows you to locate files by searching a specified directory and any subdirectories beneath it. You will discover that this command is useful for finding information that might be in any of a number of subdirectories on your system, especially when your filenames are a good indication of file contents.

The general format of the **find** command when attempting to locate a file and display its location is the following:

find *pathname* **-name** *filename* **-print**

The *pathname* entry specifies the directories you wish to search. The **-name** entry specifies that you wish to specify a *filename*. The *filename* entry can specify either a single file or can specify a number of files with the use of pattern-matching characters (as described in Chapter 2). If you wish to search for a number of files with pattern-matching characters, you must

General User Tasks

enclose the *filename* in " " (double quotes). The **-print** entry specifies that you wish to display the location of the file or files.

As an example of using the **find** command, suppose that you are user **chang** and wish to locate all the report files in your directory hierarchy. To do so, enter the following:

$ **find /usr/chang -name "report*" -print**
```
/usr/chang/reports88
/usr/chang/reports88/reportjan
/usr/chang/reports88/reportjan.tmp
/usr/chang/reports88/reportmay
/usr/chang/reports88/reportmay.tmp
/usr/chang/reports88/reportsept
/usr/chang/reports88/reportdec
/usr/chang/reports89
/usr/chang/reports89/reportjan
/usr/chang/reports89/reportmay
/usr/chang/reports89/reportsept
/usr/chang/reports89/reportsept.tmp
/usr/chang/reports89/reportdec
/usr/chang/reports90
/usr/chang/reports90/reportjan
/usr/chang/reports90/reportmay
/usr/chang/reports90/reportmay.tmp
/usr/chang/reports90/reportsept
$
```

You can also use the **find** command to search for files and then have a command executed on the files selected. The general format for this function is the following:

find *pathname* **-name** *filename* **-print** **-exec** *command* {} \;

The *pathname* entry specifies the directories you wish to search. The **-name** entry specifies that you wish to specify a filename. The *filename* entry can specify either a single file or can specify a number of files with the use of pattern-matching characters. If you wish to search for a number of files with pattern-matching characters, you must enclose the *filename* in " " (double quotes). The **-print** entry specifies that you wish to display the pathnames of the files acted on by the command. The **-exec** entry specifies that you wish to execute a command upon the selected files. The *command* entry

specifies the command you wish to execute upon the selected files. The {}
(braces) indicate that the output of the **find** command should be a
command-line argument for *command*. The **\;** (backslash and semicolon)
are an escape sequence. The semicolon specifies the end of the *command*,
and the backslash prevents the shell from interpreting the semicolon.

For example, suppose that you are user **chang** and want to delete all the
temporary files shown in the preceding example. Those files begin with the
word **report** and end with **.tmp**. To do so, enter the following:

$ find /usr/chang -name "report*.tmp" -print -exec rm {} \;
```
/usr/chang/reports88/reportjan.tmp
/usr/chang/reports88/reportmay.tmp
/usr/chang/reports89/reportsept.tmp
/usr/chang/reports90/reportmay.tmp
$ _
```

There are many more functions that the **find** command provides. For more
information, see the **find** reference page.

Part 2
Communications Tasks

Chapter 10
Using Simple Communications Facilities

This chapter shows you how to use simple facilities to communicate with users on your system or on remote systems.

After completing this chapter, you will be able to do the following:

- Determine who can currently receive messages or participate in online talk sessions
- Send messages to users logged in on the system
- Conduct online conversations with users on local or remote systems
- Control messages and online talk sessions for your display station

Sending Messages (write)

You can send a message to anyone currently logged in on the local system. To find out who is currently logged in, use the **who** command. For information about this command, see "Displaying Information About Users and Their Processes" in Chapter 6.

Once you know that the intended recipient of your message is logged in, use the **write** command to send the message. The **write** command is most useful for sending short messages that need immediate attention. For those messages that are longer, not as pressing, or need to be distributed to more than one user, use the **mail** command. For more information on the **mail** command, see Appendix D.

The **write** command has the following general format:

write *username*

The following procedure shows you how to send a message, using **me** as the sender and **chang** as the recipient:

1. Enter the **write** command at the shell prompt as follows:

   write chang

   This command sends an alerting sound and the following notice to Chang's screen:

   ```
   message from me tty04 Feb 8 10:32:45
   ```

   You may also receive an alerting sound, indicating that the connection is established and that you can enter your message.

2. Type the message. If your message is more than one line, every time you press **<Return>** a line will be sent to Chang's screen.

   A typical message on Chang's screen might be the following:

   ```
   Our presentation this afternoon will be at 2:00.
   See you in the conference room at 1:55 to discuss
   our strategy.
   ```

Using Simple Communications Facilities

3. When you have finished typing your message, press **<Ctrl-d>** to tell Chang that your message is complete and that you are ending the connection. The text EOF displays on Chang's screen, and your system prompt returns.

   Refer to the documentation you received with your system if pressing **<Ctrl-d>** does not produce the EOF text on the recipient's screen.

If the person to whom you sent the message is not currently logged into the system, the following message is displayed on the screen:

```
user is not logged on
```

If you receive this message, you can still communicate with the individual by sending a note with the **mail** command. This command sends a note to the recipient's mail box and it can be read upon demand. See Appendix D for information about sending mail messages.

Note: At some sites, you may be able to use the **write** command to send a message to users on remote systems. Ask your system administrator whether the **write** command runs on remote as well as local systems.

Having a Conversation

The **write** command allows you to have a conversation (sending messages back and forth) with another user. If you expect to have a conversation, both of you should agree on a symbol that indicates your message is completed. For example, you might both end your messages with the letter **o** for "over." (You cannot press **<Ctrl-d>** to denote "over" because it will terminate the connection.) You should also agree on a different symbol, such as **oo** for "over and out," to identify the end of the conversation.

When the conversation is over, press **<Ctrl-d>** to break the connection. If you inadvertently press **<Ctrl-d>** at any other time during the conversation, you or the user with whom you are conversing must reestablish the connection by again issuing the **write** command.

Communications Tasks

The following procedure shows you how to have a conversation, using **me** as the sender and **lucy** as the recipient:

1. Enter the **write** command as follows:

   $ **write lucy**

   This command sends an alerting sound and the following notice to Lucy's screen:

   ```
   message from me tty04 Feb 8 11:20:45
   ```

   You may also receive an alerting sound, indicating that the connection is established and that you can enter your message. A common convention is for Lucy to indicate that she is ready to receive your message by entering **write me**. This will produce the following message on your screen:

   ```
   message from lucy tty02 Feb 8 11:21:30
   ```

   However, if Lucy does not respond, you can still send your message.

2. Type the message. If your message is more than one line, every time you press **<Return>** a line will be sent to Lucy's screen.

3. When you have finished typing your message, use the **(o)** signal to tell Lucy that you are ready for her reply. A typical message on Lucy's screen might be the following:

   ```
   Ready to go to lunch? (o)
   ```

4. If she has not already done so, Lucy enters the following command to establish a connection:

   $ **write me**

   This will produce the following message on your screen:

   ```
   message from lucy tty02 Feb 8 11:22:23
   ```

   When Lucy has finished her message, she ends it with the **(o)** signal. Conversation can then continue as previously described until you or Lucy decides to end the conversation by using the **oo** signal.

Using Simple Communications Facilities

5. Press **<Ctrl-d>** to tell Lucy that you are ending the connection. The text EOF displays on Lucy's screen, and your system prompt returns. Lucy also presses **<Ctrl-d>** and the conversation is over.

There may be times when you may wish not to receive messages. For information on how to stop being interrupted by messages, see "Controlling Messages and Online Talk Sessions (**mesg**)" later in this chapter.

For more information, see the **write** reference page.

Retaining a Local Connection

After opening a connection to a specified user, you can continue to send messages to that user until you press **<Ctrl-d>**. In between messages to the original recipient, you can also send messages to other users on the system by prefixing the **write** command with an **!** (exclamation point), like this:

!write *username*

The exclamation point is the shell escape symbol. If you are already running one process started by a specific command, prefixing an exclamation point to a second command tells the shell to execute that second process while the first process continues to run. For example, entering **!write user2** instructs the shell to send a message to **user2** even though you are still conversing with **user1**.

Note: After you use the **!write** command and have finished entering your message, you *must* end the message to the second user with **<Ctrl-d>**. This is because you cannot connect with two users simultaneously.

You can execute any OSF/1 operating system command from this shell by preceding the command with an exclamation point. For example, if you are communicating with another user and need to look at a file mentioned in the conversation, you can enter the following to display the contents of that file:

!more *filename*

The following procedure shows you how to retain a connection with Amy while writing a message to another user, Tony:

1. Contact Amy with the following command:

   $ **write amy**

2. After receiving the alerting sounds indicating that the connection is established, enter your message. You can continue to communicate with Amy simply by continuing to type your messages and pressing **<Return>**. *Do not* press **<Ctrl-d>** until you want to break the connection.

3. While conversing with Amy, you can also send a message to Tony with the following command:

   !write tony

   Type your message to Tony, press **<Return>**, and then press **<Ctrl-d>** to break the connection.

4. You can now continue your conversation with Amy simply by typing the text of the message and pressing **<Return>**. (You do not have to issue the **write** command again because the connection established in step 1 is still open.)

5. When you are ready to break the connection to Amy, press **<Ctrl-d>**.

Sending a Long Message

If you want to send a long message, we recommend that you use the **mail** command, described in Appendix D, because it is most efficient. However, should you wish to, you can create a file to contain the text and then send that file with the **write** command. The following procedure shows you how to send a message contained in a file with the **write** command:

1. Create a file, using the text editor of your choice.
2. Write the text.

3. Use the **write** command to send the message, and enter the username of the recipient, a < (less-than symbol), and the name of the file. For example, to send a message file named **letter** in your current directory to **tony**, enter:

   $ **write tony < letter**
   $ _

System Errors

Sometimes the system cannot send a message. For example, if the recipient is not logged in, the message cannot be delivered. If, however, the failure is the result of a system error, the following message appears on your screen:

cannot write to *username* on *systemname*

If this message is displayed, see your system administrator.

Conducting an Online Talk Session (talk)

The **talk** command allows two users on the same system or on different systems to have an interactive conversation. During an online talk session, a send window and a receive window are opened on each user's display station. Each user is then able to type into the send window while the talk command displays what the other user is typing.

If you want talk to a user on your local system, enter the **talk** command in the following format:

talk *username*

If you want talk to a user on a remote system, enter:

talk *username@systemname*

Communications Tasks

If you want to talk to a user who is logged in more than once, the *ttyname* can be used to indicate the specific terminal name, as in the following:

talk *username ttyname*

When you initiate the conversation, a message is sent to the second user, inviting a conversation. If you have also specified a *ttyname*, the invitation message is sent only to the specified terminal. Otherwise, the invitation is sent to the login terminal of the second user. If a conversation is desired, the second user enters the **talk** command and specifies the first user's account name and system name (if a remote system).

Once an invitation is accepted, the two windows are displayed on each user's terminal. One window displays what is typed by the first user; the other window displays what is typed by the second user.

To end the conversation, either user can press **<Ctrl-c>** and the connection is closed.

In the following example, user **juan** (on system **concord**) wishes to have a conversation with **lucy** (on remote system **boston**):

1. Juan enters the following command to talk with Lucy:

   $ **talk lucy@boston**

   The following message is displayed on Lucy's display station:

   ```
   Message from TalkDaemon@concord at 14:25
   talk: connection requested by juan@concord
   talk: respond with: talk juan@concord
   ```

2. To accept the invitation, Lucy enters the following command to talk with Juan:

   $ **talk juan@concord**

   The **talk** command displays two windows (a split screen) on Juan's and Lucy's display stations so that they are now able to have an interactive conversation. One window displays Juan's text while the other window displays Lucy's text.

3. When Juan and Lucy wish to end the conversation, they both press <Ctrl-c> to return to the shell prompt.

There may be times when you may not wish to be involved in online conversations. For information on how to halt online talk sessions, see "Controlling Messages and Online Talk Sessions (**mesg**)" next in this chapter. For more information, see the **talk** reference page.

Controlling Messages and Online Talk Sessions (mesg)

Unless you specify otherwise, the system automatically sends you all the messages and enables all online talk sessions. Sometimes, however, receiving a message or an online talk request on your display can interrupt your current work, so you may occasionally prefer not to receive them. You use the **mesg** command to turn off the message and online talk facilities, to turn them back on again, and to check the current status of your display station. For more information, see "Using the **mesg** Command" next in this chapter.

The procedure that starts up the message and the talk facilities is included as part of the OSF/1 operating system. This start-up procedure contains a default value that lets you receive messages and invitations to online talk sessions. If you prefer not to do so, you can change this default. For more information, see "Changing the **mesg** Start-Up Procedure" later in this chapter.

Using the mesg Command

You can use the **mesg** command in the following ways:

- To check the current status of the message and talk facilities for your account
- To turn off the message and talk facilities, thereby rejecting them
- To turn the message and talk facilities back on, thereby again receiving messages

Communications Tasks

To check your current status, enter the **mesg** command by itself, without any options. To turn off the message and talk facilities for your account, enter the command with the **n** option. (There is an optional dash before the **n**.) To turn the message and talk facilities back on for your account, enter the command with the **y** option.

To check and/or change your message and talk facility status, perform the following procedure:

1. Check your message status by entering:

   $ **mesg**

   The system will notify you, as defined by locale, whether you can or cannot receive messages. In the United States, for example, the system displays the following message indicating that message and talk sessions are enabled for your account:

   ```
   is y
   ```

2. To change the setting, enter **mesg** [-]**y** (for affirmative) or **mesg** [-]**n** (for negative). For example, to reject messages and online talk sessions, enter:

   $ **mesg** [-]**n**

   When you change the setting to **mesg** [-]**n**, someone attempting to contact you through the message and talk facilities receives the message `Permission denied`. However, to enhance system security and efficiency, a person with superuser authority can still send you messages.

For more information, see the **mesg** reference page.

Changing the mesg Start-Up Procedure

The shell start-up procedures for the Korn, Bourne, and C shells included with the OSF/1 operating system contain a default value that lets you receive messages and conduct online talk sessions. If you prefer not to do so, you can change this default.

To change the default value so that you cannot receive any messages or online talk requests, add a **mesg [-]n** notation to the login script that activates the shell you use. You can find your login script in your login directory.

For detailed information about login scripts, see Chapter 8. In the meantime, see Table 10-1 for information about login scripts. To find out what shell you are using, match the prompt on your screen with the default prompt in the table. Then, look in your login directory to find the correct login script to edit.

Note: The shell prompt on your screen may vary from the ones listed in Table 10-1. If so, see your system administrator to find out your default shell. Then, you can edit the appropriate file.

For example, assume that your shell prompt is a $ (dollar sign). In Table 10-1, both the Bourne and the Korn shells display the dollar sign. To find out what login script to edit, look in your login directory. Assume that you find **.kshrc** in your login directory. You now know that you should edit this file to inhibit receiving message or online talk session requests.

Table 10–1. Login Script Information

Shell Prompt	Shell Name	Login Script to Edit
%	C Shell	.cshrc
$	Bourne Shell	.profile
$	Korn Shell	.kshrc

To modify your message and online talk start-up procedure, perform the following:

1. Enter the following command to move to your login directory:

   $ **cd**
   $ _

2. Use any editor to display the appropriate login script. If you wish to use the **vi** editor, see Appendix A.

   The system will display the contents of your login script.

3. If necessary, move the cursor to the end of the file. On a separate line, enter:

   mesg [-]n

4. Save the file and exit the editor.

Adding **mesg [-]n** to your login script overrides the default value in the shell start-up procedure so that you no longer automatically receive messages. Once you have turned the message and talk facilities off in your login script, they will remain off every time you log in. If you choose to turn them back on temporarily, you can do so by entering the **mesg [-]y** command on the command line. When you log out, however, they are both turned off, and they remain off until you enter **mesg [-]y** again.

Chapter 11
Using the UUCP Networking Utilities

This chapter shows you how to use the UUCP networking utilities. You use these utilities to communicate with systems other than your own.

After completing this chapter, you will be able to do the following:

- Identify and connect to remote systems
- Communicate with a remote system
- Run commands on a remote system
- Transmit files between the local system and remote systems
- Get status information about the remote connection or the file transfer

Note: Any UUCP networking utilities operation you perform is subject to the security features in effect on both the local and remote systems. In addition, your system may contain enhanced security features that may affect whether you can connect with other systems. If so, see your system administrator for details.

Introduction to the UUCP Networking Utilities

The UUCP networking utilities (UUCP) include a set of directories, files, programs, and commands that let you communicate with remote systems. UUCP enables two computer systems to communicate in three different ways:

- Over hardwired lines
- Over telephone lines using modems
- Over networks

UUCP enables you to perform tasks as background processes. This means that, once a UUCP task is running, you can use your workstation for other jobs. For example, you can send a file to a remote system for printing and, while it prints, edit another document stored on the same remote computer.

UUCP commands are also used to manage network-related tasks such as installing and maintaining the UUCP software. For information about these operations, see your system administrator.

Identifying Compatible Systems (uuname)

In order for a local system to communicate with a remote system using UUCP, the remote system must be connected to your local system. Additionally, the remote system must support UUCP. Systems that are based on the UNIX operating system normally have UUCP available. Communications via UUCP with a system not based on the UNIX operating system may require additional hardware or software. Once UUCP has been installed on your system, the **Systems** file (normally stored in the **/etc/uucp** directory) contains the list of remote sites you can access through UUCP commands.

Use the **uuname** command to identify compatible remote systems with which you can communicate using the UUCP networking utilities. The **uuname** command has the following general format:

uuname

The entries that your local system (the computer at which you are currently working) displays in response to the **uuname** command are the names your system manager has assigned to the computers linked by UUCP. For example, if you enter the **uuname** command, the names of compatible remote systems will appear in a list like the following (your output will vary):

```
$ uuname
venus
merlin
hera
zeus
research
cad
archives
$ _
```

You can use one option, the **-l** flag, which displays the name of your local system only. For example, the following command displays the name of a local system (your output will vary):

```
$ uuname -l
lowell
$ _
```

For additional information, see the **uuname** reference page.

Pathnames Used With UUCP Commands

Pathnames used with UUCP commands are essentially the same as pathnames used with OSF/1 operating system commands. However, UUCP pathnames often include the name of the remote system.

Keep the following conventions in mind as you specify pathnames when using UUCP:

- *Full pathname*. A full pathname lists all the directories along the route from the root directory to a specific directory or file, ending with the

Communications Tasks

name of the final directory or file. By convention, the elements in a pathname are separated by **/** (slashes).

- *Relative pathname*. A relative (or partial) pathname lists the route to a specific directory or file relative to the current directory. Relative pathnames may not always work with all UUCP commands. If you are having trouble accessing a file with a relative pathname, reenter the command using the full pathname to the file.

- ~*user pathname*. The ~ (tilde) is a shorthand way of identifying part of a pathname. In this case, ~*user pathname* refers to the login directory of the person identified as *user*.

- ~**uucp**/*filename*. In this case, the entries preceding the *filename* refer to the public directory on the designated system. UUCP uses this directory, named **/var/spool/uucppublic**, for sending and receiving information. The ~**uucp** entry is a shorthand way of specifying the public directory.

- *System_name!pathname*. This is the syntax UUCP uses to identify the path to a file on another system. The following example identifies the file **new** in the directory **/research** on a system named **merlin**:

    merlin!/research/new

- *System_name!system_name!pathname*. This is the pathname to a file on another system that goes through one or more other intermediate systems. You may think of the **!** (exclamation point) character as specifying the pathnames for nodes, very much as the **/** (slash) character specifies the pathnames for files.

    In the following example, the pathname specifies the file **cells** in directory **/research** on system **merlin**, which is reached first through system **zeus** and then through system **venus**.

    zeus!venus!merlin!/research/cells

    In the C shell, the **!** character has a special meaning. As a result, when specifying system names, you must type the name of the system, a **** (backslash), an **!** (exclamation point), and the pathname as follows:

    zeus\!venus\!merlin\!/research/cells

Communicating With a Remote System

UUCP has several commands that enable you to communicate with computers other than your own. Using these commands, you can do the following:

- Connect, over a hardwired asynchronous line, to
  - Another workstation
  - Another computer running an operating system that (like OSF/1) is based on the UNIX operating system
  - A computer running a system not based on the UNIX operating system, given proper hardware and software
- Connect, over a telephone line, to a remote system, or to a remote workstation, using modems at both ends of the connection
- Connect over a network to
  - Another workstation
  - Another computer running an operating system that (like OSF/1) is based on the UNIX operating system
  - A computer running a system not based on the UNIX operating system, given proper hardware and software

You can make remote connections over both a hardwired line, a telephone line, or a network using either the **cu** command or the **tip** command. Both **cu** and **tip** provide very similar functions, so it is a matter of choice which command you use. The **ct** command, on the other hand, is used only to connect to a remote terminal over a telephone line, by using a modem. The following sections describe the **cu**, **tip**, and the **ct** commands, respectively.

Note: Any connection operation you perform is subject to the security features in effect on both the local and remote systems.

Connecting to a Remote Computer With the cu Command

The **cu** command enables you to connect with a specified remote computer, log into it, and then perform tasks on it while you remain physically working at your local computer. You are thus logged in on both systems at the same time, and you can switch back and forth between the two computers, performing tasks on both concurrently.

If the remote system is running under the OSF/1 operating system, you can enter regular OSF/1 commands on the remote computer to change directories, list directory contents, view files, send files to the print queue, and so on. You can also use special local commands with **cu**, both to enter OSF/1 commands on your local system and to perform tasks such as transferring files between the two systems. You preface these commands with a ~ (tilde). For more information, see "Using the **cu** Local Commands" later in this chapter.

For example, suppose you want to transfer a copy of a file from your local system to a remote system for printing. While the first file is printing, you want to edit a second file on the remote system and then send a copy of that file over to your local computer. Following is an overview of the steps you would perform in an operation of this kind:

1. While logged into your own workstation, connect with the **cu** command to a specific remote system and then log into that system.

2. Enter the appropriate local ~ (tilde) command to transfer the file from the local to the remote system for printing.

3. Enter the OSF/1 **more** command on the remote system to display the file on the screen, or **lpr** to print the file. You can also enter any other OSF/1 command on the remote computer, such as **cd** to change to a different directory, or **ls** to list the contents of a directory.

4. Now you can edit another file on the remote computer while the first file is printing. Because the communications link remains open, you can also move easily between the local and the remote systems, checking the status of a job in progress on your local system, monitoring the printing job on the remote system, and so on.

5. When you have finished editing the second file on the remote system, use the appropriate local command to send a copy of the updated file back to your local computer. You can then continue with other tasks on both your local computer and the remote system.

Using the UUCP Networking Utilities

To connect to a remote computer, enter the **cu** command in the following format:

cu [*flag*] *system_name*

The *flag* entry specifies an option that modifies the operation of the command. The *system_name* specifies the system to which you wish to be connected. Table 11-1 describes **cu** command flags and entries.

This form of the command enables you to connect to a remote system over a hardwired line. If your system manager has set up UUCP so that you can communicate with remote systems over a telephone line, this version of the **cu** command also enables you to connect to a remote system using a modem.

Note: For two systems to be connected over a telephone line using the **cu** [*flag*] *system_name* form of the command, both systems must be attached to modems, and both systems must be set up for this type of communication. For information about customizing the files in the UUCP supporting database for remote communications, see your system administrator.

Most of the time you will connect to a remote system using the *system_name*, as shown previously. However, you may occasionally need to connect to a remote system whose name you do not know.

In that case, you can enter the **cu** command and connect with a remote system by specifying the name of the device (the hardwired line that actually connects your computer with the specified remote computer). The standard device name is prefixed by **tty**. Most hardwired communication lines have names that are variations of the **tty** device name, such as **tty00**, **tty01**, and so on.

When you enter **cu** with the name of a device, you must include the name of the device, or line, preceded by the **-l** flag. Use the following format:

cu -l*line*

The **-l***line* flag specifies the device to which you wish to be connected.

Communications Tasks

Occasionally, you may need to communicate with a remote computer that does not support UUCP. You can use a version of the **cu** command to establish such a connection under the following conditions:

- The remote computer must run under an operating system (such as OSF/1) that is based on the UNIX operating system.
- Both the local and the remote system must be connected to working modems.
- You must know the telephone number of the remote modem and have a valid login on that system.

Under these circumstances, you can connect to the remote computer by using the following form of the **cu** command:

cu [*flag*] *telno*

The *flag* entry specifies an option that modifies the operation of the command. The *telno* entry is the telephone number of the remote modem. Table 11-1 describes **cu** command flags and the *telno* entry. For examples of **cu** command use, see ''The **cu** Examples'' next in this chapter.

Table 11-1. The cu Command Flags and Entries

Flag/Entry	Description
-s*speed*	**Specify Transmission Speed**
	Specifies the rate at which data is transmitted to the remote system. The default transmission speed is generally "Any," which instructs **cu** to use the rate appropriate for the default (or specified) transmission line.
	Most modems operate at 300, 1200, or 2400 baud, while most hardwired lines are set to 1200 baud or higher. When transferring data (such as a file) between a local and a remote computer, you may occasionally need to specify a 300-baud transmission speed (the lower baud rate results in less interference on the line).
	Note that you should *not* have to set the transmission rate as an ordinary practice. The default rate, set

Using the UUCP Networking Utilities

Flag/Entry	Description
	when UUCP is installed and customized for your site, should be sufficient for most of your work.
-l*line*	**Specify Transmission Line or Device**
	Specifies the name of a device to be used as the line of communication between the local and the remote system. The default device is generally a hardwired asynchronous line, or a telephone line associated with an automatic dialer such as a modem. If your site has a number of lines of communication between local and remote computers, you may occasionally want to specify a particular device, or line, for your **cu** link.
	Note that under ordinary circumstances you should *not* have to specify a line or device. The default device established when UUCP is installed should be sufficient.
	However, if you want to connect to a remote computer and are not certain of the system name, you can enter the **cu** command with the **-l** flag and a variation of the standard device name **tty** (for example, **-ltty01** or **-lttyab**). Check with your system administrator for the device names used at your site.
	Because you use the **-l***line* flag when you do not know a system name, do not use the *system_name* entry in conjunction with the **-l***line* flag. If you do, **cu** connects to the first available line for the requested system name, ignoring the specified line.
system_name	**Remote System Name (for Hardwired or Modem Connections)**
	Specifies the name of the remote system, recognized by UUCP, with which you want to establish a connection. This is the assigned name of the system, such as **gumby**, **homer**, **phoebus**, and so on. UUCP establishes this connection either over a hardwired line, or over a telephone line using a modem, depending on how your system administrator has set

Communications Tasks

Flag/Entry	Description
	up communications between your local system and the specified remote system.
telno	**UUCP Number of Modem on an Unrecognized System** Specifies the telephone number you want to use to establish a remote connection using a modem. In this case, the remote computer uses OSF/1 (or another operating system based on the UNIX operating system), but it was not set up to communicate with your local system through UUCP. The *telno* entry can be either a local or a long-distance telephone number.

For detailed information, see the **cu** reference page.

The cu Examples

Example 1: Connecting to a System with a Known Name

To connect to the remote system **hera**, log in, and then display the contents of directory called **/user/sales/reports**, do the following:

1. Enter the following:

    $ **cu hera**

    The system displays the message

    ```
    Connected
    ```

    and the screen displays the login prompt for the remote system.

    When connecting to some remote systems, you may need to press **<Return>** one or more times before the remote system displays its login prompt.

2. Log in on the remote system.

    You are now logged in and ready to work concurrently on both your local system and the remote system **hera**. You can enter any OSF/1 command on the remote system simply by entering that command following the prompt.

3. To display the contents of a directory called **/user/sales/reports** on system **hera**, enter:

   $ **ls /user/sales/reports**

   If you also wish to enter a command on your local system, type a ~ (tilde) followed by an **!** (exclamation point) before the command. See ''Using the **cu** Local Commands'' next in this chapter for more information.

Example 2: Connecting to a System with an Unknown Name

Assume that you want to connect to a remote system using hardwired device **tty02**:

1. To connect with the remote system, enter:

   $ **cu -ltty02**

   The system displays the `Connected` message.

   When connecting to some remote systems, you may need to press **<Return>** one or more times before the remote system displays its login prompt.

2. When the remote system displays its login prompt, log in and begin your work. Remember that the connection to your local system is still open, so you can perform tasks on both systems concurrently.

Example 3: Connecting to a non-UUCP System (Local and Long Distance)

Assume that you want to connect to a remote system with a local telephone number.

1. To connect to a remote system whose telephone number is 461-1492, enter the following:

   $ **cu 4611492**

OSF/1 User's Guide   11–11

2. After the system displays the Connected message, press **<Return>**.

    When connecting to some remote systems, you may need to press **<Return>** one or more times before the remote system displays its login prompt.

3. When the remote system displays its login prompt, log in and begin your work.

In the following example, assume that you want to connect to a remote system with a long-distance telephone number:

1. To connect to a remote system whose telephone number is 1-612-223-1612, where dialing 9 is required to get an outside dial tone, and you want to transmit data at 300 baud, enter:

    $ **cu -s300 9=16122231612**

2. After the system displays the Connected message, press **<Return>** until the login prompt appears, and log in on the remote system.

Using the cu Local Commands

Once you have entered **cu**, connected to the remote system, and logged into it, you can enter regular OSF/1 commands on either the remote system or the local system. You can also enter special **cu** commands on the local system to transmit files between the two computers.

When you are logged into a remote computer using a **cu** link, enter OSF/1 commands on the remote computer simply by entering the command at the prompt. For example, to list the contents of a directory on the remote system, you would use the **ls** command.

However, suppose you want to display the contents of a directory on your local computer while linked to a remote system through the **cu** command. In that case, you must type a ~ (tilde) and an ! (exclamation point) preceding **ls** to indicate that **cu** should execute the command on your local system. You would therefore enter the **ls** command like this:

~!**ls**

Using the UUCP Networking Utilities

Another way to perform the same operation is to enter the ~ and ! (or %, which is used with three local commands), as in the following:

~!

The system displays the name of your local computer in this form:

~[*system_name*]!

You then enter the **ls** command. The complete entry, requesting a list of the contents of your current working directory on local system **hera**, would therefore look like this:

~[hera]!**ls**

Table 11-2 lists some local commands to use with the **cu** command.

Table 11-2. The cu Local Commands

Command	Description
~.	**Terminate Remote Connection**
	The ~. (tilde and dot) characters log you out of the remote computer and then terminate the remote connection.
	Entering the ~. characters always terminates the **cu** process. However, in some cases where you are connected to the remote system over a telephone line using a modem, ~. does not always successfully log you out of the remote system. For this reason, it is generally a good idea to press <**Ctrl-d**> to log out. Then enter ~. at the prompt and press <**Return**> to terminate the remote connection.
~!	**Escape to Local System**
	The ~! (tilde and exclamation point) sequence returns you to the local system after you have been working on the remote system. Type ~! at the prompt and then enter any command you wish. Then, when

OSF/1 User's Guide   11–13

Communications Tasks

Command	Description
	you want to return to the remote system, press <Ctrl-d> to leave the local computer and work on the remote system. Once you have established the **cu** connection, toggle back and forth between the two computers by entering ~! (to go from remote to local) and <Ctrl-d> (to go from local to remote).
~!*cmd*	**Execute** *cmd* **Locally**
	The ~!*cmd* sequence tells **cu** to execute the command on the local system. Once you have established the **cu** link, you can run commands on your local computer only by typing a tilde and an exclamation point before the name of the command.
~%cd *directory_name*	**Change Local Directory**
	The ~%cd *directory_name* command changes your local working directory from the current directory to the directory specified with the *directory_name* entry. If you do not specify a directory, **cu** changes to your home directory.
~%take *from* [*to*]	**Copy from Remote to Local**
	The ~%take *from* [*to*] command "takes" a specified file, copying it from the remote system to a specified file on the local system. If you do not type a name for the file on the local system (the *to* entry), the command copies the specified file from the remote to the local system under the same filename.
~%put *from* [*to*]	**Copy from Local to Remote**
	The ~%put *from* [*to*] command "puts" a specified file, copying it from the *local* system to the remote system. If you do not enter a target filename, the command copies the file to the remote system under the same filename. Note that, in the case of the ~%put command, the source file is on the local computer.

Note: You can transfer only ASCII files with the ~%take and ~%put commands. To transfer other types of files, use the **uucp** command, discussed in "Sending and Receiving Files

Using the UUCP Networking Utilities

(uucp)'' later in this chapter. In addition, neither ˜%**take** nor ˜%**put** checks to ensure that the system transfers the file(s) without errors. As a result, for the most reliable file transfers, we recommend that you use the **uucp** command.

For detailed information about the **cu** local commands, see the **cu** reference page.

The cu Local Commands Examples

Example Set 1: Running Commands on Your Local System

Suppose that you want to view a file on your local system. To do so, perform the following procedure:

1. Enter **cu** and log in on the remote system.

2. To display the contents of the file **status10** in the directory **/usr/msg/memos/** on your local computer **venus**, enter:

   ~!

   The system responds with the following prompt:

   ~[venus]!

3. Enter the **more** command and the name of the file (in this case, the complete pathname of the file):

   ~[venus]!**more /usr/msg/memos/status10**

For another example, assume that you want to change from one directory to another directory on your local computer. To do so, perform the following procedure:

1. Enter **cu** and log in on the remote system.

2. Now change from your current local working directory **/usr/msg** to directory **/adm/msg**, also on your local system **zeus**. Enter the following:

   ~%

OSF/1 User's Guide   11–15

The system responds with the name of your local system, prompting you to enter the command:

~[zeus]%

3. Enter the **cd** command and the name of the directory following the ~[zeus]% prompt:

~[zeus]%**cd /adm/msg**

Example Set 2: Copying Files from Remote to Local Systems

To copy the file **test1** from a remote system to your local system, perform the following procedure:

1. Enter the **cu** command and then log in on the remote system.

2. To transfer a copy of the file **/u/amy/test1** from the remote system to your local system, enter:

~%**take/u/amy/test1**

where **/u/amy** is also the name of an existing directory on your local system. This command copies the file to the local system under the same filename, **test1**.

If you wish to copy the same file but call it **tmptest** in a different directory on your local system, enter the following instead:

~%**take/u/amy/test1 /usr/dev/amy/tmptest**

Example Set 3: Copying Files from Local to Remote Systems

To copy the file **/usr/pubs/geo/ch2a** from your local system to a remote system, do the following:

1. Enter the **cu** command and then log in on the remote system.

2. To copy the file **/usr/pubs/geo/ch2a** from the local system to the remote system to which you are connected, enter:

~%**put/usr/pubs/geo/ch2a**

Using the UUCP Networking Utilities

where **/usr/pubs/geo** is also the name of an existing directory on the remote system. This command copies the file to the remote system under the same filename, **ch2a**.

If you wish to copy the same file, but call it **part2** in a different directory on the remote system, enter the following instead:

~%put /usr/pubs/geo/ch2a /u/geo/part2

Note: When you use ~%**put** and ~%**take** to transfer files, make sure that the target directory (the one to which you are copying the source files) already exists on the specified system. Unlike the **uucp** command, these **cu** local commands do not create intermediate directories during file transfers.

Additional Information About the cu Command

The following are some examples of **cu** features that you may find helpful. For more information, see the **cu** reference page.

- Remember not to use the *system_name* entry in conjunction with the **-l***line* flag. On the other hand, you can use the **-s***speed* flag with either the **-l** flag or the *system_name* entry, but not with both.

  If you do use the **-s***speed* flag with both the **-l** flag and the *system_name* entry, **cu** connects to the first available line for the requested system name, and ignores the specified line and speed.

- You can enter **cu** to connect system X to system Y, log into system Y, and then enter **cu** again on system Y to connect to system Z. You then have one local computer (system X) and two remote computers (systems Y and Z).

  You can run OSF/1 commands on system Z simply by logging in and entering the command. You can run commands on system X by prefixing the command with a single tilde (~*cmd*). You can also run commands on system Y by prefixing the command with two tildes (~~*cmd*).

  In general, a single tilde causes the specified command to be executed on the original local computer, and two tildes cause the command to be executed on the next system on which you executed **cu**.

- Remember that the ~! sequence takes you from the remote system to the local system. To return to the remote system from the local computer, press **<Ctrl-d>**.

Connecting to a Remote Computer With the tip Command

The **tip** command enables you to connect with a specified remote computer, log into it, and then perform tasks on it while you remain physically working at your local computer. You are thus logged in on both systems at the same time, and you can switch back and forth between the two computers, performing tasks on both concurrently.

If the remote system is running under the OSF/1 operating system, you can enter regular OSF/1 commands on the remote computer to change directories, list directory contents, view files, send files to the print queue, and so on. You can also use special **tip** "local commands" both to enter OSF/1 commands on your local system and to perform tasks such as transferring files between the two systems. You preface these commands with a ~ (tilde). For more information, see "Using the **tip** Local Commands" later in this chapter.

For example, suppose you want to transfer a copy of a file from your local system to a remote system for printing. While the first file is printing, you want to edit a second file on the remote system and then send a copy of that file over to your local computer. Following is an overview of the steps you would perform in an operation of this kind:

1. While logged into your own workstation, connect to a specific remote system and then log into that system.

2. Enter the appropriate local ~ (tilde) command to transfer the file from the local to the remote system for printing.

3. Enter the OSF/1 **more** command on the remote system to display the file on the screen, or **lpr** to print the file. You can also enter any other OSF/1 command on the remote computer, such as **cd** to change to a different directory, or **ls** to list the contents of a directory.

4. Now you can edit another file on the remote computer while the first file is printing. Because the communications link remains open, you can also move easily between the local and the remote systems,

Using the UUCP Networking Utilities

checking the status of a job in progress on your local system, monitoring the printing job on the remote system, and so on.

5. When you have finished editing the second file on the remote system, use the appropriate local command to send a copy of the updated file back to your local computer. You can then continue with other tasks on both your local computer and the remote system.

To connect to a remote computer, enter the **tip** command in the following format:

tip [*flag*] *system_name*

The *flag* entry specifies an option that modifies the operation of the command. The *system_name* specifies the system to which you want to be connected. Table 11-3 describes **tip** command-line entries.

This form of the command enables you to connect to a remote system over a hardwired line. If your system manager has set up UUCP so that you can communicate with remote systems over a telephone line, this version of the **tip** command also enables you to connect to a remote system using a modem.

Note: For two systems to be connected over a telephone line using the **tip** [*flag*] *system_name* form of the command, both systems must be attached to modems, and both systems must be set up for this type of communication. For information about customizing the files in the UUCP supporting database for remote communications, see your system administrator.

Occasionally, you may need to communicate with a remote computer that does not support UUCP. You can use a version of the **tip** command to establish such a connection under the following conditions:

- The remote computer must run under an operating system based on the UNIX operating system, such as OSF/1.
- Both the local and the remote system must be connected to working modems.
- You must know the telephone number of the remote modem and have a valid login on that system.

Under these circumstances, you can connect to the remote computer by using the following form of the **tip** command:

tip [*flag*] *telno*

The *flag* entry specifies an option that modifies the operation of the command. The *telno* entry is the telephone number of the remote modem. Table 11-3 describes **tip** command flags and the *telno* entry.

In general, however, you will probably find that the form of the **tip** command that connects you to a specified system is sufficient for your work.

Table 11-3. The tip Command Flags and Entries

Flag/Entry	Description
-baud_rate	**Specify Transmission Speed**
	Specifies the rate at which data is transmitted to the remote system. The default transmission speed is generally "Any," which instructs **tip** to use the rate appropriate for the default (or specified) transmission line.
	Most modems operate at 300, 1200, or 2400 baud, while most hardwired lines are set to 1200 baud or higher. When transferring data (such as a file) between a local and a remote computer, you may occasionally need to specify a 300-baud transmission speed (the lower baud rate results in less interference on the line).
	Note that you should *not* have to set the transmission rate as an ordinary practice. The default rate, set when UUCP is installed and customized for your site, should be sufficient for most of your work.
system_name	**Remote System Name (for Hardwired or Modem Connections)**
	Specifies the name of the remote system, recognized by UUCP, with which you want to

Using the UUCP Networking Utilities

Flag/Entry	Description
	establish a connection. This is the assigned name of the system, such as **gumby**, **homer**, **phoebus**, and so on. UUCP establishes this connection either over a hardwired line, or over a telephone line using a modem, depending on how your system administrator has set up communications between your local system and the specified remote system.
telno	**UUCP Number of Modem on an Unrecognized System**
	Specifies the telephone number you want to use to establish a remote connection using a modem. In this case, the remote computer uses OSF/1 (or another operating system based on the UNIX operating system), but it was not set up to communicate with your local system through UUCP. The *telno* entry can be either a local or a long-distance telephone number.

For detailed information about the **tip** command, see the **tip** reference page.

The tip Examples

Example 1: Connecting to a System with a Known Name

To connect to the remote system **ames**, log in, and then display the contents of directory called **/user/car/sales**, do the following:

1. Enter the following:

   $ **tip ames**

   The system displays the message

   ```
   Connected
   ```

   and the screen displays the login prompt for the remote system.

When connecting to some remote systems, you may need to press **<Return>** one or more times before the remote system displays its login prompt.

2. Log in on the remote system.

   You are now logged in and ready to work concurrently on both your local system and the remote system **ames**. You can enter any OSF/1 command on the remote system simply by entering that command following the prompt.

3. To display the contents of a directory called **/user/car/sales** on system **ames**, enter:

   $ **ls /user/car/sales**

   If you also wish to enter a command on your local system, type a ~ (tilde) followed by an **!** (exclamation point) before the command. See "Using the **tip** Local Commands" next in this chapter for more information.

Example 2: Connecting to a non-UUCP System (Local and Long Distance)

Assume that you wish to connect to a remote system with a local telephone number.

1. To connect to a remote system whose telephone number is 543-4592, enter the following:

   $ **tip 5434592**

2. After the system displays the Connected message, press **<Return>**.

   When connecting to some remote systems, you may need to press **<Return>** one or more times before the remote system displays its login prompt.

3. When the remote system displays its login prompt, log in and begin your work.

Using the UUCP Networking Utilities

In the following example, assume that you wish to connect to a remote system with a long-distance telephone number:

1. To connect to a remote system whose telephone number is 1-512-360-1522, where dialing 9 is required to get an outside dial tone, and you want to transmit data at 300 baud, enter:

   $ **tip -s300 9,15123601522**

2. After the system displays the Connected message, press **<Return>** until the login prompt appears, and log in on the remote system.

Using the tip Local Commands

Once you have entered **tip**, connected to the remote system, and logged into it, you can enter regular OSF/1 commands on either the remote system or the local system. You can also enter special **tip** commands on the local system to transmit files between the two computers.

When you are logged into a remote computer using a **tip** link, you enter OSF/1 commands on the remote computer simply by entering the command at the prompt. For example, to list the contents of a directory on the remote system, you would use the **ls** command.

However, suppose you want to display the contents of a directory on your local computer while linked to a remote system through the **tip** command. In that case, you must type a ~ (tilde) and an ! (exclamation point) preceding **ls** to indicate that UUCP should execute the command on your local system. You would therefore enter the **ls** command like this:

~!ls

Another way to perform the same operation is to enter the ~ and ! as in the following:

~!

The system displays the name of your local computer in this form:

~[*system_name*]!

OSF/1 User's Guide   11–23

Communications Tasks

You then enter the **ls** command.

The complete entry, requesting a list of the contents of your current working directory on local system **ames**, would therefore look like this:

~[ames] !**ls**

Table 11-4 lists some of the local commands you can use with the **tip** command.

Table 11–4. The tip Local Commands

Command	Description
~<Ctrl-d>	**Terminate Remote Connection** The ~<Ctrl-d> sequence (tilde and control-d) logs you out of the remote computer and then terminates the remote connection. Entering the ~<Ctrl-d> sequence always terminates the **tip** process. However, in some cases where you are connected to the remote system over a telephone line using a modem, ~<Ctrl-d> does not always successfully log you out of the remote system. For this reason, it is generally a good idea to press <Ctrl-d> to log out. Then, enter ~<Ctrl-d> at the prompt and press <Return> to terminate the remote connection.
~!	**Escape to Local System** The ~! (tilde and exclamation point) sequence returns you to the local system after you have been working on the remote system. Enter ~! at the prompt and then enter any command you wish. Then, when you want to return to the remote system, press <Ctrl-d> to leave the local computer and work on the remote system. Once you have established the **tip** connection, toggle back and forth between the two computers by entering ~!(to go from remote to local) and <Ctrl-d> (to go from local to remote).

Using the UUCP Networking Utilities

Command	Description
~!cmd	**Execute** *cmd* **Locally** The ~!*cmd* sequence tells **tip** to execute the command on the local system. Once you have established the **tip** link, you can run commands on your local computer only by typing a tilde and an exclamation point before the name of the command.
~c[*directory_name*]	**Change Local Directory** The ~c command changes your local working directory from the current directory to the directory specified with the *directory_name* entry. If you do not specify a directory, **tip** changes to your home directory.
~<	**Copy from Remote to Local** The ~< command copies the specified file from the remote system to the local system. The **tip** command prompts you for name of the local file.
~>	**Copy from Local to Remote** The ~> command copies the specified file from the local system to the remote system. The **tip** command prompts you for name of the remote file.
~t *from* [*to*]	**Copy from Remote to Local** The ~t *from* [*to*] command "takes" a specified file, copying it from the remote system to a specified file on the local system. If you do not type a name for the file on the local system (the *to* entry), the command copies the specified file from the remote to the local system under the same filename.
~p *from* [*to*]	**Copy from Local to Remote** The ~p *from* [*to*] command "puts" a specified file, copying it from the *local* system to the remote system. If you do not enter a target filename, the command copies the file to the remote system under the same filename.

Note: You can transfer only ASCII files with the ~t and ~p commands. To transfer other types of files, use the **uucp** command, discussed later in this chapter in "Sending and

OSF/1 User's Guide   11-25

Communications Tasks

Receiving Files (**uucp**)." In addition, neither **~t** nor **~p** checks to ensure that the system transfers the file(s) without errors. As a result, for the most reliable file transfers, use the **uucp** command.

For detailed information about **tip** local commands, see the **tip** reference page.

The tip Local Commands Examples

Example Set 1: Running Commands on Your Local System

Suppose that you want to view a file on your local system. To do so, perform the following procedure:

1. Enter **tip** and log in on the remote system.

2. To display the contents of the file **status10** in the **/usr/msg/memos/** directory on your local computer **venus**, enter:

    ~!

    The system responds with the following prompt:

    ~[venus]!

3. Enter the **more** command and the name of the file (in this case, the complete pathname of the file):

    ~[venus]!**more /usr/msg/memos/status10**

For another example, assume that you want to change from one directory to another directory on your local computer. To do so, perform the following procedure:

1. Enter **tip** and log in on the remote system.

2. Now change from your current local working directory **/usr/msg** to directory **/adm/msg**, also on your local system **zeus**. Enter the following:

    ~!

Using the UUCP Networking Utilities

The system responds with the name of your local system, prompting you to enter the command:

~[zeus]!

3. Enter the **c** command and the name of the directory following the ~[zeus]! prompt:

~[zeus]!**c /adm/msg**

Example Set 2: Copying Files from Remote to Local Systems

To copy the file **test1** from a remote system to your local system, perform the following procedure:

1. Enter **tip** and log in on the remote system.

2. To transfer a copy of the file **/u/amy/test1** from the remote system to your local system, enter:

   ~t/u/amy/test1

   where **/u/amy** is also the name of an existing directory on your local system. This command copies the file to the local system under the same filename, **test1**.

   If you want to copy the same file but call it **tmptest** in a different directory on your local system, enter the following instead:

   ~t/u/amy/test1 /usr/dev/amy/tmptest

Example Set 3: Copying Files from Local to Remote Systems

To copy the file **/usr/pubs/geo/ch2a** from your local system to a remote system, do the following:

1. Enter **tip** and log in on the remote system.

2. To copy the file **/usr/pubs/geo/ch2a** from the local system to the remote system to which you are connected, enter:

   ~p/usr/pubs/geo/ch2a

OSF/1 User's Guide 11–27

Communications Tasks

where **/usr/pubs/geo** is also the name of an existing directory on the remote system. This command copies the file to the remote system under the same filename, **ch2a**.

If you wish to copy the same file but call it **part2** in a different directory on on your local system, enter the following instead:

~p/usr/pubs/geo/ch2a /u/geo/part2

Note: When you use the ~p and ~t commands to transfer files, make sure that the target directory (the one to which you are copying the source files) already exists on the specified system. Unlike the **uucp** command, these **tip** local commands do not create intermediate directories during file transfers.

Additional Information About the tip Command

The following are some examples of **tip** features that you may find helpful:

- You can enter **tip** to connect system X to system Y, log into system Y, and then enter **tip** again on system Y to connect to system Z. You then have one local computer (system X) and two remote computers (systems Y and Z).

  You can run OSF/1 commands on system Z simply by logging in and entering the command. You can run commands on system X by prefixing the command with a single tilde (~cmd). You can also run commands on system Y by prefixing the command with two tildes (~~cmd).

  In general, a single tilde causes the specified command to be executed on the original local computer, and two tildes cause the command to be executed on the next system on which you executed **tip**.

- Remember that the ~! sequence takes you from the remote system to the local system. To return to the remote system from the local computer, press **<Ctrl-d>**.

For more information about the **tip** command, see the **tip** reference page.

Connecting a Remote Terminal to Your System Using a Modem (ct)

The **ct** command enables a user on a remote ASCII terminal to communicate with your system over a telephone line attached to a modem at each end of the connection. The user on the remote terminal can then log in and work on your system.

The following is a brief overview of **ct** command operations:

1. The user on the remote terminal generally contacts a user on your system (with a regular phone call) and asks that user to enter the **ct** command.

2. The user on the local system enters **ct** with the appropriate telephone number to call the modem attached to the remote terminal.

3. When the connection is established, **ct** enters an OSF/1 login prompt that is displayed on the remote terminal screen.

4. The user on the remote terminal enters his or her OSF/1 login name at the prompt, and OSF/1 opens a new shell. The user at the remote terminal then works on your system just like a local user.

Note: Normally, a user on the remote terminal calls the user on the local system to request a **ct** session. However, if such connections occur regularly at your site, your system manager may prefer to set up UUCP in such a way that a specified local system automatically enters **ct** to one or more specified terminals at certain designated times. For information about customizing UUCP for use at your site, see your system administrator.

The **ct** command is useful in the following situations:

- When a user working offsite needs to communicate with your system under strictly supervised conditions. Because the local system contacts the remote terminal, the user on that terminal does not need to know the telephone number of the local system. Additionally, the local user entering **ct** can monitor the work of the remote user.

- When the cost for the telephone connection should be charged either to the local site or to a specific account on the remote terminal.

  For example, assume that the user on the remote terminal has the appropriate access permissions and can make outgoing calls on the attached modem. That user can call the specified system, log in, and

Communications Tasks

enter the **ct** command with the phone number of the remote terminal, but *without* the **-h** flag (see Table 11-5). The local system hangs up the initial link so that the remote terminal is free for an incoming call, and then calls back to the terminal. This process is similar to making a collect call.

When you enter **ct** to connect to a remote terminal, you will find the following features of the command useful under certain circumstances:

- You can instruct **ct** to continue dialing the number until the connection is established or a set amount of time has elapsed.

- You can specify more than one telephone number at a time to instruct **ct** to continue dialing each modem until a connection is established over one of the lines.

Normally, **ct** dials the number specified in the command line, reaches the modem attached to the remote terminal, and displays the OSF/1 login prompt. If there are no free lines, however, **ct** displays a message to that effect and asks if you want to wait for one.

If you reply **no**, **ct** hangs up. If you reply that you do want to wait for a free line, **ct** prompts for the number of minutes to wait. The command continues to dial the remote system at 1-minute intervals until the connection is established or the specified amount of time has elapsed.

To connect to a remote terminal, enter the **ct** command in the following format:

ct [*flags*] *telno*

The *flags* entry specifies options that modify the operation of the command. The *telno* entry is the telephone number of the remote modem. Table 11-5 describes **ct** command-line entries.

Table 11–5. The ct Command Flags and Entries

Flag/Entry	Description
-w*minutes*	**Specify Wait Time**
	Specifies the maximum amount of time that **ct** waits for a line. You enter the command and then the **-w** flag, followed immediately by the amount of time, which you enter as minutes. For example, to specify a wait time of 5 minutes, you enter:
	-w5
	The **ct** command then dials the remote modem at 1-minute intervals until either the connection is established or the specified number of minutes has passed.
	Entering this flag on the command line suppresses the messages that **ct** normally displays if it cannot make the connection. Instead of asking whether to wait for a free line and then prompting for the wait time, **ct** continues to dial for the specified amount of time.
-h	**No Hangup**
	Normally, **ct** hangs up on the current call in order to respond to a call coming in to your modem from another modem. The **-h** flag instructs **ct** not to break the current connection in order to answer an incoming call.
-s*speed*	**Specify Transmission Rate**
	Specifies the rate at which **ct** transmits data. The default speed is 1200 baud. Enter this flag when you want to connect to a remote terminal using a modem set to another baud rate, such as 300 baud (often used to transfer files) or 2400 baud (for high-speed transmissions).

Communications Tasks

Flag/Entry	Description
telno	**Specify Telephone Number**
	Specifies the phone number of the remote modem. You can enter a local or a long-distance number, and you can specify secondary dial tones such as 9 for an outside line, or an access code.
	Use an = (equal sign) following a secondary dial tone (**9=**), and an appropriately placed - (dash) for delays (**687-5092**). Telephone numbers may contain up to 31 characters, and may include digits from 0 to 9, and any of the characters - (dash), = (equal sign), * (asterisk), and # (number sign).

For a complete description of the **ct** command, see the **ct** reference page.

The ct Examples

Example 1: Dialing an Internal Number

Suppose that you want to connect to a remote terminal modem within your company with the internal telephone number 7-6092. To do so, perform the following procedure:

1. Enter the following:

   $ **ct 76092**

   The system displays:

   ```
   Allocated dialer at 1200 baud
   Confirm hang_up? (y to hang_up)
   ```

2. Press **y** to hang up any other phone lines currently in use and establish your **ct** connection. Press **n** to cancel the command.

Example 2: Dialing an External Local Number

Suppose that you want to connect to a remote terminal modem with a local telephone number, specifying 9 for an outside line and a 2-minute wait for the modem line. To do so, perform the following procedure:

1. Enter the following:

   $ ct -w2 9=6340043

   The system displays:

   ```
   Allocated dialer at 1200 baud
   Confirm hang_up? (y to hang_up)
   ```

2. Press **y** to hang up any other phone lines currently in use and establish your **ct** connection. Press **n** to cancel the command.

Example 3: Dialing a Long-Distance Number

Suppose that you want to connect to a remote terminal with a long-distance number, specifying 9 for an outside line and a 5-minute wait. To do so, perform the following procedure:

1. Enter the following:

   $ ct -w5 9=15023597824

   The system displays:

   ```
   Allocated dialer at 1200 baud
   Confirm hang_up? (y to hang_up)
   ```

2. Press **y** to hang up any other phone lines currently in use and establish your **ct** connection. Press **n** to cancel the command.

For additional information about the **ct** command, see the **ct** reference page.

Communications Tasks

Running Remote Commands (uux)

The **uux** command allows you to run a command on a designated remote system while continuing with other work on your local system.

The command first gathers various files from the designated systems, if necessary. It then runs a specified OSF/1 command on a designated system. (If the specified command does not exist on the designated system, the **uux** command will not execute.) If the command you enter on the designated system produces some type of output, such as the **cat** or **diff** command, you can instruct **uux** to place that output in a specified file on any specified OSF/1 system.

Note: You can use the **uux** command on any OSF/1 system configured to run the specified command. For security reasons, however, certain sites may restrict the use of particular commands. Some systems, for example, may permit access only to the **mail** command.

You can enter the **uux** command in either of the following formats:

- **uux** [*flags*] "*commandstring* > *destination_name*"
- **uux** [*flags*] *commandstring* \{*destination_name*\}

The *flags* entry specifies options that modify the operation of the command. The *commandstring* entry specifies the name of the command you wish to run on the remote system. The *destination_name* specifies the system and file in which you wish to store the output of the remote command.

In the first format, notice the set of double quotes (" ") when you use the > (greater than) symbol to direct the output of the remote command to the destination name.

In the second format, you must type a backslash, a left brace, the destination name followed by a second backslash, and a right brace: \{*destination_name*\}. You need to include the backslashes because the left and right braces are special characters to the shell command interpreter. For examples of these forms, see "Additional Information About the **uux** Command" later in this chapter.

Table 11-6 describes **uux** command-line entries.

Table 11-6. The uux Command Flags and Entries

Flag/Entry	Description
-n	**No Notification Message**
	Normally, the **uux** command notifies you through the mail system about whether the command executed successfully on the designated system. The **-n** flag instructs **uux** not to send you this notification.
	The **-n** flag and the **-z** flag are mutually exclusive. You may use one or the other with **uux**, but not both.
-z	**Failure Message Only**
	Instructs **uux** to notify you only if the command fails to execute successfully on the designated system. In that case, **uux** sends you notification about the failure through the mail.
	The **-n** flag and the **-z** flag are mutually exclusive. You may use one or the other with **uux**, but not both.
-j	**Display Job ID**
	Displays the job identification number of the process that is running the remote command. You can use this job ID with the **uustat** command to check the status of the remote command, or use it with the **uustat -k** ("kill") flag to terminate the remote command before it finishes executing.
	For information about the **uustat** command, see "Getting Status Information about UUCP Jobs (**uustat**)" later in this chapter.
commandstring	**Name of Remote Command and System It Runs On**
	Specifies any OSF/1 command accepted by the designated system.
	In the Bourne and Korn shells, to specify the command and the system on which you want to run the command, type the name of the system, an **!** (exclamation point), and the command name as follows:
	system_name!commandstring

Communications Tasks

Flag/Entry	Description
	For C shell users, to specify the command and the system on which you want to run the command, type the name of the system, a \ (backslash), an ! (exclamation point), and the command name as follows:
	system_name\!commandstring
	For more information on these formats, see "The **uux** Examples" and "Additional Information About the **uux** Command" next in this chapter.
destination_name	**Name of Destination System and File**
	Specifies the system and file in which you want to store the output of the remote command.
	Suppose, for example, that you want a listing of all the files in a certain directory on a remote system. Rather than having the OSF/1 **ls** command simply display the filenames on the remote system, you can specify that you want the **uux** command to place the directory listing in a file on your own system by entering the appropriate destination name.
	In the Bourne and Korn shells, to specify the system and the file in which you want to store the output, type the name of the system, an ! (exclamation point), and the pathname as follows:
	system_name!pathname
	In the C shell, to specify the system and the file in which you want to store the output, type the name of the system, a \ (backslash), an ! (exclamation point), and the pathname as follows:
	system_name\!pathname
	For more information on these formats, see "The **uux** Examples" and "Additional Information About the **uux** Command" next in this chapter.
	When specifying the pathname, you may use a full name or a pathname preceded by ˜*user*. In this case,

Using the UUCP Networking Utilities

Flag/Entry	Description
	replace the *user* entry with a login name that refers to the user's login directory.
	Note that, when specifying an output file, it must be writable. This means that the permission for the file should allow you to place data in it. If you are uncertain about the permission status of a specific target output file, direct the results of the command to the **/var/spool/uucppublic** public directory. Remember that ~**uucp**/ is a shorthand way of specifying the **/var/spool/uucppublic** public directory.

For a complete description of the **uux** command, see the **uux** reference page.

The uux Examples

Example 1: Concatenating Two Files and Storing the Output in a Third File

Suppose that you wish to concatenate two files (one on system **zeus** and one on system **hera**) and then direct the output to a third file on system **zeus**. Also assume that you are using the Bourne or the Korn shell.

To do so, enter the following command in either of the following forms:

$ uux "zeus!cat zeus!/u/amy/f1 hera!/usr/amy/f2 > zeus!/u/amy/catout"

or

$ uux zeus!cat zeus!/u/amy/f1 hera!/usr/amy/f2 \{zeus!/u/amy/catout\}

Either form of **uux** executes the **cat** command, which is stored on system **zeus**. The **cat** command combines the file **f1**, located in the directory **/u/amy** on **zeus**, with the file **f2**, located in **/usr/amy** on system **hera**. The command then places the new file on system **zeus** under the filename **catout** in the directory **/u/amy**.

OSF/1 User's Guide   11–37

Communications Tasks

To perform the same operation in the C shell, enter either one of the following forms:

% **uux "zeus\\!cat zeus\\!/u/amy/f1 hera\\!/usr/amy/f2 > zeus\\!/u/amy/catout"**

or

% **uux zeus\\!cat zeus\\!/u/amy/f1 hera\\!/usr/amy/f2 \\{zeus\\!/u/amy/catout\\}**

Note that, if you request a command that the remote system cannot run, you will receive a mail message to that effect from the remote system.

Example 2: Copying a File from a Remote System

Assume that you are using the C shell. To copy the file **report6** on remote system **boston** and place the output in the file **report6** in the public directory on your local system, enter either of the following forms:

% **uux "cp boston\\!/reports/report6 > ~uucp/report6"**

or

% **uux cp boston\\!/reports/report6 \\{~uucp/report6\\}**

Additional Information About the uux Command

The following are some examples of **uux** features that you may find helpful:

- To run commands on more than one system, enter the information on separate command lines as follows:

  $ uux merlin!print /reports/memos/charles
  $ uux zeus!print /test/examples/examp1
  $ _

- In addition to the two forms of the destination name that you can use with the **uux** command (see Table 11-6), you can also represent your local system in several different ways. The **uux** command assumes your local system is the default, so the easiest way to represent the local system is not to specify it in the command line.

Using the UUCP Networking Utilities

For example, assume that you want to run the **diff** command, which is on your local system **hera**. You then want to compare the file **/u/f1** on system **venus** with the file **/u/f2** on system **merlin**. Lastly, you want to specify that the output of the **diff** command should be placed in the file **/u/f3** on your local computer. To accomplish this, you enter:

$ **uux "diff venus!/u/f1 merlin!/u/f2 > /u/f3"**

Note that because your local system is the default, you need not enter both the system name and the exclamation point. However, if you want to specify your local system, you could enter it this way:

$ **uux "hera!diff venus!/u/f1 merlin!/u/f2 > hera!/u/f3"**

You can also enter the destination name in the following form:

$ **uux hera!diff venus!/u/f1 merlin!/u/f2 \{hera!/u/f3\}**

You can also represent the local system by using just an exclamation point, as in the following example:

$ **uux "!diff venus!/u/f1 merlin!/u/f2 > !/u/f3"**

- When specifying the pathname for a file you want to use as the source in running commands such as **diff** or **cat**, you can include the following shell pattern-matching characters, which the remote system can interpret:

  ? (question mark)
  * (asterisk)
  [(left bracket)
  ] (right bracket)

  Precede these characters with a \ (backslash), or enclose them with " " (double quotes), so that the local shell cannot interpret the characters before **uux** sends the command to the remote system.

  Do not use pattern-matching characters in destination names.

OSF/1 User's Guide   11-39

- If you use the following shell characters, precede each special character with a \ (backslash) or place " " (double quotes) around the entire command string:

  < (less than)
  > (greater than)
  ; (semicolon)
  | (pipe)

  Do not use the shell redirection characters (<< and >>) because they do not work in the UUCP program.

For additional information about the **uux** command, see the **uux** reference page.

Sending and Receiving Files (uucp)

In general, you will probably use the UUCP networking utilities primarily to send and receive files. The **uucp** command and its options enable you to copy one or more source files from one computer running under the OSF/1 operating system (or some other system based on the UNIX operating system) to one or more destination files on a system similarly based on the UNIX operating system that supports UUCP.

You can use **uucp** to copy files between and among systems in the following ways:

- Between a local system and a remote system
- Between two remote systems
- Between two systems through an intermediate system
- Within your local system

Note: Any sending and receiving operation you perform is subject to the security features in effect on both the local and remote systems.

The **uucp** command has the following format:

uucp [*flags*] *source_name(s) destination_name*

Using the UUCP Networking Utilities

The *flags* entry specifies options that modify the operation of the command. The *source_name* entry specifies the system and the pathname of the file you wish to copy to the remote system. The *destination_name* specifies the system, directory, and file in which you wish to copy the source file. Table 11-7 describes **uucp** command-line entries.

Table 11-7. The uucp Command Flags and Entries

Flag/Entry	Description
-d	**Copy Files and Create Intermediate Directories**
	Creates any intermediate directories needed to copy a source file to a destination file on a remote system. For example, instead of first creating a directory and then copying a file to it, you can simply enter **uucp** with the destination pathname, and the required directory will be created.
	The **-d** flag is the default.
-f	**Copy File Without Creating Intermediate Directories**
	Instructs **uucp** not to create any intermediate directories during the file transfer. Use this flag if the destination directory already exists and you do not want **uucp** to write over it.
-j	**Display Job ID**
	Displays the job identification number of the transfer operation. You can use this job ID with the **uustat** command to check the status of the transfer, or use it with **uustat -k** ("kill") to terminate the transfer before it is completed. See "Getting Status Information about UUCP Jobs (**uustat**)" later in this chapter for information about the **uustat** command.
-m	**Mail Message to Sender**
	Specifies that a mail message should be sent to you when the source file is successfully copied to the destination file on a remote system. The message

Flag/Entry	Description
	goes to your mail box, **/usr/mail/**username. The **mail** command does not send a message for a local transfer.
-nusername	**Notify Recipient**
	Notifies the recipient on the remote system identified by the username entry that a file has been sent. The mail system does not send a message for a local transfer.
source_name	**Pathname of Source File**
	Specifies the pathname of the file that you want to send or receive. For detailed information about pathnames used with the UUCP networking utilities, see "Pathnames Used with UUCP Commands" earlier in this chapter.
	In the Bourne and Korn shells, to specify the source_name, type the name of the system, an **!** (exclamation point), and the pathname as follows:
	system_name!pathname
	In the C shell, to specify the source_name, type the name of the system, a \ (backslash), an **!** (exclamation point), and the pathname as follows:
	system_name\!pathname
	For all shell users, if the pathname of the source file is on your local system, you do not have to specify system_name.
destination_name	**Pathname of Destination File**
	Specifies the pathname of the file (or directory) to which the copy is being sent.
	In the Bourne and Korn shells, to specify the destination_name, type the name of the system, an **!** (exclamation point), and the pathname as follows:
	system_name!pathname

Using the UUCP Networking Utilities

Flag/Entry	Description
	In the C shell, to specify the *destination_name*, type the name of the system, a \ (backslash), an ! (exclamation point), and the pathname as follows: *system_name*\!*pathname* For all shell users, if the pathname of the source file is on your local system, you do not have to specify *system_name*. For detailed information about pathnames used with the UUCP networking utilities, see "Pathnames Used with UUCP Commands" earlier in this chapter.

For information about other **uucp** options, see the **uucp** reference page.

Note: You may find that file transfers may fail because of security restrictions. Because the **uucp** command does not display error messages for file transfers that fail because of security restrictions, you must use the **uustat** or **uulog** commands to check on the status of **uucp** jobs. See the appropriate sections later in this chapter for information about **uustat** and **uulog** commands. Also see "The **uucp** Command and System Security" next in this chapter for information on system security.

The uucp Command and System Security

You can always transfer your own protected files as well as files in protected directories that you own. However, you may have problems sending and receiving files that you do not own because of system security restrictions. For example, after attempting to copy a file from your local directory to a remote system directory, you may find that the file has not been copied because the remote file system is protected.

Security restrictions are defined by the system administrator in a special file to prevent unwarranted use by remote users. As a result, you may find that only certain parts of the local or remote file system are accessible.

To minimize problems with file transfers, many sites make the public UUCP directory **/var/spool/uucppublic** available for receiving and sending files. This directory gives everyone read and write access, thereby bypassing potential security restrictions. You can use a ~ (tilde) and the name of the command (~**uucp**) as a shorthand way of specifying this directory.

The uucp Examples (Bourne and Korn Shells)

Example 1: Copying a File from a Local to a Remote System

Assume that you wish to copy a local file called **/meteors** to the file **/solar/stats** in the public directory on the remote system **galaxy**. To copy this file directly, enter:

$ **uucp /meteors galaxy!~uucp/solar/stats**

Note that the ~**uucp** entry preceding the name **/solar/stats** is a shorthand method of specifying the public directory. You can also enter the full destination pathname:

$ **galaxy!/var/spool/uucppublic/solar/stats**

Example 2: Copying a File Through an Intermediate System

Assume that you wish to send a copy of **/meteors** to the file **/solar/stats** on system **galaxy** by way of the intermediate system **milkyway**. To do so, enter:

$ **uucp /meteors milkyway!galaxy!~uucp/solar/stats**

UUCP routes the transfer from your system through system **milkyway** and then to the public directory on system **galaxy**.

Example 3: Copying a File from a Remote System

Assume that you wish to get the file **/cells/type1** from system **biochem** and store it in a file called **/drmsg/research** on your local system. To do so, enter:

$ **uucp biochem!/cells/type1 /drmsg/research**

Example 4: Copying Multiple Files from a Remote System

Assume that you wish to copy multiple files from the remote system **zeus** to your local public directory. To do so, enter:

$ **uucp zeus!/u/amy/reports* ~uucp**

The uucp Examples (C Shell)

Example 1: Copying a File from a Local to a Remote System

To copy **marchsales** on your local system to the public directory on remote system **hera**, enter:

% **uucp marchsales hera\!~uucp**

Example 2: Copying a File from a Remote to a Local System

To copy **report3** from the **/usr/reports** directory on system **hera** to the public directory on your own system, enter:

% **uucp hera\!/usr/reports/report3 ~uucp**

Example 3: Copying Multiple Files from a Remote to a Local System

Assume that the **/user/amy/reports** directory on the remote system **zeus** contains a number of files with names beginning with the character string **report**. To copy all these files to your local public directory, enter either of the following forms:

% **uucp zeus\!/user/amy/report'*' ~uucp**

or

% **uucp "zeus\!/user/amy/report*" ~uucp**

In the first format, the pattern-matching character * (asterisk) in the pathname of the source files is enclosed in single quotes. In the second format, the entire pathname of the source files is enclosed in double quotes. In both examples, the multiple source files are copied to the public directory on the local system.

Another Method for Transferring and Handling Files (uuto, uupick)

In addition to the **uucp** command, the UUCP networking utilities provide another command that enables you to copy files from one OSF/1 system to another OSF/1 system. The **uuto** command actually uses **uucp** to transfer the specified file(s), but **uuto** makes the whole process easier for both the sender and the recipient.

The **uuto** command sends a specified file or files from one system to a specific user on another system. The command places the copied file(s) in the public directory on the recipient's system, and the system notifies the recipient that a file has arrived.

Once the file is in the UUCP public directory, the user enters the **uupick** command, which displays a message that file *name* has arrived from system *name*. The user then enters one of the **uupick** options for handling the file, such as deleting it or moving it to another directory.

Following is an overview of the way in which you can use the **uuto** and **uupick** commands to send and receive a file:

1. To send a file, enter the **uuto** command to copy one or more files to a specific username on another system.

2. The **uucp** command then sends the file(s) to **/var/spool/uucppublic**, the UUCP public directory. In this case, **uucp** also creates (if it does not already exist) an additional directory called **receive**, plus the directory */username/system*. The full pathname to the copied file is, therefore,

   /var/spool/uucppublic/receive/*username/system/file*

   The **rmail** command then notifies the recipient that a file (or files) has arrived.

3. The recipient enters the **uupick** command.

4. The **uupick** command searches the public directory for files sent to the recipient and notifies the recipient about each file it locates.

5. Using a series of **uupick** options, the recipient saves or deletes each file.

Using the UUCP Networking Utilities

You can also use the **uuto** and **uupick** commands to transfer files to a specific user on the local system. Again, **uuto** places the copied file(s) in the UUCP public directory on the local system. More information on **uuto** and **uupick** follows. Refer also to the reference pages for these commands.

Note: Any transfer operation you perform is subject to the security features in effect on both the local and remote systems.

Sending Files to a Specific ID (uuto)

The **uuto** command copies one or more source files from one OSF/1 system to a specific user on another OSF/1 system. The command stores the file in the public directory on the destination system until the specified user enters the **uupick** command to locate and handle the file.

The **uuto** command has the following general format:

uuto [*flags*] *file_name destination_name*

The *flags* entry specifies options that modify the operation of the command. The *file_name* entry specifies the pathname of the source file. The *destination_name* specifies the system, directory, and file in which you wish to copy the source file. Table 11-8 describes **uuto** command-line entries.

Table 11–8. The uuto Command Flags and Entries

Flag/Entry	Description
-m	**Mail Message to Sender** Notifies you, the sender, when the **uuto** command has successfully copied the source file(s) to the specified username on the specified system.
-p	**Copy File to Spool Directory** Sends the source file(s) to the spool directory on your local system before actually transferring the copy of the

OSF/1 User's Guide   11–47

Communications Tasks

Flag/Entry	Description
	file(s) to the public directory on the specified system. Without this flag, **uuto** copies the source file(s) to the following directory:
	/var/spool/uucppublic/receive/*username*/*system*/*file(s)*.
file_name	**Pathname of Source File**
	Specifies the pathname of the source file. This may be a simple filename if the file you are sending is in the directory from which you are entering the **uuto** command. Otherwise, enter the complete pathname of the file.
destination_name	**Pathname of Destination**
	The *destination_name* is the pathname to the specific location to which you want to copy the source file. This pathname *must* include the username of the person to whom you are sending the file.
	The *destination_name* has the following form:
	system!*username*
	where *system* is the name of the remote computer and *username* is the username of the recipient. When copying a file from one location to another location on your local system, the *destination_name* can be simply the name of the user to whom you are sending the file.

For more information about **uuto**, see the **uuto** reference page.

The uuto Examples

Example 1: Sending a File to a Remote System

To send the file **/usr/bin/data/private** to a user with the ID **monique** on remote system **venus**, enter:

$ **uuto /usr/bin/data/private venus!monique**

The **uuto** command copies the file and sends it to the public directory on system **venus**. The **rmail** command then sends user **monique** a mail message that the file has arrived. Monique enters the **uupick** command to locate and handle the transferred file.

For more information about using **uupick**, see "Locating Files for a Specific ID (**uupick**)" next in this chapter.

Example 2: Sending a File Within Your System

To send the file **/usr/research/file1** to user **amy**, enter:

$ **uuto /usr/research/file1 amy**

Note that no mail message is sent to Amy or any recipient in a local transfer of this kind.

Locating Files for a Specific ID (uupick)

When **uuto** copies a file or files to your user ID, UUCP places the file(s) in the **/var/spool/uucppublic/receive**/*username*/*system*/*file(s)* public directory on your local system, and **rmail** notifies you that the file has arrived. When you receive this message, enter the **uupick** command to complete the transfer and handle the file(s).

Following is the general format of the **uupick** command:

uupick

As you can see, **uupick** does not have command flags. It does, however, have options that enable you to handle the file(s) sent to you with **uuto**.

Communications Tasks

Following is a list of the **uupick** user options. Note that the option is *not* preceded by a dash.

* (asterisk)
newline (**<Return>**)
a [*dir*]
d
m[*dir*]
p
q or **<Ctrl-d>**
!*command*

After notifying you that a file has been sent from *system*, the **uupick** command displays a **?** (question mark) as a prompt. This indicates that you can now enter one of the file-handling options shown previously. Table 11-9 describes these **uupick** command options.

Table 11-9. The uupick Command Options

Options	Description
*	**Display uupick Options** Instructs **uupick** to display all **uupick** file-handling options.
<Return>	**Next File** Pressing **<Return>** signals **uupick** to move on to the next file in the directory.
a [*dir*]	**Move All Files** Enables you to move all your **uuto** files currently in the public directory into a specified directory on your local system or a remote system. The default is your current directory (that is, the directory you were in when you entered the **uupick** command). You can use either a full pathname or a relative pathname to specify the directory.
d	**Delete File** The **d** option enables you to delete the specified file.

11-50   OSF/1 User's Guide

Using the UUCP Networking Utilities

Options	Description
m [*dir*]	**Move Specified File**
	Enables you to move a specified file to a specified directory. Again, the default is your current directory, and you may use either full or relative pathnames.
p	**Display File**
	Enables you to display the file on your workstation.
q or <Ctrl-d>	**Quit uupick**
	The **q** option enables you to leave the **uupick** command without actually doing anything about the file(s) in the public directory. You can also press <Ctrl-d> to quit the command.
!*command*	**Run Specified Command**
	Enables you to leave the **uupick** command and return to the OSF/1 prompt to run a specified OSF/1 command. After the command executes, the system automatically returns to **uupick** so you can continue handling the **uuto** files in the public directory.

For more information about **uupick**, see the **uupick** reference page.

A uupick Example

Assume that a mail message informs you that a file has been sent. A user on system **boston** has sent you the file **sales**. To retrieve the file, do the following:

1. Enter the **uupick** command:

   $ **uupick**

   The following message is displayed:

   ```
   from system boston: file sales
   ?
   ```

2. At the ? prompt, enter a **uupick** user option to indicate how you want to handle the file. For now, you wish to move the file to your current directory. As a result, you enter:

? m

3. Enter **q** at the ? prompt to stop reviewing files.

Displaying the Status of UUCP Jobs

UUCP has two commands that enable you to get information about the status of a particular operation: **uustat** and **uulog**.

The **uustat** command reports the status of various UUCP networking utilities operations, including the following:

- File transfers initiated with the **uucp** command, discussed earlier in this chapter in "Sending and Receiving Files (**uucp**)."

- Commands invoked with the **uux** command that are running on designated systems, discussed earlier in this chapter in "Running Remote Commands (**uux**)."

- Files copied with the **uuto** command, discussed earlier in this chapter in "Another Method for Transferring and Handling Files (**uuto, uupick**)."

For more information on the **uustat** command, see the following section.

Getting Status Information About UUCP Jobs (uustat)

The **uustat** command displays information about the progress of various jobs initiated with UUCP networking utilities commands. This command is particularly useful in monitoring file transfers requested with the **uucp** and **uuto** commands, and command executions requested with the **uux** command.

In addition, **uustat** gives you limited control over jobs that you have queued to run on a remote computer. Not only can you check the general

Using the UUCP Networking Utilities

status of UUCP connections to other systems and the progress of UUCP file transfers and command executions, but you can also use **uustat** to cancel copy requests invoked with the **uucp** command.

The status reports generated by **uustat** are displayed on your workstation screen in this basic form:

jobid date/time status system_name username size file

For more information on status reports, see ''Additional Information About the **uustat** Command'' later in this chapter.

Note: Any status display operation you perform is subject to the security features in effect on both the local and remote systems.

The **uustat** command has the following general format:

uustat [*flags*]

The *flags* entry specifies options that modify the operation of the command. You may enter **uustat** with one or more flags. Following are some of the available flags, which are mutually exclusive:

-a
-k *jobid*
-m
-q
-r *jobid*

You can also use either or both of the following flags with **uustat**:

-u*user*
-s*file*

Table 11-10 describes the **uustat** command flags.

OSF/1 User's Guide   11-53

Table 11-10. The uustat Command Flags

Flags	Description
-a	**Display All Jobs in Queue (-a)** Displays information about all the jobs in the "holding" queue, regardless of the user who entered the original UUCP command. The holding queue lists those jobs that have not executed or are not scheduled for execution. The holding queue lists all jobs that have not executed during a set period of time. For information about the UUCP queues, refer to "Additional Information about the **uustat** Command" later in this chapter.
-k *jobid*	**Cancel Job** Cancels (kills) the UUCP process specified by the *jobid*. This is useful, for example, when you want to cancel a file transfer or copy request, a remote printing job, and so on. You can cancel a job only if you are the user who entered the original UUCP command specified by the *jobid*. (A system administrator with superuser authority can also cancel UUCP requests.)
-m	**Most Recent Attempt** Reports on the status of your most recent attempt to communicate with another computer through the UUCP facility. For example, the status is reported as successful if the UUCP request executed. If the job was not completed, UUCP reports an error message, such as `Login failed`.
-q	**Jobs Currently in Queue** Lists the jobs currently queued for each computer. These jobs are waiting to execute, or are in the process of executing. If a status file exists for the computer, UUCP reports its date, time, and the status information. Once the process is completed, UUCP removes the job listing from the current queue.

Using the UUCP Networking Utilities

Flags	Description
-r *jobid*	**Rejuvenate Specified Job**
	Rejuvenates the UUCP process specified by the job identification number. This flag enables you to mark files in the holding queue with the current date and time, thus ensuring that the cleanup operation does not delete these files until the job's modification time reaches the end of the allotted period.
	For information about the UUCP queues, refer to "Additional Information About the **uustat** Command" later in this chapter. For information about cleaning up UUCP queues, see your system administrator.
-s *system*	**Jobs on Specified System**
	Reports the status of all UUCP requests that users have entered to run on the computer specified by the *system* entry.
-u *username*	**Jobs Requested by Specified User**
	Reports the status of all UUCP requests entered to run that were specified by the user named in the *username* entry.
	You can use both the **-s***system* and the **-u***username* flags with the **uustat** command to get a status report on all UUCP requests entered by a specified user on a specified system.

For detailed information about the flags available with the **uustat** command, see the **uustat** reference page.

The uustat Examples

Example 1: Displaying All Jobs in the Holding Queue

To display the status of all UUCP jobs in the holding queue, enter the following:

$ **uustat -a**

Communications Tasks

Refer to "Additional Information About the **uustat** Command" next in this chapter for a sample of the output generated by this command.

Example 2: Displaying All Jobs in the Current Queue

To report the status of all the UUCP jobs either currently executing or queued to run on each system, enter:

$ **uustat -q**

Sample output for this example is shown in "Additional Information About the **uustat** Command."

Example 3: Displaying All Jobs in the Holding Queue for a Specific System

To report the status of all jobs in the holding queue for system **venus**, enter:

$ **uustat -svenus**

See "Additional Information About the **uustat** Command" for the sample output for this command.

Example 4: Displaying All Jobs Requested by a Specific User

To report the status of jobs requested by user **amy**, enter:

$ **uustat -uamy**

Additional Information About the uustat Command

The **uustat** command produces information about the status of various requests that users have entered with one of the UUCP commands. The type of information that **uustat** displays depends on the flag you enter with it.

Because the **-q** and **-a** flags produce different types of listings, this section distinguishes between the following types of output information:

- The output of the **uustat -q** command is called the current queue. The current queue lists the UUCP jobs either queued to run or currently executing on one or more remote systems.

Using the UUCP Networking Utilities

- The output of the **uustat -a** command is called the holding queue. The holding queue lists all jobs that have not executed during a set period of time.

Note: After the set time period has elapsed, the entries in the holding queue can be deleted with the UUCP **uucleanup** command. For detailed information about cleaning up UUCP queues, see your system administrator.

The following list describes the kind of output displayed when you use selected **uustat** flags:

- When you enter the **uustat -a** command to examine the status of all UUCP jobs in the holding queue, the system displays the following type of output:

```
heraC3113     11/06-17:47 S hera    lorenzo 289   D.venus471afd8
zeusN3130     11/06-09:14 R zeus    chang   338   D.venus471bc0a
merlinC3120   11/05-16:02 S merlin  amy     828   /u/amy/tt
merlinC3119   11/05-12:32 S merlin  msg           rmail amy
```

The first field is the job ID of the operation, which is followed in the second field by the date and time that the UUCP command was entered. The third field is either an S or an R, depending on whether the job is to send or receive a file.

The fourth field is the name of the system on which the command was entered, followed by the *username* of the person who entered the command in the fifth field.

The sixth field is the size of the file, or, in the case of a remote execution like the last entry in the example, the name of the remote command. When the size is given, as in the first three lines of the example output, the filename is also displayed.

The filename can be either the name given by the user, as in the **/u/amy/tt** entry, or a name that UUCP assigns internally to data files associated with remote executions, such as **D.venus471afd8**.

OSF/1 User's Guide   11–57

- When you enter the **uustat -q** command to report the status of all the UUCP jobs either currently executing or queued to run on each system, the following type of output is displayed:

  ```
  merlin    2C          09/12-09:14    SUCCESSFUL
  hera      4C          09/12-10:02    NO DEVICES AVAILABLE
  zeus      1C   (2)    09/12-10:12    CAN'T ACCESS DEVICE
  ```

  This output tells how many command (**C.**) files are waiting for each system. The date and time refer to the last time UUCP tried to communicate with that system, and the message at the end of the line reports the status of each interaction. The number in parentheses (2) in the third line of this example indicates that the file has been in the queue for 2 days.

- When you enter the **uustat -s**_system_ command, UUCP displays the following type of output for the specified system:

  ```
  arthurC3114 11/06-16:50 S arthur   daemon 427 D.venus471994d
  arthurN3219 11/05-10:12 S arthur   msg    278 D.hera471eac5
  ```

- The **uustat -u**_user_ command produces output similar to that produced by the **-s** flag.

- In a status report, a number in parentheses next to the number of a command file (a **C.** file) or an execute file (an **X.** file) represents the age in days of the oldest **C.** or **X.** file for that system.

  The "retry" field indicates how many times the local system has tried to communicate with a specified remote system since the last successful UUCP connection.

The following list provides additional information about **uustat** flags:

- The **-k** _jobid_ flag cancels a process only when that job is still on the local computer. Once the UUCP facility has moved the request to a remote computer for execution, you cannot use this flag to kill the remote job.

- Entering **uustat** without any flags displays the status information for your personal UUCP jobs (that is, for all the UUCP commands that you have entered since the last time the holding queue was cleaned up).

For more information about the **uustat** command, see your system administrator and the **uustat** reference page.

Chapter 12
Using TCP/IP Commands

This chapter shows you how to use TCP/IP (Transmission Control Protocol/Internet Protocol) on a network, such as Ethernet. You use TCP/IP to communicate with systems other than your own.

After completing this chapter, you will be able to do the following:

- Display information about users
- Display information about remote systems
- Transfer files between systems
- Copy files between systems
- Log into remote systems
- Run commands on remote systems
- Display who is on remote systems

This chapter discusses a few of the basic commands you need to perform the tasks previously listed.

Note: Any TCP/IP operation you perform is subject to the security features in effect on both the local and remote systems.

Requesting Information About Users (finger)

To request information about current users on a specified system, use the **finger** command. The **finger** command has the following general format:

finger [*user*]@*system_name*

The *user* entry specifies the user about whom you wish to obtain information. The @*system_name* entry species the system on which the user resides. If you do not provide a username, the **finger** command provides a list of all the current users.

If you do not specify a username, the system displays the following information:

- Login name
- Full name
- Terminal name and write status (an * indicates that write status is denied)
- Idle time
- Login time
- User's office location

If you specify a user or a list of users, **finger** displays the preceding information as well as the following:

- User's home directory and login shell
- Any plan that users have placed in the file **.plan** in their home directory, and the project on which they are working from the file **.project** in the home directory.

For example, assume that you wish to display information about users on remote system **boston**. To do so, enter:

$ **finger** **@boston**

Information similar to the following is displayed:

```
[boston]
Login     Name         TTY  Idle    When      Office
amy       Amy Wilson   p0      4    Thu 10:00  345
chang     Peter Chang  p1   2:58    Thu 10:16  103
```

For another example, assume that you wish to display information about user **geo** on system **zeus**. To do so, enter:

$ **finger geo@zeus**

Information similar to the following is displayed:

```
Login name: geo               In real life: George Garcia
Directory: /users/geo         Shell: /usr/bin/csh
On since May 24 10:16:07 on pts/4 from :0.0
58 minutes Idle Time
No Plan.
```

Note: If you do not specify a *system_name*, **finger** displays information for users on your local system.

For more information, see the **finger** reference page.

Requesting Information About Remote Systems (ruptime)

Note: To use the **ruptime** command, your system must be running the **rwhod** daemon.

To determine the status of the network and various remote systems, you can use the **ruptime** command. The **ruptime** command displays the operational systems on your network, as well as providing system statistics. In other words, it displays the status of each host on a local network.

The **ruptime** command displays the following information:

- System name and status (up or down)
- The length of time the system has been up
- The number of users currently on the system
- Load average statistics

The general format of the **ruptime** command is the following:

ruptime

For example, to get a status report on the hosts on the local network, enter the following:

$ **ruptime**

Information similar to the following is displayed:

```
host1    up        5:15,    4 users,    load 0.09, 0.04, 0.04
host2    up        7:45,    3 users,    load 0.08, 0.07, 0.04
host3    up        2:28,    0 users,    load 0.01, 0.02, 0.03
host4    up     3+01:44,    1 user,     load 0.01, 0.02, 0.03
host7    up        7:43,    1 user,     load 0.06, 0.12, 0.11
```

The **ruptime** command has flags that determine the kind and order of information that is displayed. For more information, see the **ruptime** reference page.

Transferring Files with ftp

You can transfer files between two OSF/1 systems or between an OSF/1 system and any system supporting the **ftp** command. This transfer operation includes the following steps:

1. The **ftp** command makes a connection to the other system.
2. Once the connection is made, you issue subcommands that instruct the system to transfer the file or files.

Using TCP/IP Commands

See "Using **ftp** Subcommands" next in this chapter for information about these subcommands.

Note: Any transfer operation you perform is subject to the security features in effect on both the local and remote systems.

The **ftp** command has the following general format:

ftp *system_name*

The *system_name* entry is the name of the system you want to reach. This may be another OSF/1 system, or another type of system to which you have a connection. (A remote system is sometimes called the host computer.) If you do not specify a *system_name* on the command line, you must use the **open** subcommand (see Table 12-1) inside the **ftp** program to make a connection with a remote system.

When you see the ftp> prompt, enter the subcommands that you need to make the file transfer. See "Using ftp Subcommands" for information about these subcommands.

The **ftp** command has flags that can be specified on the command line for more complex operations. For full details on those flags, see the **ftp** reference page.

As an overview of **ftp** operations, assume that you wish to reach system **host2** and log in. To do so, perform the following:

1. Enter the following:

   $ **ftp host2**

   When the connection is made, the system displays

   Connected to host2.

   and prompts for a login name:

   Name(host2:*local user_name*)

Communications Tasks

2. To log into the remote system with your local username, press **<Return>**. For example, if you used **smith** on the local system, press **<Return>** when you see the following:

   Name(host2:smith)

   To log into the remote system with a different username, type the name after the displayed information and press **<Return>**. To log in as **sam**, add the name as shown:

   Name(host2:smith) **sam**

3. When prompted, enter a valid password. The prompt for this example is

   Password(host2:sam)

4. The prompt changes to the following:

   ftp>

   You now may enter any **ftp** subcommand. See the list of subcommands and the steps for transferring files that follow.

Using ftp Subcommands

Once you log into the remote system, you can transfer files or do other tasks related to file transfer at the ftp> prompt.

The following is the procedure for using **ftp** subcommands:

1. Enter the subcommand for file transfer or a related task, adding any required filename or pathname.
2. Continue entering subcommands until all the work is finished.
3. To exit **ftp**, enter the **quit** subcommand.

Table 12-1 describes the **ftp** subcommands that let you transfer files and perform related tasks, such as changing the type of file transfer, displaying information, and changing directory and filenames.

12–6   OSF/1 User's Guide

Table 12-1. The ftp Subcommands

Subcommand	Description
![command [parameters]]	Invokes an interactive shell on the local host. An optional command, with one or more optional parameters, can be given with the shell command.
? [subcommand]	Displays a message describing the subcommand. If you do not specify subcommand, **ftp** displays a list of known subcommands.
account [password]	Sends a supplemental password that a remote host other than an OSF/1 system may require before granting access to its resources. If the password is not supplied with the command, the user is prompted for the password. The password does not appear on the screen.
ascii	Sets the file transfer type to network ASCII. This is the default.
binary	Sets the file transfer type to binary image. This may be more efficient when transferring non-ASCII files.
bye	Ends the file transfer session and exits **ftp**. Same as **quit**.
cd remotedirectory	Changes the working directory on the remote host to the specified directory.
cdup	Changes the working directory on the remote host to the parent of the current directory.

Subcommand	Description
delete *remotefile*	Deletes the specified remote file.
dir [*remotedirectory*][*localfile*]	Writes a listing of the contents of the *remotedirectory* to the file *localfile*. If *directory* is not specified, **dir** lists the contents of the current remote directory. If *localfile* is not specified or is a - (dash), **dir** displays the listing on the local terminal. (Same as **ls**.)
get *remotefile* [*localfile*]	Transfers a file from the remote host to the local host. The *remotefile* argument can be specified in one of two ways: 1) as a file that exists on the remote host, if a default host was already specified, or 2) as *host:file*, where *host* is the remote host and *file* is the name of the file to copy to the local system. If this form of the argument is used, the last host specified becomes the default host for later transfers in this **tftp** session. If *localfile* is not specified, the remote filename is used locally.
help [*subcommand*]	Displays help information. Refer to the **?** subcommand.
lcd [*directory*]	Changes the working directory on the local host. If you do not specify a directory, **ftp** uses your home directory.
ls [*remotedirectory*] [*localfile*]	Writes a listing of the contents of the *remotedirectory* to the file *localfile*. If *directory* is not specified, **ls** lists the contents of the current remote directory. If *localfile* is not specified or is a - (dash), **ls** displays the listing on the local terminal. (Same as **dir**.)

Using TCP/IP Commands

Subcommand	Description
mget *remotefile* [*localfile*]	Copies the remote file to the local host. If *localfile* is not specified, the remote filename is used locally. The **mget** command allows you to use pattern-matching characters to specify files.
mkdir [*remotedirectory*]	Creates the directory *remotedirectory* on the foreign host.
mput *localfile* [*remotefile*]	Stores a local file on the remote host. If you do not specify *remotefile*, **ftp** uses the local filename to name the remote file. The **mput** command allows you to use pattern-matching characters to specify files.
nlist [*remote_directory*] [*local_file*]	Prints an abbreviated list of the files of a directory on the remote machine. If *remote_directory* is left unspecified, the current working directory is used. If interactive prompting is on, **ftp** prompts the user to verify that the last argument is indeed the target local file for receiving **nlist** output. If no local file is specified, the output is sent to the terminal.
open *host* [*port*]	Establishes a connection with the remote system, if you have not specified it on the command line. If the optional port number is specified, **ftp** will attempt to connect to a server at that port. If the autologin feature is set (the default), **ftp** will attempt to automatically log the user into the remote system.
put *localfile* [*remotefile*]	Transfers a file from the local host to the remote host. The *remotefile* argument can be specified in one of two ways: 1) as a file that exists on the remote host, if

Communications Tasks

Subcommand	Description
	a default host was already specified, or 2) as *host:remotefile*, where *host* is the remote host and *remotefile* is the name of the file on the remote system. If this form of the argument is used, the last host specified becomes the default host for later transfers in this **tftp** session. In either of these cases, the remote filename must be a full pathname, even if the local and remote files have the same name.
pwd	Displays the name of the current directory on the foreign host.
quit	Ends the file transfer session and exits **ftp**. A synonym for **bye**.
recv *remotefile* [*localfile*]	Copies the remote file to the local host. A synonym for **get**.
rename *source destination*	Renames a file on the foreign host.
rmdir *remotedirectory*	Removes the directory *remotedirectory* at the foreign host.
runique	Toggles, creating unique filenames for local destination files during **get** operations. If unique local filenames is off (the default), **ftp** overwrites local files. Otherwise, if a local file has the same name as specified for a local destination file, **ftp** modifies the specified name of the local destination file with a **.1** extension. If a local file is already using the new name, **ftp** appends the extension **.2** to the specified name, and so on. If **ftp** cannot find a unique name, **ftp** reports an error and the transfer does not take place.

12–10   OSF/1 User's Guide

Using TCP/IP Commands

Subcommand	Description
	Note that **runique** does not affect local filenames generated from a shell command.
send *localfile* [*remotefile*]	Stores a local file on the remote host. A synonym for **put**.
status	Displays the current status of **ftp**, including the current transfer mode (**ascii** or **binary**), connection status, time-out value, and so on.
sunique	Toggles, creating unique filenames for remote destination files during **put** operations. If unique remote filenames is off (the default), **ftp** overwrites remote files. Otherwise, if a remote file has the same name as specified for a remote destination file, the remote FTP server modifies the name of the remote destination file. This renaming mechanism is the same as the **runique** command and must be supported on the remote system.
verbose	Toggles verbose mode. When verbose mode is on (the default), **ftp** displays all responses from the remote FTP server. Additionally, **ftp** displays statistics on all file transfers when the transfers complete.

The following example shows how you can log into a remote system, check the current working directory, list its contents, transfer a file, and then end the session. Assume that you are user **tony** on **host1** and that you wish to work on remote system **host2**.

1. Enter the following command:

    $ **ftp host2**

OSF/1 User's Guide   12–11

Communications Tasks

If the connection to **host2** is successful, information similar to the following is displayed on the local system:

```
Connected to host2.
220 host2 FTP Server systemname ready.
Name (host2:tony): tony
Password:
```

2. Enter your name and password when prompted by the system. A message similar to the following is then displayed on your local system:

```
230 User tony logged in
ftp>
```

3. To set the file transfer type to binary, enter the **binary** subcommand after the ftp> prompt:

   ftp> **binary**

   A message similar to the following is displayed on your local system:

   ```
   200 Type set to I
   ```

4. To check the current working directory, enter the **pwd** command after the ftp> prompt:

   ftp> **pwd**

   A message similar to the following is displayed on your local system:

   ```
   257 "u/tony" is current directory
   ```

5. To list the contents of the current working directory, enter the **ls** command after the ftp> prompt:

   ftp> **ls -l**

Using TCP/IP Commands

A message similar to the following is displayed on your local system, along with the output of the **ls -l** command:

```
200 PORT command successful.
150 Opening BINARY mode data connection for /usr/bin/ls
(192.9.200.1,1026) (0 bytes).
total 2
-rw-r--r--   1 tony      system       101 Jun  5 10:03 file1
-rw-r--r--   1 tony      system       171 Jun  5 10:03 file2
226 Transfer complete.
```

6. To transfer the file **sales** from the remote host to the local host, enter the **get** subcommand. Note the file is being renamed **newsales** on your local system:

   ftp> **get sales newsales**

   A message similar to the following is displayed on your local system:

   ```
   200 PORT command successful.
   150 Opening BINARY mode data connection for testfile
   (192.9.200.1,1029) (1201 bytes).
   226 Transfer complete.
   25 bytes received in 0.0039 seconds (6.3 Kbytes/s)
   ```

7. To end the **ftp** session, enter the **quit** subcommand:

   ftp> **quit**
   221 Goodbye.
   $ _

OSF/1 User's Guide   12-13

Communications Tasks

Transferring Files With tftp

In addition to the **ftp** command, the OSF/1 operating system provides another way to transfer files. With the **tftp** command, you can transfer files between two OSF/1 systems.

Both **ftp** and **tftp** perform similar functions. However, **tftp** performs those functions without logging you into the remote system.

The **tftp** command has two general forms:

- Interactive form
- Command-line form

The following sections describe both the interactive and the command-line forms of the **tftp** command.

Note: Any transfer operation you perform is subject to the security features in effect on both the local and remote systems.

Interactive tftp

With interactive **tftp**, the file transfer operation includes the following steps:

1. The **tftp** command makes a connection to the other system.
2. Once the connection is made, you issue subcommands that instruct the system to transfer the file or files.

   See "Using **tftp** Subcommands" next in this chapter for information about these subcommands.

The interactive **tftp** command has the following general format:

tftp *system_name*

The *system_name* entry is the name of the system you want to reach. This may be another OSF/1 system or another type of system to which you have a connection. (A remote system is sometimes called the host computer.) If

12–14   OSF/1 User's Guide

you do not specify a *system_name* on the command line, you must use either the **get** or the **put** subcommands to make a connection with a remote system.

When you see the `tftp>` prompt, enter the subcommands that you need to make the file transfer. See ''Using **tftp** Subcommands'' next in this chapter for information about these subcommands.

Assume that you wish to reach system **host3**. To do so, perform the following:

1. Enter the following:

    $ **tftp host3**

    When the connection is made, the system displays the following prompt:

    `tftp >`

2. You now may enter any **tftp** subcommand. See the list of subcommands in Table 12-2.

Using tftp Subcommands

When the `tftp>` prompt appears, you can transfer files or do other tasks related to file transfer.

The following is the procedure for using **tftp** subcommands:

1. Enter the subcommand for file transfer or a related task, adding any required filename or pathname.
2. Continue entering subcommands until all the work is finished.
3. To exit **tftp**, enter the **quit** subcommand.

Table 12-2 describes the **tftp** subcommands that let you transfer files and perform related tasks, such as changing the type of file transfer.

Communications Tasks

Table 12–2. The tftp Subcommands

Subcommand	Description
? [*subcommand*]	Displays help information. If a subcommand is specified, only information about that subcommand is displayed.
ascii	Sets the file transfer type to network ASCII. This is the default.
binary	Sets the file transfer type to binary image. This may be more efficient when transferring non-ASCII files.
get *remotefile* [*localfile*]	Transfers a file or set of files from the remote host to the local host. The *remotefile* argument can be specified in one of the following two ways: • As a file that exists on the remote host if a default host was already specified. • As *host:file*, where *host* is the remote host and *file* is the name of the file to copy to the local system. If this form of the argument is used, the last host specified becomes the default host for later transfers in this **tftp** session.
mode *type*	Sets the *type* of transfer mode to that specified, either **ascii** or **binary**. A transfer mode of **ascii** is the default.
put *localfile* [*remotefile*]	Transfers a file or set of files from the local host on to the remote host. The *remotefile* argument can be specified in one of the following two ways: • As a file or directory that exists on the remote host if a default host was already specified. • As *host:remotefile*, where *host* is the remote host and *remotefile* is the name of the file or directory on the remote system. If this form of the argument is used, the last host specified becomes the default host for later transfers in this **tftp** session.

Using TCP/IP Commands

Subcommand	Description
	In either of these cases, the remote filename or directory name must be a fully specified pathname, even if the local and remote directories have the same name. If a remote directory is specified, the remote host is assumed to be an OSF/1 machine.
quit	Exits **tftp**.
status	Shows the current status of **tftp**, including the current transfer mode (**ascii** or **binary**), connection status, time-out value, and so on.
verbose	Turns verbose mode, which displays additional information during file transfer, on or off.

The following example shows how you can connect to a remote system, **host4**, and then transfer a remote file to your local system:

1. Enter the following command:

    $ **tftp host4**

    If the connection to **host4** is successful, the `tftp>` prompt is displayed:

    `tftp> _`

2. To transfer a file **memo6** from the remote host to the current directory on your system, enter the **get** subcommand. Note that the file is being renamed **newmemo** on your local system.

    `tftp>` **get /user/chang/memo6 newmemo**
    `Received 7212 bytes in 9.4 seconds`

3. To end the **tftp** session, enter the **quit** subcommand:

    `tftp>` **quit**
    `$ _`

For more information, see the **tftp** reference page.

OSF/1 User's Guide   12–17

Communications Tasks

Command-Line tftp

With the command-line form of **tftp**, you use flags instead of subcommands to specify file transfer operations. There are two kinds of commands flags you can use:

- Those that put (or write) a local file on to a remote system: **-p** or **-w**.

  Because the **-p** or the **-w** flag can be used interchangeably, this section discusses the **-p** flag only.

- Those that get (or read) remote files on to a local system: **-g** or **-r**.

  Because the **-g** or the **-r** flag can be used interchangeably, this section discusses the **-g** flag only.

If you wish to perform a local-to-remote file transfer, the general form of the command line is the following:

tftp -p *localfile remotehost remotefile* [*mode*]

The **-p** flag specifies that you wish to transfer a local file to a remote system. The *localfile* entry specifies the local file you want to transfer. The *remotehost* entry is the name of the remote system to which you want to transfer the file. This may be another OSF/1 system or another type of system to which you have a connection. The *remotefile* entry specifies the name of the file on the remote system. The *mode* entry specifies whether the file transfer is **netascii** (ASCII) or **image** (binary).

If you wish to perform a remote to local file transfer, the general form of the command line is the following:

tftp -g *remotefile remotehost localfile* [*mode*]

The **-g** flag specifies that you want to transfer a remote file to a local system. The *remotefile* entry specifies the file on the remote system that you want to transfer to the local system. The *remotehost* entry is the name of the remote system from which you want to transfer the file. This may be another OSF/1 system or another type of system to which you have a connection. The *localfile* entry specifies the name of the file on the local system. The *mode* entry specifies whether the file transfer is **netascii** (ASCII) or **image** (binary).

Using TCP/IP Commands

The following example shows how you can transfer a binary file. To transfer the file **core** in the current directory to the **/tmp** directory on system **host3**, enter:

$ **tftp -p core host3 /tmp/core image**
```
Sent 309295 bytes in 15 seconds
$ _
```

For more information, see the **tftp** reference page.

Copying Files (rcp)

You can copy files or directories between two OSF/1 systems with the **rcp** command.

Note: Any copy operation you perform is subject to the security features in effect on both the local and remote systems.

To copy a file from a local to a remote system, use the following general format:

rcp *localfile hostname:file*

The *localfile* entry specifies the local file that you want to copy. The *hostname:file* entry is the name of the remote system, as well as the name you want to give the copied file.

To copy a file from a remote system to your local system, use the following general format:

rcp *hostname:file localfile*

The *hostname:file* entry is the name of the remote system as well as the name of the file you want to copy. The *localfile* entry specifies the name the file will have on the local system. The **rcp** command also allows you to copy directory trees by specifying the **-r** flag on the command line.

Communications Tasks

To copy a directory tree from a local system to a remote system, use the following general format:

rcp -r *localdirectory hostname:directory*

The **-r** flag specifies that you want to copy a directory and all its subdirectories. The *localdirectory* specifies the directory tree on your local system that you want to copy. The *hostname:directory* specifies the directory name on the remote system to which you want to copy the directory tree.

To copy a directory tree from a remote system to your local system, use the following general format:

rcp -r *hostname:directory localdirectory*

The **-r** flag specifies that you want to copy a directory and all its subdirectories. The *hostname:directory* specifies the remote system as well as the directory tree you want to copy. The *localdirectory* specifies the name of the directory on your local system to which you want to copy the directory tree.

To use **rcp**, one of the following must be true:

- Your local system is listed in the **/etc/hosts.equiv** file on the remote system. As a result, your local system is considered as *trusted*. The **/etc/hosts.equiv** file is maintained by the system administrator.

- Your system is listed in the **.rhosts** file in your home directory on the remote system.

The following example copies the file **newreport** from the local directory **/usr/reports/newreport** to the file **/usr/amy/newreport** on the remote system **host7**:

```
$ rcp /usr/reports/newreport host7:/usr/amy/newreport
$ _
```

This example copies the directory **/usr/reports** from the local host to the directory **user/status/newreports** on remote system **host2**:

```
$ rcp -r /usr/reports host2:/user/status/newreports
$ _
```

Logging Into Remote Systems

The OSF/1 operating system provides the following two commands that allow you to log into remote systems:

- The **rlogin** command allows you to log into an OSF/1 or OSF/1 compatible system.

- The **telnet** command allows you to log into an OSF/1 system or any system supporting **telnet**.

The following sections describe the preceding commands.

Note: Any login operation you perform is subject to the security features in effect on the remote systems.

Logging In With rlogin

You can log into another system with the **rlogin** command. Once logged in, you may enter any commands you wish, subject to security restraints. The **rlogin** command has the following basic format:

rlogin [**-l** *user*] *system_name*

The **-l** *user* flag changes the remote username to the one you specify. This practice is useful when you have permission to access files that belong to another user. If you do not specify the **-l** flag, your username is used by default. The *system_name* entry specifies that system with which you want to establish a login session.

Assume that you want to reach system **boston** and log in as yourself. To do so, perform the following:

1. Enter the following:

   $ **rlogin boston**
   Password:

2. Enter your password.

   When the system prompt appears, you are logged into the remote system and can perform any tasks you wish, subject to security restraints.

3. To close the connection and exit from the program, press **<Ctrl-d>**.

Assume that you want to reach system **ames** and log in as another user, **chang**. To do so, perform the following:

1. Enter the following:

   $ **rlogin -l chang ames**
   Password:

2. Enter Chang's password.

   When the system prompt appears, you are logged into the remote system and can perform any tasks you wish, subject to security restraints.

3. To close the connection and exit from the program, press **<Ctrl-d>**.

When using **rlogin**, there are times when you may not be prompted for a password during the login sequence:

- If your local system is listed in the **/etc/hosts.equiv** file on the remote system, then your local system is regarded as a *trusted* system, and you will not need to supply a password. The **/etc/hosts.equiv** file is maintained by the system administrator.

- If the name of your system and, optionally, your username are listed in the **.rhosts** file in your home directory on the remote system, then you will not need to supply a password.

For more information, see the **rlogin** reference page.

Logging In With telnet

You can log into another system with the **telnet** command. The **telnet** command implements the TELNET protocol, which opens a connection to the system.

A **telnet** remote login session consists of the following steps:

1. The **telnet** command logs into a remote system.
2. Once logged in, you can enter any commands you wish, subject to security restraints.
3. You can also enter **telnet** subcommands that allow you to manage the remote session.

The **telnet** command has the following basic format:

telnet *system_name*

The *system_name* entry specifies that system with which you want to establish a login session. If you omit the *system_name*, you can use the **open** subcommand (see Table 12-3) to create a connection after you enter the **telnet** program.

Assume that you wish to reach system **syst2** and log in. To do so, perform the following:

1. Enter the following:

   $ **telnet syst2**

   When the command is accepted, several lines of message text appear on the display, ending with the login prompt.

2. When prompted, enter your password. By default, **telnet** enters your login name when connecting you to the remote system.

   When the system prompt appears, you are logged into the remote system and can perform any tasks you wish, subject to security features, or use **telnet** subcommands. For information on **telnet** subcommands, see "Using **telnet** Subcommands" next in this chapter.

3. To close the connection and exit from the program, press **<Ctrl-]>**, and then enter **q** at the **telnet** prompt. If you are at the `telnet>` prompt or at the system prompt, you can also press **<Ctrl-d>** to close the connection and exit.

Using telnet Subcommands

Table 12-3 contains a partial list of **telnet** subcommands. Before entering each subcommand, press **<Ctrl-t>**. The **<Ctrl-t>** escape sequence tells the program that subsequent information is not text. Otherwise, the program would interpret subcommands as text.

For each of the subcommands, you only need to type enough letters to uniquely identify the command. (For example, **q** is sufficient for the **quit** command.) For a complete list of **telnet** subcommands, see the **telnet** reference page.

Table 12–3. The telnet Subcommands

Subcommand	Description
? [*subcommand*]	Displays help information. If a subcommand is specified, only information about that subcommand is displayed.
close	Closes the connection and returns to **telnet** command mode.
display [*argument*]	Displays all of the **set** and **toggle** values if no *argument* is specified; otherwise, lists only those values that match *argument*. For information on the **set** and **toggle** commands, see the **telnet** reference page.
open *host* [*port*]	Opens a connection to the specified *host*. The host specification can be either a hostname or an Internet address in dotted-decimal form. If no *port* is given, **telnet** attempts to contact a TELNET server at the default port.
quit	Closes a connection and exits the **telnet** program. A **<Ctrl-d>** in command mode also closes the connection and exits.
status	Shows the status of **telnet**, including the current mode and the currently connected remote host.
z	Opens a shell on the local host. The shell started is the one specified by the **SHELL** environment variable. When you exit the shell using **<Ctrl-d>**, **telnet** returns to the remote session.

The following example shows you how to log into remote system **host3**, check the status of the **telnet** program with the **status** subcommand, and then quit the program:

1. Enter the following:

    $ **telnet host3**

    ```
    Trying...
    Connected to host3
    ```

Communications Tasks

```
Escape Character is '^]'.
host3 TCP Telnet service.
login: (Entered automatically)
password:
```

2. Enter your password.

3. Press **<Ctrl-t>** to receive the `telnet>` prompt.

4. Enter the **status** subcommand at the prompt:

   `telnet >`**status**

   Information similar to the following is then displayed on your screen:

   ```
   Connected to host3.
   Operating in character-at-a-time mode.
   Escape character is '^T'.
   ```

   To enter another subcommand, press **<Ctrl-t>**. To display the remote prompt, press **<Return>**.

5. To quit the **telnet** session from the system prompt, press **<Ctrl-d>**.

   To quit the **telnet** session from the `telnet` subcommand prompt, enter **q**, or press **<Ctrl-d>**.

Executing Commands Remotely (rsh)

The **rsh** command allows you to run a command on a designated remote system. Use **rsh** when you want to run a single noninteractive command on an OSF/1-based remote system. If you want to run an interactive command or a series of commands, use the **rlogin** command instead.

The **rsh** command has the following general format:

rsh [**-l** *user*] *system_name command*

The **-l** *user* flag changes the remote username to the one you specify. This practice is useful when you want to perform operations that are accessible to the specified user. If you do not specify the **-l** flag, your username is used by default. The *system_name* entry specifies that system on which you want to run the command. The *command* entry specifies the command you want to run.

Note that, if you do not specify the *command* entry, **rsh** prompts you for login information.

To use **rsh**, one of the following must be true:

- Your local system is listed in the **/etc/hosts.equiv** file on the remote system. As a result, your local system is considered as *trusted*. The **/etc/hosts.equiv** file is maintained by the system administrator.

- Your system is listed in the **.rhosts** file in your home directory on the remote system.

Assume that you want to append the remote file **test2** on remote system **host2** to the local file **test3**. To do so, enter the following:

$ **rsh host2 cat test2 >> test3**
$ _

Displaying Who Is on Remote Systems (rwho)

Note: To use the **rwho** command, your system must be running the **rwhod** daemon.

The **rwho** command displays the users logged into hosts on the local network. This command displays the following information:

- Username

- Remote system name

- Start date and time for all currently active users (those that have been active during the last hour)

- Number of minutes currently active users have been idle (if they have been inactive for more than 3 minutes but less than an hour)

Communications Tasks

The **rwho** command has the following general format:

rwho [**-a**]

The **-a** flag specifies that you want to display all users, including those who have been idle for an hour or more.

Assume that you want to display all users currently logged into systems on the local network. To do so, enter the following:

```
$ rwho
sue      syst2:pts5      Jan 17 06:30 :20
sue      syst7:console   Jan 17 06:25 :25
lorenzo  syst1:pts0      Jan 17 11:20 :51
steve    syst1:pts8      Jan 16 15:33 :42
helmut   syst4:console   Jan 17 16:32
tom      syst1:console   Jan 17 13:14 :31
ling     syst1:pts7      Jan 17 13:15 :47
server   syst2:console   Jan 17 06:58 :20
alice    syst2:pts6      Jan 17 09:22
$ _
```

For more information, see the **rwho** reference page.

Part 3
System Administration Tasks for the User

Chapter 13
Adding and Removing Users and Groups

This chapter shows you how to add and remove users and groups. Before new users can log in successfully, they must be made known to the system. Likewise, when users or groups no longer have privileges on the system, you must remove their identity from the system.

Adding and removing individual users and groups is a routine but critical activity that is usually performed by the system administrator. However, there may be times when you will be required to perform such activities.

Because adding and removing users requires a higher familiarity with the system than is expected from most general users, we urge you to see your system administrator before attempting any operation in this chapter. Your system administrator can provide you with essential information needed for certain procedures and perhaps step you through the appropriate procedures.

You must have superuser privileges to add and remove users from the system. To become a superuser, you must be logged in as **root**. To obtain the password for **root**, see your system administrator. For more information on superuser privileges and logging in as a superuser, see "Superuser Concepts" in Chapter 5.

After completing this chapter, you will be able to do the following:

- Add new users to the system (interactively and manually)
- Create an environment for new users
- Add groups to the system
- Remove users and their environments from the system
- Become familiar with the files that are affected by adding and removing users

Note: Your system may contain enhanced security features that require an alternate procedure for adding and removing users. If so, see your system administrator for details.

Adding Users

You can add a user to your system either interactively or manually. In most cases, you will want to add a new user interactively because it automates many of the tasks involved in adding a new user to your system. However, for those times that you want to control the process more closely, you may want to add a user manually. See your system administrator for information on which procedure to use.

Before adding a new user account, perform the following tasks:

- Verify the existence of the file system where the user's login directory will reside. If the file system does not exist, see your system administrator.
- Verify the existence of the group that the new user will join. If the group does not exist, create the group now by following the instructions in "Adding a New Group to the **/etc/group** File" later in this chapter.

Once the file system and user's group exist, you can add a new user to your system. The following sections describe both the interactive and manual procedures.

Adding a New User Interactively

To add a new user interactively, use the **adduser** command, which automates many of the tasks involved in adding a new user to your system. The **adduser** command performs the following tasks:

- Adds a new user account to the system password file (**/etc/passwd**)
- Creates a login directory for the user
- Creates **.cshrc**, **.login**, and **.profile** files in the user's login directory
- Adds the user to a specific group in the system group file (**/etc/group**)
- Allows you to create a password for the user (optional) and places that password in encrypted form in the **/etc/passwd** file

To access and use the **adduser** program, follow these steps:

1. As **root**, enter the following command:

   # **adduser**

2. Respond to the prompts that the program displays. The program is simple to use, and the prompts are self-explanatory. You will be prompted for the following information:

   - User's login name
   - User's full name
   - User's group
   - User's login directory
   - User's password (optional)

By default, the **adduser** command allows you to set up the account with a user password. However, if you do not specify a password with the **adduser** command, we recommend that you use the **passwd** command to create a password for the new user. For information on the **passwd** command, see "Assigning an Initial Password" later in this chapter. For more information, see the **adduser** reference page.

OSF/1 User's Guide

Adding a New User Manually

To add a new user manually, perform the following tasks:

1. Add an entry in the **/etc/passwd** file for the new user.
2. Modify entries in the **/etc/group** file or add a new entry for the new user.
3. Create the user's login directory and supply the default shell scripts for the user's working environment.
4. Create the user's mail file.
5. Protect the user account by assigning a password.

The following subsections describe these tasks and provide instructions for editing the files manually.

Adding a User Account to the /etc/passwd File

For every new user, you must add a line to the **/etc/passwd** file. This file is a very important component of your system because it identifies each user (including **root**). If **/etc/passwd** is inaccessible or if it gets corrupted, you risk disabling **root** and other users from logging in.

Use the **vipw** command to modify the **/etc/passwd** file. The **vipw** command ensures that no other user or process can access the **/etc/passwd** file while you are editing it. Before writing your changes back to the disk, **vipw** performs several consistency checks. By default, **vipw** invokes the **vi** editor. If you prefer to use another editor, assign the name of that editor to the environment variable **EDITOR** in your **.login** (or **.profile**) file. For additional information, see the **vipw** reference page. The following subsection describes **/etc/passwd** file entries.

The /etc/passwd File Entries

Each entry in the **/etc/passwd** file is a single line that contains seven fields per line. The fields are separated by colons, and the last field ends with a newline character. The following text shows the format of each entry and describes the meaning of each field:

username:*password*:*UID*:*GID*:*user_info*:*login_directory*:*login_shell*

username
: The name for the new user account. The *username* must be unique and consist of from 1 to 8 bytes. Digits and letters of your alphabet are allowed.

password
: You cannot enter a password directly. Leave the *password* field empty, or enter an * (asterisk). If the password field contains an * (asterisk), a login to that account is disabled. An empty *password* field allows anyone who knows the login name to log into your system as that user. See ''Assigning an Initial Password'' later in this chapter for instructions on assigning a user password with the **passwd** command. The **passwd** command encrypts the specified password and inserts it in the user's *password* field. *Never* try to edit in a password.

UID
: The user ID for this account. This is an integer between 0 (zero) and 32,767 and must be unique for your system. The user ID 0 (zero) is reserved for **root**. We recommend that you assign user IDs in ascending order beginning with 100. Lower numbers are used for pseudo-users like **bin** or **daemon**.

GID
: The group ID for this account. This is also an integer between 0 (zero) and 32,767. The group ID 0 (zero) is reserved for the group **root**. We recommend that you assign group IDs in ascending order beginning with 100.

user_info
: This field contains additional user information such as the full username, office address, telephone extension, and private phone number. The **finger** command displays the information contained in the *user_info* field. For additional information, see the **finger** reference page. Users can change the contents of their *user_info* field

login_directory with the **chfn** command. For additional information, see the **passwd** reference page.

The absolute pathname of the directory where the user is located immediately after logging in. The **login** command assigns this pathname to the shell variable **$HOME**; users, however, can change the value of **$HOME**. If a user changes the value, then the home directory and the login directory are two different directories.

You create the login directory after adding a new user account to the **/etc/passwd** file. Typically, the username is used as the name of the login directory. For additional information on creating a login directory, refer to the **chgrp**, **chmod**, **chown**, and **mkdir** reference pages.

login_shell The absolute pathname of the program that gets started after the user has logged in. Normally, a shell is started. If you leave this field empty, the shell, **/bin/sh**, is started. For information on the shell, refer to the **sh** reference page. Users can change their login shell with the **chsh** command. For additional information, refer to the **passwd** reference page.

A Sample Entry in the /etc/passwd File

Following is an example of how an entry would look in the **/etc/passwd** file:

```
smith:*:201:120:Harold Smith,dev,x1234:/users/smith:/usr/bin/bsh
```

The user account `smith` has user ID 201 and group ID 120. The login directory is `/users/smith` and the Bourne shell (`/usr/bin/bsh`) is defined as the command interpreter. Since the password field contains an * (asterisk), the user `smith` cannot log into the system. See "Assigning an Initial Password" later in this chapter for instructions on how to add a usable password to the **/etc/passwd** file with the **passwd** command.

Adding a User Account to the /etc/group File

The **/etc/group** file serves two purposes:

- It assigns a name to a group ID defined in the **/etc/passwd** file.
- It allows users to be members of more than one group by simply adding the usernames to the corresponding group entries.

Before adding a user account to the **/etc/group** file, examine the file to verify that the group to which you intend to add the new account exists:

- If the group already exists (there is a line entry in the file for that group), then simply add the new user's name to the *user* field within the group's line entry.
- If the group does not exist (there is no line entry in the file for that group), then create a new entry for the group and include the new user's name within that entry in the **/etc/group** file.

To add or edit an **/etc/group** file entry, open and edit the file manually. As a precaution, before you modify the **/etc/group** file, copy it to a file called **/etc/group.old**. As a result, if there are problems with the edited file, you have the reliable older version ready for use. The following subsection describes **/etc/group** file entries.

The /etc/group File Entries

Each entry in the **/etc/group** file is a single line that contains four fields. The fields are separated by colons, and the last field ends with a newline character. The following text shows the format of each entry and describes the meaning of each field:

groupname:*password*:*GID*:*user1*[,*user2*,...,*userN*]

groupname	The name of the group defined by this entry. The *groupname* consists of from 1 to 8 bytes. Digits and the letters of your alphabet are allowed.
password	Leave the *password* field empty. Entries in this field are ignored.

OSF/1 User's Guide   13-7

System Administration Tasks for the User

GID	The group ID for this group. This is an integer between 0 (zero) and 32,767. The group ID 0 (zero) is reserved for **root**. The group ID must be unique.
usernames	The *usernames* belonging to this group as defined in the **/etc/passwd** file. If more than one user belongs to the group, the user accounts are separated by commas. The last user account ends with a newline character. The user list is often so long that it extends over several screen lines.

A user can be a member of more than one group.

Sample Entries in the /etc/group File

If you add a user account to an existing group, specify the username in the *user* field of that group's line entry. The following two line entries in the **/etc/group** file specify that user `jerry` is a member of two groups: `tools` and `dep11`:

```
tools::120:rosy,peter,harold,maude,jerry
dep11::121:bill,mary,ann,peter,dave,jerry
```

If the group does not already exist, add a new entry for the group in the **/etc/group** file. For example, to create a new entry for a group called **software** with the user **jerry** as a member, you would add this line to the **/etc/group** file:

software::122:jerry

Creating the Login ($HOME) Directory

Each user on your system needs a login (**$HOME**) directory. Use the following steps to create this directory manually:

1. Verify that the file system intended for user directories already exists before creating any login directories. If the file system does not exist, see your system administrator.

13–8   OSF/1 User's Guide

Adding and Removing Users and Groups

2. Change your working directory to the target location in the file system. For example, enter:

   # **cd /users**
   # _

3. Make a directory for the user. For example, enter:

   # **mkdir jerry**
   # _

4. Change ownership of the directory to the user. For example, enter:

   # **chown jerry jerry**
   # _

5. Change membership of the user to the desired group. For example, enter:

   # **chgrp tools jerry**
   # _

6. Request a listing of the directory attributes. For example, enter:

   # **ls -lgd jerry**

7. Read the listing and confirm that the attributes correspond to the user's needs. For example, here is output from the previous command:

   drwxr-xr-x 2   jerry   tools   24 Jan   9 10:48 jerry

Providing the Default Shell Scripts

Users can customize their working environment by modifying their login scripts. When a user logs into the system, the invoked login shell looks for start-up files in the login directory. If the shell finds a login script, it reads the file and executes the commands.

System Administration Tasks for the User

With the exception of the **/etc/profile** file, each login script begins with a . (dot). Table 13-1 displays each shell, the corresponding login script, and command control.

Table 13–1. Shells and Their Login Scripts

Shell	Login Script	Command Control
csh	.login .chsrc	Login shell Login shell and subshells
ksh	.profile .kshrc	Login shell Login shell and subshells
bsh	/etc/profile .profile	Login shell Login shell

The system uses these login scripts to initialize local and global environment variables, shell variables, and the terminal type. The distributed software sometimes provides a set of default start-up files for your use. See your system administrator for information about where to find the directory containing these files.

If your distribution software does not contain these files, see your system administrator. Once these files are available, you need only to copy them to the login directory of each new user account.

To copy the login scripts for a new user to the user's login directory, follow these steps:

1. Copy the login scripts for each shell to the new user's login directory by entering the **cp** command. Assume that the **/usr/skel** contains the default login scripts. As a result, to copy the Bourne Shell's **.profile** login script to user **jerry**'s directory, enter:

   # **cp /usr/skel/.profile /users/jerry**
   # _

2. Change directory to the new user's login directory and change file ownership and access permissions from **root** to the new user. For

Adding and Removing Users and Groups

example, to make these changes to the **.profile** file for user **jerry**, enter this sequence of commands:

 # cd /users/jerry
 # chmod 644 .profile
 # chown jerry .profile
_

3. Confirm that the changes were made and get a long listing of the user **jerry** files. For example, enter:

 # ls -al /users/jerry

Creating a Mail File

The mail file must be created in the **/usr/spool/mail** directory. The username must be used as the filename for the mail file. The **mail** command writes all mail arriving for the specified username in the corresponding mail file. When a user wants to read mail, the **mail** command opens and reads from that user's mail file.

The following example illustrates the sequence of commands and output for creating a mail file for user **jerry**:

 # cd /usr/spool/mail
 # touch jerry
 # chown jerry jerry
 # chgrp tools jerry
 # chmod 600 jerry
 # ls -lg jerry
-rw-------   1 jerry   tools   0 Jan 11 17:54 jerry
_

The last line in the previous example specifies that user `jerry` owns the mail file, he has read/write (-rw) permission for it, he belongs to the `tools` group, and the file was created on `Jan 11`. Once the file exists, Jerry can read incoming mail messages and delete the ones that he does not want to keep. With the exception of **root**, only Jerry has access to this file.

System Administration Tasks for the User

Assigning an Initial Password

Use the **passwd** command to assign an initial password for a new user account. When you enter the command, the program prompts for the password. Each password should have at least 6 bytes, and can include digits, symbols, and the letters of the alphabet. After you enter the password, the program prompts you to retype it. The second entry serves as verification.

To assign an initial password, follow these steps:

1. Enter the **passwd** command using this syntax:

   passwd *username*

2. In response to the program's prompt, enter the new password for the user. For example, the program displays these prompts:

   ```
   New password:
   Retype new password:
   ```

   The echo is disabled while you enter the password, thus ensuring password confidentiality. Be sure to tell the user what the password is.

Refer to the **passwd** reference page for a description of the **passwd** command.

Removing a User

There are several tasks that you perform and several files that you edit when you remove a user from your system. You must do the following:

- Remove the user's files and directories
- Remove the user's entry from the **/etc/group** file
- Remove the user's entry from the **/etc/passwd** file

The following subsections describe each task and provide instructions for editing the files manually.

Removing the User's Files and Directories

Before removing anything that belongs to the user, follow these steps:

1. Make sure that the associated files and directories are no longer being used by other users on your system.
2. Make sure that the user's login directory and, if necessary, other directories are backed up to diskette or tape. See your system administrator for details.

To remove the user's login directory with all of its files and subdirectories, use the **rm -r** *login_dir* command. For example, to remove the login directory and its entire tree substructure for user **mary**, enter:

rm -r /users/mary

To remove the user's mail file, use the **rm** *mail_file* command. For example, to remove user **mary**'s mail file, enter:

rm /usr/spool/mail/mary

Make sure that there are no files left that were owned by the user. To check this, use the **find** command. The **find** command locates user files that are either links (identified by a notation of >1), user files within directories (identified by a notation of 1), or user directories (identified by a notation of 2).

If your search locates any user files or directories, use the **chown** command to change the file or directory ownership to a different user (one who still needs to access the file). If you have no reason to save or maintain these files, then remove them.

Removing the User's Account from the /etc/group File

Because users can be members of more than one group, you must modify all line entries in the **/etc/group** file that contain the username within the *user* field. However, you should always create a copy of the **/etc/group** file before you modify it.

System Administration Tasks for the User

Removing the User's Account from the /etc/passwd File

After you remove the user's account from the **/etc/passwd** file, the user account vanishes and the system no longer has a means of identifying the user. To remove the user's account, simply delete the line entry in the **/etc/passwd** file that identifies the user. Use the **vipw** command to edit the **/etc/passwd** file.

Check with the system administrator before attempting to remove a user's account to verify whether your site maintains monthly system accounting. If so, *do not* remove the user's line entry from the **/etc/passwd** file until the monthly accounting has been done. Since the accounting commands access the **/etc/passwd** file, removing the user entry would create inaccuracies in your accounting.

However, since your primary goal is to restrict the user from gaining access to the system, you can immediately suspend the user from logging in. To do this, edit the **/etc/passwd** file and substitute an * (asterisk) for the encrypted user password.

Adding and Removing Groups

Whenever you add or remove a group, you must modify the **/etc/group** file. There are two primary reasons for grouping user accounts:

- Several users work together on the same files and directories; grouping these users together simplifies file and directory access.

- Only certain users are allowed access to system files or directories; grouping these users together simplifies the identification of those privileged users.

The following subsections tell you how to add and remove groups and which commands to use.

Adding a New Group to the /etc/group File

When you want to add a new group, you must add a new entry within the **/etc/group** file. You have two options for adding the entry:

- Use the **addgroup** command to perform the work interactively.
- Use an editor (**vi**, for example) to perform the work manually.

Before adding a new group manually, you need to make some decisions. For example, you must have answers to the following questions:

- What will you name the group? The group name must be unique.
- What number will you assign as the group ID (GID)? The number must be unique within the **/etc/group** file.
- When can you include this information within the **/etc/passwd** file?

When you have answers to these questions (see your system administrator, if necessary), you can proceed with the actual task. The following subsections describe how to do this.

Adding a New Group Interactively with the addgroup Program

To add a new group to the **/etc/group** file interactively, follow these steps:

1. As **root**, enter the following command:

   # **addgroup**

   The program immediately displays its first prompt:

   Enter name for new group:

2. Enter the name of the group. For example, enter:

   Enter name for new group: **doc**

System Administration Tasks for the User

The program next prompts you for a group ID:

```
Enter group number for new group [184]:
```

3. Enter the group ID or accept the default value by pressing **<Return>**.

Adding a New Group Manually

To add a new group to the **/etc/group** file manually, follow these steps:

1. Change the directory to the **/etc** directory.

2. As **root**, copy the **/etc/group** file with the **cp** command. For example, enter:

   # **cp /etc/group /etc/group.new**
   #

3. Open the new file and add the required line entry. See "The **/etc/group** File Entries" earlier in this chapter for a listing of required fields within each line entry in the **/etc/group** file.

4. Close the new file and copy it by overwriting the original **/etc/group** file. For example, enter:

   # **cp /etc/group.new /etc/group**
   #

5. Edit the **/etc/passwd** file to include the new group identification number within the *GID* field of each user who is a member of the group. See "The **/etc/passwd** File Entries" in this chapter for a description of the **/etc/passwd** fields.

A Sample Entry in the /etc/group File

To add a new group called **editors** to your system, add the following line to the **/etc/group** file:

editors::150:

This entry is valid if the group name **editors** does not already exist (and is therefore unique within the file), and if the group ID (**150**) is unique and is the next ascending number available for an entry in the **/etc/group** file.

Removing a Group

To remove a group that no longer has any members, delete the corresponding line from the **/etc/group** file.

To remove a group that still has members, follow these steps:

1. Edit the **/etc/passwd** file line entry for each member of the group. You can either assign a new group number or delete the current group number. If you assign a new group number, make sure that it corresponds to a current (or new) group entry in the **/etc/group** file.

2. Remove the original group line entry from the **/etc/group** file.

Chapter 14

Shutting Down and Rebooting Your System

This chapter describes the process of shutting down and automatically rebooting your system. When you reboot the operating system, you are initiating a set of critical tasks that the system must perform in order to operate successfully.

Shutting down and rebooting the system is a critical task usually performed by the system administrator. However, there may be times when you will be required to perform such an activity.

Because shutting down and rebooting the system requires a higher familiarity with the system than is expected from most general users, we urge you to see your system administrator before attempting any operation in this chapter. Your system administrator can provide you with the essential information needed for performing the procedures correctly, and perhaps step you through the process.

You must have superuser privileges to shut down and reboot the system. To become a superuser, you must be logged in as **root**. To obtain the password for **root**, see your system administrator. For more information on superuser privileges and logging in as a superuser, see "Superuser Concepts" in Chapter 5.

After completing this chapter, you will be able to do the following:

- Understand the basic concepts necessary to shut down and reboot the system
- Stop and automatically reboot your system by using a simplified procedure

This chapter does not contain information about installing the system or performing an initial boot. In addition, it does not attempt to discuss the options for shutdown and rebooting that are available to you depending upon your system configuration. Instead, the chapter presents introductory concepts, and provides a simplified procedure for shutdown and automatic reboot. For detailed information about installation, initial boot, and options for rebooting, see your system administrator.

Shutdown and Reboot Concepts

Shutting down and rebooting the system are critical activities that you may be required to perform. This section covers the concepts that will help you understand what happens during shutdown and rebooting.

In most circumstances, you can shut down the system easily and with minimal disruption to other system users. This is called a controlled shutdown. There are several good reasons for performing a controlled shutdown, namely:

- New software or hardware needs to be added to your configuration. The system is shut down so that additions can be made.
- The system may be on the brink of failure. The system is shut down to examine the problem.
- System performance is degrading rapidly. The system is shut down so that the appropriate changes can be made.
- The file system is possibly corrupt. The system is shut down so that the problems can be fixed.

In each of these and similar situations, consult your system administrator.

Similarly, there are circumstances that are out of your control whereby the system shuts itself down suddenly, causing substantial disruption to users.

This is called an unexpected shutdown. For information on unexpected shutdowns and the procedures necessary for rebooting, see your system administrator.

For controlled shutdowns, there are practical and reasonable ways to shut down your system from either single-user or multiuser mode. Single-user mode is usually used for system maintenance. Under most circumstances, the operating system runs in multiuser mode.

After a controlled shutdown, the system will either be automatically rebooted or manually rebooted. The procedure described next in ''Shutdown and Automatic Reboot Procedure'' performs a controlled shutdown from multiuser mode, and then automatically reboots the system to multiuser mode. See your system administrator for information on manual reboots.

When your system is automatically rebooted, a number of operations are performed. Although certain boot operations are hardware dependent, there are some features that typically apply to all systems. For example:

- The system boots automatically or manually.

  In an automatic boot, the system controls the entire operation. With an automatic boot, the system begins the initialization process and continues until completion or failure. See ''Shutdown and Automatic Reboot Procedure'' for an example of automatic rebooting.

  In a manual boot, the system controls the initial operation, turns control of the procedure over to you, then reinstates control in order to complete the operation. See your system administrator for information on manual booting.

  In an automatic or a manual boot, the operation either succeeds or fails:

  — If the boot operation succeeds, the system initializes. In single-user mode, the system displays the **root** prompt (#) on the console or on the workstation screen. In a multiuser mode, the system displays the login prompt or a start-up display. The prompt or start-up display differs according to the hardware capability and the available start-up software.

  — If the boot operation fails, the system displays an error message followed by a prompt on the console or terminal. In the worst case, the system hangs.

System Administration Tasks for the User

- The user mode that you boot to or that the system boot software defaults to determines who has access to the system, when access is available, what is accessible, and how initialization tasks are handled.

    — In a boot to a multiuser mode, the system loads the kernel and moves through various phases such as hardware and virtual memory initialization, resource allocation, configuration, module loading, and so on. At the conclusion of these activities, the system is fully enabled and accessible to users.

    — In a boot to single-user mode, the software loads the kernel and proceeds through the initialization tasks and creates a Bourne shell (**/sbin/sh**), turns control over to you, and waits for you to exit the shell with the **exit** command or **<Ctrl-d>** before continuing with its start-up tasks.

    Normally, you boot to single-user mode in order to perform specific administrative tasks that are best accomplished without the threat of parallel activity by other users. You perform these tasks manually before exiting the Bourne shell. When you finish your work, you return control to the system, start-up tasks are continued, and mulituser mode is enabled.

Under the best of circumstances, the boot operation succeeds and you move on to other tasks. Under less favorable circumstances, the boot operation flounders or fails completely. In that case, see your system administrator.

The following section describes a straightforward procedure for shutting down and automatically rebooting your system.

Shutdown and Automatic Reboot Procedure

To shut down the system from a multiuser run level, warn all users, and automatically reboot the system to a multiuser run level, follow these steps:

1. Log on as **root**.

2. Change the directory to the root directory:

    # **cd /**

Shutting Down and Rebooting Your System

3. Enter the **shutdown** command using this syntax:

   /usr/sbin/shutdown -r +*Time Message*

For example, to shut down the system in 15 minutes and automatically reboot, with a warning to users that the system is going down for a reboot, enter this command:

/usr/sbin/shutdown -r +15 Rebooting the system

In this case, the system begins to notify users of the impending shutdown, disables logins, and proceeds with the standard shutdown activities involved in bringing the system to the single-user run level. When it completes these activities, **shutdown** automatically reboots the system to a multiuser run level. As part of the reboot operation, **fsck** runs a consistency check on all mounted file systems. If problems are not encountered, the system reboots to a multiuser run level.

Note: If the **fsck** command finds file system inconsistencies, it displays a warning message, recommending that you run **fsck** again from the single-user run level before operating the system in a multiuser run level. If this occurs, see your system administrator.

Chapter 15
Backing Up the System

This chapter describes the importance of performing system backups. Performing a system backup is the process of copying files onto a removable backup medium, such as cartridge tape. In case of data loss, you can copy these files back onto your system.

Performing system backups is a routine but critical activity that is usually performed by system administrators or computer facilities personnel. At some sites, however, individual users may be responsible for their own backups.

After completing this chapter, you will be able to do the following:

- Know why backups are important
- Have an introductory understanding of backup concepts and media
- Be able to perform a backup of multiple files and directories
- Be able to perform a restore of multiple directories

For detailed information on system backups at your site, see your system administrator.

System Administration Tasks for the User

Why Backups are Essential

The hard work that you and others perform on the system is stored in files and directories. These represent a very significant investment of time and effort. At the same time, all computer files are potentially easy to change or erase, either intentionally or by accident. Even if all users on your system are scrupulous, there will be times when files will be inadvertently deleted, or when a file system will be destroyed by an unforeseen hardware failure or a system crash.

To protect against these problems, your system administrator should regularly perform backups by copying files onto a removable medium. Common backup mediums are the following: cartridge tape, 9-track tape, optical disks, and floppy disks. This medium is stored at a remote location for safekeeping.

Should data be lost, the removable medium is brought back from the remote location and mounted on the system so that the data can be copied back onto the system. This process of copying lost data back onto the system is called "restoring."

Backups are also useful for preserving data that is no longer current. For example, suppose that you have just completed a large project. After the files from the old project are backed up, you can delete them to make room on the system for new project files. In addition, at a later date, should you need the old project files, you can have them restored.

There are two kinds of backups:

- Full (archive) backup

  This is a backup of all files on your system.

- Incremental backup

  This is a backup of only those files that have been modified since the last archive backup.

At some companies, performing backups is the responsibility of the system administrator or a computer facilities team. At other companies, an individual user may back up files in addition to the regularly scheduled system backups.

Your system's backup schedule depends upon the volume of use. For example, on a small system that has only one user, a weekly archival backup might be adequate. For large installations with heavy volume, a weekly archival backup and a daily incremental backup might be adequate. See your system administrator about the backup schedule.

To show you how a weekly archive backup and a daily incremental backup help preserve data, assume the following about your site. Weekly archival backups are done on Fridays, and incremental backups are performed daily. Also assume that your file system was destroyed on Tuesday. To restore the file system, your system administrator would do the following:

- Restore Friday's archive backup
- Restore Monday's incremental backup

Work done after Monday's incremental backup would be lost, but would only represent at most one day's work.

The following section describes how to back up and restore multiple files and directories. It is assumed that your system has regularly scheduled archival backups, but that you may perform individual backups for your own personal use.

Sample Backup Procedures

This section shows you how to back up and restore multiple files and directories with the **tar** command. The aim of this section is to provide you with a simple backup and restore procedure that is not hardware or site dependent.

We strongly recommend that you check with your system administrator before performing any backup or restore procedures. This is because your site may have its own shell procedures for the purpose, or it may be using other OSF/1 commands such as **cpio**, **dump**, or **restore**. Your system administrator can provide you with the essential information needed, and perhaps step you through the process.

Note that this section does not provide you with a procedure for backup and restoration of file systems or for performing a complete backup/restore procedure. For those procedures, see your system administrator.

System Administration Tasks for the User

Before you perform a backup, see your system administrator for some vital information. Specifically, you must:

- Know the device name of the backup medium. Typical names might be similar to the following: **/dev/mt1** (tape drive) and **/dev/rz0a** (disk drive). Be aware that device names are all unique to your site.
- If the device medium is a cartridge tape or 9-track tape, know whether it is a high-density, medium-density, or low-density tape.
- Ensure that you have write permission for the backup medium.
- Ensure that the backup medium is loaded and properly formatted prior to its use.

Backing Up Multiple Files

To back up multiple files, use the following format for the **tar** command:

tar cvf *devicename filenames*

The **c** flag specifies that you want to write to the beginning of the medium. The **v** flag specifies that **tar** display information about each file it archives. The **f** flag specifies that the next argument in the command line is the name of the medium upon which you intend to back up your file. The *devicename* entry is the device name of the medium. If the device is a tape, you can specify one of the following density levels immediately after the device name: **h** (high), **m** (medium), or **l** (low). The *filenames* entry can be a list of filenames in the current directory, a list of absolute pathnames, or a combination of both. You may also use pattern-matching characters to specify files. See Chapter 2 for information on pattern matching.

The following example backs up all files in the current directory that begin with the name **report** to a high-density tape medium named **/dev/mt1**:

```
$ tar cvf /dev/mt1h report*
a reportjan 5 blocks
a reportfeb 4 blocks
a reportmar 6 blocks
a reportapr 8 blocks
a reportmay 4 blocks
a reportjun 5 blocks
```

```
a reportjuly 6 blocks
a reportaug 5 blocks
a reportsept 4 blocks
$ _
```

The following example backs up all files beginning with the name **memo** in the directory **/user/chang/status** to the floppy disk **/dev/rz2**:

$ tar cvf /dev/rz2 /user/chang/status/memo*
```
a /user/chang/status/memo1 2 blocks
a /user/chang/status/memo2  5 blocks
a /user/chang/status/memo3 9 blocks
a /user/chang/status/memo4 8 blocks
a /user/chang/status/memo5 3 blocks
a /user/chang/status/memo6 7 blocks
$ _
```

Backing Up Directories

Note: The **tar** command backs up the specified directories as well as any subdirectories below them.

To back up directories, use the following format of the **tar** command:

tar cvf *devicename directorynames*

The **c** flag specifies that you want to write to the beginning of the medium. The **v** flag specifies that **tar** display information about each file it archives. The **f** flag specifies that the next argument in the command line is the name of the medium upon which you intend to back up your file. The *devicename* entry is the device name of the medium. If the device is a tape, you can specify one of the following density levels immediately after the device name: **h** (high), **m** (medium), or **l** (low). The *directorynames* entry specifies the absolute pathname of one or more directories.

The following example backs up the directory **/usr/soshanna** to a medium-density tape named **/dev/mt2**:

$ tar cvf /dev/mt2m /usr/soshanna
```
a /usr/soshanna/reportjan 5 blocks
a /usr/soshanna/reportfeb  4 blocks
a /usr/soshanna/reportmar 3 blocks
a /usr/soshanna/reportapr 6 blocks
```

System Administration Tasks for the User

```
a /usr/soshanna/reportmay 4 blocks
a /usr/soshanna/reportjun 5 blocks
a /usr/soshanna/reportjuly 6 blocks
a /usr/soshanna/reportaug 5 blocks
a /usr/soshanna/reportsept 4 blocks
a /usr/soshanna/plans 5 blocks
a /usr/soshanna/designs 9 blocks
a /usr/soshanna/status 7 blocks
$ _
```

The following example backs up the directories **/user/al** and **/user/juan** and all subdirectories beneath them to the high-density tape medium named **/dev/mt3**:

```
$ tar cvf /dev/mt3h /user/juan /user/al
a /user/al
a /user/al/memo1 3 blocks
a /user/al/memo2 4 blocks
a /user/al/schedule 2 blocks
a /user/al/cars/Q1 4 blocks
a /user/al/cars/Q2 3 blocks
a /user/al/cars/Q3 3 blocks
a /user/al/cars/Q4 5 blocks
a /user/juan
a /user/juan/memojan 2 blocks
a /user/juan/memofeb 3 blocks
a /user/juan/memomar 4 blocks
a /user/juan/reports
a /user/juan/reports1 5 blocks
a /user/juan/reports2 3 blocks
a /user/juan/reports3 2 blocks
a /user/juan/reports4 6 blocks
$ _
```

Listing the Contents of a Backup Medium

To list the contents of a backup medium, use the following format for the **tar** command:

tar tvf *devicename* [*directorynames*]

Backing Up the System

The **t** flag specifies that you want to list the files on the backup medium. The **v** flag specifies that, in addition to filenames, you wish to display complete information about each file on the medium. The **f** flag specifies that the next argument in the command line is the name of the medium upon which the files reside. The *devicename* entry is the device name of the medium. If the device is a tape, you can specify one of the following density levels immediately after the device name: **h** (high), **m** (medium), or **l** (low). The *directorynames* entry is optional and specifies the absolute pathname of one or more directories. If you wish to display information about the entire contents of the tape, *do not* specify a directory name.

Assume that you want to list the contents of the medium you just backed up in the previous example. Before doing so, ensure that the tape (**/dev/mt3**) upon which you backed up the directories is mounted and accessible. Then, enter the following command:

```
$ tar tvf /dev/mt3h
drwxrwxr-x 9236/1000   4 Sep 24 14:41:57 1991 /user/al
-rw-rw-r-- 9236/1000   3 Sep 06 11:52:02 1991 /user/al/memo1
-rw-rw-r-- 9236/1000   4 Sep 09 10:43:06 1991 /user/al/memo2
-rw-rw-r-- 9236/1000   2 Aug 14 08:22:01 1991 /user/al/schedule
-rw-rw-r-- 9236/1000   4 Mar 29 16:33:44 1991 /user/al/cars/Q1
-rw-rw-r-- 9236/1000   3 Jun 28 17:14:18 1991 /user/al/cars/Q2
-rw-rw-r-- 9236/1000   3 Sep 30 18:45:03 1991 /user/al/cars/Q3
-rw-rw-r-- 9236/1000   5 Dec 30 17:01:49 1991 /user/al/cars/Q4
drwxrwxr-x 9236/1000   4 Jan 05 10:18:45 1990 /user/juan
-rw-rw-r-- 9236/1000   2 Jan 31 09:06:24 1990 /user/juan/memojan
-rw-rw-r-- 9236/1000   3 Feb 28 16:10:58 1990 /user/juan/memofeb
-rw-rw-r-- 9236/1000   4 Mar 30 09:29:12 1990 /user/juan/memomar
drwxrwxr-x 9236/1000   4 Jan 30 11:56:45 1990 /user/juan/reports
-rw-rw-r-- 9236/1000   5 Mar 07 09:35:16 1990 /user/juan/reports1
-rw-rw-r-- 9236/1000   3 May 23 13:31:34 1990 /user/juan/reports2
-rw-rw-r-- 9236/1000   2 Aug 15 07:50:21 1990 /user/juan/reports3
-rw-rw-r-- 9236/1000   6 Jan 23 08:55:18 1991 /user/juan/reports4
$ _
```

Restoring Multiple Directories

To restore directories, use the following format for the **tar** command:

tar xvf *devicename* [*directorynames*]

System Administration Tasks for the User

The **x** flag specifies that you want to restore files from the specified medium. The **v** flag specifies that **tar** display information about each file it archives. The **f** flag specifies that the next argument in the command line is the name of the medium upon which you intend to back up your file. The *devicename* entry is the device name of the medium. If the device is a tape, you can specify one of the following density levels immediately after the device name: **h** (high), **m** (medium), or **l** (low). The *directorynames* entry is optional and specifies the absolute pathname of one or more directories. If you wish to restore the entire contents of the tape, do not specify a directory name.

Assume that the directories you backed up in a previous example (**/user/al** and **/user/juan** and all subdirectories beneath them) have been inadvertently deleted and that it is your job to restore them.

Before performing the restore procedure, ensure that the tape (**/dev/mt3**) upon which you backed up the directories is mounted and accessible. Then, enter the following command:

```
$ tar xvf /dev/mt4h
a /user/al
/user/al/memo1 3 blocks
/user/al/memo2 4 blocks
/user/al/schedule 2 blocks
/user/al/cars/Q1 4 blocks
/user/al/cars/Q2 3 blocks
/user/al/cars/Q3 3 blocks
/user/al/cars/Q4 5 blocks
/user/juan
/user/juan/memojan 2 blocks
/user/juan/memofeb 3 blocks
/user/juan/memomar 4 blocks
/user/juan/reports
/user/juan/reports1 5 blocks
/user/juan/reports2 3 blocks
/user/juan/reports3 2 blocks
/user/juan/reports4 6 blocks
$ _
```

For more information, on performing backups and restores, see the **tar** reference page.

Appendix A
A Beginner's Guide to Using vi

From writing memos to modifying C programs, editing text files is one of the most common uses of any computer system, and **vi** is particularly well-suited for the day-to-day tasks of most computer users. Using **vi**, you can quickly and easily open a file, edit it, and save the results. The **vi** editor operates basically the same way on all UNIX based systems, so learning it will allow you to edit on any system.

While **vi** does not have some of the features of proprietary text editors and word processors, it is a full-featured text editor with the following major features:

- Fast processing, especially on start-up and global operations
- Full-screen editing and scrolling capability, unlike the line editors **ed** and **ex**, on which **vi** is based
- Separate text entry and edit modes
- Global substitution and complex editing commands using the underlying **ex** commands
- Access to operating system level commands
- Customizability of system parameters and keyboard mappings

The **vi** editor works in two modes: command mode and input mode. Command mode is the mode **vi** starts in, and the normal mode for **vi**. In command mode, the characters you type are treated as commands for manipulating the text. In input mode, the characters you type are actually placed into the text.

This appendix shows you how to use the basic features of **vi**. When you finish reading it, you will understand the basic editing models used by **vi** and be able to do the following:

- Open or create a file for editing
- Move the cursor within the file
- Enter new text into the file
- Change existing text within the file
- Search for simple strings within the file
- Move and copy text
- Make simple global substitutions in the file
- Write out all or part of the text to a file
- Delete, move, or copy blocks of text
- Customize your editing environment

This appendix provides only an introduction to the features of **vi**. If you want to learn more, see the **vi** reference page. You may also read one of the many books that describe its advanced features.

This appendix is divided into three sections. The first section gets you started using **vi**. The second section shows you some advanced techniques for speeding up your work. The third section shows you how to take advantage of the power of the underlying **ex** commands.

Getting Started

This section will show you how to open a file with **vi**, move around within it, create some text, change that text, and save your changes. When you are done reading this section, you will be able to use **vi** to create any text file or make simple changes to any existing file.

Before you get started, you will create a file to edit. Create that file with the **cat** command as follows:

$ **cat > my.file**
You can use this text file
to experiment with vi.
<Ctrl-d>
$ _

We will use your newly created file in the examples that follow.

Opening a File

Whether creating a new file or opening an existing file, the syntax for using **vi** is the same:

vi [*file*]

To open the file **my.file**, enter the **vi** command as follows:

$ **vi my.file**

Your screen should look like the following:

```
You can use this text file
to experiment with vi.
~
~
~
 .
 .
 .
~
~
~
"my.file" 2 lines, 46 characters
```

You should see the text of your sample file at the top of the screen, and a number of lines following it that begin with a ~ (tilde). The lines beginning with tildes are the remaining blank lines on your screen. The line at the very bottom of the screen shows the name of the file, the number of lines in the file, and the number of characters.

To quit **vi** at this point, enter:

:q

Exiting **vi** is described in more detail later in this appendix.

Moving Within the File

If you have closed **my.file**, reopen it as described in the previous section. The text cursor should be on the first character of the file: the Y in You.

When you start up **vi**, it is in command mode. In command mode, the characters you enter are treated as commands rather than text input to the file. You can use the keys <h>, <j>, <k>, and <l> to move the cursor one character at a time to the left, down, up, and right, respectively. Try moving the cursor to the first letter of the word experiment by typing:

lllj

A Beginner's Guide to Using vi

Note that, if your keyboard is equipped with arrow keys, you may be able to use them to move left, right, up, or down. However, using **<h>**, **<j>**, **<k>**, and **<l>** allows you to keep your fingers on the main section of the keyboard for faster typing. Also note that there is no need to press **<Return>** after most **vi** commands. In fact, when you are in command mode, pressing **<Return>** moves the cursor to the first character of the next line.

You can also move the cursor by whole word boundaries. The **<w>** command moves to the beginning of the next word. Move the cursor to the beginning of the word with by typing:

w

You can also use the **<b>** command to move back to the next beginning of a word. For example, move to the beginning of the word experiment again by typing:

b

Now see what happens when you do not use the **<b>** command from the beginning of a word by typing:

llllb

The cursor returns to the beginning of the word experiment.

The word motion commands will wrap to the next or previous text line when appropriate. Try moving the cursor to the beginning of the word text by typing:

bbb

There are a few other interesting movement commands you should know about at this point. The **<0>** and **<$>** commands move to the beginning and end of the current text lines. The **<)>** and **<(>** commands move to the beginning of the next and previous sentences. And the **<}>** and **<{>** commands move to the beginning of the next and previous paragraphs.

In larger files, you can move the cursor by whole screenfuls and scroll the screen at the same time by using the **<Ctrl-f>** and **<Ctrl-b>** commands. The **<Ctrl-f>** command moves the cursor to scroll the text one screen forward, and **<Ctrl-b>** moves the cursor one screen backward.

The **vi** editor has many more movement commands. When you have learned the basics, you should look at a more advanced book or read the **vi** reference page for a full list.

Entering New Text

To enter new text into a file, you must change to input mode. In input mode, the characters you type are added directly to the text of the file. You can always get back from input mode to command mode by pressing **<Esc>**. If you ever lose track of which mode you are in, press **<Esc>** a couple of times to get back into command mode. If your system is so configured, you will hear a bell when you press **<Esc>** while in command mode.

Add the word **new** just before `text` in the file. First, move the cursor to the `t` in `text`. Then, enter input mode by typing:

i

Next, enter the word **new**, plus a space character:

new<Space>

Now exit input mode by pressing:

<Esc>

The cursor should now be on the space between the words `new` and `text`.

The **<i>** command starts inserting text *before* the character with the cursor. To insert text *after* the character with the cursor, use the **<a>** command. You need the **<a>** command to add text to the end of a line.

The **<o>** command creates a new line below the line with the cursor and allows you to insert text at the start of that new line. To add a sentence to the end of this file, first move the cursor to the next line by typing:

j

The cursor should be on the `i` in `vi`. Then, enter input mode by typing:

o

A Beginner's Guide to Using vi

Enter the new sentence, which can include return characters as follows, and press **<Esc>** to return to command mode when you are finished. If you make a mistake, you can use **<Backspace>** to correct it.

New text can be easily entered<Return>
while in input mode.< Esc>

Your screen should now look like the following:

```
You can use this new text file
to experiment with vi.
New text can be easily entered
while in input mode.
~
~
~
       .
       .
       .
~
~
~
"my.file" 4 lines, 102 characters
```

There is also an **<O>** command, which creates a new line above the current line and starts inserting text at the start of the new line. This is most useful for adding new text to the top of the file, but can be used anywhere.

There are two other commands that start input mode: **<I>** and **<A>**. The **<I>** command starts inserting text before the first character of the current line. The **<A>** command starts inserting text after the last character of the current line.

Editing Text

Up to this point you have only learned how to add new text to the file, but what if you need to change some text? The **vi** editor provides commands for both deleting and changing blocks of text. For example, to remove the word `easily`, move the cursor to the first character of the word and type:

dw

This is a combination of the delete command **<d>**, and the motion command **<w>**. In fact, many **vi** commands can be combined with motion commands to specify the duration of the action. The general form of a **vi** command follows:

[number][command]motion

The *command* entry represents an action command, *motion* represents a motion command, and *number* optionally represents the number of times to perform the command. You also can use this general form to move the cursor in larger steps. For example, to move the cursor forward five words, enter:

5w

Deleting Multiple Words

Using the general form of commands, you can delete the last five words of this text file by moving to the beginning of the last line and entering:

5dw

Note that it takes five words to delete the whole line, rather than four. This is because the trailing period counts as a word.

There is a special shortcut for deleting whole lines at a time. It is the **dd** command. The **dd** command can also be used with a number to delete multiple lines.

Changing Text

The command for changing text, **<c>**, can be used to combine the actions of deleting and returning to input mode. It follows the same general form as the **<d>** command. To change the text new text to almost new demo, you can move the cursor to the first character in the word new. Then, enter the command:

2cw

The text will not immediately disappear. Instead, a $ (dollar sign) is placed at the end of the change range (the last t in text), and you are placed in input mode. The text you type will overwrite the existing text up to the dollar sign and then extend the text as needed. Enter the new text by typing:

almost new demo<Esc>

Both the **<c>** and **<d>** commands can be used together with any of the motion commands to give you more editing power.

Undoing a Command

If you make a change and then realize it was in error, you may still be able to correct it. The **<u>** command undoes the last command entered. Try undoing the last command by typing:

u

The string almost new demo will be changed back to new text.

Finishing Your Edit Session

After you finish making changes, you need to save those changes and quit **vi**. To save your changes and quit **vi**, enter:

:wq<Return>

Note that the format of this command is much different than other **vi** commands. That is because it is not a **vi** command. It is an **ex** command. When you press **<:>**, you should note that it appears at the bottom of the screen. The **<:>** command begins all **ex** commands from within **vi**. The **wq** command writes the file and quits the editing session. You need to press **<Return>** after the command to signify to **ex** that you are finished entering the command. You will learn more about **ex** commands later in this appendix.

If you want to quit **vi** without saving your changes, you can do so by entering:

:q!<Return>

Now you have learned enough about **vi** to edit any file. The following sections show you some advanced techniques that can improve your productivity and allow you to customize your environment.

Using Advanced Techniques

This section will show you how to search for strings, move text, and copy and paste text. As you deal with larger documents, all these tasks increase your ability to work efficiently. At the end of this section is a short list of some other useful advanced features of **vi**.

Searching for Strings

In a large document, searching for a particular text string can be very time consuming. The **</>** command prompts for a string to search for in the file. When you press **<Return>**, **vi** searches the file for the next occurrence of the string you entered.

To try searching for a string, first move to the top of the document. If you do not have it open, reopen the file **my.file**. Then, type **</>** followed by the string **th** and press **<Return>** as follows:

/th<Return>

As soon as you enter **</>**, it will be displayed on the bottom of the screen. As you type the string **th**, it will be echoed at the bottom of the screen. You can use **<Backspace>** to fix mistakes as you type the search string. After pressing **<Return>**, the cursor is moved to the first occurrence of the string.

The **<n>** command searches for the next occurrence of the last string you searched for. Try it now by entering:

n

The cursor should move to the next occurrence of the string, which is the th in the word with. You can also use **<N>** like **<n>** to search the other direction through the file.

The **<?>** command can be used in the same way as **</>** to specify a search string for a backward search through the file. When you search backward, the **<n>** command moves the cursor backward to the next occurrence of the string, and the **<N>** command moves the cursor forward.

Moving Text

The first step to moving a block of text is to select text for moving. In fact, you already know how to do this. The **<d>** command not only deletes a block of text but also copies it to a paste buffer. Once in the paste buffer, the text can be moved by repositioning the cursor and then using the **<p>** command to place the text after the current cursor position.

To delete the first line of the file, move there and type:

dd

The line is deleted and copied into the paste buffer, and the cursor is moved to the next line in the file. To paste the line following the current line, type:

p

The **<P>** command can be used to paste text before the cursor rather than after it.

If you delete a letter or word-size block, it will be pasted into the new position within the current line. For example, to move the word can to just before the word with, you could use the following command sequence:

/can<Return>
dw
/with<Return>
P

Copying Text

You copy text in the same manner as you move it, except that, instead of using the delete text command **<d>**, you use the yank text command **<y>**. The **<y>** command copies the specified text into the paste buffer without deleting it from the text. It follows the same syntax as the **<d>** command. You can also use the shortcut **yy** to copy an entire text line into the paste buffer, in the same way as **dd**.

For example, you can copy the first two lines of the file to a position immediately underneath them. To do so, enter the following command sequence from the first line of the file:

2yy
j
p

Note that you must move down one line using **<j>**; otherwise, the two lines will be pasted after the first line rather than after the second.

Other vi Features

You may want to try some of the other features of **vi**. The reference page for **vi** lists its available commands. You may want to pay particular attention to the following:

J	Joins the following line to the current line.
.	Repeats the last command.
s	Substitutes the current character with the following entered text.
x	Deletes the current character.
~	Changes the alphabetic case of the current character.
!!	Executes an OSF/1 command on the current line of text and replaces the text with the output.
<Ctrl-l>	Refreshes the screen when problems with the screen display features of **vi** occur. Anytime your screen is displaying confusing output, press **<Ctrl-l>**.

Using the Underlying ex Commands

The **vi** screen editor is based upon the **ex** line editor. The underlying **ex** line editor can bring the power of global changes to your entire text file or any large piece of it. Commands from **ex** can be accessed within **vi** by using the **vi** command **<:>**. You were introduced to **ex** commands earlier in this appendix with the **:wq** and **:q!** commands for writing and quitting an editing session.

The **<:>** command causes **ex** to prompt for a single command line at the bottom of the editor screen with a : (colon). Each **ex** command is ended by pressing **<Return>**. You can also enter **ex** more permanently with the **vi** command **<Q>**. This command turns processing over to **ex** until you explicitly return to **vi**. This often happens accidentally. If it should happen to you, you can return to **vi** by typing **vi** at the **:** (colon) prompt followed by **<Return>** as follows:

: vi<Return>

An **ex** command acts on a block of lines in your text file according to the following general syntax:

: [*address*[*,address*]]*command*

The *command*, along with any of its arguments, acts on the lines between and including the first and second *address*. If only one address is specified, the command acts only on the specified line. If no address is specified, the command acts only on the current line. Addresses can be specified in a number of ways. Some of the more common address specifications are the following:

line number	Specifies an address by absolute line number.
/pattern/	Specifies the next line that contains the pattern.
.	Specifies the line that the cursor is on.
$	Specifies the last line of the file.
address±lines	Specifies a relative offset from the addressed line.
%	Specifies all the lines in the file, and is used once in place of both addresses.

The following subsections show some of the most generally useful **ex** commands and some of the customization features offered by **ex**. You should read the reference page for **ex** for a more detailed list of commands.

Making Substitutions

The most common substitution task, possibly the most common **ex** task, is a global substitution of one word or phrase for another. You can do this with the **<s>** command. If you have closed the file **my.file**, reopen it at this point. To change every occurrence of is to was, use the following command:

: %s/is/was/g<Return>

The **vi** command **<:>** prompts for an **ex** command. This substitution command is applied to all lines in the file by the **%** address. The **/** (slash) is used as a separator. (Any other character can be used.) The **g** argument at the end of the command causes the substitution to occur on each instance of the pattern within each line. Without the **g** argument, substitution occurs only once on each line.

You should be careful when making substitutions to ensure that you get what you want. Note that, in the previous command line, the word this has changed to thwas because every occurrence of is was changed to was.

You can add a **c** argument along with the **g** argument to prompt for confirmation before each substitution. The format of the confirmation is a bit complex; however, it is well worth using when you wish to be scrupulous about making global changes.

As an example of confirming a substitution, change the word thwas back to this by issuing the following command:

:%s/thwas/was/gc<Return>

The following prompt appears at the bottom of the screen:

```
You can use thwas text file
              ^^^
```

Note that the was of thwas is emphasized as the text to substitute. As shown in the following example, type **y** and press **<Return>**. You are then prompted for the second substitution:

```
You can use thwas text file
              ^^^y<Return>
You can use thwas text file
              ^^^
```

Type **y** and press **<Return>**, and in response to the Hit return to continue prompt, press **<Return>** once again as follows:

```
You can use thwas text file
4~            ^^^y
You can use thwas text file
4~            ^^^y<Return>
[Hit return to continue]<Return>
```

You will find that the two occurrences of the word thwas have been changed back to this. In addition, you will also be back in command mode with your cursor at the place of the last substitution.

Now try another substitution on our example file. Then, add three lines of new text to the file by using the **<$>** (go to beginning of last line), **<o>** (create new line), **<yy>** (yank), and **<p>** (paste) commands as follows:

:$<Return>
o
Some new text with a mispelling. <Esc>
yy
p
p
p

You now should have four lines of new text, all containing the incorrectly spelled mispelling.

To fix the spelling error, enter the following command:

:$-3,$s/mispelling/misspelling/<Return>

The address **$-3** indicates the line that is three lines above the last line, and the second address **$** indicates the last line. You do not need to use the **g** operator in this case, since the change is only necessary once on each line.

Writing a Whole File or Parts of a File

The **:wq** command is a special **ex** command that writes the whole file. It combines the features of the write command **w** and the quit command **q**. The only argument that the quit command can take is the exclamation point (**!**). It forces the session to quit even if changes made to the file would be lost by quitting.

The **w** command can also take addresses and a filename argument, which allows you to save part of your text to another file. For example, to save the first three lines of your text to the new file **my.new.file**, use the following command:

:1,3w my.new.file\<Return\>

Deleting a Block of Text

The delete command in **ex** is **d**, just as in **vi**. To delete from the current line to the end of the file, use the following command:

:.,$d\<Return\>

Moving and Copying Blocks of Text

The **ex** command **d** saves the deleted text to the same paste buffer as the **vi** command. You can also use the **ex** copy command **ya** (for yank), and the paste command **pu** (for put) to copy and paste text.

Customizing Your Environment

The **ex** editor provides two mechanisms for customizing your **vi** environment. You can use the **:set** command to set environment variables, and the **:map** command to map a key sequence to a **vi** command key.

Environment variables are set either by assigning them as *option* or **no***option* for Boolean variables, or by assigning them as *option=value*. The full set of environment variables is described in the **ex** reference page. Table A-1 lists some of the more common variables.

Table A–1. Selected vi Environment Variables

Variable	Description
errorbells	Specifies that, when an error is made, a bell sounds. This is the default setting.
ignorecase	Specifies that, when searches are performed, the case of characters should be ignored. The default variable setting is **noignorecase**.
number	Specifies that line numbers are to be displayed at the left margin. The default variable setting is **nonumber**.
showmatch	Specifies that, when you type a matching parenthesis or brace, the cursor moves to the matching character and then returns. The default variable setting is **noshowmatch**.
tabstop	Specifies the amount of space between tab stops. The default setting is 8 spaces.
wrapscan	Specifies that searches should wrap around the beginning or end of the file. This is the default variable setting.
wrapmargin	Creates an automatic right margin located a specified number of characters from the right-hand side of your workstation screen. Whenever your cursor reaches the specified right-hand margin, an automatic new line is generated, and the word you are keying is brought to the next line. We recommend that you set the **wrapmargin** variable to a value with which you are comfortable. Otherwise, **vi** will use the default setting of 0. Using the default setting means that your cursor jumps to the next line when it reaches the end of your workstation screen; however, parts of the word you are keying may be on separate lines.

Try displaying the line numbers of your example file by entering the following command:

:set number<Return>

Remove the line numbers by entering:

:set nonumber<Return>

The **:map** command sets a single **vi** command key to a **vi** command sequence. The syntax for the **:map** command follows:

:map *key sequence*<**Return**>

This command sequence replaces any existing command for that key. The command sequence should be identical to the keystrokes you want to map, except that special keys such as **<Return>**, **<Esc>**, and keys modified with **<Ctrl>** must be quoted first with **<Ctrl-V>**. Because the **<q>** and **<v>** keys do not have commands associated with them, they are good keys to map.

For example, to map a key sequence that inserts a line into your text that says **This space held for new text**, you could use the following command:

:map q oThis space held for new text<Ctrl-V><Esc><Return>

Note the use of **<Ctrl-V>** to quote the **<Esc>** character.

Saving Your Customizations

You can make your environment customizations permanent by placing the appropriate **ex** commands in a file named **.exrc** in your home directory. Commands placed in this file will take effect every time you enter **vi** or **ex**. In this file, you do not need to use the **vi** command **<:>**, since these commands are read directly by the underlying **ex** editor.

For example, to customize your environment to always display line numbers for your files, to use the map sequence shown in the previous section, and to set an automatic right margin of five spaces, you would first open the **.exrc** file with **vi** in your home directory, and add the following lines of text:

set number
map q oThis space held for new text<Ctrl-V><Esc>
set wrapmargin=5

After you write this file, open your example file by reinvoking **vi** to verify that it works.

Appendix B
Creating and Editing Files With ed

This appendix explains how to create, edit (modify), display, and save text files with **ed**, a line editing program. If your system has another editing program, you may wish to learn how to do these tasks with that program.

A good way to learn how **ed** works is to try the examples in this appendix on your system. Since the examples build upon each other, it is important for you to work through them in sequence. Also, to make what you see on the screen consistent with what you see in this guide, it is important to do the examples just as they are given.

In the examples, everything you should type is printed in boldface. When you are told in the text to *enter* something, you should type all of the information for that line and then press **<Return>**.

Because **ed** is a line editor, you can work with the contents of a file only one line at a time. Regardless of what text is on the screen, you can edit only the *current* line. If you have experience with a screen editing program, you should pay careful attention to the differences between that program and **ed**. For example, with the **ed** program, you cannot use the ↑ and ↓ keys to change your current line.

Understanding Text Files and the Edit Buffer

A file is a collection of data stored together in the computer under an assigned name. You can think of a file as the computer equivalent of an ordinary file folder. It may contain the text of a letter, a report, or some other document, or the source code for a computer program.

The edit buffer is a temporary storage area that holds a file while you work with it; it is the computer equivalent of the top of your desk. When you work with a text file, you place it in the edit buffer, make your changes to the file (edit it), and then transfer (copy) the contents of the buffer to a permanent storage area.

The rest of this appendix explains how to create, display, save, and edit (modify) text files.

Creating and Saving Text Files

To create and save a text file, perform the following steps:

1. At the shell prompt, enter:

    ed *filename*

    where *filename* is the name of the file you want to create or edit.

2. When you receive the **?***filename* message, enter:

    a

3. Enter your text.
4. To stop adding text, enter a **.** (period) at the start of a new line.
5. To copy the contents of the edit buffer into the file *filename*, enter:

    w

6. To end the **ed** program, enter:

   q

Starting the ed Program

To start the **ed** program, enter a command of the form **ed** *filename* after the $ (shell) prompt.

In the following example, the **ed afile** command starts the **ed** program and indicates that you want to work with a file named **afile**:

$ **ed afile**
?afile
_

The **ed** program responds with the message ?afile, which means that the file does not now exist. You can now use the **a** (append) subcommand (described in the next section) to create **afile** and put text into it.

Entering Text—The a (Append) Subcommand

To put text into your file, enter **a**. The **a** subcommand tells **ed** to add, or append, the text you type to the edit buffer. Note that, if your file had already contained text, the **a** subcommand would add the new text to the end of the file.

Type your text, pressing **<Return>** at the end of each line. When you have entered all of your text, enter a **.** (period) at the start of a new line.

Note: If you do not press **<Return>** at the end of each line, the **ed** program automatically moves your cursor to the next line after you fill a line with characters. However, **ed** treats everything you type before you press **<Return>** as one line, regardless of how many lines it takes up on the screen; that is, the line *wraps around* to the beginning of the next line (based upon your workstation display settings).

The following example shows how to enter text into the file **afile**:

**a
The only way to stop
appending is to type a
line that contains only
a period.
.**

If you stop adding text to the buffer and then decide you want to add some more, enter another **a** subcommand. Type the text and then enter a period at the start of a new line to stop adding text to the buffer.

If you make errors as you type your text, you can correct them before you press **<Return>**. Use **<Backspace>** to erase the incorrect character(s). Then type the correct characters in their place.

Displaying Text—The p (Print) Subcommand

Use the **p** (print) subcommand to display the contents of the edit buffer.

To display a single line, use the subcommand *n***p** (where *n* is the number of the line):

2p
```
appending is to type a
```

To display a series of lines, use the *n,m***p** subcommand, where *n* is the starting line number and *m* is the ending line number:

1,3p
```
The only way to stop
appending is to type a
line that contains only
```

Creating and Editing Files With ed

To display everything from a specific line to the end of the buffer, use the *n*,**$p** subcommand, where *n* is the starting line number and **$** stands for the last line of the buffer.

In the following example, **1,$p** displays everything in the buffer:

1,$p
The only way to stop
appending is to type a
line that contains only
a period.
_

Note: Many examples in the rest of this appendix use **1,$p** to display the buffer's contents. In these examples, the **1,$p** subcommand is optional and convenient. It lets you verify that the subcommands in examples work as they should. Another convenient **ed** convention is **,p**, which is equivalent to **1,$p**; that is, it displays the contents of the buffer.

Saving Text—The w (Write) Subcommand

The **w** (write) subcommand writes, or copies, the contents of the buffer into a file. You can save all or part of a file under its original name or under a different name. In either case, **ed** replaces the original contents of the file you specify with the data copied from the buffer.

Saving Text Under the Same Filename

To save the contents of the buffer under the original name for the file, enter **w**, as follows:

w
78
_

The **ed** program copies the contents of the buffer into the file named **afile** and displays the number of characters copied into the file (78). This number includes blanks and characters such as **<Return>** (sometimes called "newline"), which are not visible on the screen.

The **w** subcommand does not affect the contents of the edit buffer. You can save a copy of the file and then continue to work with the contents of the buffer. The stored file is not changed until the next time you use **w** to copy the contents of the buffer into it. As a safeguard, it is a good practice to save a file periodically while you work on it. Then, if you make changes (or mistakes) that you do not want to save, you can start over with the most recently saved version of the file.

Note: The **u** (undo) subcommand restores the buffer to the state it was in before it was last modified by an **ed** subcommand. The subcommands that **u** can reverse are **a, c, d, g, G, i, j, m, r, s, t, v,** and **V**.

Saving Text Under a Different Filename

Often, you may need more than one copy of the same file. For example, you could have the original text of a letter in two files—one to keep as it is, and the other to be revised.

If you have followed the previous examples, you have a file named **afile** that contains the original text of your document. To create another copy of the file (while its contents are still in the buffer), use a subcommand of the form **w** *filename*, as the following example shows:

w bfile
78
_

At this point, **afile** and **bfile** have the same contents, since each is a copy of the same buffer contents. However, because **afile** and **bfile** are separate files, you can change the contents of one without affecting the contents of the other.

Creating and Editing Files With ed

Saving Part of a File

To save part of a file, use a subcommand of the form *n,m*w *filename*, where:

n   is the beginning line number of the part of the file you want to save.

m   is the ending line number of the part of the file you want to save (or the number of a single line, if that is all you want to save).

filename   is the name of a different file (optional).

In the following example, the **w** subcommand copies lines **1** and **2** from the buffer into a new file named **cfile**:

1,2w cfile
44
_

Then **ed** displays the number of characters written into **cfile** (**44**).

Leaving the ed Program—The q (Quit) Subcommand

Caution: You lose the contents of the buffer when you leave the **ed** program. To save a copy of the data in the buffer, use the **w** subcommand to copy the buffer into a file before you leave the **ed** program.

To leave the **ed** program, enter the **q** (quit) subcommand:

q
$ _

The **q** subcommand returns you to the $ (shell) prompt.

If you have changed the buffer but have not saved a copy of its contents, the **q** subcommand responds with **?**, an error message. At that point, you can either save a copy of the buffer with the **w** subcommand, or enter **q** again, which lets you leave the **ed** program without saving a copy of the buffer.

Loading Files into the Edit Buffer

Before you can edit a file, you must load it into the edit buffer. You can load a file either at the time you start the **ed** program or while the program is running.

To load a file into the edit buffer at the time you start the **ed** program, enter the following:

ed *filename*

This starts **ed** and loads the file *filename* into the edit buffer.

To load a file into the edit buffer while **ed** is running, you can enter one of the following:

- **e** *filename*

    This loads the file *filename* into the buffer, erasing any previous contents of the buffer.

- *n***r** *filename*

    This reads the named file into the buffer after line *n*. If you do not specify *n*, **ed** adds the file to the end of the buffer.

Using the ed (Edit) Command

To load a file into the edit buffer when you start the **ed** program, simply type the name of the file after the **ed** command. The **ed** command in the following example invokes the **ed** program and loads the file **afile** into the edit buffer:

$ **ed afile**
78
_

The **ed** program displays the number of characters that it read into the edit buffer (78).

Creating and Editing Files With ed

If **ed** cannot find the file, it displays ?*filename*. To create that file, use the **a** (append) subcommand described earlier in "Entering Text—The **a** (Append) Subcommand," and the **w** (write) subcommand described earlier in "Saving Text—The **w** (Write) Subcommand."

Using the e (Edit) Subcommand

Once you start the **ed** program, you can use the **e** (edit) subcommand to load a file into the buffer. The **e** subcommand replaces the contents of the buffer with the new file. (Compare the **e** subcommand with the **r** subcommand, described next in "Using the **r** (Read) Subcommand," which adds the new file to the buffer.)

Caution: When you load a new file into the buffer, the new file replaces the buffer's previous contents. Save a copy of the buffer with the **w** subcommand before you read a new file into the buffer.

In the following example, the subcommand **e cfile** reads the file **cfile** into the edit buffer, replacing **afile**. The **e afile** subcommand then loads **afile** back into the buffer, deleting **cfile**. The **ed** program returns the number of characters read into the buffer after each **e** subcommand (44 and 78):

e cfile
44
e afile
78
_

If **ed** cannot find the file, it returns ?*filename*. To create that file, use the **a** (append) subcommand, described earlier in "Entering Text—The **a** (Append) Subcommand," and the **w** (write) subcommand, described earlier in "Saving Text—The **w** (Write) Subcommand."

You can edit any number of files, one at a time, without leaving the **ed** program. Use the **e** subcommand to load a file into the buffer. After making your changes to the file, use the **w** subcommand to save a copy of the revised file. See "Saving Text—The **w** (Write) Subcommand" for information about the **w** subcommand. Then use the **e** subcommand again to load another file into the buffer.

Using the r (Read) Subcommand

Once you have started the **ed** program, you can use the **r** (read) subcommand to read a file into the buffer. The **r** subcommand adds the contents of the file to the contents of the buffer. The **r** subcommand does not delete the buffer. (Compare the **r** subcommand with the **e** subcommand, described earlier in "Using the **e** (Edit) Subcommand," which deletes the buffer before it reads in another file.)

With the **r** subcommand, you can read a file into the buffer at a particular place. For example, the **4r cfile** subcommand reads the file **cfile** into the buffer following line 4. The **ed** program then renumbers all of the lines in the buffer. If you do not use a line number, the **r** subcommand adds the new file to the end of the buffer's contents.

The following example shows how to use the **r** subcommand with a line number:

1,$p
The only way to stop
appending is to type a
line that contains only
a period.
3r cfile
44
1,$p
The only way to stop
appending is to type a
line that contains only
The only way to stop
appending is to type a
a period.
_

The **1,$p** subcommand displays the four lines of **afile**. Next, the **3r cfile** subcommand loads the contents of **cfile** into the buffer, following line 3, and shows that it read 44 characters into the buffer. The next **1,$p** subcommand displays the buffer's contents again, letting you verify that the **r** subcommand read **cfile** into the buffer after line 3.

If you are working the examples on your system, do the following before you go to the next section:

1. Save the contents of the buffer in the file **cfile**:

   w cfile

2. Load **afile** into the buffer:

   e afile

Displaying and Changing the Current Line

The **ed** program is a line editor. This means that **ed** lets you work with the contents of the buffer one line at a time. The line you can work with at any given time is called the current line, and it is represented by the . (period). To work with different parts of a file, you must change the current line.

To display the current line, enter:

p

To display the line number of the current line, enter:

.=

Note: You cannot use ↑ and ↓ to change the current line. To change the current line, use the **ed** subcommands described in the following sections.

To change your position in the buffer, do one of the following:

- To set your current line to line number n, enter:

  n

- To move the current line forward through the buffer one line at a time press **<Return>**.

- To move the current line backward through the buffer one line at a time, enter a - (dash) character.
- To move the current line *n* lines forward through the buffer, enter:

    .+n

- To move the current line *n* lines backward through the buffer, enter:

    .-n

Finding Your Position in the Buffer

When you first load a file into the buffer, the last line of the file is the current line. As you work with the file, you usually change the current line many times. You can display the current line or its line number at any time.

To display the current line, enter **p**, as shown:

p
a period.
_

The **p** subcommand displays the current line (a period.). Because the current line has not been changed since you read **afile** into the buffer, the current line is the last line of the buffer.

Enter **.=** to display the line number of the current line, as shown:

.=
4
_

Since **afile** has four lines, and the current line is the last line in the buffer, the **.=** subcommand displays 4.

Creating and Editing Files With ed

You also can use the **$** (the symbol that stands for the last line in the buffer) with the = subcommand to determine the number of the last line in the buffer:

```
$=
4
_
```

The **$=** subcommand is an easy way to find out how many lines are in the buffer. Note that the **ed $** symbol has no relationship to the $ shell prompt.

Changing Your Position in the Buffer

You can change your position in the buffer (change your current line) in one of two ways:

- Specify a line number (an absolute position)
- Move forward or backward relative to your current line

To move the current line to a specific line, enter the line number; **ed** displays the new current line. In the following example, the first line of **afile** becomes the current line:

```
1
The only way to stop
_
```

Pressing **<Return>** advances one line through the buffer and displays the new current line, as the following example shows:

```
appending is to type a

line that contains only

a period.

?
_
```

OSF/1 User's Guide   B–13

Note that, when you try to move beyond the last line of the buffer, **ed** returns ?, an error message. You cannot move beyond the end of the buffer.

To set the current line to the last line of the buffer, enter **$**.

To move the current line backward through the buffer one line at a time, enter **-** (dashes) one after the other, as the following example shows:

```
-
line that contains only
-
appending is to type a
-
The only way to stop
-
?_
```

When you try to move beyond the first line in the buffer, you receive the ? message. You cannot move beyond the top of the buffer.

To move the current line forward through the buffer more than one line at a time, enter **.n** (where *n* is the number of lines you want to move):

```
.2
line that contains only

_
```

Note that **.2** is an abbreviation for **.+2**.

To move the current line backward through the buffer more than one line at a time, enter: **.-n** (where *n* is the number of lines you want to move):

```
.-2
The only way to stop

_
```

Locating Text

If you do not know the number of the line that contains a particular word or another string of characters, you can locate the line with a context search.

To make a context search, do one of the following:

- To search forward, enter:

    /string to find/

- To search backward, enter:

    ?string to find?

Searching Forward Through the Buffer

To search forward through the buffer, enter the string enclosed in // (slashes):

/only/
```
line that contains only
_
```

The context search (**/only/**) begins on the first line after the current line, then locates and displays the next line that contains the string **only**. That line becomes the current line.

If **ed** does not find the string between the first line of the search and the last line of the buffer, then it continues the search at line 1 and searches to the current line. If **ed** searches the entire buffer without finding the string, it displays the ? error message:

/random/
```
?
_
```

Once you have searched for a string, you can search for the same string again by entering **//**. The following example shows one search for the string **only**, and then a second search for the same string:

```
/only/
The only way to stop
//
line that contains only
_
```

Searching Backward Through the Buffer

Searching backward through the buffer is much like searching forward, except that you enclose the string in question marks (**??**):

```
?appending?
appending is to type a
_
```

The context search begins on the first line before the current line, and locates the first line that contains the string **appending**. That line becomes the current line. If **ed** searches the entire buffer without finding the string, it stops the search at the current line and displays the message **?**.

Once you have searched backward for a string, you can search backward for the same string again by entering **??**. This is because **ed** remembers search strings.

Changing the Direction of a Search

You can change the direction of a search for a particular string by using the **/** (slash) and **?** (question mark) search characters alternately:

```
/only/
line that contains only
??
```

B–16   OSF/1 User's Guide

Creating and Editing Files With ed

```
The only way to stop
```

If you go too far while searching for a character string, it is convenient to be able to change the direction of your search.

Making Substitutions—The s (Substitute) Subcommand

Use the **s** (substitute) subcommand to replace a character string (a group of one or more characters) with another. The **s** subcommand works with one or more lines at a time, and is especially useful for correcting typing or spelling errors.

To make substitutions, do one of the following:

- To substitute *newstring* for *oldstring* at the first occurrence of *oldstring* in the current line, enter:

  s/*oldstring*/*newstring*/

- To substitute *newstring* for *oldstring* at the first occurrence of *oldstring* on line number *n*, enter:

  *n***s**/*oldstring*/*newstring*/

- To substitute *newstring* for *oldstring* at the first occurrence of *oldstring* in each of the lines *n* through *m*, enter:

  *n,m***s**/*oldstring*/*newstring*/

Substituting on the Current Line

To make a substitution on the current line, first make sure that the line you want to change is the current line. In the following example, the **/appending/** (search) subcommand locates the line to be changed. Then the **s/appending/adding text/p** (substitute) subcommand substitutes the string **adding text** for the string **appending** on the current line. The print (**p**) subcommand displays the changed line.

/appending/
```
appending is to type a
```
s/appending/adding text/
p
```
adding text is to type a
_
```

Note: For convenience, you can add the **p** (print) subcommand to the **s** subcommand (for example, **s/appending/adding text/p**). This saves you from having to type a separate **p** subcommand to see the result of the substitution.

A simple **s** subcommand changes only the first occurrence of the string on a given line. To learn how to change all occurrences of a string on the line, see "Changing Every Occurrence of a String" later in this appendix.

Substituting on a Specific Line

To make a substitution on a specific line, use a subcommand of the following form:

ns/oldstring/newstring/

where *n* is the number of the line on which the substitution is to be made. In the following example, the **s** subcommand moves to line number 1, replaces the string **stop** with the string **quit**, and displays the new line:

1s/stop/quit/p
```
The only way to quit
_
```

The **s** subcommand changes only the first occurrence of the string on a given line. To learn how to change all occurrences of a string on the line, see "Changing Every Occurrence of a String."

Substituting on Multiple Lines

To make a substitution on multiple lines, use a subcommand of the following form:

n,ms/oldstring/newstring/

where *n* is the first line of the group and *m* is the last. In the following example, the **s** subcommand replaces the first occurrence of the string **to** with the string **TO** on every line in the buffer.

1,$s/to/TO/
1,$p
```
The only way TO quit
adding text is TO type a
line that contains only
a period.
```

The **1,$p** subcommand displays the contents of the buffer, which lets you verify that the substitutions were made.

Changing Every Occurrence of a String

Ordinarily, the **s** (substitute) subcommand changes only the first occurrence of a string on a given line. However, the **g** (global) operator lets you change every occurrence of a string on a line or in a group of lines.

To make a global substitution on a single line, use a subcommand of the following form:

ns/oldstring/newstring/

In the following example, **3s/on/ON/gp** changes each occurrence of the string **on** to **ON** in line 3 and displays the new line:

3s/on/ON/gp
```
line that cONtains ONly
_
```

To make a global substitution on multiple lines, specify the group of lines with a subcommand of the form:

*n,ms/oldstring/newstring/*g

In the following example, **1,$s/TO/to/g** changes the string **TO** into the string **to** in every line in the buffer:

1,$s/TO/to/g
1,$p
```
The only way to quit
adding text is to type a
line that cONtains ONly
a period.
_
```

Removing Characters

You can use the **s** (substitute) subcommand to remove a string of characters (that is, to replace the string with *nothing*). To remove characters, use a subcommand of the form **s/***oldstring***//** with no space between the **//** (last two slashes).

In the following example, **ed** removes the string **adding** from line number 2 and then displays the changed line:

2s/adding//
```
text is to type a
_
```

B–20   OSF/1 User's Guide

Substituting at Line Beginnings and Ends

Two special characters let you make substitutions at the beginning or end of a line:

^ (circumflex)   Makes a substitution at the beginning of the line.

$ (dollar sign)   Makes a substitution at the end of the line. (In this context, the $ character does not stand for the last line in the buffer.)

To make a substitution at the beginning of a line, use the **s/^/**newstring subcommand. In the following example, one **s** subcommand adds the string **Remember,** to the start of line number 1. Another **s** subcommand adds the string **adding** to the start of line 2:

1s/^/Remember, /p
```
Remember, The only way to quit
```
2s/^/adding/p
```
adding text is to type a
```
```
─
```

To make a substitution at the end of a line, use a subcommand of the form **s/$/**newstring. In the following example, the **s** subcommand adds the string **Then press Enter.** to the end of line number 4:

4s/$/ Then press Enter./p
```
a period.  Then press Enter.
```
```
─
```

Notice that the substituted string includes two blanks before the word **Then** to separate the two sentences.

Using a Context Search

If you do not know the number of the line you want to change, you can locate it with a context search. See ''Locating Text'' earlier in this appendix for more information on context searches.

For convenience, you can combine a context search and a substitution into a single subcommand: /string to find/s/oldstring/newstring/.

In the following example, **ed** locates the line that contains the string **, The** and replaces that string with **,the**:

/, The/s/, The/, the/p
```
Remember, the only way to quit
-
```

Also, you can use the search string as the string to be replaced with a subcommand of the form /string to find/s//newstring/. In the following example, **ed** locates the line that contains the string **cONtains ONly**, replaces that string with **containsonly**, and prints the changed line:

/cONtains ONly/s//contains only/p
```
line that contains only
-
```

Deleting Lines—The d (Delete) Subcommand

Use the **d** (delete) subcommand to remove one or more lines from the buffer. The general form of the **d** subcommand is the following:

*starting line,ending line***d**

After you delete lines, **ed** sets the current line to the first line following the lines that were deleted. If you delete the last line from the buffer, the last remaining line in the buffer becomes the current line. After a deletion, **ed** renumbers the remaining lines in the buffer.

To delete lines from the buffer, do the following:

- To delete the current line, enter:

    d

Creating and Editing Files With ed

- To delete line number *n* from the buffer, enter:

  *n***d**

- To delete lines numbered *n* through *m* from the buffer, enter:

  *n,m***d**

Deleting the Current Line

If you want to delete the current line, simply enter **d**. In the following example, the **1,$p** subcommand displays the entire contents of the buffer, and the **$** subcommand makes the last line of the buffer the current line:

1,$p
```
Remember, the only way to quit
adding is to type a
line that contains only
a period.   Then press Enter.
$
a period.   Then press Enter
d

_
```

The **d** subcommand then deletes the current line (in this case, the last line in the buffer).

Deleting a Specific Line

If you know the number of the line you want to delete, use a subcommand of the form *n*d to make the deletion. In the following example, the **2d** subcommand deletes line 2 from the buffer:

2d
1,$p
```
Remember, the only way to quit
line that contains only
_
```

The **1,$p** subcommand displays the contents of the buffer, showing that the line was deleted.

Deleting Multiple Lines

To delete a group of lines from the buffer, use a subcommand of the form *n*,*m***d**, where *n* is the starting line number and *m* is the ending line number of the group to be deleted.

In the following example, the **1,2d** subcommand deletes lines 1 and 2:

1,2d
1,$p
```
?
_
```

The **1,$p** subcommand displays the ? message, indicating that the buffer is empty.

If you are following the examples on your system, you should restore the contents of the buffer before you move on to the next section. The following example shows you how to restore the contents of the buffer:

e afile
?
e afile
78
_

This command sequence reads a copy of the original file **afile** into the buffer.

Moving Text—The m (Move) Subcommand

Use the **m** (move) subcommand to move a group of lines from one place to another in the buffer. After a move, the last line moved becomes the current line.

To move text, enter a subcommand of the form $x,y\mathbf{m}z$ where:

x is the first line of the group to be moved.
y is the last line of the group to be moved.
z is the line the moved lines are to follow.

In the following example, the **1,2m4** subcommand moves the first two lines of the buffer to the position following line 4:

1,2m4
1,$p
```
line that contains only
a period.
The only way to stop
appending is to type a
```
_

The **1,$p** subcommand displays the contents of the buffer, showing that the move is complete.

To move a group of lines to the top of the buffer, use 0 (zero) as the line number for the moved lines to follow. In the next example, the **3,4m0** subcommand moves lines 3 and 4 to the top of the buffer:

3,4m0
1,$p
```
The only way to stop
appending is to type a
line that contains only
a period.
_
```

The **1,$p** subcommand displays the contents of the buffer, showing that the move was made.

To move a group of lines to the end of the buffer, use **$** as the line number for the moved lines to follow:

1,2m$
1,$p
```
line that contains only
a period.
The only way to stop
appending is to type a
_
```

Changing Lines of Text—The c (Change) Subcommand

Use the **c** (change) subcommand to replace one or more lines with one or more new lines. The **c** subcommand first deletes the line(s) you want to replace and then lets you enter the new lines, just as if you were using the **a** (append) subcommand. When you have entered all of the new text, type a **.** (period) on a line by itself. The general form of the **c** subcommand is the following:

*starting line,ending line***c**

To change lines of text, do the following:

1. Enter a subcommand of the form:

   *n,m*c

   where:

   n is the number of the first line of the group to be deleted.
   m is the number of the last line of the group (or the only line) to be deleted.

2. Type the new line(s), pressing **<Return>** at the end of each line.

3. Enter a period on a line by itself.

Changing a Single Line

To change a single line of text, use only one line number with the **c** (change) subcommand. You can replace the single line with as many new lines as you like.

In the following example, the **2c** subcommand deletes line 2 from the buffer, and then you can enter new text:

2c
appending new material is to
use the proper keys to create a
.
1,$p
```
The only way to stop
appending new material is to
use the proper keys to create a
line that contains only
a period.
```

The period on a line by itself stops **ed** from adding text to the buffer. The **1,$p** subcommand displays the entire contents of the buffer, showing that the change was made.

Changing Multiple Lines

To change more than one line of text, give the starting and ending line numbers of the group of lines to be with the **c** subcommand. You can replace the group of lines with one or more new lines.

In the following example, the **2,3c** subcommand deletes lines 2 and 3 from the buffer, and then you can enter new text:

2,3c
adding text is to type a
.
1,$p
```
The only way to stop
adding text is to type a
line that contains only
a period.
_
```

The period on a line by itself stops **ed** from adding text to the buffer. The **1,$p** subcommand displays the entire contents of the buffer, showing that the change was made.

Inserting Text—The i (Insert) Subcommand

Use the **i** (insert) subcommand to insert one or more new lines into the buffer. To locate the place in the buffer for the lines to be inserted, you can use either a line number or a context search. The **i** subcommand inserts new lines before the specified line. (Compare the **i** subcommand with the **a** subcommand, explained earlier in "Entering Text—The **a** (Append) Subcommand," which inserts new lines after the specified line.)

Creating and Editing Files With ed

To insert text, do the following:

1. Enter a subcommand of one of the following types:

   *n***i**

   where *n* is the number of the line the new lines will be inserted above.

   /*string***/i**

   where *string* is a group of characters contained in the line the new lines will be inserted above.

2. Enter the new lines.
3. Enter a period at the start of a new line.

Using Line Numbers

If you know the number of the line where you want to insert new lines, you can use an insert subcommand of the form *n***i** (where *n* is a line number). The new lines you type go into the buffer before line number *n*. To end the **i** subcommand, type a **.** (period) on a line by itself.

In the following example, the **1,$p** subcommand prints the contents of the buffer. Then the **4i** subcommand inserts new lines before line number 4.

1,$p
```
The only way to stop
adding text is to type a
line that contains only
a period.
```
4i
--repeat, only--

```
.
1,$p
The only way to stop
adding text is to type a
line that contains only
--repeat, only--
a period.
_
```

After **4i**, you enter the new line of text and type a period on the next line to end the **i** subcommand. A second **1,$p** subcommand displays the contents of the buffer again, showing that the new text was inserted.

Using a Context Search

Another way to specify where the **i** subcommand inserts new lines is to use a context search. With a subcommand of the form **/***string***/i**, you can locate the line that contains *string* and insert new lines before that line. When you finish inserting new lines, type a period on a line by itself.

In the following example, the **/period/i** subcommand inserts new text before the line that contains the string **period**:

/period/i
and in the first position--
```
.
1,$p
The only way to stop
adding text is to type a
line that contains only
--repeat, only--
and in the first position--
a period.
_
```

The **1,$p** subcommand displays the entire contents of the buffer, showing that the **i** subcommand has inserted the new text.

Copying Lines—The t (Transfer) Subcommand

With the **t** (transfer) subcommand, you can copy lines from one place in the buffer and insert the copies elsewhere. The **t** subcommand does not affect the original lines. The general form of the **t** subcommand is the following:

*starting line,ending line***t***line to follow*

To copy lines, enter a subcommand of the form:

*n,m***t***x*

where:

n is the first line of the group to be copied.
m is the last line of the group to be copied.
x is the line the copied lines are to follow.

To copy lines to the top of the buffer, use 0 (zero) as the line number for the copied lines to follow. To copy lines to the bottom of the buffer, use **$** as the line number for the copied lines to follow.

In the following example, the **1,3t4** subcommand copies lines 1 through 3, and inserts the copies after line 4:

1,3t4
1,$p
```
The only way to stop
adding text is to type a
line that contains only
--repeat, only--
The only way to stop
adding text is to type a
line that contains only
and in the first position--
a period.

-
```

The **1,$p** subcommand displays the entire contents of the buffer, showing that **ed** has made and inserted the copies, and that the original lines are not affected.

Using System Commands from ed

Sometimes you may find it convenient to use a system command without leaving the **ed** program. Use the **!** (exclamation point) character to leave the **ed** program temporarily.

To use a system command from **ed**, enter the following:

!command

In the following example, the **!ls** command temporarily suspends the **ed** program and runs the **ls** (list) system command (a command that lists the files in the current directory):

!ls
```
afile
bfile
cfile
!
_
```

The **ls** command displays the names of the files in the current directory (**afile, bfile,** and **cfile**), and then displays another **!** character. The **ls** command is finished, and you can continue to use **ed**.

You can use any system command from within the **ed** program. You can even run another **ed** program, edit a file, and then return to the original **ed** program. From the second **ed** program, you can run a third **ed** program, use a system command, and so forth.

Ending the ed Program

This completes the introduction to the **ed** program. To save your file and end the **ed** program, do the following steps:

1. Enter the following to save your file:

   w

2. Enter the following to exit **ed**:

   q

For a full discussion of the **w** and **q** subcommands, see "Saving Text—The **w** (Write) Subcommand" and "Leaving the **ed** Program—The **q** (Quit) Subcommand," respectively.

For information about other features of **ed**, see the **ed** reference page. For information about printing the files you create with **ed**, see "Printing Files (**lpr**, **lpq**, **lprm**)" in Chapter 3.

Appendix C
Using Internationalization Features

This appendix describes the internationalization features of the OSF/1 operating system. These features provide users with the ability to process data and to interact with the system in a manner appropriate to their native language, customs, and geographic region (their locale).

After completing this appendix, you will be able to do the following:

- Understand the concept of locale
- Understand what functions are affected by locale
- Determine whether a locale has been set (if necessary)
- Set your locale (if necessary)
- Change your locale or aspects of your locale (if necessary)

If your site is in the United States and you plan to use American English language and its conventions, there is no need to set a locale because the system default is American English.

If your site is outside the United States, the locale will most likely have already been specified by the system administrator. If the locale has already been set, you may wish to only skim this appendix for background information on internationalization. On the other hand, if the locale has not been specified, you will find this appendix to be essential.

Understanding Locale

Because OSF/1 is an internationalized operating system, it is capable of presenting information in a variety of ways. Users tell OSF/1 how to process and present information in a way appropriate to their language, country, and cultural customs by specifying a locale. See "Setting Locale" later in this appendix for information about how to specify locale.

A locale generally consists of three parts: language, territory, and code set. All three are important for specifying how information is to be processed and displayed:

- Language specifies the language used for the locale (for example, German, French, English).
- Territory specifies the geographic area (for example, Germany, France, Great Britain).
- Code Set specifies the coded character set that is used for this locale.

Language, territory, and code set are all important in defining a locale. The language tells the system to display the messages in the appropriate language and to define the appropriate collating sequence. The territory defines the date and time conventions as well as the numeric and monetary formats. The code set provides information about how data is encoded and, therefore, how the system should process the data.

You may find some background information on code sets useful here.

The ASCII code set has traditionally been used on UNIX based systems to express American English. Each letter of the English alphabet (A to Z, a to z) as well as digits, control characters, and symbols are uniquely expressed by 7 of the 8 bits of a standard byte.

However, one of the most sweeping changes for internationalization support is the addition of new code sets, or the expansion of old ones, to include non-English characters. Because so many programs rely on ASCII in one way or another, all commonly used sets begin with ASCII and then build from there.

The 8-bit code sets (those that use all 8 bits of a byte) can support European, Middle Eastern, and other alphabetic languages. The most popular standard sets are a series called ISO 8859. The first in the series is called ISO 8859/1, the second is ISO 8859/2, and so on through ISO 8859/9. The ISO 8859/1 code set is often called Latin-1.

Asian code sets can support ideographic languages such as Japanese and Chinese. In these languages, each word is written using one or more unique ideographic symbols. There are thousands of such symbols in these languages, and most characters require 2 or more bytes.

When you specify a locale, you specify a locale name that defines the language, territory, and code set of the locale. The following is the general format of the locale name:

lang_terr.codeset

where:

lang A 2-letter, lowercase abbreviation for the language name. The abbreviations come from *ISO 639 Code for the Representation of Names of Languages*. Examples:

    en   English

    fr   French

    ja   Japanese

    de   German (from Deutsch)

terr A 2-letter, uppercase abbreviation for the territory name. The abbreviations come from *ISO 3116 Codes for the Representation of Names of Countries*. Examples:

    US   United States

    JP   Japan

    NL   The Netherlands

    ES   Spain (from España)

codeset The name of the code set. Examples:

    ASCII

    ISO 8859-1   ISO 8859/1

    SJIS   Shift Japanese Industrial Standard

    AJEC   Advanced Japanese EUC

Here are examples of full locale names:

```
fr_FR.ISO8859-1 (French, France)
ja_JP.SJIS (Japanese, Japan)
```

To set a locale, you define an environment variable that uses the locale name. For information on how to set locale, as well as a complete list of locale names, see "Setting Locale" later in this appendix.

The following section describes how the locale specification affects the way data is processed and displayed.

How Locale Affects Processing and Display of Data

As previously mentioned, the locale specified on your system influences how information is processed and displayed in a locale. The following functions are affected by locale:

- Collation
- Date and time conventions
- Numeric and monetary formats
- Program messages
- Yes/No prompts

The following subsections describe these functions.

Collation

Collation, or sorting, is the action of arranging the elements of a set into a particular order. Collation always follows a set of rules. The rules for sorting English words are few and simple. Each letter sorts to one, and only one, place; and uppercase and lowercase letters are not distinguished. The ASCII collating sequence for the letters A to Z is the same as the English collating sequence, except that ASCII distinguishes between uppercase and lowercase characters.

Other languages include a variety of collation methods. Here are a few examples:

- **Multi-Level.** In this system, a group of characters all sort to the same primary location. If there is a tie, one or more additional sorts is applied.

  For example, in French, *a, á, à*, and *â* all sort to the same primary location. If two strings collate to the same primary location, the secondary sort goes into effect. These words are in correct French order:

  a
  à
  abord
  âpre
  après
  âpreté
  azur

- **One-to-Two Character Mappings.** This system requires that certain single characters be treated as if they were two characters. For example, in German, ß (scharfes-S) is collated as if it were *ss*.

- **N-to-One Character Mappings.** Some languages treat a string of characters as if it were one single collating element. For example, in Spanish, the *ch* and *ll* sequences are treated as their own elements within the alphabet. Dictionaries have separate sections for them (that is, there are entries for *a, b, c, ch, d,* and so on). The following words are in correct Spanish order:

  canto
  construir
  curioso
  chapa
  chocolate
  dama

- **Don't-Care Character Mappings.** In some cases, certain characters may be ignored in collation. For example, if a - (dash) were defined as a don't-care character, the strings *re-locate* and *relocate* would sort to the same place.

In addition to these collation rules, some languages use basically the same rules as English, but still need more than a plain ASCII sort. For example, in

OSF/1 User's Guide   C–5

Danish, there are three characters that appear *after* z in the alphabet: æ, ø, and å. This means that you cannot assume that the range [A to Z, a to z] includes every letter.

Date and Time Conventions

Users around the world express dates and times with different formatting conventions. When specifying day and month names, Americans generally express dates using this format:

Tuesday, May 22, 1990

while the French would use this format:

mardi, 22 mai 1990

The following examples show common methods for formatting the date, March 22, 1990. These formats, however, are not the only way to write the date in the listed country:

3/20/90	American: month/day/year order
20/3/90	British: day/month/year order
20.3.90	French: day.month.year order
20-III-90	Italian: day-month-year order; uses the Roman numeral for the month
90/3/20	Japanese: year/month/day order
2/3/20	Japanese Emperor: same order, but the year is the number years the current emperor has been reigning, rather than the Gregorian calendar year

As with dates, there are many conventions for expressing the time of day. Americans use the 12-hour clock with its a.m. and p.m. designations, while most other people in Europe and Asia use the 24-hour clock for written times.

In addition to the 12-hour/24-hour clock differences, punctuation for written times can vary. For example:

3:20 p.m.   American
15h20   French
15.20   German
15:20   Japanese

Numeric and Monetary Formatting

The characters used to format numeric and monetary values vary from place to place. For example, Americans use a . (period) as the radix character (that is, the character that separates whole and fractional quantities), and a , (comma) as a thousands separator. In many European countries, these definitions are reversed.

For example, here are sample numeric formats:

1,234.56   American; comma as thousands separator; period as radix character
1.234,56   French: period as thousands separator; comma as radix character

And here are sample monetary formats:

$1,234.56   American: dollars
kr1.234,56   Norwegian: krona
SFrs.1,234.56 Swiss: Swiss francs

In addition, users sometimes need more than two places for fractional digits with monetary amounts.

Program Messages

One of the most basic user needs is the ability to interact with the system in the local language. This means that it must be possible to see all program messages in the local language and for the program to accept input in that language. Often, programs are written with the English messages hardcoded into the program. In an internationalized system, the messages are put in a separate module and replaced with calls to a messaging system.

Yes/No Prompts

Many programs ask questions that need a positive or negative response. Those programs typically look for the English string literals *y* or *yes*, *n* or *no*.

An internationalized program lets users enter the characters or words that are appropriate to their language. For example, in France, an affirmative response for a prompt could be *o* for *oui*.

Determining Whether a Locale Has Been Set

If your system is functioning in accordance with the language and conventions of your country, you can assume that the locale has been set correctly. On the other hand, if you are not sure whether your locale has been set, enter one of the following commands to display active environment variables:

- The **set** command if in the Bourne or the Korn shells
- The **setenv** command if in the C shell

For information on the **set** and the **setenv** commands, see Chapter 7.

The following variables specify the locale:

LANG
LC_ALL
LC_COLLATE
LC_TYPE
LC_NUMERIC
LC_MONETARY
LC_TIME
LC_MESSAGES

These variables define language, collation, code set, language of prompt and system messages, as well as the numeric, monetary, and time formats for the locale. In most cases, only the **LANG** variable will have been set. For more information on these variables, see ''Setting Locale'' and ''Locale Functions.''

Setting Locale

A locale can be set either by an individual user or by a system administrator. If your system administrator sets the locale at your site, it is likely that a default locale has been specified for your system, as well as for all systems at your site. Depending on the implementation, users may or may not have the freedom to override the default. The rest of this section assumes that you have the authority to set the locale.

To set a locale, you must assign a locale name to one or more environment variables. The simplest case is to assign a value to a variable called **LANG** because this variable covers all the pieces of a locale.

Table C-1 lists the locale names provided by OSF/1. Every locale name (except for the C locale and the POSIX locale) specifies language, territory, and code set. For information on the locale name format, see ''Understanding Locale'' at the beginning of this appendix.

Table C-1. OSF/1 Locale Names

Language	Locale Name
C	**C**
POSIX	**POSIX**
Danish	**da_DK.ISO8859-1**
Dutch	**nl_NL.ISO8859-1**
Dutch_Belgium	**nl_BE.ISO8859-1**
English_U.K.	**en_GB.ISO8859-1**
English_U.S.A.	**en_US.ISO8859-1**
Finnish	**fi_FI.ISO8859-1**
French_Belgium	**fr_BE.ISO8859-1**
French_Canada	**fr_CA.ISO8859-1**
French_France	**fr_FR.ISO8859-1**
French_Switzerland	**fr_CH.ISO8859-1**

Language	Locale Name
German_Germany	de_DE.ISO8859-1
German_Switzerland	de_CH.ISO8859-1
Greek	el_GR.ISO8859-7
Icelandic	is_IS.ISO8859-1
Italian	it_IT.ISO8859-1
Japanese_SJIS	ja_JP.SJIS
Japanese_EUC	ja_JP.AJEC
Japanese_English	en_JP.ISO8859-1
Korean	ko_KR.eucKR
Norwegian	no_NO.ISO8859-1
Portuguese	pt_PT.ISO8859-1
Spanish	es_ES.ISO8859-1
Swedish	sv_SE.ISO8859-1
Taiwanese	zh_TW.eucTW
Turkish	tr_TR.ISO8859-9

Note: The C locale mentioned in Table C-1 is the system default if no locales are set on your system. The C locale specifies American English with uninternationalized ASCII-based behavior. The main difference between the C locale and the American English locale (**en_US.ISO8859-1**) is that the latter has enhanced error messages.

The following example sets the locale to French for the C shell in which it is invoked and all child processes of that shell:

% setenv LANG fr_FR.ISO8859-1

If you want another shell to have a different locale, you can reset **LANG** in that particular shell. Here is an example of setting the locale to French in the Korn shell:

$ LANG=fr_FR.ISO8859-1
$ export $LANG

Using Internationalization Features

Note that setting the **LANG** variable on the command line sets the locale only for the current shell and all its child processes.

To set your locale whenever you log in, edit the appropriate login script for your shell. For the the C shell, set the **LANG** variable in the **.login** file. For the Bourne or the Korn shells, set the **LANG** variable in the **.profile** file.

In most cases, assigning a value to the **LANG** variable is the only variable you must specify to set the locale. This is because when you set the locale with the **LANG** variable, the behavior is automatically set for the following functions:

- Character classification
- Collation
- Date and time conventions
- Numeric and monetary formats
- Program messages
- Yes/No prompts

However, to change the default behavior of any of the preceding functions within a locale, you can do so by setting the variables that are associated with these functions. See the following subsection for more information.

Locale Functions

When you set the locale with the **LANG** variable, the appropriate behavior for character classification, collation, date and time conventions, numeric and monetary formats, program messages, and the yes/no prompts is set up for your locale. If you need to change any of the default functions, you can do so by setting the variables that are associated with these functions. Table C-2 describes the environment variables that influence locale functions.

Table C–2. Environment Variables That Influence Locale Functions

Environment Variable	Description
LC_COLLATE	Specifies the collating sequence to use when sorting strings and when character ranges occur in patterns.
LC_CTYPE	Specifies the character classification information to use.
LC_NUMERIC	Specifies the numeric format.
LC_MONETARY	Specifies the monetary format.
LC_TIME	Specifies the date and time format.
LC_MESSAGES	Specifies the language in which system messages will appear. In addition, this variable specifies the strings that indicate *yes* and *no* in yes/no prompts.
LC_ALL	Specifies the behavior for all aspects of the locale. In general, use of this variable is *not recommended*. See the "Caution" section that follows for more information.

As with the **LANG** variable, all of the environment variables can be assigned locale names. For example, suppose that your company is in the southern United States, but your company's prevalent language is Spanish. As a result, you can set the locale with the **LANG** variable for Spanish, but set the numeric and monetary format for American English. To do this, you would make the following variable assignments for the C shell:

setenv LANG es_ES.ISO8859-1
setenv LC_NUMERIC en_US.ISO8859-1
setenv LC_MONETARY en_US.ISO8859-1

In addition, you can also add a field (*@modifier*) to a locale name to select a specific version of locale-specific data. For example, a locale might sort data two ways: in dictionary order and in telephone-book order. Suppose your site is in France and the standard setup for this locale uses dictionary

Using Internationalization Features

order, but you need to use a telephone-book order defined by your site. You might set your environment variables this way in the C shell:

setenv LC_COLLATE fr_FR.ISO8859-1@phone
setenv LANG fr_FR.ISO8859-1

The collating sequence specified by **fr_FR.ISO8859-1@phone** is defined by your site.

The explicit setting of **LC_COLLATE** overrides **LANG**'s implicit setting of that portion of the locale.

Caution: Use the **LC_ALL** environment variable with care. This variable overrides all other locale-dependent environment variables even if you set it before category-specific variables. For example, suppose that you make the following assignments:

setenv LC_ALL fr_FR.ISO8859-1
setenv LC_MESSAGES en_US.ISO8859-1

In this case, **LC_ALL** overrides the explicit setting of **LC_MESSAGES**. The only way to cancel the influence of **LC_ALL** in a process is to unset the variable (for example, **unsetenv LC_ALL**). In general, it is best to use **LANG** rather than **LC_ALL**.

Limitations of Locale Variables

The ability to set locale allows you to tailor your environment, but it *does not* protect you from making mistakes. For example, there is nothing to protect you from setting the **LANG** variable to a Swedish locale, and the **LC_CTYPE** variable to a Japanese locale. It is likely, though, that the results would not be what you intend.

Likewise, there currently is no way to tie locale information to data. This means that the system has no way of knowing what locale you had set when you created a file, and so it will not prevent you from processing that data in inappropriate ways later. For example, suppose **LANG** was set to a German locale when you created file **foo**. Now suppose you have reset **LANG** to a French locale and then use the **grep** command to search for a text string in file **foo**. The **grep** command will use French rules on the German data in the file. There is nothing to prevent you from doing this, or even to warn you that this probably is not what you intend. As a result, if you set the locale, be sure your variable settings are consistent with each other.

Your Terminal Setup and Locale

If your system is used for different locales, you must make sure that the terminal is properly set up for the current login session. The terminal is properly set up when the system software controlling it can process data in the code set of the selected locale without errors.

You must verify the terminal setup each time that you begin a login session. If you do not, you may encounter problems. For example, you may not be able to type at the keyboard, or data may be displayed on the terminal in an unintelligible or unexpected format. To verify the terminal setup, you check the code set that the locale is using (the active code set) against the software that controls the terminal line.

The active code set can be specified by any of the environment variables related to locale (**LANG, LC_COLLATE, LC_CTYPE, LC_MESSAGES, LC_MONETARY, LC_TIME**, or **LC_ALL**). You can inquire about the current values of these variables by using the **locale** command. If you need to change the variable values, you can do this by using the appropriate shell commands (**printenv** for the C shell, and **set** for the Bourne and Korn shells). If your system is exclusively or primarily used for a particular locale, it is likely that the locale variables are specified in the local login script (the **.login** file for the C shell and **.profile** file for the Bourne and Korn shells). If this is true, you can view the file and modify the variable values by using any editor.

The software for terminal line control is selected at system startup. The system first intializes a terminal with software modules that are named in a database for the automatic configuration of such devices. Then, when the login shell is started, it adds any modules that it finds in the local login script. You can display the names of all the modules that are currently selected for a locale by using the **strconf** command. To see if some of the terminal line software is specified in the local login script, you can view the file by using an editor.

Instructions for checking and changing the terminal setup follow. The instructions assume that you will be performing these tasks interactively. If you choose to edit the login script, you can find instructions for doing this in the *OSF/1 System Administrator's Guide*. However, editing the login script is a more complicated way to change the terminal setup, and you should consult with your system administrator first.

Background on OSF/1 Terminal Devices

Before you try to verify your terminal setup, you should know more about terminal devices in an OSF/1 system. Terminals, like disk drives and printers, are peripheral devices that the system provides to users. When the user types at a terminal, the device driver, which is the software module in the operating system (**kernel**) that controls the device, accepts the input. The terminal device driver enlists other kernel modules for any processing of the data that is required. When the kernel has finished its processing, it sends the data to the user process, which is the executable version of the user program (application, shell, windowing software, and so on). Once the user process has finished its manipulation of the data, it sends this back to the terminal device as output. An example of output from a user process are the characters displayed on a terminal screen.

Terminal devices in OSF/1 are designed using a programming facility called "STREAMS." STREAMS allows developers to code device functions into several separate modules that can be used in different combinations for different devices. The modules that are used for operating a particular terminal device are determined by the device type, locale, and other processing requirements. When a user process sends data to the terminal device, or the terminal device sends data to the user process, this data flows over a communications path called a stream. This terminal device stream includes the STREAMS modules that are required for the processing of input and output data. Figure C-1 illustrates a terminal device stream in the OSF/1 kernel.

Figure C–1. Terminal Device Stream in OSF/1

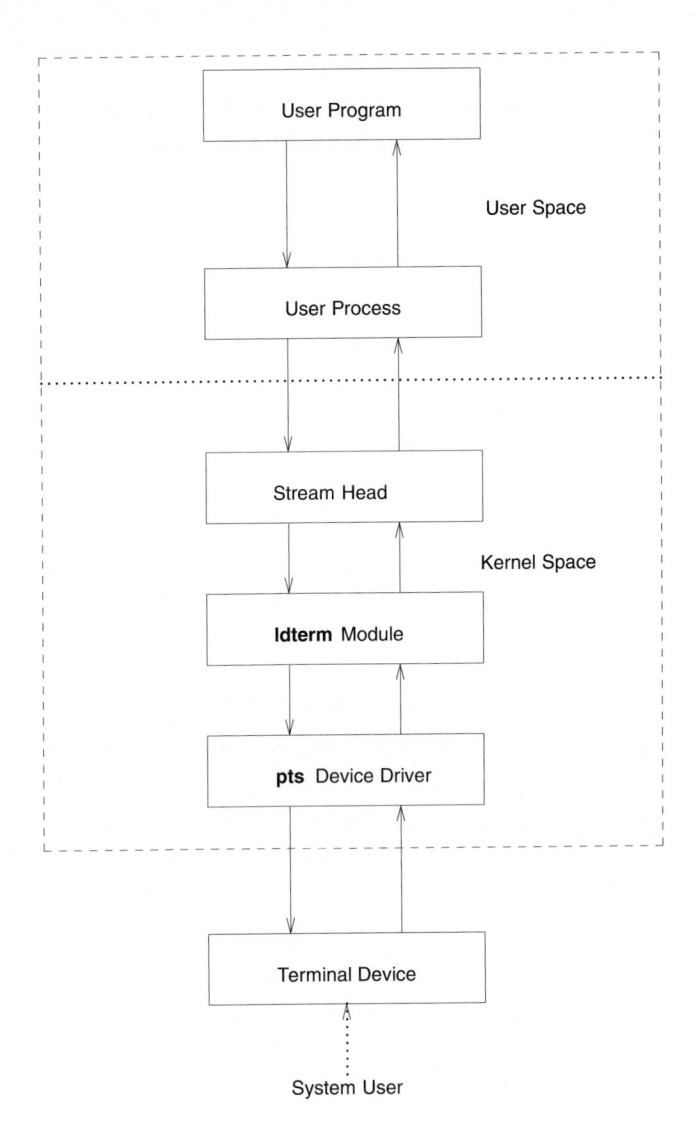

```
            ┌─────────────────┐
            │  User Program   │
            └─────────────────┘
                                    User Space
            ┌─────────────────┐
            │  User Process   │
            └─────────────────┘
·········································
            ┌─────────────────┐
            │   Stream Head   │
            └─────────────────┘
                                    Kernel Space
            ┌─────────────────┐
            │  ldterm Module  │
            └─────────────────┘

            ┌─────────────────┐
            │ pts Device Driver│
            └─────────────────┘

            ┌─────────────────┐
            │ Terminal Device │
            └─────────────────┘
                  System User
```

The terminal device stream in Figure C-1 consists of the following:

- The stream head module. This module allows user processes to communicate with the terminal device driver.

- The line discipline module. This module interprets input and output to the terminal. Some of its functions include formatting typed character strings, processing erase and kill characters typed at the keyboard, and echoing (writing) characters to the terminal screen. OSF/1 provides the **ldterm** module for the line discipline.

  The **ldterm** module can process the single-byte and multibyte characters that are contained in the code sets that applications and keyboards use. However, these characters must be in the Extended UNIX Codes (EUC) format. EUC is a character encoding method for data in internationalized systems. If the applications or keyboard on a system do not use or convert to EUC, conversion modules must be included in the terminal device stream. Otherwise, **ldterm** will not recognize and accept input and output.

- The terminal device driver. As previously explained, this software device driver controls the transmission of input and output to the terminal device. OSF/1 provides the **tty** driver for the terminal device driver.

A terminal device stream can contain any number of modules. It can include other software device drivers, as well as the terminal device driver.

As previously mentioned, terminals are automatically set up when the system is started. This occurs because the system administrator has arranged for it to happen through the **autopush** facility. This facility creates a database of information that is used to build terminal device streams. When a terminal device is opened, the system takes the modules named in the database and *pushes* them on the terminal device stream. (See the **autopush** reference page in the *OSF/1 System and Network Administrator's Reference* for more information.) You may never have to change the stream that was initially built for a terminal. However, you must check it.

Determining the Active Code Set

To determine which code set is active for the current login session, you look at the environment variables for the selected locale. To do this, you display the variables using the appropriate shell command. For example, in the C shell, you enter the following command line:

% **locale**

The systems displays a list of current settings for the locale's environment variables that is similar to the following:

```
LANG=
LC_COLLATE="C"
LC_CTYPE="C"
LC_MONETARY="C"
LC_NUMERIC="C"
LC_TIME="C"
LC_MESSAGES="C"
LC_ALL=
```

To see which code set is currently being used, you look for the **LC_CTYPE, LC_COLLATE, LANG,** or **LC_ALL** variable. As explained earlier in "Locale Functions," the code set is designated by the third part of the locale name specified in the variable. Also, one or more of the **LC_CTYPE, LC_COLLATE, LANG,** or **LC_ALL** variables can be set for a locale. If more than one of these variables have been set, the active code set is specified in the variable that takes precedence. The order of precedence is as follows:

- **LANG**
- **LC_CTYPE**
- **LC_COLLATE**
- **LC_ALL**

If **LANG** is the only one of the preceding variables that is set, its value specifies the active code set. When **LC_TYPE** is also set and it specifies a different code set than **LANG**, its value overrides the **LANG** value's setting for the code set. When **LC_COLLATE** is set in addition to **LANG** and **LC_CTYPE** and it specifies a different code set from either, its value

Using Internationalization Features

overrides both of the other values' settings for the code set. When the **LC_ALL** variable is set, its value overrides any setting for the code set that is different in the variables of lesser precedence.

Changing the Active Code Set

System users do not typically change the active code set. However, if you must do this, you can by resetting the ruling environment variable.

To reset the ruling variable value, you use the appropriate shell command. The following example shows how to reset the **LC_CTYPE** value for the C shell:

% **setenv LC_CTYPE C**

Checking the Terminal Device Stream

To check the terminal device stream, you use the **strconf** command. This system command allows you to query a terminal device for the configuration of the associated device stream. (See the **strchg, strconf** reference page in the *OSF/1 System and Network Administrator's Reference*.) In the C shell, the command line is as follows:

% **strconf**

The system displays the requested information:

```
% ldterm
  pts
```

The display shows that the line discipline module **ldterm** and the terminal device driver **pts** are included on the terminal device stream. The name of the terminal device driver may be different in your installation. In any case, the terminal device stream that is shown is configured correctly for the system in our example. It will process the US ASCII code set in the C locale.

OSF/1 User's Guide   C–19

In the next example, the terminal is set up for the Japanese locale, **ja_JP.SJIS**. The shell and applications running on the system use SJIS. The terminal keyboard also uses this code set. You are in the Korn shell and enter the **strconf** command. The information displayed for the terminal device stream is as follows:

```
uc_sjis
ldterm
lc_sjis
com
```

In addition to the **ldterm** module and **tty** driver, the terminal device stream contains the **uc_sjis** and **lc_sjis** conversion modules. The **uc_jis** module translates characters between SJIS for the user process and EUC for the **ldterm** module. The **lc_sjis** module translates characters between EUC for the **ldterm** module and the SJIS for the **tty** driver. The terminal in our example is appropriately set up for working in the **ja_JP.SJIS** locale where the applications and keyboard use SJIS.

Once you have checked the terminal software modules, you must check the information that the **ldterm** module currently has about the format of the EUC characters that it is to process.

The **ldterm** module accepts data formatted in four different EUC code sets. These code sets are defined as belonging to classes: EUC code set classes 0, 1, 2, and 3. The characters in EUC code set class 1 have a single-byte format like US ASCII. The characters in EUC code set classes 1 to 3 have multibyte formats, although an application or the keyboard can use these formats to send single-byte characters.

The **ldterm** module needs to know the "character widths" of the characters in the EUC code sets that it will be handling. The character widths for an EUC code set specify the number of bytes that are required for encoding characters and the number of columns that are required for displaying characters.

To see what the **ldterm** module currently has for the character widths of the EUC code sets that it will accept, you use the **eucset** command. This command queries and sets EUC code set character widths. (See the **eucset** reference page in the *OSF/1 Command Reference*.)

$ **eucset -p**

Using Internationalization Features

The system displays the current settings. For SJIS, the settings are the following:

cswidth 2:2,2:1,0:0

If you query the system about the terminal device stream and the EUC code set information, and find that either or both are incorrect, you must make the appropriate changes.

Changing the Terminal Device Stream Configuration

If you need to change the configuration of the terminal device stream, you can do so by using the **stty**, **strchg**, and **eucset** commands. For example, if you are working in the **ja_JP.SJIS** locale and find that the required code conversion modules (the **uc_sjis** and **uc_sjis** modules) are not included in the stream, you can change the configuration by taking the following steps.

First, you use the **stty** command to save the parameters that the **ldterm** module uses for I/O control. (See the **stty** reference page in the *OSF/1 Command Reference*.) If you are in the Korn shell, the command line is as follows:

$ oldvar = 'stty -g'

The **stty** command line saves the current settings of the terminal's I/O control parameters to a Korn shell variable, **oldvar**. The I/O control parameters must be saved because the terminal loses track of them when its line discipline module is popped, and reconfiguring the terminal device stream requires popping this module. You will restore the saved parameters after the stream is reconfigured.

Note that the variable name **oldvar** is simply a name that the system user gave to the variable. It could have been any name that was in the proper format for a Korn shell variable. You must enclose the variable name in single quotes.

Next, you use the **strchg** command to pop all of the modules on the terminal device stream. You must remove all of the modules currently existing on the stream because you cannot reconstruct it until all the existing modules have been removed. You enter the command line as follows:

$ **strchg -p -a**

The **-p** flag in the command line indicates that the the **strchg** command must pop modules, while the **-a** flag in the command line indicates that it must pop *all* of the modules. Note that the **pts** device driver will never be removed from the stream.

Next, you reconfigure the terminal device stream. To do this, you use the **strchg** command again. The command line as follows:

$ **strchg -h lc_sjis ldterm uc_sjis**

The **-h** flag in the command line indicates that the **strchg** command must push the modules needed for the desired configuration. The modules to be pushed on the stream are listed after the flag. Notice that the modules are listed in the order that they will be pushed on the stream. The **lc_sjis** module will be pushed first, above the terminal device driver at the bottom of the stream. The **ldterm** module will be pushed next. The **uc_sjis** module will be pushed last, above the **ldterm** module at the top of the stream.

Next, you use the **eucset** command to provide the **ldterm** module with EUC character width information:

$ **eucset 2:2,2:1,0:0**

The **eucset** command line shows the encoding and display widths of the kanji and katakana character sets that are part of SJIS. The character widths are represented in the command line as pairs of numbers separated by colons (**2:2,2:1**, and **0:0**). Kanji characters are to be sent as EUC code set class 1 characters. Katakana characters are to be sent as EUC code set class 2 characters. The pair of numbers (**0:0**) indicates that SJIS does not have a character set that fits the EUC code set class 3 format. Also, notice that the **eucset** command does not show any character widths for the ASCII

Using Internationalization Features

character set that is also part of SJIS. These characters belong to EUC code set class 0, which is understood by the **ldterm** module to have the character widths **1:1**.

Finally, you use the **stty** command to reset the terminal's I/O control parameters. The command line is as follows:

$ **stty $oldvar**

The command line indicates that the **stty** command must retrieve the parameter settings previously saved in the **oldvar** variable.

Once you check the terminal setup and make any needed changes, you need not do anything special. You can simply proceed with your work.

Appendix D
Sending and Receiving Mail

This appendix tells you how to use the electronic mail system. It provides an overview of how the mail system operates and how to address messages for local or remote delivery. It also gives instructions to help you

- Compose and send messages to other users
- Receive and read messages from other users
- Organize the messages that you receive
- Change the mail program to your preferences

Before you can use the mail system, it must be installed and running on your operating system.

Understanding the Mail System

The OSF/1 operating system mail system is a series of programs that allows you to create, send, and receive messages to and from other people on your computer or on other computers connected to your computer. It is similar in concept (although not in how it works) to delivery of letters through a national postal system. The following sections use that similarity to help you become familiar with the parts of the mail system and how you can use them in your daily communications.

Parts of the Mail System

The following subsections describe the operation of the mail system as it is initially installed. Both you and the person responsible for the operation of the mail system can change the operation of the mail system. See "Changing Mail to Meet Your Needs" later in this appendix for changes that you can make to the operation of the mail system.

Figure D-1 shows the major parts of the mail system. These parts work together to help you write, send, receive, and organize your daily correspondence. Understanding the role of each of these parts will help you use the mail system to handle your correspondence most effectively.

Sending and Receiving Mail

Figure D-1. Parts of the Mail System

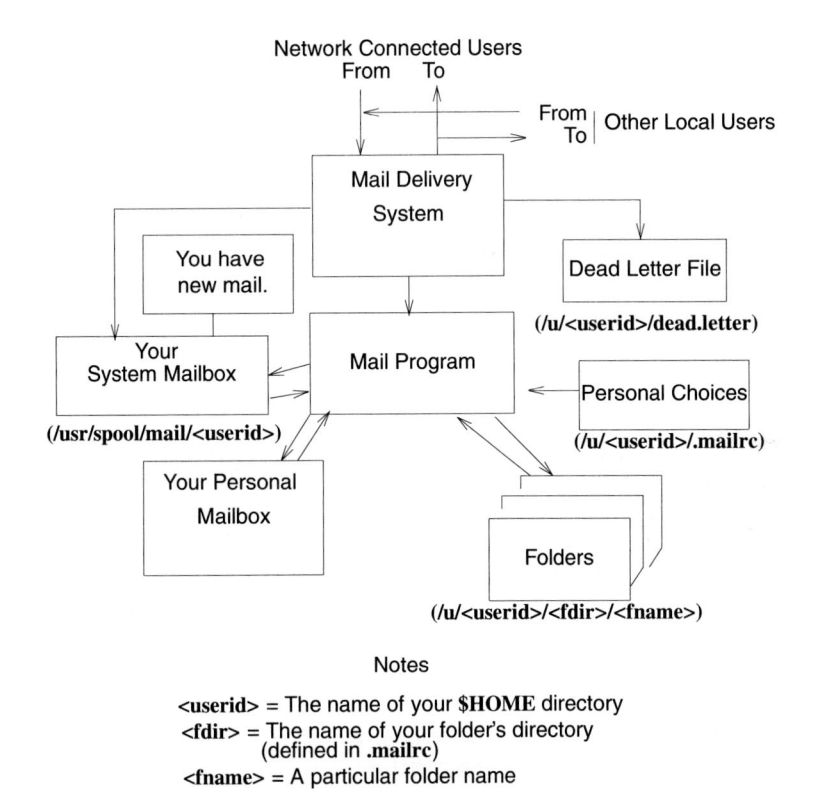

```
                    Network Connected Users
                        From    To
                         ↑      ↑
                         │      │
                         ←──────┤        From │ Other Local Users
                                ├──────→   To │
                         ┌──────┴──────┐
                         │Mail Delivery│
                         │   System    │
         ┌───────────────┤             ├───────────────┐
         │   ┌───────────┤             │               │
         │   │ You have  └──────┬──────┘   ┌───────────────────┐
         │   │ new mail. │      │          │ Dead Letter File  │
         │   └───────────┘      │          └───────────────────┘
         │                      ▼          (/u/<userid>/dead.letter)
    ┌────┴────────┐      ┌─────────────┐
    │   Your      │◄─────┤    Mail     │
    │System Mailbox│     │   Program   │◄─── Personal Choices
    └─────────────┘      └──────┬──────┘      (/u/<userid>/.mailrc)
  (/usr/spool/mail/<userid>)    │
                                │
                     ┌──────────┴──┐
                     │Your Personal│
                     │   Mailbox   │     ┌─────────┐
                     │             │     │ Folders │
                     └─────────────┘     └─────────┘
                                      (/u/<userid>/<fdir>/<fname>)
```

Notes

<userid> = The name of your $HOME directory
<fdir> = The name of your folder's directory
(defined in **.mailrc**)
<fname> = A particular folder name

OSF/1 User's Guide

Delivery System

The delivery system is a set of programs that routes mail to the correct system mailbox. You can send and receive system mail without knowing how to use the delivery system programs.

For example, imagine an ordinary letter being sent from one person to another through a post office. In this case, the sender and receiver of the letter do not worry about details like which trucks carry the mail or which personnel sort the mail. All the sender has to do is address the letter correctly, and the letter will be delivered. If the letter cannot be delivered, the sender will be notified of that fact.

Likewise, to use the OSF/1 operating system mail system, you do not need to know all the details about how the mail is delivered. You need only be concerned about writing, sending, and receiving messages. If you provide the proper address, as described later in ''Addressing Mail,'' the delivery system either delivers your message or notifies you if the message cannot be delivered.

The dead.letter File

When the delivery system cannot deliver a message that you sent, it places the message in the **dead.letter** file in your **$HOME** directory. If **dead.letter** does not exist, the delivery system creates the file; otherwise, it adds the message to the file. In addition, the delivery system displays a message to indicate that the message could not be delivered. Reasons for delivery failure include the following:

- User unknown

    The username specified in the address of the message is not a defined username or alias on the specified system.

- Host unknown

    The host and/or domain portion of the address of the message is not correct. This can be either a syntax error or a bad host or domain name.

The system also uses **dead.letter** to save partially completed messages when you exit the **mail** editor with the ~q command. In this case, the previous content of **dead.letter** is replaced with the partially completed message.

Note: Do not use the **dead.letter** file to store messages. The content of this file changes frequently. Use the **mail** editor ~d command (see "Resending Undelivered Messages") to retrieve the contents of **dead.letter**.

System Mailbox

The system mailbox is similar in concept to the postal mailbox into which the post office delivers letters addressed to a particular person. In the OSF/1 operating system mail system, the system mailbox is a file assigned to a particular user. The file is created when mail arrives for a username; it is deleted when all messages have been removed from the file. However, you can specify that the file not be deleted (see "Changing Mail to Meet Your Needs"). A separate system mailbox can exist for each username defined in **/etc/passwd**. The mail system keeps all system mailboxes in the directory **/usr/spool/mail**. Each system mailbox is named by the username associated with it. For example, if your username is **mark**, then your system mailbox is **/usr/spool/mail/mark**.

When mail arrives for your username, the mail system puts the mail in your system mailbox. If you are logged in when the mail arrives, the mail system writes a message to your terminal. If you are not logged in, the mail system writes the message to your terminal when you next log in. If you do not change it, the message is the following:

```
[YOU HAVE NEW MAIL]
```

Use the **mail** command (see "Receiving Mail") to read and remove messages from your system mailbox. Do not use the system mailbox to store messages. Instead, store messages in your personal mailbox and in folders.

Personal Mailbox

The personal mailbox is similar in concept to an in-basket in an office. You put mail in the in-basket after you have received it but before you have filed it. The personal mailbox is a working storage place for mail that still requires action.

In the mail system, the personal mailbox is a file assigned to a particular user. The mail system creates the file with the name *$HOME*/**mbox** (where *$HOME* is the user's login directory) when the user receives mail from his or her system mailbox. For example, if your home directory is **/u/george**, the mail system creates the file **/u/george/mbox** as your personal mailbox. The system deletes this file when all messages are removed from the personal mailbox.

When you use the **mail** program to view mail in your system mailbox (see "Receiving Mail"), **mail** automatically puts all messages that you have read but did not delete into your personal mailbox. The messages remain in your personal mailbox until you move them to a folder or delete them. See "Receiving Mail" for information about handling the contents of your personal mailbox.

Folders

Folders provide a way to save messages in an organized fashion. You can create as many folders as you need. Name each folder with a name that pertains to the subject matter of the messages that it contains, similar to file folders in an office. Using the **mail** program, you can put a message into a folder from

- Your system mailbox
- Your personal mailbox
- The **dead.letter** file
- Another folder

Sending and Receiving Mail

Like the mailboxes, each folder is a text file. The mail system puts each folder in the directory that you specify in your **.mailrc** file (see "Creating and Using Folders" for more information). You must create this directory before using folders to store messages. Once the directory exists, **mail** creates the folders in that directory as needed.

Personal Choices

The mail system allows you to modify the way it operates in order to suit your needs. These choices include

- What information to include in message headings
- Whether to forward incoming mail to another username
- How you want the messages handled
- Other characteristics pertaining to your terminal

Refer to "Changing Mail to Meet Your Needs" and to "Forwarding Your Mail" for information about specifying these and other personal choices.

The mail Program

The **mail** program allows you to create, send, and receive messages to communicate with other users connected to your system (either directly or through a network). It includes a line-oriented editor (described in "Using the Mail Editor") for creating messages and provides a command-oriented interface for processing the contents of your system mailbox, your personal mailbox, any folders you may have, and **dead.letter**. "Sending Mail" describes how you use **mail** to create and send a message. "Receiving Mail" describes how to use **mail** to process the contents of any mailbox or folder.

Addressing Mail

Using **mail**, you can send messages and files to another user on your local system, on another system connected to your system in a network, or on another system connected to another network that has a connection to your network. The command always has the following form to start composing a message to another user:

$ **mail** *address*

However, you must supply a different form of the *address* parameter, depending upon where the person receiving the message is located. The concept is similar to how you might address a note to a fellow worker in an office.

For example, to send a note to someone in your department (a small department of six to eight people), you might simply write his or her name on the envelope and put it in the mail system:

    Hal

However, if Hal is in another department, you may have to provide more information on the envelope:

    Hal
    Payroll

If Hal is in another plant, you may need even more information to ensure that the message gets to him:

    Hal
    Payroll
    Gaithersburg

Addressing of messages with **mail** operates in a similar fashion, as the next few subsections show.

Addressing for Users on Your Local System

To send a message to a user on your local system (that is, to someone whose username appears in **/etc/passwd** on your system), specify the username for the address:

$ **mail** *login_ID*

For example, if user **hal** is on your system, enter the following command to create and send a message to **hal**:

$ **mail hal**

This command activates **mail**, allows you to create a message to **hal**, and then tries to send the message to the local username **hal**. If the message is delivered successfully, you receive no notification. If **hal** is not on your system, the mail system returns an error message and puts the unsent message in your system mailbox.

Addressing for Users on Your Network

To send a message to a user on another system connected to your system through a network, you must know the name of the other system in addition to the username (on the other system) of the person to whom you are sending the message. Refer to "Determining the Name of Another System" to find out the name of the other system and whether you can directly address the other system. If you can directly address the other system, use the username of the recipient, followed by the @ (at sign), followed by the name of the remote system as the address for sending the message:

$ **mail** *username@system_name*

For example, if user **hal** is on system **zeus**, enter the following command to create and send a message to **hal**:

$ **mail hal@zeus**

This command activates **mail**, allows you to create a message to **hal**, and then tries to send the message to username **hal** on system **zeus**. If the message is delivered successfully, you receive no notification. If **hal** is not a user on **zeus**, you receive no error message; however, the mail system returns the undelivered message to your system mailbox, together with an explanation of why it could not be delivered.

Determining the Name of Another System

The name of the system for mail routing is determined by a configuration file on that system. By convention, the name is often set to the node name of that system; however, it may be defined differently in the configuration file. To find out the node name of another system, use the **uname -a** command on the other system. Contact the person responsible for the mail system on the other system to find out the name defined in the configuration file on that system.

In addition, your local system must have access to information that defines the other system on the network. To determine if your local system has this information, use the **host** command. For example, to find out if your system has routing information for system **zeus**, enter:

$ **host zeus**

If your system responds with a message like the following, it has the proper information and you can send a message to that system:

```
zeus is 192.9.200.4    (300,11,310,4)
```

If your system does not have information about the requested system, it responds with the following message:

```
zeus: unknown host
```

If you receive this message, the requested system name

- May not be correct. (Check your typing.)
- May be on your network, but not defined to your system. (Contact the person responsible for setting up your network.)

Sending and Receiving Mail

- May be on another network and require more detailed addressing to define it. (See "Addressing for Users on a Different Network.")
- May not be connected to a network that is connected to your network.

You may also receive that message if the network is not operating and your local system depends on a remote system to supply network addresses.

Addressing for Users on a Different Network

If the network to which your system is connected is also connected to other networks, you can send mail to users on those networks. If the networks use a central database of names, you do not need any additional information to send mail to users on the connected networks. Use the same addressing as for users on your local network:

$ **mail** *username@system_name*

This type of addressing works well when the nature of the network allows a central database of names to be maintained. However, for networks that span large, unrelated local networks in widespread locations, a central database of names is not possible. To send mail to someone in such a network, more addressing information is needed. The address must be in the following format:

$ **mail** *username@system_name.domain_name*

The additional information in this format is the *domain_name*. This information defines the remote network, relative to your local network, within the defined structure for the larger group of interconnected networks.

This information may be as simple as an added network name. For example, if your local network (named **olympus** for this example) is connected to a second network (named **valhalla**), you could enter the following command to send a note to user **kelley** at system **odin** on the second network:

$ **mail kelley@odin.valhalla**

OSF/1 User's Guide   D–11

Similarly, user **kelley** could respond to user **hal** on **zeus** by entering:

$ **mail hal@zeus.olympus**

Frequently, however, the domain name is more than another network name. It becomes the path through the logical arrangement of domains in the network through which your message must travel. It does *not* represent the actual route that the message travels, only the position of the destination network in the interconnected network structure.

The largest and most common example of this type of interconnection is a network of business, government, and educational institutions called the Internet. At the highest structural level of this network, it divides into several large domains, including

- COM for commercial entities
- EDU for educational institutions
- GOV for government agencies
- BITNET for connection to the BITNET network
- CSNET for connection to the CSNET network

Figure D-2 shows a high-level view of some parts of the Internet network, showing detail for some imaginary branches to illustrate the domain naming concept.

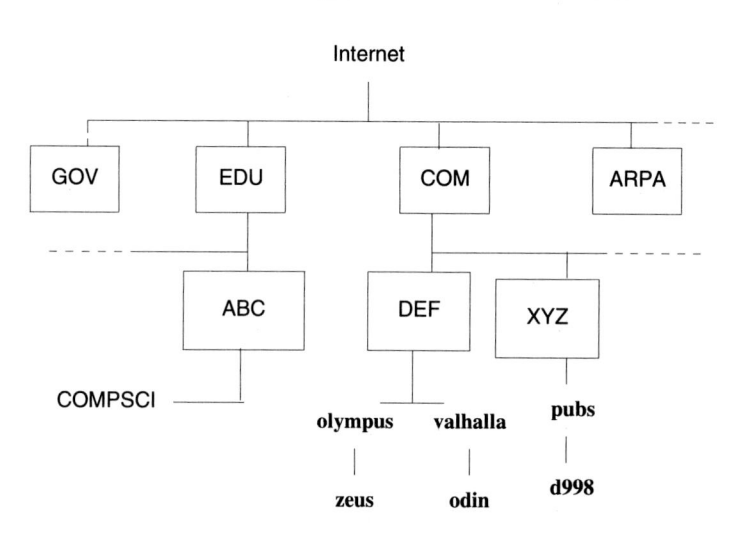

Figure D-2. General Domain Naming Structure with Example Connections

```
                        Internet
                           │
        ┌──────────┬───────┴───────┬──────────┐
      ┌───┐      ┌───┐           ┌───┐      ┌────┐
      │GOV│      │EDU│           │COM│      │ARPA│
      └───┘      └───┘           └───┘      └────┘
                   │       ┌───────┼───────┐
                 ┌───┐   ┌───┐   ┌───┐
                 │ABC│   │DEF│   │XYZ│
                 └───┘   └───┘   └───┘
        COMPSCI────┘       │       │
                        olympus  valhalla   pubs
                           │       │         │
                          zeus    odin      d998
```

In this example, the domain **pubs** is connected to the larger domain **XYZ** and is not directly connected to **olympus** as was **valhalla** in the previous example. Therefore, enter the following command to send a note to user **ed** at system **odin** from system **d998**:

$ **mail ed@odin.valhalla.DEF**

Similarly, user **ed** responds to user **cath** on **d998** by entering:

$ **mail cath@d998.pubs.XYZ**

Each of these addresses specifies only that part of the address needed to reach the destination from the domain **COM**. The routing programs at that domain recognize the domains **DEF** and **XYZ**. However, someone at **COMPSCI** sending a message to **cath** must enter the following command:

$ **mail cath@d998.pubs.XYZ.COM**

This example shows the complete address for user **cath** in the example network.

Addressing for Users Connected with a UUCP Link

To send a message to a user on another system connected to your system by UUCP, you must know the name of the other system and the physical route to that other system in addition to the username (on the other system) of the person to whom you are sending the message. The person responsible for connecting your system to the other system should be able to provide the proper routing information to address the other system.

Addressing When Your Computer Has a UUCP Link

If your local computer has a UUCP connection that can be used to reach the remote site, use the following format to address a message:

$ **mail** *uucp_route*!*username*

The variable parameter *username* is the username on the remote system of the person who is to receive the message. The variable parameter *uucp_route* describes the physical route that the message must follow along the UUCP network to reach the remote system. If your system is connected to the remote system without any intermediate UUCP systems between, then this parameter is just the name of the remote system. If your message must travel through one or more intermediate UUCP systems before reaching the desired remote system, this parameter is a list of each of the intermediate systems, starting with the nearest system and proceeding to the farthest system, separated by an **!** (exclamation point).

For example, if your local system has a UUCP link to a system called **merlin** and there are no other UUCP systems between your system and **merlin**, enter the following command to send a message to **ken** on that system:

$ **mail merlin!ken**

However, if the message must travel through systems **arthur** and **lancelot** (in that order) before reaching **merlin**, enter the following command to send the message:

$ **mail arthur!lancelot!merlin!ken**

Addressing When the UUCP Link is on Another Computer

In a local area or wide area network environment, one of the systems on the network may have a UUCP connection to a remote UUCP system. You can use that UUCP connection to send a message to a user on that remote UUCP system. Use the following command format to send a message:

$ **mail** @*systemA*:@*systemB*.**UUCP**:*username*@*systemC*

This format sends mail first to *systemA*, then to *systemB*, which routes it on a UUCP link to *systemC*. The **.UUCP** addition to the address for *systemB* indicates that the UUCP mailer at that system handles the routing of the message to *systemC*. The system addresses in this format are in the addressing format described earlier in "Addressing for Users on Your Network" and "Addressing for Users on a Different Network." Notice that, in this format, you are not sending mail to a user at any of the intermediate systems, so no username precedes the @ in the domain address.

Figure D-3 shows an example network that uses domain addressing for much of the mail, but has a UUCP link that routes mail to systems **depta** and **deptb**. The system **deptb** is connected to another system; that is, **deptc** by a local area network. The following commands illustrate addressing using this example network.

For **ed** at **odin** to send messages to **fred** at **depta**, **dick** at **deptb**, and **bill** at **deptc**, he would enter the following commands:

$ **mail @odin.UUCP:fred@depta**
$ **mail @odin.UUCP:@depta.UUCP:dick@deptb**
$ **mail @odin.UUCP:@depta.UUCP:@deptb:bill@deptc**

These people respond with the following commands:

$ **mail @depta.UUCP:ed@odin**
$ **mail @deptb.UUCP:@depta.UUCP:ed@odin**
$ **mail @deptb.UUCP:@depta.UUCP:ed@odin**

Similarly, **cath** at **d998** can send mail to the same people by entering the following commands:

$ **mail @odin.UUCP.valhalla.DEF:fred@depta**
$ **mail @odin.UUCP.valhalla.DEF:@depta.UUCP:dick@deptb**
$ **mail @odin.UUCP.valhalla.DEF:@depta.UUCP:@deptb:bill@deptc**

These people respond with the following commands:

$ **mail @depta.UUCP:@odin:cath@d998.pubs.XYZ**
$ **mail @deptb.UUCP:@depta.UUCP:@odin:cath@d998.pubs.XYZ**
$ **mail @deptb.UUCP:@depta.UUCP:@odin:cath@d998.pubs.XYZ**

Figure D-3. Example of UUCP Connection on a Network

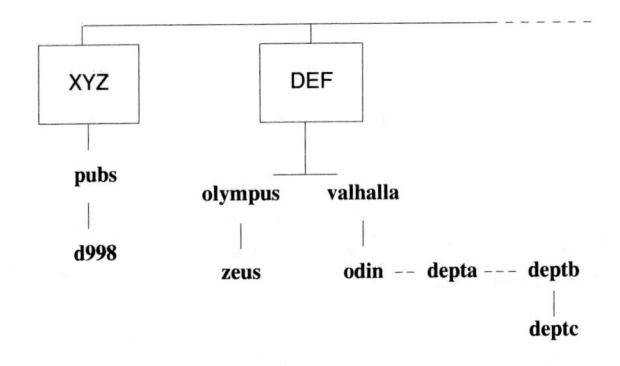

```
            XYZ             DEF
             |               |
            pubs       olympus   valhalla
             |            |         |
            d998        zeus      odin -- depta --- deptb
                                                     |
                                                    deptc
```

Creating Aliases and Distribution Lists

If you send mail on a large network or often send the same message to a large number of people, entering long addresses for each receiver can become tedious. To simplify this process you can create an alias or a distribution list:

Alias   A name that you define that can be used in place of
                    a user address when addressing mail.

Distribution list   A name that you define that can be used in place of
                    a group of user addresses when addressing mail.

Sending and Receiving Mail

Aliases and distribution lists are used the same way and defined in similar ways; the only difference is the number of addresses defined for an alias (one address) and a distribution list (more than one address).

Defining an Alias or Distribution List

To define an alias or a distribution list that you can use when sending mail, edit the file **.mailrc** in your home (login) directory. This file contains many commands that **mail** reads when you start it from the command line. These commands are discussed later in ''Changing Mail to Meet Your Needs.''

To define an alias, add a line in the following format to **.mailrc**:

alias *name user_addr*

To define a distribution list, add a line in the following format to **.mailrc**:

alias *name user_addr1 user_addr2 ... user_addrn*

In this format, the variable parameter *name* can be any alphanumeric string that you choose. It should be short and easy to remember, but it cannot be the same as any of the other defined aliases in this file. Duplicate names are redefined to match the last definition in this file.

> **Note:** If you define a *name* that is the same as a username on your system (as listed in **/etc/passwd**), you will *not* be able to send mail to that username. The alias name takes precedence over any defined usernames.

The variable parameters *user_addrx* can be any address that can be used with the **mail** command as defined earlier in ''Addressing Mail.'' For example, to define an alias for user **cath** using the alias name **catherine**, you might enter the following command in **.mailrc**:

alias catherine @deptb.UUCP:@depta.UUCP:@odin:cath@d998.pubs.XYZ

With this line in **.mailrc**, you can send mail to user **cath** by entering the command:

$ **mail catherine**

Similarly, to define a distribution list that sends a common message to a group of people, you might enter the following command in **.mailrc**:

alias dept geo anne mel@gtwn mark@mark.austin

With this line in **.mailrc**, you can enter the following command:

$ **mail dept**

This command sends the same message to users **geo** and **anne** on the local system, to **mel** on system **gtwn**, and to **mark** on system **mark** in subdomain **austin**.

In addition, you can use a previously defined alias in a distribution list. Therefore, you could add the first alias above to the distribution list to include user **cath** in the distribution list:

alias dept geo anne mel@gtwn mark@mark.austin catherine

You can also define aliases that are longer than one line by adding another line that defines the same alias. The second definition is added to the first; it does *not* replace the first definition. For example, the following entries define the same distribution list **dept** as in the previous example:

alias dept geo anne mel@gtwn
alias dept mark@mark.austin catherine

Sending Mail

Use the mail system to send information to another user. The other user need not be logged into the system when you send the information. You can use the **mail** command in one of two ways to send information. For short messages or letters that do not require a lot of formatting and editing, use the **mail** command's built-in editor to both compose and send the message. For larger letters, use your favorite editor to create the letter and then send the resulting file using the **mail** command.

Composing and Sending a Message

The **mail** command provides a simple, line-oriented editor for entering messages. See "Using the Mail Editor" later in the appendix for more information. Use the following procedure to use this editor to compose and send a message:

1. Enter the **mail** command on the command line followed by the address of the person or persons who will receive the message.

    $ **mail** *address*

    The system places the cursor on a new line and waits for input from the keyboard.

2. Type the message (see "Using the Mail Editor" for information about using the built-in editor).

3. When you are finished with the message, press **<Return>** and then **<Ctrl-d>**. The system adds appropriate header information and sends the message. The command-line prompt appears again.

For example, enter the following command to compose and send a message to user **amy** on system **zeus** on a local network:

$ **mail amy@zeus**

Sending a File

Use the **mail** command to send any text file to another user. The file may be a letter you have written using your favorite editor, a source file for a program you have written, or any other file in text format. To send a text file to another user, enter the following **mail** command:

mail *address* < *filename*

The system reads the input file, *filename*, adds appropriate header information, and sends the message. The command-line prompt appears again.

For example, enter the following command to send the file **letter** to user **amy** on your local system:

$ **mail amy < letter**

Receiving Mail

When mail arrives for you from another user, the mail system puts the mail in your system mailbox. If you are logged in, it also sends a message to your terminal periodically to tell you that new mail has arrived. If you are not logged in, a message is sent to your terminal the next time that you log in. If you do not change it, the message is

[YOU HAVE NEW MAIL]

To receive mail, do the following:

1. Enter the **mail** command without parameters:

   $ **mail**

   The system displays a listing of the messages in your system mailbox.

2. Enter the **t** command to display the text of a particular message.

3. Enter the **q** command to exit the mailbox and return to the command line. The **mail** program saves the messages that you read in your personal mailbox if you did not delete them.

Use the **mail** command without parameters to view the contents of your system mailbox. If no mail is in your system mailbox, the mail system responds with the message:

No mail for *username*

For example, if your username is **carol**, the following message displays if no mail is in your system mailbox:

$ **mail**
No mail for carol
$

Sending and Receiving Mail

If there is mail in your mailbox when you enter the **mail** command, the mail system displays a listing of the messages in your system mailbox. The listing shows information about who sent the message, when it was received, how large the message is, and what the subject is (if included in the message).

For example, user **geo** enters the **mail** command and receives the following display:

```
Mail   Type ? for help.
"/usr/spool/mail/geo": 2 messages 2 new
>N  1 amy     Mon Sep 17 14:36   13/359 "Dept Meeting"
 N  2 amy     Mon Sep 17 16:28   13/416 "Meeting Delayed"
&
```

The first line is the Mail program banner. It indicates that you can enter a ? (question mark) to get the help screen. The second line indicates the name of the mailbox file being used (/usr/spool/mail/geo is the system mailbox for user geo), the number of messages in the mailbox and their status. The following lines list information for each message in the mailbox. One line describes one message. The information about each message is arranged in fields, as shown in Table D-1. Fr From this listing you can look at, save, reply to, or delete any of the messages. Refer to ''Processing Messages in a Mailbox'' for a description of what you can do while in the mailbox.

Type **q** at the & prompt to exit the mailbox.

Table D-1. Mailbox Information

Field	Description
Pointer	The > (redirection symbol) in this field for a particular message indicates that the message is the current message in the mailbox. The current message is the default message for mailbox commands if no other message number is specified (see "Processing Messages in a Mailbox").

Field	Description
Status	A one-letter indicator of the status of the message:
	M Indicates that the message will be stored in your personal mailbox. N Indicates that the message is a new message. P Indicates that the message will be held (preserved) in your system mailbox. U Indicates that the message is an unread message. The message has been listed in the mailbox before, but you have not looked at the contents of the message. R Indicates that you have read the message. * Indicates that you have saved or written the message to a file or folder. No indicator indicates that the message is unresolved.
Message Number	An integer that mailbox commands use to refer to the message (see "Processing Messages in a Mailbox").
Address	The address of the person who sent the message.
Date	The date the message was received, including day of the week, month, date, and time.
Size	Size of the message in number of lines and number of characters, including heading information.
Subject	The contents of the subject field of the message (if the message has one).

Forwarding Your Mail

If you are going to be away from your normal network address for an extended period of time, you may want to have your network mail sent to another network address while you are away. Sending your incoming mail to a different address (or addresses) is called "forwarding." The new address may be the address of a co-worker who will handle your messages while you are away, or it may be the network address where you will be working while away from your normal address.

Sending and Receiving Mail

When you choose to forward your network mail, you do not receive a copy of any incoming mail in your mailbox. All mail goes directly to the address or addresses that you indicate.

Use the following procedure to forward your incoming network mail to another address:

1. Use the **cd** command with no parameters to ensure that you are in your home directory. The following command sequence illustrates that action for the username **geo**:

    $ **cd**
    $ **pwd**
    /u/geo
    $ _

2. While in your home directory, create a file called **.forward** that contains the network address or addresses that are to receive your forwarded network mail. This file must contain valid addresses. If it is a null file (zero length), your mail is not forwarded and is stored in your mailbox. If it contains addresses that are not valid, you do not receive the mail, but the sender receives an error message and the mail is put in **dead.letter** in the sender's home directory.

    As an example of creating a **.forward** file, the following command sequence uses the **cat** command to create that file. (Note that the entry **EOF** indicates the End-of-File character, frequently **<Ctrl-d>**, entered on a line by itself.) In this case, incoming mail will be forwarded to user **mark** on the local system and to user **amy** on system **zeus**.

    $ **cat > .forward**
    mark
    amy@zeus
    EOF
    $ _

   Once this file exists, you will receive no more mail. All mail is sent to the addresses in **.forward**. When you return to your normal network address, remove this file to resume receiving mail:

    $ **rm .forward**

OSF/1 User's Guide   D–23

Note: The file **.forward** does not appear in a simple listing of the files in your home directory. Use the **ls -a** command to see all files that begin with a **.** (dot).

Looking at Your Personal Mailbox

Messages that you have read but do not delete are saved in your personal mailbox. Use the **mail -f** command to view the contents of your personal mailbox as follows:

1. Enter the **mail** command with the **-f** flag:

   $ **mail -f**

   The system displays a listing of the messages in your personal mailbox.

2. Enter the **t** command to display the text of a particular message.
3. Enter the **q** command to exit the mailbox and return to the command line.

Use the **mail -f** command to view the contents of your personal mailbox. If the personal mailbox does not yet exist, the system responds with an error message:

/u/*userid*/mbox: No such file or directory

If the personal mailbox exists but is empty, the mailbox handler becomes active and displays a mailbox header similar to the following:

```
Mail    Type ? for help.
"/u/geo/mbox": 0 messages
&
```

Enter the **q** command to return to the command line.

If there is mail in your personal mailbox when you enter the **mail -f** command, the mail system displays a listing of the messages in your personal mailbox. The listing shows information similar to that shown when you look at your system mailbox (as described earlier in "Receiving Mail").

D–24   OSF/1 User's Guide

From this listing you can look at, save, reply to, or delete any of the messages. Refer to "Processing Messages in a Mailbox" later in this appendix for a description of what you can do while in the mailbox.

Enter **q** at the & prompt to exit the mailbox.

Looking at a Mail Folder

Use the **mail -f** command to view the contents of a defined mail folder. See "Creating and Using Folders" later in this appendix for information on how to create a folder.

To look at a mail folder, perform the following:

1. Enter the **mail** command with the **-f** flag and the name of the folder using a **+** (plus sign) to indicate the folder name:

   $ **mail -f +***folder*

   The system displays a listing of the messages in the indicated folder.

2. Enter the **t** command to display the text of a particular message.

3. Enter the **q** command to exit the folder and return to the command line.

Use the **mail -f** command to view the contents of a mail folder. For example, to view the contents of the defined folder **status** in your folder directory (defined in **.mailrc**), enter the following command:

$ **mail -f +status**

If the folder does not yet exist, the system responds with an error message:

/u/*userid*/letters/*folder*: No such file or directory

If the folder exists but is empty or contains information that is not in the correct format, the mailbox handler becomes active and displays a mailbox header similar to the following:

```
Mail  Type ? for help.
"/u/geo/letters/reports": 0 messages
&
```

Enter the **q** command to return to the command line.

If there is mail in the folder when you enter the **mail -f** command, the mail system displays a listing of the messages in the folder. The listing shows information similar to that shown when you look at your system mailbox (as described earlier in "Receiving Mail").

From this listing you can look at, save, reply to, or delete any of the messages. Refer to "Processing Messages in a Mailbox" next for a description of what you can do while in the mailbox.

Enter **q** at the & prompt to exit the mailbox.

Processing Messages in a Mailbox

You can use the **mail** command to process the contents of

- Your system mailbox
- Your personal mailbox
- Any mail folder that you have created

Using this program you can read, delete, store, and respond to messages you receive through the mail system. The following subsections explain how to perform these tasks.

Using Mailbox Commands

When the **mail** program is processing a mailbox, it displays the mailbox prompt to indicate that it is waiting for input. The mailbox prompt is the & (ampersand) that appears at the beginning of a new line. When this prompt appears, you can enter any of the mailbox commands described in this appendix or on the **mail** reference page.

Specifying Groups of Messages

Many mailbox commands operate on a message or group of messages. You can specify the message(s) using information displayed in the listing of the contents of the mailbox, such as message number or sender. Enter the **h** command (as described later in "Displaying the Contents of a Mailbox") to display the listing. Commands that allow groups of messages use the parameter *message_list* in the command format in this appendix. For example, the format of the **f** command (display information about messages) appears as

& **f** *message_list*

In this format, *message_list* can be one of the following:

- One or more message numbers separated by spaces:

    & **f** 1 2 4 7

- A range of message numbers indicated by the first and last numbers in the range separated by a - (dash):

    & **f** 2-5

    is the same as

    & **f** 2 3 4 5

OSF/1 User's Guide

- One or more addresses separated by spaces to apply the command to messages received from those addresses:

  & f amy geo@zeus

  The characters entered for an address do not need to exactly match the address. They must only be contained in the address field of the messages in either uppercase or lowercase characters. Therefore, the request for address **amy** matches all of the following addresses (and many others):

  amy
  AmY
  amy@zeus
  hamy

- A string, preceded by a / (slash), to match against the Subject: field of the messages:

  & f /meet

  applies the command to all messages whose subject field contains the letters meet in uppercase or lowercase characters. The characters entered for a match pattern do not need to exactly match the subject field. They must only be contained in the subject field of the messages in either uppercase or lowercase characters. Therefore, the request for subject meet matches all of the following subjects (and many others):

  ```
  Meeting on Thursday
  Come to meeting tomorrow
  MEET ME IN ST. LOUIS
  ```

Specifying File or Folder Names

Many mailbox commands allow you to specify a file or folder name to be used with the command. Commands that allow a file or folder name use the parameter *fname* in the command format in this appendix. For example, the format of the **file** command (change mailbox files) appears as

& **file** *fname*

In this format, *fname* can be one of the following:

- The pathname of the new mailbox relative to the current directory. For example, if the current directory is your home directory, enter the following command to change to your personal mailbox:

  & **file mbox**

  The program changes to that mailbox and displays a list of the contents of that mailbox.

- The absolute pathname of the new mailbox. For example, if your username is **george**, enter the following command to change to your system mailbox:

  & **file /usr/spool/mail/george**

- The shorthand form of a folder name in your directory defined for folders (described later in "Creating and Using Folders"). For example, if you define your folder directory as **letters**, enter the following command to change to the folder **reports**:

  & **file +reports**

  The **+** (plus sign) is a shorthand form for the full pathname of the folder directory. Therefore, this command performs the same function as if it had been entered as:

  & **file /u/george/letters/reports**

Looking at a Mailbox

To start the **mail** program with one of the main types of mailboxes, refer to the following procedures:

- For system mailbox information, see "Receiving Mail."
- For personal mailbox information, see "Looking at Your Personal Mailbox."
- For folders information, see "Looking at a Mail Folder."

Leaving the Mailbox

You can leave the mailbox and return to the shell using one of two commands:

- Enter the **q** command to leave the mailbox and return to the shell. When you leave the mailbox, all messages that you marked to be deleted are removed from the mailbox and cannot be recovered. For example, the following command processes the mailbox commands and returns you to the shell:

  & **q**

- Enter the **x** command to leave the mailbox and return to the shell *without changing the original contents of the mailbox*. The program ignores any requests to delete messages. For example, the following command returns you to the shell without changing the content of the mailbox:

  & **x**

Getting Help

While using **mail** to look at a mailbox, display a summary of many mailbox commands by entering the **?** command:

& ?

You can also display a list of all mailbox commands (with no explanation of what they do) by entering the **l** (list) command:

& l

Finding the Name of the Current Mailbox

Although the **mail** command displays the name of the current mailbox when it is started, you may lose track of what the current mailbox is. Use the **file** command without parameters to find out the name of the current mailbox. When you enter this command, it responds with the name of the current mailbox, the number of messages, and whether any messages have been marked to be deleted.

For example, if the current mailbox is **/u/george/mbox**, the system displays the following when you enter the **file** command:

& **file**
/u/george/mbox: 2 messages 1 deleted
&

This message indicates that **/u/george/mbox** contains two messages and that one of those messages will be deleted when you finish with this mailbox.

Changing Mailboxes

Once the program is started with one mailbox, use the **file** command to change to another mailbox. The format of this command is as follows:

file *fname*

Refer to "Specifying File or Folder Names" earlier in the appendix for an explanation of the *fname* parameter.

Note: When you change mailboxes, any messages that you marked to be deleted are deleted when you leave that mailbox. If you return to that mailbox, the deleted messages cannot be recovered.

Reading a Message from a Mailbox

To look at a message, enter the number of that message at the mailbox prompt (&). Pressing **<Return>** only at the mailbox prompt displays the current message. If the mailbox listing is

```
Mail  Type ? for help.
"/usr/spool/mail/geo": 2 messages 2 new
>N  1 amy    Thu Sep 17 14:36   13/359 "Dept Meeting"
 N  2 amy    Thu Sep 17 16:28   13/416 "Meeting Delayed"
&
```

pressing **<Return>** displays the message "Dept Meeting" because message number **1** is the current message (indicated by the > in the first column). Entering the number **2** displays the message "Meeting Delayed":

```
& 2
Message 2:
From geo Mon Sep 17 14:38 CDT 1990
Received: by zeus
        id AA00716; Mon, 17 Sep 90 14:38:53 CDT
Date: Mon, 17 Sep 90 14:38:53 CDT
From: amy
```

```
Message-Id: <8709171938.AA00716@zeus>
To: geo
Subject: Meeting Delayed
Status: R

The department meeting scheduled for 1:30 PM tomorrow
has been postponed to 3:30 PM.  It will still be held
in the planning conference room.

EOF:_
```

The EOF: prompt indicates that **pg** is being used to display the message. See ''Controlling the Display Scroll'' later in this appendix to change this option. Press **<Return>** to return to the mailbox prompt.

Looking at the Next Message

Enter the **n** command to look at the next message in the mailbox. The next message then becomes the current message. For example, if the current message is message number 6, then the following command displays message number 7 and makes message number 7 the current message:

& **n**

Looking at More Than One Message

To display more than one message in succession, enter the **t** command with a list or range of message numbers. The format for this command is as follows:

& **t** *message_list*

Refer to ''Specifying Groups of Messages'' earlier in this appendix for an explanation of the *message_list* parameter.

Note: When displaying more than one message at a time, be sure to include the **set crt** command in your **.mailrc** file (as described later in "Changing Mail to Meet Your Needs"). You can also enter this command at the mailbox prompt. If you do not use this command, the displayed messages scroll up and off the screen without pausing for you to read them.

Displaying the Contents of a Mailbox

When the **mail** program starts, it lists what is currently in the mailbox that it is using (as described earlier in "Receiving Mail"). You can see this list again by entering the **h** command. This command is useful to help you keep track of messages in the mailbox as you perform actions on them. Messages that you delete are not shown in the listing.

Only a certain number of messages (about 20) can be listed at a time. The actual number is determined by the terminal type being used, and by the **set screen** command (as described later in "Controlling the Display Scroll"). If the mailbox contains more than that number of messages, information about only the first group of messages will be displayed. To see information about the rest of the messages, enter the **h** command with a number that is in the next range of message numbers (21 to 40 in this case).

For example, suppose the mailbox contains 25 messages and the current list shows messages numbered 1 to 20. The following command displays information about messages numbered 21 to 25:

& **h 21**

To return to the first group of messages, enter the following command:

& **h 1**

You can also change the group of messages by displaying any of the messages in the desired group. For example, if you display message number 5, then the first group of messages becomes the current group of messages. Entering the **h** command shows information about messages 1 to 20.

Displaying Information About Selected Messages

If you have a large number of messages in your mailbox, you may want to display the heading information only about groups of messages. Enter the **f** command with a list or range of message numbers. The format for this command is as follows:

& **f** *message_list*

Refer to "Specifying Groups of Messages" earlier in this appendix for an explanation of the *message_list* parameter.

Deleting and Recalling Messages

Enter the **d** command to delete messages from a mailbox. The format of this command is as follows:

& **d** *message_list*

Note: If you delete a message and either change to another mailbox or quit the mailbox (with the **q** command), the deleted message cannot be recalled.

Once a message is deleted, but *before leaving* the current mailbox, you can recall that message and undelete it with the **u** command. The format of this command is as follows:

& **u** *message_list*

Refer to "Specifying Groups of Messages" for an explanation of the *message_list* parameter.

Entering **d** without a message list deletes the current message. Entering **u** without a message list recalls the last deleted message. You can also enter the **dt** command to delete the current message and automatically display the next message. For example, if the current message is message number 4, then the following command deletes message 4 and displays message 5:

& **dt**

Saving Messages in a File or Folder

You can add the contents of a message to a file or folder using one of two commands. One command includes the message headings in the file or folder; the other command adds only the text of the message to the file or folder. Both of these commands add information to the end of an existing file or else create a new file. They do not destroy information currently in the file.

Enter the **s** command to save a message, including header information, to a file or folder. The format of this command is as follows:

& **s** *message_list fname*

Use the **w** command to save a message without header information (text of the message only) to a file or folder. The format of this command is as follows:

& **w** *message_list fname*

Sending and Receiving Mail

Refer to "Specifying Groups of Messages" earlier in this appendix for an explanation of the *message_list* parameter. Refer to "Specifying File or Folder Names" earlier in this appendix for an explanation of the *fname* parameter.

For example, the following command saves messages 1, 2, 3, and 4 with their header information to a file called **notes** in the current directory:

& s 1-4 notes
```
"notes" [Appended] 62/1610
```

As an additional example, if message number 6 contains the following information, perform the next instruction:

```
From root Fri Sep 11 12:55 CDT 1990
Received: by zeus
        id AA00549; Fri, 11 Sep 90 12:55:25 CDT
Received: by thor
        id AA00178; Fri, 11 Sep 90 12:57:15 CDT
Date: Fri, 11 Sep 90 12:57:15 CDT
From: su@thor.8d33
Message-Id: <8709111757.AA00178@thor>
To: geo@zeus
Status: RO

Please change your password.
```

Enter the following command to save the entire message to a folder called **admin** in your folder directory (defined as /u/george/letters in your **.mailrc** file):

& s 6 +admin
```
"/u/george/letters/admin" [New file] 14/321
```

OSF/1 User's Guide   D–37

Enter the following command to save the text only to a file called **text** in the current directory:

& **w 6 text**
```
"text" [New file] 12/30
```

The **text** file contains the following:

```
Please change your password.
```

Editing a Message

You can use your favorite editor to add information to a note in your mailbox. When you leave the editor, you return to the mailbox prompt to continue processing the messages in the mailbox.

Two mailbox commands, **e** and **v**, allow you to activate one of two editors to edit the text of a message.

The **e** command activates the **ex** editor, or other editor that you define (as described later in ''Changing Mail to Meet Your Needs''). This command has the following format:

e [*message_number*]

The **v** command activates the **vi** editor, or other editor that you define (as described later in''Changing Mail to Meet Your Needs''). This command has the following format:

v [*message_number*]

For each of these commands, *message_number* is the number of the message that you want to edit. If you do not specify a message number, **mail** activates the editor using the current message.

Creating a Message

While using the **mail** command to process a mailbox, you can create a new message by activating the **mail** editor (as described later in "Using the Mail Editor"). Use one of the following three commands to activate the editor from the mailbox prompt depending upon the purpose of the message:

- **R** Responds to the sender of a message
- **r** Responds to the sender and all others who received copies of a message
- **m** Creates a new message independent from any received messages

Responding to the Sender Only

Enter the **R** command to send a response message to the originator of a message. This command creates a new message addressed to the sender of the selected message and with a `Subject:` field that refers to the selected message. Then it activates the **mail** editor to allow you to enter text into the new message. The format of this command is as follows:

& **R** [*message_number*]

The *message_number* parameter is the message number of the message to which you want to reply. If you do not specify a message number, **mail** creates a reply to the current message.

For example, suppose message number 4 is as follows:

```
From root Thu Sep 17 14:45 CDT 1990
Received: by zeus
        id AA00731; Thu, 17 Sep 90 14:44:59 CDT
Received: by thor
        id AA00614; Thu, 17 Sep 90 14:47:53 CDT
Date: Thu, 17 Sep 90 14:47:53 CDT
From: amy@thor
Message-Id: <8709171947.AA00614@thor>
```

```
To: geo@zeus
Subject: Department Meeting
Cc: mark@zeus, mel@gtwn
Status: RO

Please plan to attend a department meeting tomorrow
at 1:30 PM in the planning conference room.
```

In this case, you would enter the following as a reply message to **amy@thor**:

```
& R 4
To:   amy@thor
Subject: Re:  Department Meeting
```

I'll be there.
EOF

When you enter the **EOF** (**<Ctrl-d>** on many terminals), the program sends the message to **amy@thor** and returns you to the mailbox prompt.

Responding to the Sender and Recipients

Enter the **r** command to respond to the originator of a message and send a copy of your response to everyone on the Cc: list. The **r** command creates a new message that is addressed to the sender of the selected message and copied to the people on the Cc: list. The Subject: field of the new message refers to the selected message. The **r** command also activates the **mail** editor so you can enter text into the new message. The format of this command is as follows:

& **r** [*message_number*]

The *message_number* parameter is the number of the message to which you want to reply. If you do not specify a message number, **mail** creates a reply to the current message.

Sending and Receiving Mail

For example, using message number 4 in the previous example, the following sequence generates a reply message to **amy@thor** as well as to **mark@zeus** and **mel@gtwn**:

```
& r 4
To:  amy@thor
Cc: mark@zeus mel@gtwn
Subject: Re:  Department Meeting
```

I'll be there.
EOF

When you enter the **EOF** (**<Ctrl-d>** on many terminals), the program sends a copy of the message to all addressees and returns you to the mailbox prompt.

Creating a New Message

Enter the **m** command to create a new message while processing a mailbox. The format for this command is as follows:

& **m** *address*

The *address* parameter is any proper user address as described earlier in "Addressing Mail." This command starts the **mail** editor to create a new message as described earlier in "Sending Mail."

Listing Defined Aliases

While processing a mailbox, you can get a listing of the aliases that are defined for this **mail** session by entering the **a** command. The format for this command is as follows:

& **a**

This command displays all aliases and their corresponding addresses, one alias per line. Refer to "Addressing Mail" earlier in this appendix for information about defining an alias to be used as an address.

Using the Mail Editor

The **mail** command provides a line-oriented editor for composing messages. This editor allows you to enter each line of the message and then press **<Return>** to get a new line to enter more text. You cannot change a line once you have entered it. However, before pressing **<Return>**, you can change information on that one line by using **<Backspace>** and **<Delete>** to erase the information, and then enter the correct information.

Starting the Mail Editor

You can start the **mail** editor in one of two ways. From the command line you can start the editor to compose and send a message to another user as described earlier in "Composing and Sending a Message." The format of this command is as follows:

mail *address*

You can also use the **mail** editor to compose a reply to mail that you receive using the **R**, **r**, or **m** commands, as described earlier in "Creating a Message."

Sending a Message

When the editor is active and it contains some message text that you have entered, you can send that message and quit the editor with the following procedure:

1. Press **<Return>** to get the cursor at the beginning of a new line.

Sending and Receiving Mail

2. Enter an **EOF** character (**<Ctrl-d>** on many terminals). The system sends the message and returns you to either the mailbox handling program or to the shell, depending upon where you were when you started the editor.

You can change the editor to allow a **.** (dot) to be used as an additional EOF character in the preceding procedure as described later in "Changing Mail to Meet Your Needs."

Quitting Without Sending the Message

When the editor is active, you can use the following procedure to quit the editor without sending the message:

1. Press **<Enter>** to get the cursor at the beginning of a new line.
2. Enter the **~q** command. The system saves the message in the **dead.letter** file and returns you to the shell.

Getting Help

While using the **mail** editor to create a message, you can display a summary of the editor commands by entering the following command on a line by itself:

~?

Using the Escape Character

The editor includes many control commands that allow you to perform other operations on the message. Each of these commands must be entered on a new line, and each begins with the special escape character ~ (tilde). You can change this escape character to any other character by including the **set escape** command in your **.mailrc** file (as described later in "Changing Mail to Meet Your Needs"). To start a new line in your message with the escape character, use two escape characters together.

OSF/1 User's Guide   D–43

For example, the following text:

```
This is a tilde (~) and this is two tildes (~~).  However,
~~ results in sending only one tilde.
```

would be received as the following message:

```
This is a tilde (~) and this is two tildes (~~).  However,
~ results in sending only one tilde.
```

Displaying a Message

To look at lines of the message that you have entered (or that have been read from another file), use the ~p command. When you enter this command on a line by itself in the **mail** editor, the editor displays the contents of the message including the header information for the message. The text scrolls up from the bottom of the display.

If the message is larger than one screen and you have not set the page size for your terminal, the text scrolls off the top of the screen until it displays the last screen of the message, followed by the **mail** editor's (Continue) prompt. To look at the content of large messages, enter the **mail** editor commands to view the message with your favorite editor as described next in ''Changing a Message.''

Changing a Message

You cannot change information on a line once you have pressed **<Return>** and gone on to the next line. You can, however, change the content of your message before sending it by editing the message with another editor. The following subsections describe how to activate different editors from the **mail** editor.

Using a Different Editor

To change information that you have already entered, you can activate a different editor without leaving the **mail** editor. Once you have activated a different editor, you can use it to change the message or add new information to the message. When you leave the different editor, you return to the **mail** editor to continue composing, or to send, your message.

Enter the following commands on a new line in the **mail** editor to activate one of the different editors to edit the text of the current message:

~e This command activates the **ex** editor, or other editor that you define.

~v This command activates the **vi** editor, or other editor that you define.

When you save the message and quit the different editor, you return to the **mail** editor. You can then continue to compose the message, or enter one of the other **mail** editor commands to process the message.

Defining a Different Editor

The **mail** editor allows you to define two different editors to use when changing a message from within the **mail** program. You define either or both editors with the **set** command in your **.mailrc** file as follows. If you do not define these editors in **.mailrc**, **mail** tries to use the editors shown as the default in the following list:

set EDITOR=pathname   This command in your **.mailrc** file defines the editor that you activate with the ~e command. The value of *pathname* must be the full pathname to the editor program that you want to use. Default: **/usr/bin/ex**

set VISUAL=pathname   This command in your **.mailrc** file defines the editor that you activate with the ~v command. The value of *pathname* must be the full pathname to the editor program that you want to use. Default: **/usr/bin/vi**

For example, the following entry in your **.mailrc** file defines the **ed** editor for use with the ~e command:

set EDITOR=/usr/bin/ed

Reformatting a Message

After you have entered a message and before sending it, you may want to reformat the message to improve its appearance. Use the ~| command along with the **fmt** shell program to reformat the message. Enter the following command on a new line to reformat the message:

~| fmt

This command uses the **fmt** command to change the appearance of the message by reformatting the information for each paragraph within defined margins (a blank line must separate each paragraph).

Note: Do not use the **fmt** command if a message contains embedded messages or preformatted information from external files (as described later in "Including Another Message"). This command reformats the heading information in embedded messages and may change the format of preformatted information.

Checking for Misspelling

If you have the text formatting set of programs installed on your system, you can use the **spell** program to check your message for misspelled words with the following procedure:

1. Write the message to a temporary file. For example, to write the message to the **spellchk** file, use the following command:

    ~w spellchk

Sending and Receiving Mail

2. Run the **spell** program using the temporary file as input. For example, the following command uses the temporary file **spellchk** as input to the **spell** program:

   ~! spell spellchk

   The **spell** program responds with a list of words that are not in its list of known words, followed by an **!** (exclamation point) to indicate that you have returned to the **mail** program.

3. Examine the list of words to determine if you need to use an editor to correct any of them (described earlier in ''Changing a Message'').

4. Erase the temporary file. The following command erases the temporary file in the preceding example:

   ~! rm spellchk

Changing the Header

The header of the message contains routing information and a short statement of the subject. You must specify at least one recipient of the message, but the other information is not required. The information in the header may include the following:

To:	This field contains the address or addresses to which the message is to be sent.
Subject:	This field contains a short summary of the topic of the message.
Cc:	This field contains the address or addresses of persons who are to receive copies of the message. This field is included as part of the message sent to all who receive the message.
Bcc:	This field contains the address or addresses of persons who are to receive ''blind'' copies of the message. This field is *not* included as part of the message sent to all who receive the message.

OSF/1 User's Guide

You can set up **mail** to automatically ask you for the information for these fields by entering commands in your **.mailrc** file (described later in "Changing Mail to Meet Your Needs"). If you have not changed **.mailrc** or if you need to change the information that you entered in these fields, use the commands described in the following subsections to change the information in these fields.

Editing the Header Information

To add to or change information in more than one of the header fields, enter the ~**h** command. When you enter this command on a new line, the system displays each of the four header fields, one at a time. You can view the contents of each field, delete information from that field (using **<Backspace>**) or add information to that field when the field and its contents are displayed. Pressing **<Return>** saves any changes to that field and displays the next field and its contents. When you press **<Return>** for the last field (Bcc:), you return to the editor.

For example, when composing a message, enter the ~**h** command to change the Subject: and Cc: fields:

```
~h
To: mark@austin_
```

The system responds with the contents of the To: field (mark@austin) and places the cursor at the end of that field. You could edit or add to this field at this time, but this information is correct. Press **<Return>**. The system responds with the contents of the Subject: field:

```
Subject: Fishng Trip_
```

Note: If you have changed this field before, the cursor may not be at the end of the field.

Sending and Receiving Mail

In this case, we want to correct the misspelling in the indicated subject. The cursor is at the end of the `Subject:` field. Position the cursor under the `n` in `Fishng`. Reenter the rest of the subject to correct it to `Fishing Trip`. Press **<Return>**. The system responds with the contents of the `Cc:` field:

`Cc: mel@gtwn_`

To add another person to the copy list, ensure that the cursor is at the end of the list, enter a space, and then enter the address of the new person. For example:

`Cc: mel@gtwn` **geo@austin**

This entry expands the copy list to two persons. When you have completed the copy list, press **<Return>**. The system responds with the contents of the `Bcc:` field. Press **<Return>**. The system responds with the (`Continue`) prompt and returns you to the **mail** editor at the current end of the message.

Adding to the To: List

Enter the ~t command to add one or more addresses to the `To:` list. For example, the `To:` list for a message may contain the following address:

`To: mark@austin`

To add to this list, enter the following command:

~t geo@austin mel@gtwn

This command changes the `To:` list as follows:

`To: mark@austin geo@austin mel@gtwn`

You cannot use the ~t command to change or delete the contents of the `To:` list.

OSF/1 User's Guide   D–49

Setting the Subject: Field

Enter the ~s command to set the Subject: field to a particular phrase or sentence. Entering this command replaces the previous contents (if any) of the Subject: field. For example, the Subject: field for a message may contain the following phrase:

```
Subject: Vacation
```

To change the Subject: field, enter the following command:

~sFishing Trip

This command changes the Subject: field to the following:

```
Subject: Fishing Trip
```

You cannot append to the Subject: field with this command.

Adding to the Cc: List

Enter the ~c command to add one or more addresses to the Cc: list. For example, the Cc: list for a message may contain the following addresses:

```
Cc: mark@austin amy
```

To add to this list, enter the following command:

~cgeo@austin mel@gtwn

This command changes the Cc: list to the following:

```
Cc: mark@austin amy geo@austin mel@gtwn
```

You cannot use the ~c command to change or delete the contents of the Cc: list.

Adding to the Bcc: List

Enter the ~**b** command to add one or more addresses to the Bcc: list. For example, the Bcc: list for a message may contain the following address:

Bcc: mark@austin

To add to this list, enter the following command:

~**b geo@austin mel@gtwn**

This command changes the Bcc: list to the following:

Bcc: mark@austin geo@austin mel@gtwn

You cannot use the ~**b** command to change or delete the contents of the Bcc: list.

Including Information from Another File

You can include information from other files in the message you are currently writing. This feature allows you to include data, such as a schedule, from another file. Enter the ~**r** command to read the contents of a file into the current message. The format of this command is as follows:

~**r** *filename*

For example, to read the contents of the **schedule** file and append that information to the current end of the message, enter the following command:

~**r schedule**

Including Another Message

You can include another message within the current message for reference purposes, or to forward the other message to another user.

Enter the ~m command to include another message in the current message for reference purposes. This command reads the indicated message and appends it to the current end of the message. The included message is indented one tab character from the normal left margin of the message. The format of this command is as follows:

~m*numlist*

Enter the ~f command to include another message in the current message to forward the message to another user. This command reads the indicated message and appends it to the current end of the message, but *does not indent* the appended message. Also enter this command to append messages for reference whose margins are too wide to embed with the ~m command. The format of this command is as follows:

~f*numlist*

Note: To use the commands ~m and ~f that include other messages within your message, you must enter the editor from the mailbox (using either the **r**, **R**, or **m** mailbox commands). See "Creating a Message" earlier in this appendix for information about using the mailbox commands.

In the preceding formats, the *numlist* parameter is a list of integers that refer to valid message numbers in the mailbox or folder currently being handled by **mail**. You can enter simple ranges of numbers also. For example, the following commands embed the indicated messages if those message numbers exist in the current mailbox or folder:

~m 1   Appends message number **1** to the current end of the message being written. Message number **1** is indented one tab from the left margin.

~m 1 3   Appends message number **1** and then message number **3** to the current end of the message being written. Both messages are indented one tab from the left margin.

~f 1-4   Appends message numbers **1** to **4** to the current end of the message being written. These messages are aligned with the left margin (not indented).

Resending Undelivered Messages

When **mail** cannot deliver a message that you send, it places that message in a file named **dead.letter** in your home (login) directory. This file can also contain a partial letter that was saved when you quit by entering the ~q command from the **mail** editor. To read the contents of the **dead.letter** file into the current message, enter the ~d command.

~d

This command appends the contents of **dead.letter** to the current end of the message and responds with the (Continue) prompt. You can then continue to add to, or send, the message.

Changing Mail to Meet Your Needs

The person responsible for managing your system defines the initial configuration of the **mail** program. You may, however, alter the way the **mail** program operates to meet your personal requirements. The characteristics of a **mail** session that you can change include

- Whether **mail** prompts for the subject of a message
- Whether **mail** prompts for users to get a copy of a message
- If any aliases or distribution lists are defined
- How many lines are displayed when reading messages
- What information is listed in messages
- Whether a folder directory is selected in which to store messages
- Whether a log file is set up to record outgoing messages

- Whether different editors can be used for entering messages
- How to exit the **mail** editor
- How **mail** stores messages

The system manager uses the **/usr/share/lib/Mail.rc** file to define the initial configuration. This file contains **mail** commands that perform the tasks mentioned in the previous list. Although the initial configuration can meet the needs of most users, you can easily alter it by creating a file in your home (login) directory with the name **.mailrc**. Commands in this file override similar commands in **/usr/share/lib/Mail.rc** when you run **mail**.

Another way of executing **mail** commands that are stored in a file is by using the **source** command. When reading mail, you can issue this command from the **mail** command line as follows:

& **source** *pathname*

where *pathname* is the path and file containing the **mail** commands. Commands in this file override the previous settings of any similar commands for the duration of the current session. You may also alter the characteristics of the current **mail** session by entering commands at the mailbox prompt (&).

Commands for Customizing Mail

There are four **mail** commands that alter the characteristics of the **mail** session. These are **set**, **unset**, **alias**, and **ignore**.

The set and unset Commands

The **set** command and its inverse, the **unset** command, are used in conjunction with *options*. Enter the **set** command to enable options, and the **unset** command to disable options. You can also use the **set** command to assign a value to an option.

Sending and Receiving Mail

The format for using the **set** command to enable options is as follows:

set [*option_list*]

The *option_list* may be one or more options that you want to enable. Entering **set** without the *option_list* shows what options are already enabled. Refer "Checking Mail Characteristics" later in this appendix to see when to enter **set** with no *option_list*.

The format for the **unset** command is as follows:

unset *option_list*

You must include the *option_list* with the **unset** command.

For example, to cause **mail** to prompt for a Subject: field, enter the following command:

& **set ask**

To also cause **mail** to prompt for a Cc: field, enter the following command:

& **set ask askcc**

To suppress both of these prompts, enter the following command:

& **unset ask askcc**

The format for entering the **set** command to assign a value to an option is as follows:

set *option=value*

An example of a *valued option* is shown in the following entry:

& **set toplines=10**

With this entry in your **.mailrc** file, the **top** command displays only the first 10 lines of a message. (See "Controlling the Display Scroll" later in this appendix.)

The alias Command

Enter the **alias** command in your **.mailrc** file to define alias names and distribution lists. The **alias** command allows you to send messages without entering long addresses or long lists of addresses. "Creating Aliases and Distribution Lists," earlier in this appendix, describes how to use the **alias** command.

You can define a distribution list with the **alias** command that includes your own address. If you send a message using the distribution list, however, the mail system does not normally send a copy to your mailbox. Enter the following **set** command to enable sending a copy to yourself also:

set metoo

With this entry in **.mailrc**, anytime you send a message using an alias name that includes you, a copy of the message will be put in your mailbox.

The ignore Command

Enter the **ignore** command to define what information is listed in message headers. The message headers are the fields like To: and From: at the tops of messages. Refer to "Controlling What Information is Displayed" later in this appendix, to see how to use the **ignore** command.

Checking Mail Characteristics

The characteristics of a **mail** session are determined by many commands and options. Commands in **.mailrc** and **/usr/share/lib/Mail.rc** affect each **mail** session; so do any commands you entered during the current session. You can avoid confusion by reviewing the characteristics of a mail session as described in this section.

Before running **mail**, you can enter the **pg** command to view **/usr/share/lib/Mail.rc** and see what **mail** commands are in it. You can also look at your **.mailrc** file.

Sending and Receiving Mail

When reading your mail, enter the **set** command without any arguments to list all of the options that are currently enabled. From this list you can also see if a folder directory is selected, and if a log file is set up to record outgoing messages. For example, entering the **set** command from the mailbox prompt (&) could produce a display as follows:

```
& set
ask
metoo
toplines   10
&
```

You can see from this list that two options are enabled: `ask` and `metoo`. Notice that there is no `askcc` entry in the list. This indicates that the `askcc` option is not enabled. You can also see that the `toplines` option has been assigned the value 10.

Two other commands from the **mail** command line provide current command settings. The **ignore** command with no arguments lists all header fields that are not included when you enter a **t** or **p** command to display a message. The **alias** command without any arguments lists all alias names that are currently defined.

The information listed by the **set**, **ignore**, and **alias** commands includes system default settings, settings from the **/usr/share/lib/Mail.rc** file, settings from your **.mailrc** file, and any settings you made during the current **mail** session.

Prompting for a Subject: Field

When you start **mail** to begin writing a message to another user, the program may or may not ask you for a `Subject:` field with a prompt similar to the following:

```
Subject:
```

If this prompt appears, you can fill in a summary of the subject matter of the message, and that summary is included at the start of the message that you send. Whether this prompt appears or not is determined by the presence of the **ask** option. To enable the subject prompt, enter the following line in your **.mailrc** file:

set ask

To prevent **mail** from displaying this prompt, either delete the **set ask** statement from **.mailrc** or enter the following line in **.mailrc**:

unset ask

Prompting for a Cc: Field

You can set up **mail** so that when you send a message, **mail** prompts you for the names of other users whom you want to receive copies of the message. This prompt is similar to the following:

```
Cc:
```

This prompt appears if the **askcc** option is set in the system file **/usr/share/lib/Mail.rc** or in your **.mailrc** file as shown:

set askcc

To suppress this prompt, either delete the **set askcc** entry from your **.mailrc** file or include the following entry in **.mailrc**:

unset askcc

Changing How Mail Displays a Message

You can set several options from your **.mailrc** file to control how much information **mail** displays at different times. You can also enter the **ignore** command in your **.mailrc** file to keep header fields from being displayed.

The following subsections show you how to use **mail** commands to control display functions.

Controlling the Display Scroll

Each message in your mailbox has a one-line heading in the message list. If you have more than 24 messages, the first headings from the message list scroll past the top of your screen whenever you display the message list. The **set screen** command controls how many lines of the list are displayed at a time. For example, with the following entry in **.mailrc**:

set screen=20

the **h** command displays 20 message headers, then waits for you to press **<Return>** before displaying the next 20 headers.

A similar situation occurs when you display a long message. If you display a message with more than 24 lines, then the first lines of the message scroll past the top of the screen. You can enter the **pg** program from within **mail** to browse through long messages if you include the **set crt** command in **.mailrc**.

The **set crt** command has the following form:

set crt=n

The value for n determines how many lines a message must be before the **pg** program is started. The **pg** program is invoked whenever you read messages with more than this many lines.

For example, if you enter the **t** command to read a long message, only one screen (or page) is displayed. The page is followed by a colon prompt to let you know that there are more pages. Press **<Return>** to display the next page of the message. After the last page of the message is displayed, there is a prompt similar to the following:

```
EOF:
```

At this prompt, or the colon prompt, you can enter any valid **pg** command. You can display previous pages, search the message for character strings, or quit reading the message and return to the mailbox prompt (&). Refer to the **pg** reference page for more information.

The **top** command lets you scan through messages to get more information without reading entire messages. You control how many lines of a message are displayed with the **top** command by setting the **toplines** option as follows:

set toplines=n

In this command, n is number of lines, starting from the top and including all header fields that are displayed with the **top** command.

For example, if user **amy** has the following line in her **.mailrc** file:

set toplines=10

When Amy runs **mail** to read her new messages, she receives the following display:

```
Mail  Type ? for help.
"/usr/spool/mail/amy": 2 messages 2 new
>N  1 george    Wed Jan  6  9:47  11/257 "Dept Meeting"
 N  2 mark      Wed Jan  6 12:59  17/445 "Project Planner"
&
```

Now Amy uses the **top** command to browse through her messages as shown in the following dialog:

```
& top 10
Message 1:
From george Wed Jan 9 9:47 CST 1990
Received: by zeus
        id AA00549; Wed, 9 Jan 90 9:47:46 CST
Date: Wed, 9 Jan 90 9:47:46 CST
```

```
From: george@zeus
Message-Id: <8709111757.AA00178>
To: amy@zeus
Subject: Dept Meeting

Please plan to attend the department meeting on Friday
at 1:30 in the planning conference room.  We will be

&
```

The message was not displayed completely because **toplines** was set to 10, so only lines 1 (the Received: field) through 10 (the second line of the message body) were displayed. The first line, From george Wed Jan 9 9:47CST 1990, is always present and does not count in the **toplines** option.

Controlling What Information is Displayed

Every message has several header fields at the top. These header fields are normally displayed when you read a message. However, you can enter the **ignore** command to suppress the display of header fields when a message is read with a **t** or **p** command. The format for the **ignore** command is as follows:

ignore [*field_list*]

The optional *field_list* can consist of one or more field names that you want to ignore when you display a message. For example, if Amy includes the following line in her **.mailrc** file:

ignore date from to

and the **/usr/share/lib/Mail.rc** file has the line:

ignore received message-id

the result of using the **t** command is as follows:

```
& t 10
Message 1:
From george Wed Jan 9 9:47 CST 1990
Subject: Dept Meeting

Please plan to attend the department meeting on Friday
at 1:30 in the planning conference room. We will be
discussing the new procedures for using the project
planning program developed by our department.

&
```

Many fields do not appear in the display. To display these fields, use a **T** or **P** command or the **top** command. You can enter the **ignore** command without any arguments at the **mail** command line to get a list of the currently ignored header fields.

You can set the **quiet** option so that, when you display a message, the message number is not displayed first. To do this, enter the following command in **.mailrc**:

set quiet

With the **quiet** option in **.mailrc**, the **mail** banner is not displayed when you start **mail**. The banner is the line that shows the name of the **mail** program.

Another option that suppresses the **mail** banner is the following:

set noheader

If you enter this command in **.mailrc**, the list of messages in your mailbox is not displayed when you start **mail**. The only response you will get is the mailbox prompt (&). You can get a list of messages by entering the **h** command.

Combining the delete and print Commands

After you read a message, you can delete it by entering the **d** command. You can then display the next message by entering the **p** command. You can combine these commands by entering the following line in your **.mailrc** file:

set autoprint

This causes the **d** command to delete the current message and display the next one.

Creating and Using Folders

As you read mail messages pertaining to different subjects, you can store them in appropriate folders (mail system files) and read them again during later **mail** sessions. You can create new folders during a **mail** session as necessary, but a directory for storing them must exist before defining any new folders. Since a folder directory is just a normal directory used for storing folders, you can create a new folder directory from within **mail** by entering the **mkdir** shell command as follows:

& **!mkdir** *pathname*

You must select a folder directory before storing any messages in it. To select a folder directory, set the **folder** option from the **mail** command line as follows:

& **set folder=***pathname*

You can also include the **set folder** command in **.mailrc** so that, when you invoke **mail**, the folder directory is already selected.

As you read messages, you can append them to any folder or place them into new folders within the selected folder directory. In this manner, you can sort your new messages into folders like in a file cabinet. For example, upon logging in, user **george** sees that he has new mail. He enters the **mail** command and receives the following display:

```
Mail   Type ? for help.
"/usr/spool/mail/george": 2 messages 2 new
>N  1 amy    Tue Dec 4 13:24   32/947  "New Utilities"
 N  2 mark   Wed Dec 5 15:47   16/417  "Project Schedule"
&
```

After reading the first message, **george** sees that it documents some fancy new shell procedures that **amy** has written. He decides that it should go into a special folder he uses to collect such things. User **george** has the following **set folder** command in his **.mailrc** file so that the folder directory where that folder is kept is already selected:

```
set folder=/u/george/doc
```

User **george** uses the **save** command to append the new message to the special folder **procedures** by entering a **+** (plus) symbol to indicate the folder name as follows:

& **save 1 +procedures**

He receives the message:

```
"/u/george/doc/procedures" [Appended] 32/947
```

He can access all messages saved in the procedures folder as described earlier in "Looking at a Mail Folder."

The second message is a project schedule. There is no folder yet for keeping project schedules, so **george** decides to create one. He also wants to put the folder into a directory where he has other files concerning the project. User **george** selects this directory by entering the following command:

& **set folder=/u/george/projectX**

and the new folder can be created with the **save** command as follows:

& **save 2 +schedules**

The message

`"/u/george/projectX/schedules" [New File] 16/417`

indicates that a new folder has been created.

Keeping a Record of Messages Sent

The **mail** command can automatically make a copy of any messages you send and store them in a specified file that can be read later. Since the header information is also stored, recording outgoing messages is a useful way of logging when important information was sent to others. Normally **mail** does not keep any record of messages sent.

To enable this option, enter a **set record** command in **.mailrc** as follows:

set record=*pathname*

Here the *pathname* indicates the file relative to your home (login) directory. The **mail** commands do not create directories, so any directories included in the *pathname* must already exist before using this command. Entering this command in your **.mailrc** file guarantees that copies of all of your messages will go to the same place.

If **amy** has the following lines in her **.mailrc** file:

```
set record=letters/mailout
set folder=letters
```

a copy of the messages she sends out is entered into the file **/u/amy/letters/mailout**. She can read the recorded messages by entering **mail** as follows:

$ **mail -f +mailout**

because the folder **mailout** is in the folder directory selected by the **set folder=letters** command in her **.mailrc** file.

If you set up a file to record outgoing messages, you should read the file periodically with **mail** and delete all of the unnecessary messages. Otherwise, the file will grow and eventually use up all of your storage space.

Selecting a Different Editor

The standard **mail** editor is good for entering short messages, but it does not allow you to alter text after you press **<Return>**. An alternative is to use another editor to create a file and use **mail** to send the file. However, the file will still exist after it has been sent. You can set up **mail** so that you can use any editor on your system to enter a message from within **mail**, and the message will not be left in a file when you exit **mail**.

Enter the **set** command in the **.mailrc** file with the following valued options to define two different editors:

set EDITOR=e_pathname
set VISUAL=v_pathname

In the first entry, e_pathname is the full pathname of the editor you want to activate with the ~e escape sequence or the **e** command. In the second entry, v_pathname is the full pathname of the editor you want to activate with the ~v escape sequence or the **v** command.

If Amy includes the following line in her **.mailrc** file:

set EDITOR=/usr/bin/ed

she can call up her favorite editor (from **/usr/bin/ed**) by using the ~e escape sequence from within the standard **mail** editor.

When Amy is finished entering her message, she exits from her favorite editor and returns to the standard **mail** editor. She can then press **<Ctrl-d>** to exit **mail** and send the message.

As Amy reads her mail she can edit messages to add information to them. Entering the **e** command from the mailbox prompt (&) also invokes the editor specified in the **set editor** command. After she exits the editor, Amy returns to the **mail** command line where she can save the message to a folder.

Defining How to Exit the Mail Editor

When you enter the **mail** command to send a message, you invoke the **mail** editor. From the **mail** editor you can compose your message. You can exit from the **mail** editor in one of two ways. One method is to press **<Ctrl-d>**.

Another method is to enter a **.** (dot) on a line by itself. This **.** (dot) does not appear in the message. To enable this method, enter the following line in **.mailrc**:

set dot

After you quit the **mail** editor, the message is sent and you return to the system prompt.

If you reply to a message when reading your mail, you also invoke the **mail** editor. The **set dot** command allows you to exit from the **mail** editor, but you return to the mailbox prompt (&). From there you can exit **mail** with a **quit** command, an **exit** command, or by pressing **<Ctrl-d>**.

Defining How Mail Stores Messages

The **mail** program has several defaults for how messages are stored when you exit. You can set three options in **.mailrc** to change how **mail** stores messages. These options are the **append** option, the **hold** option, and the **keepsave** option. This section describes how these options change the way **mail** stores messages.

Normally, **mail** adds messages to a mailbox at the top of the mailbox. You can cause **mail** to append messages to the end of the mailbox by entering the following in **.mailrc**:

set append

Messages are stored in different places when you exit **mail**, depending on how you exit. You can exit **mail** in three ways. One way to exit **mail** is to enter the **exit** command. Enter the **exit** command to return all messages to the mailbox you are reading. The mailbox will have the same messages the next time you read it. Another way to exit is to enter the **quit** command. Enter the **quit** command to dispose of files as described in the following paragraphs. The third way to exit **mail** is to press **<Ctrl-d>**. Using **<Ctrl-d>** is the same as using the **quit** command.

As you read messages from a mailbox, you can delete them, save them, or leave them unresolved. If you do not read a message, it remains in the mailbox, no matter how you exit **mail**.

Messages that are deleted are not saved anywhere if you exit **mail** with a **quit** command. However, if you exit with an **exit** command, deleted messages remain in the mailbox.

An unresolved message is one that you have read, but did not delete or save. If you exit **mail** with a **quit** command, any unresolved messages are stored in a file called **mbox** in your home (login) directory. You can cause **mail** to leave unresolved messages in the mailbox you are reading, instead of storing them in **mbox**, by entering the following in **.mailrc**:

set hold

The **hold** option has no effect on deleted messages.

Instead of using the **set hold** option, you can use the **hold** command to specify that a message remains in the mailbox when you exit with the **quit** command. For example, if you read message 3, but you are not sure if you want to delete it, mark it with the **hold** command:

& **hold 3**

The message remains in the mailbox instead of going to **mbox**. You can wait until the next time you read the mailbox to decide how to dispose of it.

If you set the **hold** option in **.mailrc**, you can use the **mbox** command to mark messages so that they are stored in **mbox** when you exit with the **quit** command. For example, if you are reading new mail, you can mark messages that you have read, but not discarded, by entering the **mbox** command:

& **mbox 1 3 5-7**

This example marks messages **1**, **3**, and **5** to **7** so that they are stored in **mbox** instead of remaining in the system mailbox with any unread messages or other unresolved messages.

If you save a message with a **save** or **write** command, **mail** deletes the message from the mailbox when you exit with the **quit** command. To keep the saved message in the mailbox, enter the following:

set keepsave

Now **mail** handles messages that you save just like unresolved messages. The **set hold** option causes them to be held in the mailbox. Without the **set hold** option, they are stored in **mbox**.

If you exit **mail** with the **exit** command, all messages remain in the mailbox, no matter what options are set. Also, if you save any messages, the messages remain in the files where you saved them, even if you use the **exit** command.

Glossary

access permission

A group of designations that determine who can access a particular file and how the user can access the file. See also **permissions**.

alphabetic

Pertaining to the set of letters and symbols, excluding digits, used in a language. This set usually consists of the uppercase and lowercase letters plus special symbols (such as $ and _) allowed by a particular language.

American National Standard Code for Information Interchange

(ASCII) The code developed by ANSI for information interchange among data processing systems, data communications systems, and associated equipment. The ASCII character set consists of 7-bit control characters and symbolic characters.

append

> The action that causes data to be added to the end of existing data.

application program

> A program used to perform an application or part of an application.

archive

> 1. To store programs and data for safekeeping.
> 2. A copy of one or more files or a copy of a database that is saved in case the original data is damaged or lost.

argument

> Numbers, letters, or words that expand or change the way a command works.

array

> A variable that contains an ordered group of data objects. All objects in an array have the same data type.

background process

> A mode of program execution in which the shell does not wait for program completion before prompting the user for another command.

backup

> To copy information, usually onto diskette or tape, for safekeeping.

backup copy

> A copy, usually of a file or group of files, that is kept in case the original file or files are unintentionally changed or destroyed.

Glossary

baud

The number of changes in signal levels, frequency, or phase per second on a communications channel. If each represents 1 bit of data, baud is the same as bits per second. However, it is possible for one signal change (1 baud) to equal more than 1 bit of data.

binary file

A file that contains codes that are not part of the character set. Binary files utilize all 256 possible values for each byte in the file.

block special file

A special file that provides access to an input or output device and is capable of supporting a file system.

Bourne shell

See **shell**.

buffer

An area of storage, temporarily reserved for performing input or output, into which data is read or from which data is written.

C shell

See **shell**.

cancel

To end a task before it is completed.

case sensitive

Able to distinguish between uppercase and lowercase letters.

character special file

A special file that provides access to an input or output device. The character interface is used for devices that do not use block I/O. It may also be used for alternative access to devices that normally use block I/O.

code set
> A collection of characters with assigned code values. For example, ASCII contains a specified group of characters; each character has an assigned value in the set.

collating sequence
> The sequence in which characters are ordered within the computer for sorting, combining, or comparing.

command
> A request to perform an operation or run a program. When parameters, arguments, flags, or other operands are associated with a command, the resulting character string is a single command.

command alias
> A feature that allows you to abbreviate long command lines or to rename commands.

command history
> A feature that stores commands and allows you to edit and reuse them.

command interpreter
> A program that sends instructions to the kernel; also called an interface. See also **shell**.

command search path
> A list of directories searched in order for an executable image.

communications
> See **data communications**.

computer virus
> A program or routine that inserts itself in another executable file. A virus once installed is executed by trigger mechanisms of which users are unaware.

computer worm

A program that copies itself across a computer network.

configuration

The group of machines, devices, and programs that make up a data processing system or network.

configuration file

A file that specifies the characteristics of a system or subsystem.

control character

1. A character, occurring in a particular context, that initiates, modifies, or stops any operation that affects the recording, processing, transmission, or interpretation of data (such as carriage return, font change, and end of transmission).

2. A nonprinting character that performs formatting functions in a text file.

control statement

1. A language statement that changes the normal path of execution.

2. In programming languages, a statement that is used to alter the continuous sequential execution of statements. A control statement can be a conditional statement or an imperative statement.

copy

The action by which the user makes a whole or partial duplicate of an already existing data object.

current directory

The directory that is active and can be displayed with the **pwd** command. Synonymous with **current working directory**.

current working directory

Synonym for **current directory**.

cursor

> A movable symbol (such as an underline) on a display that indicates to the user where the next typed character will be placed or where the next action will be directed.

cursor movement keys

> The directional keys used to move the cursor without altering text.

data communications

> The transmission of data according to a protocol between computers or remote devices.

default

> A value, attribute, or option that is assumed when no alternative is specified by the user.

delete character (DEL)

> A control character used primarily to obliterate an erroneous or unwanted character.

device driver

> A program that operates a specific device, such as a printer, disk drive or display.

directory

> A type of file containing the names and controlling information for other files or other directories.

dot

> A symbol (.) that indicates the current directory in a relative pathname.

dot dot

> A symbol (..) in a relative pathname that indicates the parent directory.

editor
>A program used to enter and modify programs, text, and other types of documents and data.

effective group ID
>The current group ID, but not necessarily the user's own ID. For example, a user logged in under a particular group ID may be able to change to another group ID. The ID to which the user changes becomes the effective group ID.

effective root directory
>The point where a system starts when searching for a file. Its pathname begins with a / (slash).

effective user ID
>The current user ID, but not necessarily the user's login ID. For example, a user logged in under a login ID may change to another user's ID, usually as a result of running a program. The ID to which the user changes becomes the effective user ID until the user switches back to the original login ID.

environment
>The settings for shell variables and paths set when the user logs in. These variables can be modified later by the user.

environment variable
>A variable that describes the operating environment of the process and typically includes information about the home directory, command search path, the terminal in use, and the current time zone (the **HOME**, **PATH**, **TERM**, and **TZ** variables, respectively).

equivalence class
>A grouping of characters or character strings that are considered equal for purposes of collation. For example, many languages place an uppercase character in the same equivalence class as its lowercase form, but some languages distinguish between accented and unaccented character forms for the purpose of collation.

GL–7

extended character
> A character other than a 7-bit ASCII character. An extended character can be a 1-byte code point with the eighth bit set (ordinal 128-255).

file
> A collection of related data that is stored and retrieved by an assigned name.

file descriptor
> A small positive integer that the system uses instead of the filename to identify the file.

file owner
> The user who has been marked specially as the owner of a file. Other than the superuser, this user is the only one able to change permissions on the file.

file system
> The collection of files and file management structures on a physical or logical mass storage device, such as a disk partition or logical volume.

file type
> One of the five possible types of files: ordinary file, directory, block device, character device, and first-in, first-out (FIFO or named pipe).

filename completion
> A feature that allows you to enter only a portion of a filename and the system automatically completes it or suggests a list of possible choices.

filter
> A command that reads standard input data, modifies the data, and sends it to standard output.

flag

A modifier that appears on a command line with the command name that defines the action of the command.

foreground

A mode of program execution in which the shell waits for the program specified on the command line to complete before responding to user input.

foreground process

A process that must run to completion before another command is issued to the shell.

full backup

Backup copies of all the files on a filesystem. Contrast with **incremental backups**.

full pathname

The name of any directory or file expressed as a string of directories and files beginning with the root directory. See also **pathname**, **relative pathname**.

full-screen editor

An editor that displays an entire screen at a time, and that allows data to be accessed and modified.

global

In programming languages, pertaining to the relationship between a language object and a block in which the language object has a scope extending beyond that block but contained within an encompassing block.

global search

In word processing, the process of having the system look through a document for specific characters, words, or groups of characters.

GL-9

group

    A collection of users who can share access authorities for protected resources.

hard link

    A mechanism that allows the **ln** command to assign more than one name to a file. Both the new name and the file being linked must be in the same file system.

header

1. Constant text that is formatted to be in the top margin of printed pages in a document.
2. System-defined control information that precedes user data.

home directory

1. A directory associated with an individual user.
2. The user's current directory on login or after issuing the **cd** command with no argument.

include file

    A text file that contains declarations used by a group of functions, programs, or users. Synonymous with **header file**.

incremental backup

    The process of copying files that have been opened for reasons other than read-only access since the last backup was created and that meet the backup frequency criteria.

inline editing

    A feature of some shells that allows you to edit a current or previously entered command line.

input redirection

    The specification of an input source other than the standard one.

Glossary

install

> To copy a software product from a distribution medium and configure it for use.

integer

> A positive or negative whole number or zero.

Internet Protocol (IP)

> The protocol that provides the interface from the higher level host-to-host protocols to the local network protocols. Addressing at this level is usually from host to host.

IP

> See **Internet Protocol**.

job

> A unit of work defined by a user to be done by a system. The term **job** sometimes refers to a representation of the job, such as a set of programs, files, and control statements to the operating system.

job control

> Facilities for monitoring and accessing background processes.

job number

> A number assigned to a job as it enters the system to distinguish the job from other jobs.

kernel

> The part of a system that contains programs for such tasks as input/output, management and control of hardware and the scheduling of user tasks.

keyboard

> An input device consisting of various keys that allows the user to input data, control cursor and pointer locations, and to control the dialog with the workstation.

kill

 An operating system command that stops a process.

Korn shell

 See **shell**.

language

 In internationalization contexts, the choice of language specifies the language (for example, German, French, English) and the display format for messages and the appropriate collating sequence.

line editor

 An editor that displays data one line at a time and that allows data to be accessed and modified only by entering commands.

link

 In the file system, a connection between an i-node and one or more filenames associated with it.

local

 Pertaining to a device, file, or system that is accessed directly from your system, without the use of a communications line.

local host

 The host on the network at which a particular operator is working.

locale

 A language and geographic location and the software environment required to support the local language and customs. For example, the environment required to support the French language in Canada is a locale. The locale can include information about the language, the code set used to represent the language, the collating sequence, and cultural requirements for printing numeric and date values.

log in

 To begin a session at a display station.

log out

To end a session with a computer system at a display station.

login directory

The directory you access when you log in to the system. See also **home directory**.

login shell

The program, or command interpreter, started for a user when that user logs in to the computer system.

mail

Correspondence in the form of messages transmitted between workstations over a network.

mail box

A storage location in a network to which messages for a user are sent.

message

Information from the system that informs the user of a condition that may affect further processing of a current program.

metacharacter

A character used to specify another character or series of characters.

mode

A method of operation, frequently used in UNIX based software systems to refer to read, write, execute, or search permissions of a file or directory.

mode word

An i-node field that describes the type and state of the i-node.

GL–13

modem

> A device that converts digital data from a computer to an analog signal that can be transmitted on a telecommunications line, and converts the analog signal received to data for the computer.

mount

> To make a file system accessible.

multitasking

> A mode of operation that provides for concurrent performance or interleaved execution of two or more tasks.

network

> A collection of data processing products that are connected by communications lines for information exchange between locations.

octal

> A base-eight numbering system.

operating system (OS)

> Software that controls the running of programs and that also can provide such services as resource allocation, scheduling, input and output control, and data management.

output redirection

> The specification of an output destination other than the standard one.

owner

> The user who has been marked specially as the owner of a data object or action. Other than the superuser, this user is the only one able to change the assigned permissions.

parent directory

> The directory that is one level above the current directory.

password

In computer security, a string of characters known to the computer system and a user. The user must specify it to gain access to a system and the data stored with it.

pathname

A filename specifying all directories leading to the file. See also **full pathname**, **relative pathname**.

pattern matching

Specifying a pattern of characters that the system should find.

permission code

A 3-digit octal code or a 9-letter alphabetic code that indicates access permissions. The access permissions are read, write, and execute. See also **access permission**.

permission field

One of the 3-character fields within the permissions column of a directory list. The permission field indicates the read, write, and execute permissions for the file or directory owner, for the group, and for all others.

permissions

Codes that determine how the file can be used by any users who work on the system.

pipe

1. To direct the data so that the output from one process becomes the input to another process.

2. The standard output of one command may be connected to the standard input of another command with the pipe operator. Two commands connected in this way constitute a pipeline. Pipes are unidirectional; synchronization is provided by the operating system.

printer
> A device externally attached to the system unit, used to print system output on paper.

priority
> A rank assigned to a task that determines its precedence in receiving system resources, the CPU in particular.

procedure
> A set of related control statements that cause one or more programs to be executed.

process
> In the operating system, the current state of a program that is running. This includes a memory image, the program data, variables used, general register values, the status of opened files used, and the current directory. Programs running in a process must be either operating system programs or user programs.

process ID (PID)
> A unique number assigned to a process that is running.

program
> A sequence of instructions suitable for processing by a computer. Processing can include the use of an assembler, compiler, interpreter, or translator to prepare the program for execution, and to execute it.

prompt
> A displayed symbol or message that requests information or operator action.

queue
> A line or list formed by items waiting to be processed.

quote
> To mask the special meaning of certain characters, causing them to be taken literally.

record

A collection of fields treated as a unit.

redirect

To divert data from a process to a file or device to which it would not normally go.

relative pathname

The name of a directory or file expressed as a sequence of directories followed by a filename, beginning from the current directory. Relative pathnames do not begin with a / (slash), but are relative to the current directory.

remote

Pertaining to a system or device that is accessed through a communications line.

remote host

Any host on the network except the one at which a particular operator is working.

remote system

A system that is connected to your system through a communications line.

restricted shell

A security feature that provides a controlled shell environment with limited features.

security

The protection of data, system operations, and devices from accidental or intentional ruin, damage, or exposure.

session

The period of time during which the user of a terminal can communicate with an interactive system, usually elapsed time between login and logout.

shell

A software interface between a user and the operating system of a computer. Shell programs interpret commands and user interactions on devices such as keyboards, pointing devices, and touch-sensitive screens and communicate them to the operating system. OSF/1 provides three shells: the Bourne, Korn, and C shell.

shell prompt

The character string on the command line indicating that the system can accept a command.

shell script

A series of commands, combined in a file, that carry out a particular function when the file is run or when the file is specified as an argument to a shell.

shell variables

Facilities of the shell program for assigning variable values to constant names.

Shift-Japanese Industrial Standard (SJIS)

An encoding scheme consisting of single-bytes and double-bytes used for character encoding. Because of the large number of characters in the Japanese and other Asian languages, the 8-bit byte is not sufficient for character encoding.

shutdown

The process of ending operation of a system or a subsystem by following a defined procedure.

spooling

Reading and writing input and output streams on an intermediate device in a format convenient for later processing.

Glossary

standard error (STDERR)

    The standard place where many programs place error messages.

standard input (STDIN)

    The primary source of data going into a command. Standard input comes from the keyboard, unless redirection or piping is used, in which case standard input can be from a file or the output from another command.

standard output (STDOUT)

    The primary destination of data coming from a command. Standard output goes to the display, unless redirection or piping is used, in which case standard output can be to a file or another command.

stream

    A full-duplex connection between a user process and device or pseudodevice. It consists of several linearly connected modules, and is analogous to a shell pipeline, except that data flows in both directions. The modules communicate almost exclusively by passing messages to their neighbors.

STREAMS

    A kernel mechanism from AT&T that supports the implementation of device drivers and networking protocol stacks. See also **STREAMS framework**.

subdirectory

    In the file system hierarchy, a directory contained within another directory.

superuser (su)

    A system user who operates without restrictions.

superuser authority

    The unrestricted ability to access and modify any part of the operating system, usually associated with the user who manages the system.

symbolic link

    A type of file system entry that contains the pathname of and acts as a pointer to another file or directory.

territory

    Specifies the geographic area (for example, Germany, France, Great Britain) as well as date/time conventions and numeric and monetary formats.

text editing program

    See **editor**.

transfer

    To send data to one place and to receive data at another place.

Transmission Control Protocol (TCP)

    The Internet transport-layer protocol that provides a reliable, full-duplex, connection-oriented sevice for applications. TCP uses the IP protocol to transmit information through the network.

trap

    A special statement used to catch signals in a C shell script and transfer control to a handler routine within the script.

tree structure

    A hierarchical sequence that consists of both a root directory and one or more levels of data called by way of the root.

Unix-to-Unix Copy Program (UUCP)

1. A group of programs and files that function as a background process. It includes a set of directories, files, programs, and commands that allow the user to communicate with a remote system over a dedicated line or a telephone line.

2. The command **uucp** that starts file copying from one or more sources to a single destination.

Glossary

user identification (user ID)

    1. A unique string that identifies an operator to the system. This string of characters limits the functions and information the operator can use. Often, the user ID can be substituted in commands that take a user's login name as an argument.

    2. A parameter that specifies the user ID under which the application or transaction program runs.

user process (UID)

The instance of a program that is being executed by the operating system. The process has a user context, which is address space that is accessible to it while running in user mode and a kernel context, which is maintained and available to the kernel only.

username

A string of characters that uniquely identifies a user to the system.

UUCP

See **Unix-to-Unix Copy Program**.

variable

    1. A name used to represent a data item whose value can change while the program is running.

    2. In programming languages, a language object that can take different values at different times.

    3. A quantity that can assume any of a given set of values.

working directory

Synonym for **current directory**.

workstation

A device that enables users to transmit information to or receive information from a computer.

Index

Symbols

8-bit code sets, C–2
! subcommand (**ftp**), 12–6
! subcommand (**tftp**), 12–15
$ prompt, 1–3
$ subcommand (**ftp**), 12–7
% prompt, 1–3
& operator, 6–9
&& operator, 7–10
.cshrc login script, 7–22, 8–4
.kshrc login script, 7–22, 8–27
.login login script, 7–22, 8–5
.logout script, 7–33
.profile login script, 7–22, 8–17, 8–25
/etc/group file, 13–7
/etc/passwd file, 5–3, 13–4
/etc/uucp file (UUCP), 11–2
/var/spool/uucppublic file (UUCP), 11–4, 11–46
? subcommand
    ftp, 12–7
    telnet, 12–25
    tftp, 12–16

A

absolute pathname, 2–11
account subcommand (**ftp**), 12–7
add (**a**) command (**vi** editor), A–6
addgroup command, 13–15
adding
    groups, 13–14
    users, 13–2
adduser command, 13–3
alias command
    C shell, 8–15
    Korn shell, 8–41
aliases, 8–12, 8–36
    for mail, D–16
ampersand (**&**) operator, 6–9
append subcommand (**ed** editor), B–3
apropos command, 1–13
arguments, command, 1–6
ascii subcommand
    ftp, 12–7
    tftp, 12–16
Asian code sets, C–3
autologin, 1–2
automatic reboot procedure, 14–4

B

background processes, 6–9, 11–2
backing up
    directories, 15–5
    listing contents of a backup
        medium, 15–6
    multiple files, 15–4
backup copies of files, 15–1
backup procedures, sample, 15–4
bg command (C shell), 8–15
binary subcommand
    ftp, 12–7
    tftp, 12–16
Bourne shell, 8–1, 8–17
    .logout script, 7–32
    .profile login script, 7–22,
        8–17
    built-in commands, 8–23
    built-in variables, 8–21
    login script, 8–17
    metacharacters, 8–20
breaking
    remote **cu** connection
        (UUCP), 11–13
    remote **tip** connection
        (UUCP), 11–24
built-in
    commands, 8–15, 8–23,
        8–41
    variables, 8–14, 8–21, 8–39
bye subcommand (**ftp**), 12–7

C

C shell, 8–1, 8–3
    .cshrc login script, 7–22,
        8–4
    .login login script, 7–22,
        8–5
    .logout script, 7–32
    aliases, 8–12
    built-in commands, 8–15
    built-in variables, 8–14
    command history, 8–9
    filename completion, 8–11
    login script, 8–3, 8–5
    metacharacters, 8–7
canceling commands, 1–7
cat command, 3–7, A–3
cd (change directory) command,
    4–4
cd command
    Bourne shell, 8–23
    Korn shell, 8–41
cd subcommand (**ftp**), 12–7
cdup subcommand (**ftp**), 12–7
change (**c**) command (**vi** editor),
    A–9
change (**c**) subcommand (**ed**
    editor), B–26
change word (**cw**) command (**vi**
    editor), A–9
chgrp (change group) command,
    5–23
chmod (change mode) command,
    5–5, 5–9, 5–10, 5–12, 5–15
chown (change owner) command,
    5–23

Index

close subcommand (**telnet**), 12–25
code set, C–2
collation, C–4
command history
    C shell, 8–9
    Korn shell, 8–31
command mode (**vi** editor), A–4
commands
    addgroup, 13–15
    adduser, 13–3
    alias, 8–15, 8–41
    apropos, 1–13
    bg, 8–15
    cd, 3–33, 4–4, 8–23, 8–41
    chgrp, 5–6, 5–23
    chmod, 5–6, 5–9
    chown, 5–23
    cp, 3–22, 3–23, 3–26
    date, 1–6
    df, 3–17
    diff, 3–29
    documentation, 1–11
    echo, 8–15, 8–23, 8–41
    exit (logout), 5–21
    export, 8–23, 8–41
    fc, 8–41
    fg, 6–17, 8–15
    file, 3–35
    find, 6–9, 9–5
    flags, 1–6
    grep, 2–16, 9–1
    history, 8–15, 8–41
    jobs, 6–11, 6–13, 8–15, 8–41
    kill, 6–15
    ln, 3–16, 3–18, 3–19, 3–26
    login, 1–2
    logout, 8–15
    lpq, 3–14, 3–15

lpr, 3–13
lprm (remove from print queue), 3–15
lpstat, 3–15
ls, 2–13, 3–2, 3–3, 3–4, 3–5, 3–6, 3–20, 3–21, 3–22, 3–27, 4–1, 4–3, 5–7, 5–8, 5–11
man, 1–6, 1–11, 1–12
mkdir, 4–2, 4–13
more, 3–9, 3–18
mv, 3–26, 3–27, 4–11
options, 1–6
passwd, 1–7, 1–9, 13–12
pg, 3–7
pr, 3–9
ps, 6–11
pwd, 2–8, 3–33, 4–4, 8–23, 8–41
rehash, 8–15
repeat, 8–15
rm, 3–20, 3–22, 3–32, 3–33, 3–34, 4–15
rmdir, 4–12, 4–14
set, 8–15, 8–23, 8–41
setenv, 8–15
shell built-in, 8–15, 8–23, 8–41
sort, 3–31
source, 8–15
su, 5–20
time, 8–15
times, 8–23, 8–41
touch, 3–34
trap, 8–23, 8–41
umask, 8–23, 8–41
unalias, 8–15, 8–41
unset, 8–15, 8–23, 8–41
unsetenv, 8–15

Index–3

w, 6–19
wc, 6–3
who, 6–18
whoami, 5–20
communicating with remote
    system (UUCP), 11–5
compatible communications
    systems, identifying
    (UUCP), 11–2
conditional command, running,
    7–10
connecting to an unknown remote
    system via modem (UUCP),
    11–11, 11–22
context searching
    ed editor, B–15
    vi editor, A–11
controlled shutdown, 14–2
conversation, ending with symbol,
    10–3
copying files, 3–22, 3–23, 3–24
    local system control
        (UUCP), 11–46,
        11–47
copying lines, ed editor, B–31
correcting mistakes
    in commands, 1–6
    when logging in, 1–3
correcting typing errors
    ed editor, B–4
    vi editor, A–7
creating
    directories, 4–2
    login directory, 13–8
    shell procedures (example),
        7–35

creating text files
    ed editor, B–2
    vi editor, A–3
csh.login system login script, 7–22
ct command (UUCP), flags,
    connecting to remote system
    via modem, 11–29
Ctrl-d, 5–21, 5–23
cu command (UUCP)
    flags, connecting to a remote
        computer, 11–6, 11–8
    using local commands,
        11–6, 11–12
current directory, 2–8
customizing mail, D–53

D

database security, 5–2
    group, 5–4
date and time conventions, C–6
date command, 1–6
dead.letter file, D–4
default shell script, 13–9
delete (t) subcommand (ed editor),
    B–22
Delete key, 1–6
delete line (dd) command (vi
    editor), A–8
delete subcommand (ftp), 12–8
delete word (dw) command (vi
    editor), A–8

Index

deleting a specific line
    ed editor, B–24
    vi editor, A–8
deleting current line, **ed** editor, B–23
deleting files, 3–34
deleting multiple lines
    ed editor, B–24
    vi editor, A–8
determining file type, 3–35
device name, specifying with **cu** command (UUCP), 11–8
diff (show differences) command, 3–29
dir subcommand (**ftp**), 12–8
directories, 2–8
display subcommand (**telnet**), 12–25
displaying
    current directory name, 2–8
    directory permissions, 5–7
    file permissions, 5–7
    files with formatting, 3–9
    files without formatting, 3–7
    print queue, 3–14
distribution lists for mail, D–16
dot notation, 2–12

E

echo command
    Bourne shell, 8–23
    C shell, 8–15
    Korn shell, 8–41

ed editor
    append subcommand, B–3
    change (**c**) subcommand, B–26
    context searching, B–15
    copying lines, B–31
    correcting typing errors, B–4
    creating and saving text files, B–2
    delete (**t**) subcommand, B–22
    deleting a specific line, B–24
    deleting current line, B–23
    deleting multiple lines, B–24
    displaying the current line, B–11
    edit (**e**) subcommand, B–8, B–9
    edit (**ed**) command, B–8
    edit buffer, B–2
    global (**g**) operator, B–19, B–20
    insert (**i**) subcommand, B–28
    locating text, B–15
    move (**m**) subcommand, B–25
    moving text, B–25
    print (**p**) subcommand, B–4
    quit (**q**) subcommand, B–7
    read (**r**) subcommand, B–10, B–8
    removing characters, B–20
    replacing character strings, B–17
    saving part of a file, B–7

saving text, B–5, B–6
starting the editor, B–3
substitute (**s**) subcommand,
    B–17
substitutions on multiple
    lines, B–19
transfer (**t**) subcommand,
    B–31
using system commands,
    B–32
write (**w**) subcommand,
    B–5, B–7
edit (**e**) subcommand (**ed** editor),
    B–8, B–9
edit (**ed**) command (**ed** editor),
    B–8
editing of command lines, 8–33
editor for mail, D–42
end of message/conversation (local
    communications), 10–3,
    10–5
ending a local message, 10–3,
    10–5
enhanced security features, 5–25
entering local command during
    remote connection (UUCP),
    11–13, 11–24
environment variables, locale
    LANG, C–11, C–9
    LC_ALL, C–12
    LC_COLLATE, C–12
    LC_CTYPE, C–12
    LC_MESSAGES, C–12
    LC_MONETARY, C–12
    LC_NUMERIC, C–12
    LC_TIME, C–12
errorbells environment variable,
    A–18

ex line editor, A–13
execute permission, 5–11
exit command, 5–21, 5–23
export command
    Bourne shell, 8–23
    Korn shell, 8–41

F

fc command (Korn shell), 8–41
fg command (C shell), 8–15
file, 2–1, 2–6
file (determine file type) command,
    3–35
file management, 3–1
file specifying by pattern matching,
    2–13
file system, 2–1, 2–6
filename, 2–6, 2–7
filename completion, 8–11, 8–36
filters, definition, 7–11
find command, 9–5
finding files, 9–5
finger command (TCP/IP), 12–2
flags, 1–6
foreground processes, 6–8
forgotten command names, 1–13
formatting a file, 3–9
forwarding files (UUCP), 11–44
forwarding mail, D–22
ftp command (TCP/IP), 12–5, 12–6
ftp subcommands, 12–6
full pathname, defined, 2–11

G

get subcommand
    ftp, 12–8
    tftp, 12–16
getting mail, D–20
global (**g**) operator (**ed** editor),
    B–19, B–20
grep command, 9–1
groups, adding and removing,
    13–14

H

handling copied files (UUCP),
    11–46
hard links, 3–17
help, 1–11
help subcommand (**ftp**), 12–8
history command
    C shell, 8–15
    Korn shell, 8–41
history of recently used commands,
    8–9, 8–31
HOME environment variable,
    7–18

I

i-number, 3–19
identifying compatible systems
    (UUCP), 11–2
ignorecase environment variable,
    A–18
input (**i**) command (**vi** editor), A–6
input mode (**vi** editor), A–6
insert (**i**) subcommand (**ed** editor),
    B–28
insert text (**A**) command (**vi**
    editor), A–7
insert text (**I**) command (**vi** editor),
    A–7
intermediate systems used in file
    transfers (UUCP), 11–44
internationalization, C–1
    8-bit code sets, C–2
    Asian code sets, C–3
    code set, C–2
    collation, C–4
    date and time conventions,
        C–6
    LANG environment
        variable, 7–19, C–11,
        C–9
    language, C–2
    LC_ALL environment
        variable, 7–21, C–12
    LC_COLLATE
        environment
        variable, 7–19, C–12
    LC_CTYPE environment
        variable, 7–19, C–12
    LC_MESSAGES
        environment
        variable, 7–20, C–12
    LC_MONETARY
        environment
        variable, 7–20, C–12

LC_NUMERIC
    environment
    variable, 7–20, C–12
LC_TIME environment
    variable, 7–20, C–12
locale, C–2, C–4
numeric and monetary
    formatting, C–7
program messages, C–7
territory, C–2
Internet, D–12

J

jobs command, 6–11
    C shell, 8–15
    Korn shell, 8–41

K

kill command, 6–15
Korn shell, 8–1, 8–24
    .kshrc login script, 7–22,
        8–27
    .logout script, 7–32
    .profile login script, 7–22,
        8–25
    aliases, 8–36
    built-in commands, 8–41
    built-in variables, 8–39
    command history, 8–31
    editing command lines,
        8–33

filename completion, 8–36
login script, 8–25, 8–27
metacharacters, 8–29

L

LANG environment variable,
    7–19, C–11, C–9
language, C–2
lcd subcommand (ftp), 12–8
LC_ALL environment variable,
    7–21, C–12
LC_COLLATE environment
    variable, 7–19, C–12
LC_CTYPE environment variable,
    7–19, C–12
LC_MESSAGES environment
    variable, 7–20, C–12
LC_MONETARY environment
    variable, 7–20, C–12
LC_NUMERIC environment
    variable, 7–20, C–12
LC_TIME environment variable,
    7–20, C–12
line discipline, C–17
linking files, 3–19
listing contents of a backup
    medium, 15–6
listing directory contents, 3–2, 3–3,
    3–4
lists of users to send mail to, D–16
ln (link) command, 3–18, 3–19
local commands (UUCP), 11–6,
    11–12, 11–18, 11–23

Index

local communications facility, 10–2, 10–5
local system control of file access (UUCP)
    uupick command, 11–49, 11–51
    uuto command, 11–47
locale, C–2, C–4
locales, terminal setup for handling code sets, C–14
locating text
    ed editor, B–15
    vi editor, A–11
logging in, 1–2
login directory, 2–8
login script
    .cshrc script, 7–22, 8–4
    .kshrc script, 7–22, 8–27
    .login script, 7–22, 8–5
    .profile script, 7–22, 8–17, 8–25
    Bourne shell, 8–17
    C shell, 8–3, 8–5
    csh.login system script, 7–22
    Korn shell, 8–25, 8–27
    profile system script, 7–22
LOGNAME environment variable, 7–18
logout command (C shell), 8–15
lpq (display print queue) command, 3–14
lpr command, 3–12
lprm (remove from print queue) command, 3–15
ls (list directory) command, 3–2, 3–3, 3–4, 3–6, 3–21, 5–7, 5–8
ls subcommand (**ftp**), 12–8

M

MAIL environment variable, 7–18
mail file, 13–11
man command, 1–11
map command (**vi** editor), A–19
mesg (receive local communication), 10–10
    changing default, 10–11
messages (local communications)
    ending, end-of-file symbol (EOF), 10–3, 10–5
    long, in files, 10–6
    receiving, rejecting, status, 10–9
    sending, **write** command, 10–2
    superuser override, 10–10
metacharacters
    Bourne shell, 8–20
    C shell, 8–7
    Korn shell, 8–29
mget subcommand (**ftp**), 12–8
mkdir (make directory) command, 4–2
mkdir subcommand (**ftp**), 12–9
mode subcommand (**tftp**), 12–16
more command, 3–7
move (**m**) subcommand (**ed** editor), B–25
moving
    directories, 4–11
    files, 3–26, 3–27
moving text
    ed editor, B–25
    vi editor, A–11
mput subcommand (**ftp**), 12–9
mv (move) command, 3–26, 3–27, 4–11

N

nlist subcommand (**ftp**), 12–9
noignore environment variable, A–18
nonumber environment variable, A–18
noshowmatch environment variable, A–18
number environment variable, A–18
numeric and monetary formatting, C–7

O

octal numbers, in setting permissions, 5–14
open line (o) command (**vi** editor), A–6
open previous line (O) command (**vi** e, A–7
open subcommand (**ftp**), 12–9
options, 1–6

P

parent directory, 2–11
passwd (password) command, 1–7, 13–12
password
    file, 5–3
    for logging in, 1–2
    forgotten, 1–10
    restrictions, 1–9
    security restrictions, 1–9
    selecting new, 1–8
PATH environment variable, 7–18
pathname, 2–9
    absolute, 2–11
    dot notation, 2–12
    full, 2–11
    relative, 2–11
    tilde notation, 2–13
pattern matching, file specifying, 2–13
permissions
    setting file/directory, 5–9
    specifying with umask, 5–18
pg (page) command, 3–7
PID number, 6–9
pipeline, 7–11
pipes, 7–11
pr (format) command, 3–9
print (p) subcommand (**ed** editor), B–4
printing files, 3–12
Process Identification Number (PID), 6–9
profile system login script, 7–22
program messages, C–7
ps command, 6–11
public directory (UUCP), 11–4
put subcommand
    ftp, 12–9
    tftp, 12–16

Index

pwd (print current directory)
    command, 2–8
        Bourne shell, 8–23
        Korn shell, 8–41
pwd subcommand (**ftp**), 12–10

Q

queues, printer, 3–12
quit (**q**) command (**vi** editor),
    A–10, A–4
quit (**q**) subcommand (**ed** editor),
    B–7
quit subcommand
    ftp, 12–10
    telnet, 12–25
    tftp, 12–17
quoting, 7–14
    backslash, 7–15
    double quotes (" "), 7–16
    single quotes (' '), 7–15

R

r (read) permission, 5–11
rcp command (TCP/IP), 12–19
read (**r**) subcommand (**ed** editor),
    B–10, B–8
read permission, 5–11
reboot procedure, automatic, 14–4
rebooting the system, 14–1

receiving mail, D–20
recv subcommand (**ftp**), 12–10
reexecuting commands, 8–11, 8–32
rehash command (C shell), 8–15
relative pathnames, 2–11
remote
    commands (UUCP), 11–34
    file transfers (UUCP), 11–44
    login (TCP/IP), 12–21
    login (**telnet**), 12–23
    system names (UUCP),
        11–2
removing
    absolute permissions, 5–14
    current directory, 4–15
    directories, 4–12, 4–13,
        4–14
    file links, 3–20
    files, 3–32, 3–34
    files from print queue, 3–15
    groups, 13–14
    users, 13–12
removing characters
    ed editor, B–20
    vi editor, A–8
rename subcommand (**ftp**), 12–10
renaming
    directories, 4–11
    files and directories, 3–26
repeat command (C shell), 8–15
replacing character strings
    ed editor, B–17
    vi editor, A–14
restoring a damaged file system,
    15–3
restoring multiple directories, 15–7
restrictions, password, 1–9

retaining connection (local
    communications), 10–5
returning to local system during
    remote connection (UUCP),
    11–13, 11–24
rlogin command (TCP/IP), 12–21
rm (remove file) command, 3–20,
    3–32, 3–34
rmdir (remove directory)
    command, 4–12, 4–13,
    4–14, 4–15
rmdir subcommand (**ftp**), 12–10
root directory, 2–10
rsh command (TCP/IP), 12–26
runique subcommand (**ftp**), 12–10
running
    background processes, 6–9
    foreground processes, 6–8
    shell procedures, 7–35
ruptime command (TCP/IP), 12–3
rwho command (TCP/IP), 12–27

S

s (set) permission, 5–11
sample files, creating, 2–2
saving part of a file
    ed editor, B–7
    vi editor, A–16
saving text
    ed editor, B–5, B–6
    vi editor, A–10
saving text files, **ed** editor, B–2
searching for text patterns, 9–1
security
    group, 5–2

user, 5–2
send subcommand (**ftp**), 12–11
sending
    files to a specific username
        (UUCP), 11–47
    files to remote systems,
        11–44
    local messages, 10–2
    long messages, 10–6
sending a file (**mail**), D–19
sending mail, D–19, D–42
set command
    Bourne shell, 8–23
    C shell, 8–15
    Korn shell, 8–41
set user/group ID permission, 5–11
setenv command (C shell), 8–15
setting
    file/directory permissions,
        5–9
    user mask, 5–16
shell
    aliases, 8–12, 8–36
    built-in commands, 8–15,
        8–23, 8–41
    built-in variables, 8–14,
        8–21, 8–39
    command history, 8–9, 8–31
    editing command lines,
        8–33
    features, 8–1
    filename completion, 8–11,
        8–36
    login script, 8–3, 8–5, 8–17,
        8–25, 8–27
    metacharacters, 8–7, 8–20,
        8–29

SHELL environment variable,
    7–19
shell environment variables
    HOME, 7–18
    LANG, 7–19
    LC_ALL, 7–21
    LC_COLLATE, 7–19
    LC_CTYPE, 7–19
    LC_MESSAGES, 7–20
    LC_MONETARY, 7–20
    LC_NUMERIC, 7–20
    LC_TIME, 7–20
    LOGNAME, 7–18
    MAIL, 7–18
    PATH, 7–18
    SHELL, 7–19
    TERM, 7–19
    TZ, 7–19
showing differences between files,
    3–29
showmatch environment variable,
    A–18
shutting down the system, 14–1
soft links, 3–17
sort (sort file contents) command,
    3–31
sorting file contents, 3–31
source command (C shell), 8–15
specifying files, 2–13
standard
    error, 6–5
    input, 6–3
    output, 6–3
starting the **ed** editor, B–3
starting the **vi** editor, A–3
status information (UUCP), 11–52
status subcommand
    ftp, 12–11
    telnet, 12–25

tftp, 12–17
stopping commands, 1–7
stream head, C–17
su command, 5–20
subcommands
    ftp, 12–6
    telnet, 12–24
    tftp, 12–15
subdirectories, 2–8
subshells, 7–13
substitute (**s**) subcommand (**ed**
    editor), B–17
sunique subcommand (**ftp**), 12–11
superuser privileges, 14–1
symbolic links, 3–17

T

tabstop environment variable,
    A–18
tar command, 15–4
telephone number, specifying with
    cu command (UUCP), 11–8
telnet command (TCP/IP), 12–23,
    12–24
    how to use, 12–23
telnet subcommands, 12–24,
    12–25
TERM environment variable, 7–19
terminal, setting up for handling
    code sets, C–14
terminating
    connections (local
        communications),
        10–3, 10–5
    remote **cu** connection
        (UUCP), 11–13

remote **tip** connection
(UUCP), 11–24
UUCP jobs with the **uustat**
command, 11–52
territory, C–2
text editor, 2–1
tftp command (TCP/IP), 12–14,
12–15
tftp subcommands, 12–15
tilde notation, 2–13
time command (C shell), 8–15
times command
Bourne shell, 8–23
Korn shell, 8–41
tip command (UUCP)
flags, connecting to a remote
computer, 11–18,
11–20
using local commands,
11–18, 11–23
transfer (t) subcommand (**ed**
editor), B–31
transfer-status information
(UUCP), 11–52
trap command
Bourne shell, 8–23
Korn shell, 8–41
tree structure (file system), 2–6
typing errors, correcting
ed editor, B–4
vi editor, A–7
TZ environment variable, 7–19

U

umask command, 5–16
Bourne shell, 8–23
Korn shell, 8–41
unalias command
C shell, 8–15
Korn shell, 8–41
undo (u) command (**vi** editor), A–9
unset command
Bourne shell, 8–23
C shell, 8–15
Korn shell, 8–41
unsetenv command (C shell), 8–15
username, 1–2
uuname command (UUCP),
identifying compatible
remote systems, identifying
the local, 11–2
uupick command (UUCP),
handling **uuto** files, user
responses, 11–46, 11–49,
11–51
uuto command (UUCP), copying
files, local system control,
flags, 11–46, 11–47
uux command, flags, used to run
remote commands, 11–34

V

variables, shell built-in, 8–14, 8–21, 8–39
verbose subcommand
    ftp, 12–11
    tftp, 12–17
vi command, 2–3, A–3
vi editor
    $ cursor movement command, A–5
    (cursor movement command, A–5
) cursor movement command, A–5
    / search command, A–11
    0 cursor movement command, A–5
    add (**a**) command, A–6
    b cursor movement command, A–5
    change (**c**) command, A–9
    change word (**cw**) command, A–9
    command mode, A–4
    context searching, A–11
    copying blocks of text, A–17
    copying text, A–12
    correcting typing errors, A–7
    Ctrl-b cursor movement command, A–5
    Ctrl-f cursor movement command, A–5
    customizing your environment, A–17
    delete line (**dd**) command, A–8
    delete word (**dw**) command, A–8
    deleting a block of text, A–17
    environment variables, A–18
    ex line editor commands, A–13
    getting started, A–3
    h cursor movement command, A–4
    input (**i**) command, A–6
    insert text (**A**) command, A–7
    insert text (**I**) command, A–7
    j cursor movement command, A–4
    k cursor movement command, A–4
    l cursor movement command, A–4
    locating text, A–11
    map command, A–19
    moving blocks of text, A–17
    moving text, A–11
    moving within a file, A–4
    next (**n**) search command, A–11
    open line (**o**) command, A–6
    open previous line (**O**) command, A–7
    opening text files, A–3
    paste (**p**) command, A–12
    quit (**q**) command, A–10, A–4
    saving part of a file, A–16
    saving text files, A–10

saving your customizations, A–19
searching for text, A–11
starting the editor, A–3
substituting text, A–14
undo (**u**) command, A–9
using advanced techniques, A–10
w cursor movement command, A–5
write (**w**) command, A–10
{ cursor movement command, A–5
} cursor movement command, A–5
} Esc command, A–6
vi environment variables
   errorname, A–18
   ignorecase, A–18
   noignorecase, A–18
   nonumber, A–18
   noshowmatch, A–18
   number, A–18
   showmatch, A–18
   tabstop, A–18
   wrapmargin, A–18
   wrapscan, A–18

working directory, 2–8
wrapmargin environment variable, A–18
wrapscan environment variable, A–18
write (**w**) command (**vi** editor), A–10
write (**w**) subcommand (**ed** editor), B–5, B–7
write command (local communications), 10–2
write permission, 5–11
writing shell procedures, 7–34

X

x (execute) permission, 5–11

Z

z subcommand (**telnet**), 12–25

W

w (write) permission, 5–11
w command, 6–19
who command, 6–18
whoami command, 5–20

Symbols

|| operator, 7–10